An IBM® SPSS® Companion to Political Analysis

Sixth Edition

An IBM® SPSS® Companion to Political Analysis

Sixth Edition

Phillip H. Pollock III
University of Central Florida

Barry C. Edwards
University of Central Florida

 |

FOR INFORMATION:

CQ Press
An Imprint of SAGE Publications, Inc.
2455 Teller Road
Thousand Oaks, California 91320
E-mail: order@sagepub.com

SAGE Publications Ltd.
1 Oliver's Yard
55 City Road
London EC1Y 1SP
United Kingdom

SAGE Publications India Pvt. Ltd.
B 1/I 1 Mohan Cooperative Industrial Area
Mathura Road, New Delhi 110 044
India

SAGE Publications Asia-Pacific Pte Ltd
18 Cross Street #10-10/11/12
China Square Central
Singapore 048423

Library of Congress Cataloging-in-Publication Data

Names: Pollock, Philip H., III, author. | Pollock, Philip H., III. Essentials of political analysis.

Title: An IBM SPSS companion to political analysis / Phillip H. Pollock III, University of Central Florida, Barry C. Edwards, University of Central Florida.

Other titles: International Business Machines statistical package for the social sciences companion to political analysis

Description: Sixth Edition, Revised and updated edition. | Washington, D.C. : CQ Press, A DIVISION OF SAGE, [2019] | System requirements: System requirements: Microsoft Windows-based computer; CD-ROM drive. | Companion text to: Essentials of political analysis / Philip H. Pollock. | Previous edition: 2016. | Includes bibliographical references and index.

Identifiers: LCCN 2019006730 | ISBN 9781506379654 (Paperback : alk. paper)

Subjects: LCSH: Political science—Research—Handbooks, manuals, etc. | Political statistics—Computer programs—Handbooks, manuals, etc. | Analysis of variance—Computer programs—Handbooks, manuals, etc. | SPSS (Computer file)—Handbooks, manuals, etc.

Classification: LCC JA86 .P64 2019 | DDC 320.0285/555—dc23
LC record available at https://lccn.loc.gov/2019006730

Acquisitions Editor: Scott Greenan
Content Development Editor: Scott Harris
Editorial Assistant: Lauren Younker
Production Editor: Bennie Clark Allen
Copy Editor: Christina West
Typesetter: C&M Digitals (P) Ltd.
Proofreader: Jen Grubba
Cover Designer: Dally Verghese
Marketing Manager: Erica DeLuca

CONTENTS

4 | Making Comparisons

71

5 | Making Controlled Comparisons

95

6 | Making Inferences about Sample Means

123

7 | Chi-square and Measures of Association

145

8 | Correlation and Linear Regression

169

9 | Dummy Variables and Interaction Effects

10 | Logistic Regression

11 | Doing Your Own Political Analysis

FIGURES

PREFACE

Since Philip Pollock first published *The Essentials of Political Analysis* nearly twenty years ago, his textbooks have helped countless students learn how to interpret and conduct political analysis. As its name suggests, this book, *An IBM® SPSS® Companion to the Essentials of Political Analysis, Sixth Edition*, serves as a companion to the core textbook, helping students apply general concepts of political analysis using SPSS software.

The longevity of Pollock's political analysis series is a testament to the vital union of theory and practice in teaching political science research methods. Students who appreciate the practical side of research are better prepared to contribute to class discussions of methodological concepts and problems than those who study only abstract principles. Moreover, students often develop a usable skill they can hone as they continue their academic careers or pursue employment opportunities. Whatever their professional goals, students need a solid foundation in basic political analysis techniques. They should learn to manipulate variables, explore patterns, and graph relationships. They also need a working knowledge of powerful yet easy-to-learn software, such as IBM® SPSS® Statistics.* This book instructs students in using SPSS to construct meaningful descriptions of variables and to perform substantive analysis of political relationships. The chapters cover all major topics in data analysis, from descriptive statistics to logistic regression. A final chapter describes several doable research projects, shows how to find relevant data, and lays out a framework for a well-organized research paper. After completing this book, students will have become competent SPSS users, and they will have learned a fair amount about substantive political science, too.

In its essential features—multiple datasets, guided examples, screenshots, graphics instruction, and end-of-chapter exercises—this book continues in the tradition of previous editions. As before, we continue to assume that students using this workbook have never heard of SPSS and have never used a computer to analyze data. However, previous adopters will find some changes and improvements.

DATASETS AND CHAPTER EXERCISES

The SPSS datasets that accompany this book have been thoroughly revised and updated. There are four downloadable datasets: selected variables from the 2016 General Social Survey (the GSS dataset) and the 2016 American National Election Study (the NES dataset), as well as datasets on the 50 states (the States dataset) and 169 countries in the world (the World dataset). You can find names and descriptions for all of the variables in these datasets in the Appendix.

This book has always taken a two-step approach to skill-set learning: (1) Perform the guided examples. (2) Work the exercises. Following this approach, Chapters 1 through 10 include end-of-chapter exercises for students. The exercises are designed to give students opportunities to apply their new skills and to engage students in discovering the meaning of their findings and learning to interpret them. The exercises test a full range of competencies, and most chapters include at least one more-challenging exercise. Most exercises have multiple subparts to give students the opportunity to practice the steps of a research process, including stating hypotheses, analyzing data, and discussing results.

We have included exercises that reflect current scholarly debates in American politics, international relations, comparative politics, and the judicial system. Instructors should feel free to pick and choose exercises that best match the interests and needs of their classes. The pages of this book are perforated, three-hole punched, and 8.5 × 11 inches in size so instructors can use the end-of-chapter exercises as homework assignments that students complete and submit. The formatting of this edition allows

---

*SPSS is a registered trademark of International Business Machines Corporation.

students to tear out and submit exercises without losing substantive chapter content. After completing this book, students not only are confident SPSS users, they will have also learned a fair amount about substantive political science, too.

Instructors can obtain a complete solutions manual with instructor access to the book's website (edge.sagepub.com/pollock).

CHAPTER ORGANIZATION

The chapter organization for this edition follows that of the previous edition. The "Getting Started" section, an informal preface for students, briefly explains why learning to analyze politics with SPSS is a vitally important skill, provides a roadmap of subsequent chapters, and tells students where they can download the Companion datasets featured throughout the book.

Chapter 1 introduces the SPSS Data Editor, discusses the output Viewer, and illustrates the print procedure. For the sixth edition, we've added some new material to Chapter 1. We've added a brief discussion of using keyboard shortcuts as an alternative to SPSS's graphical user interface (GUI). We've also added a section on formatting SPSS tables. SPSS now features some nice table templates, including an "Academic" style template that generates publication-style tables. Although we emphasize SPSS's GUI, we thought it appropriate to add a section on saving commands in syntax files to enable others to replicate our analysis, an increasingly important dimension of political science research.

Chapter 2 addresses how to describe the central tendency and dispersion of a variable. This chapter also shows how graphics, like bar charts and histograms, in conjunction with tables can enrich one's description of a variable. SPSS's Chart Editor makes it relatively easy to create compelling graphics. Chapter 2 also includes coverage of Case Summaries, which can be quite useful for providing insights into small datasets such as States and World. We've added a brief discussion of sample weights in Chapter 2. SPSS makes weighting observations easy and we use sample weights when analyzing GSS and NES survey data throughout the book.

Chapter 3 describes the main SPSS data transformation procedures, Recode and Compute. Students can use these procedures to create indicator variables, simplify variables, standardize variables, and create additive indexes. We demonstrate each of these operations and show how to modify variable and value labels (a new section in this edition). This chapter also discusses Visual Binning, which is a powerful and efficient alternative to Recode, especially for collapsing interval variables into ordinal categories of roughly equal size.

In Chapter 4, which covers cross-tabulations and mean comparisons, students learn bivariate analysis. This chapter shows how to use graphics, like line charts and bar charts, and box plots to supplement numeric results. Chapter 5 takes the methods introduced an important step further by showing students how to make controlled comparisons. Students use the Crosstabs and Compare Means procedures to obtain and interpret controlled comparisons. This chapter also discusses graphic support for controlled comparisons. Chapters 4 and 5 feature fresh examples and updated screenshots but cover the same procedures as prior editions.

Chapter 6 uses the One-Sample T Test and Independent-Samples T Test procedures to show students how to make inferences about the means of interval-level variables. In this edition, we show students how to visualize mean comparisons using Error Bar graphs that show point estimates and confidence intervals—it's a nice way to reinforce the core concepts of inferential statistics. We've also added a section on making inferences about proportions using an example that cuts across several subfields: public support for the government spying on U.S. citizens. The standard SPSS toolkit leaves a lot to be desired for testing inferences about proportions, but we are careful to note where SPSS provides only approximate answers and how to calculate z-scores. Like the prior edition, this edition avoids confusing students on one-tailed versus two-tailed tests of significance. Instead, Chapter 6 focuses exclusively on two-tailed tests and on the 95 percent confidence interval.

Chapter 7 covers chi-square and measures of association for nominal and ordinal variables. We cover the same methods in this chapter as covered in prior editions, but we now show students how they can depict the analyses using multiple line charts (for ordinal-level variables) and clustered bar charts (for nominal-level variables). Additionally, we've updated the featured example in this chapter to examine public support for use of force to solve international problems, a topic that's relevant to multiple subfields.

In Chapter 8, students work through guided examples to learn to use the Correlate (Bivariate) procedure and the Regression (Linear) procedure. Chapter 8 also discusses advanced scatterplot editing using the Chart Editor. The featured example in this edition looks at the correlation among different interval-level measures of democracy around the world and the effect of democratic development on global conflict levels. This chapter now concludes with a brief discussion of formatting regression results tables for presentation or publication.

Chapter 9 shows students how to use multiple regression analysis to conduct different types of analysis. Students learn how to perform regression analysis with multiple dummy variables and model interaction in multiple regression. This chapter gives students the opportunity to apply some of the variable transformation methods they learned in Chapter 3. We've added a section on graphing an interaction relationship on a scatterplot; seeing the analysis should help students properly interpret an interaction term in multiple regression results.

Chapter 10 covers binary logistic regression. Students learn how to conduct logistic regression analysis, interpret results, and visualize relationships in terms of probabilities: marginal effects at the means (MEMs) and marginal effects at representative values (MERs). In this edition, we analyze a contemporary civil rights issue: whether businesses that provide wedding services should be required to serve gay couples.

Chapter 11 guides students on conducting their own political analysis. We've revised our discussion of "doable ideas" to identify seven political science topics students can research using the four Companion datasets. Like prior editions, this chapter shows students how they can input other datasets into SPSS to conduct their own research.

These chapters are organized in the way that we typically teach our research methods courses. We prefer to cover the logic of description and hypothesis testing before introducing inferential statistics and statistical significance. We assign our students exercises and problems sets, often working with them in lab sessions. However, with a little rearranging of the chapters, this book will prove useful for instructors who do things differently. For example, if your course culminates in a significant research paper, you may prefer to assign Chapter 11 (Doing Your Own Political Analysis) at the beginning of the course, perhaps after the Introduction to SPSS (Chapter 1). As noted above, we know that political science research methods courses are often taught by instructors with different subfield interests. While focusing on the essential methods used by all subfields, we have attempted to engage varied substantive interests with our examples and exercises. Of course, one size cannot fit all, so we encourage instructors to add and subtract material to help students learn to interpret and conduct political analysis.

LEARNING TO ANALYZE POLITICS WITH SPSS

As before, each chapter is written as a step-by-step tutorial, taking students through a series of guided examples and providing many annotated screenshots. Because of the revised and updated datasets, all of the examples and screenshots have been updated. To augment the first step, we have produced a set of screencasts. These are short, tutorial videos that demonstrate essential methods using SPSS and the Companion datasets. Screencasts cover all of the guided examples—plus some other topics of interest, such as creating bubble plots and producing nicely formatted SPSS tables in Microsoft Word.

To make the screencasts as accessible as possible, we've embedded QR codes ("quick response" codes) to related screencasts in the text. With a QR reading app, students can simply point their

Screencast

Introduction to SPSS

smartphone cameras at a screencast link, which looks like a bar code stamp, and that tutorial video will play on their phone. These smartphone apps can be downloaded for free and they are built into some web browsers. We encourage students to watch screencast videos on their phones as they practice new skills on their computers.

Students can find and view all of our screencast tutorials on the book's website (edge.sagepub .com/pollock), where they can also download all of the datasets featured in this book.

The text guides students through essential methods of analyzing politics with SPSS step by step. We've prepared hundreds of screenshots to show students exactly how to use the program's GUI. To help students use the book as a reference, this edition continues to list procedures covered in each chapter. In this edition, we also highlight the procedures we discuss. For example, in Chapter 1, students learn they can select File ▶ Open ▶ Data to open one of the Companion datasets. (The underlined letters in the command show the keyboard shortcut, another convention introduced in this edition to help students get the most out of SPSS.)

Adopters can obtain a complete set of SPSS syntax files that can be run to replicate the guided examples and the exercises. Instructors may find these files useful for re-creating the graphics, for performing the exercises, or for troubleshooting students' difficulties with the examples or exercises.

SPSS 25 is featured here, but anyone running release 12 or later can profitably use this book. As far as we can tell, SPSS 25 uses the same interfaces for the core procedures discussed in this book as it did in prior versions. SPSS 25 tables and graphs, however, have a decidedly more modern design than those produced by earlier versions.

Any student who has access to SPSS, either the full version or the "Grad Pack" version, can use this book. The Grad Pack version of more recent editions of SPSS takes the place of "Student" versions of older editions of SPSS. Unlike the Student version, the Grad Pack versions of SPSS are not limited to analyzing a small number of variables and observations, so we no longer need to create pared-down versions of the companion datasets as we have for past editions of this book. To perform logistic regression analysis in Chapter 10, however, students will need access to the full version of SPSS, as this feature is not available in the Grad Pack version.

There are many commonalities across post-12 releases, including the graphic dialogs and the Chart Editor. There are currently three ways to obtain unedited charts: Chart Builder, Graphboard Template Chooser, and Legacy Dialogs. Although we have attempted to migrate to the more recent tools (for how many more releases will SPSS support routines labeled "legacy"?), the Legacy Dialogs still offer superior intuitiveness and flexibility. (One notable exception is bubble plots, which can only be created in the Graphboard Template Chooser. Bubble plots are not covered in detail in this book, but a screencast, mentioned in Chapter 8, demonstrates how to create this graphic form.) In any event, this edition carries forward the emphasis on elegant graphic displays to complement and clarify empirical results. We have sought to instruct students in using the Chart Editor to emulate the techniques advocated by Edward R. Tufte and other experts on the visual display of data.

ACCOMPANYING CORE TEXT

Instructors will find that this book makes an effective supplement to any of a variety of methods textbooks. However, it is a particularly suitable companion to our own core text, *The Essentials of Political Analysis*. The textbook's substantive chapters cover basic and intermediate methodological issues and ideas: measurement, explanations and hypotheses, univariate statistics and bivariate analysis, controlled relationships, sampling and inference, statistical significance, correlation and linear regression, and logistic regression.

As noted above, each chapter also includes end-of-chapter exercises. Students can read the textbook chapters, do the exercises, and then work through the guided examples and exercises in *An IBM® SPSS® Companion to Political Analysis*. The idea is to get students in front of the computer, experiencing political research firsthand, early in the academic term. An instructor's solutions manual, available for download online at edge.sagepub.com/pollock and free to adopters, provides solutions for all of the textbook and workbook exercises.

ACKNOWLEDGMENTS

We received more than a few friendly e-mails suggesting ways to improve this book, and we are grateful for this advice. We also thank current and past reviewers for pointing us in the right direction: Holly Brasher, University of Alabama at Birmingham; Matthew Davis, University of Delaware; Jason Kehrberg, University of Kentucky; Thad Kousser, University of California, San Diego; Nancy Martorano, University of Dayton; Matthew Streb, Northern Illinois University; Brian Vargus, Indiana University–Purdue University Indianapolis; Julian Westerhout, Illinois State University; Lindsay Benstead, Portland State University; William Field, Rutgers, The State University of New Jersey; Rob Mellen, Mississippi State University; Brian Frederick, Bridgewater State College; Krista Jenkins, Fairleigh Dickinson University; Renato Corbetta, University of Alabama at Birmingham; Changkuk Jung, SUNY College at Geneseo; and Wesley Hussey, California State University, Sacramento.

We thank our University of Central Florida colleagues Bruce Wilson and Kerstin Hamann for helping us with ideas for exercises on comparative politics. We also give special thanks to Bill Claggett of Florida State University, who attended graduate school at the University of Minnesota with Philip Pollock, for sharing his SPSS know-how with us.[1] Bill passed away in 2017. He will be missed by his students, colleagues, family, and many friends. Many encouraging people have helped us make this a better book, including all the students who have taken the Scope and Methods of Political Science course with us over the years. Any remaining errors, however, are ours.

We gratefully acknowledge the encouragement and professionalism of everyone associated with the College Division of CQ Press and SAGE Publications: Scott Greenan, acquisitions editor; Lauren Younker, editorial assistant; Scott Harris, senior content development editor; Bennie Clark Allen, production editor; Christina West, copy editor; and Erica DeLuca, marketing manager. It is a real joy to work with such a talented team. We owe an enduring debt to Charisse Kiino, vice president of editorial—without her commitment, this entire project would still be an incoherent jumble of datasets and syntax files lying fallow on an old computer.

---

[1] It was Claggett who alerted us to an ancient flaw in the Compute Variable procedure: Multiply 0 times missing, and SPSS interprets the product as 0, not as missing. This flaw—a serious defect, in our opinion—is discussed in Chapter 9.

Getting Started

To get started with this book you will need

- Access to an SPSS-compatible computer with an Internet connection

As you have learned about political research and explored techniques of political analysis, you have studied many examples of other people's work. You may have read textbook chapters that present frequency distributions, or you may have pondered research articles that use cross-tabulation, correlation, or regression analysis to investigate interesting relationships between variables. As valuable as these learning experiences are, they can be enhanced greatly by performing political analysis firsthand—handling and modifying social science datasets, learning to use data analysis software, obtaining your own descriptive statistics for variables, setting up the appropriate analysis for interesting relationships, and running the analysis and interpreting your results.

This book is designed to guide you as you learn these valuable practical skills. In this volume you will gain a working knowledge of SPSS, a data analysis package used widely in academic institutions and business environments. SPSS has been in use for many years (it first appeared in 1968), and it contains a great variety of statistical analysis routines—from basic descriptive statistics to sophisticated predictive modeling. It is extraordinarily user friendly. You can execute most of the data analysis procedures discussed in this book using SPSS's graphical user interface (GUI). Although this book assumes that you have practical knowledge of your computer's operating system and know how to perform elemental file-handling tasks, it also assumes that you have never heard of SPSS and that you have never used a computer to analyze data of any kind. By the time you complete the guided examples and the exercises in this book, you will be well on your way to becoming an SPSS aficionado. The skills you learn will be durable, and they will serve you well as you continue your educational career or enter the business world.

This book's chapters are written in tutorial fashion. Each chapter contains several guided examples, and each includes exercises at the end. You will read each chapter while sitting in front of a computer, doing the analyses described in the guided examples, and analyzing the datasets that accompany this text. Each data analysis procedure is described in step-by-step fashion, and the book has many figures that show you what your computer screen should look like as you perform the procedures. Thus, the guided examples allow you to develop your skills and to become comfortable with SPSS. The end-of-chapter exercises allow you to apply your new skills to different substantive problems.

This book will provide you with a solid foundation in data analysis. You will learn to obtain and interpret descriptive statistics (Chapter 2), to collapse and combine variables (Chapter 3), to perform cross-tabulation and mean comparison analysis (Chapter 4), and to control for other factors that might be affecting your results (Chapter 5). Techniques of statistical inference (Chapters 6 and 7) are covered, too. On the more advanced side, this book introduces correlation and linear regression (Chapter 8), and it teaches you how to use dummy variables and how to model inter-action effects in regression analysis (Chapter 9). If you are running the Full Version of SPSS, Chapter 10 provides an introduction to logistic regression, an analytic technique that has gained wide currency in recent years. Chapter 11 shows you how to read data into SPSS, and it provides guidance on writing up your results.

DOWNLOADING THE DATASETS

To access the datasets that you will analyze in this book, navigate to this site:

edge.sagepub.com/pollock

In the left navigation pane of the page, hover over the title of this book, *An IBM® SPSS® Companion to Political Analysis, 6th edition*, and click the Datasets link (Figure I-1).

Download the datasets to a USB drive or other portable storage (or download the datasets to the default location, and then copy them to a USB drive or cloud storage you can access from anywhere you plan on working with the datasets). There are four datasets.

1. **GSS** (file name: gss.sav). This dataset has selected variables from the 2016 General Social Survey (GSS), a random sample of 2,867 adults aged 18 years or older, conducted by the National Opinion Research Center and made available through the Inter-university Consortium for Political and Social Research (ICPSR) at the University of Michigan.[1] Some of the scales in the GSS dataset were constructed by the authors. All other variables retain their original names. The names and basic descriptions of variables in the GSS dataset appear in Appendix Table A-1.[2]

2. **NES** (file name: nes.sav). This dataset includes selected variables from the 2016 American National Election Study (NES), a random sample of 4,271 citizens of voting age, conducted by the University of Michigan's Institute for Social Research (ISR) and made available through the ICPSR.[3] With the exception of scales constructed by the authors, all variables in the NES dataset retain the variable names assigned to them by the ISR. The names and basic descriptions of variables in the NES dataset appear in Appendix Table A-2.[4]

3. **States Dataset** (file name: states.sav). This dataset includes variables on each of the fifty states. These variables were compiled by the authors from various sources. The names and basic descriptions of variables in the states dataset appear in Appendix Table A-3.

---

[1] The GSS Dataset (GSS) was created from the General Social Survey 1972–2016 Cumulative Data File. Smith, Tom W., Michael Hout, and Peter V. Marsden, General Social Survey, 1972–2016 [Cumulative File], ICPSR36797-v1 (Chicago, IL: National Opinion Research Center/Ann Arbor, MI: Inter-university Consortium for Political and Social Research [distributors], 2017-11-14), https://doi.org/10.3886/ICPSR36797.v1. We encourage students to explore the full version of the 2016 GSS dataset online as well as other years of the survey for additional insights.

[2] To find information on coding and question wording, visit the following link at the University of California–Berkeley's Social Data Archive and search the alphabetical variable list: http://sda.berkeley.edu/D3/GSS16/Doc/hcbk.htm.

[3] American National Election Studies, University of Michigan, and Stanford University, ANES 2016 Time Series Study, ICPSR36824-v2 (Ann Arbor, MI: Inter-university Consortium for Political and Social Research [distributor], 2017-09-19), https://doi.org/10.3886/ICPSR36824.v2.

[4] For specific coding and question wording, go to the following link and search codebooks: http://www.electionstudies.org/studypages/anes_timeseries_2016/anes_timeseries_2016.htm.

FIGURE I-1   Downloading Companion Datasets from the SAGE Edge Website

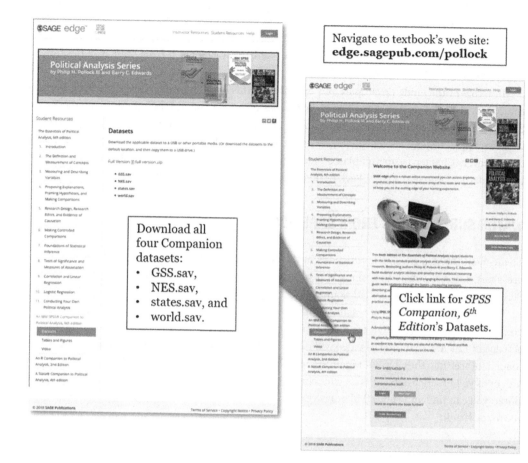

4. **World Dataset** (file name: world.sav). This dataset includes variables on 169 countries. Many of these variables are based on data compiled by Pippa Norris (John F. Kennedy School of Government, Harvard University) and made available to the scholarly community through her Internet site.[5] Other variables were compiled by the authors from various sources. The names and basic descriptions of variables in the world dataset appear in Appendix Table A-4.

As you work your way through this book, you will modify these datasets—recoding some variables, computing new variables, and otherwise tailoring the datasets to suit your purposes. You will need to make personal copies of the datasets and store them on a removable drive, such as a USB flash drive, or cloud storage that you can access from home, school, or wherever else you may want to work with the datasets.

When you begin each chapter's guided examples, or when you do the exercises, you will want to insert your personal media into the appropriate computer drive. SPSS will read the data from the drive. (Chapter 1 covers this operation in detail.) If you make any changes to a dataset, you can save the newly modified dataset directly to your drive. Alternatively, your computer lab's administrator may permit you to work on datasets that have been copied to the lab computer's desktop or to a folder designated for such a purpose. In any case, if you have modified a dataset during a data analysis session, it is important that you copy the dataset to your personal drive and take the datasets with you.

_____

[5] http://www.pippanorris.com.

SPSS FULL AND GRAD PACK VERSIONS: WHAT IS THE DIFFERENCE?

Campus computer labs run Full Version SPSS. Your institution may offer Full Version SPSS as an app, or you may have rented it. Alternatively, along with this workbook, you may have purchased a "Grad Pack" Version of SPSS, which is currently available in base, standard, and premium editions. After you install the Grad Pack Version of SPSS, you can run it from your own desktop or laptop computer.

In terms of the guided examples and exercises in this book, how does the Grad Pack Version compare with Full Version? Since this book focuses on core statistical and graphing methods, the SPSS Grad Pack, in any edition, should suffice. The base edition of the SPSS Grad Pack, however, is not equipped to perform logistic regression analysis, which is the subject of Chapter 10. If your course covers Chapter 10, or you plan on doing logistic regression analysis, you'll want to purchase the standard edition of the Grad Pack or plan to use a Full Version for that analysis.

WATCH SCREENCASTS FROM SAGE EDGE

Screencast

Introduction to SPSS

To augment the step-by-step instructions in this text, we have produced a set of screencasts. These are short, tutorial videos that show you how to use SPSS and analyze the companion datasets. Screencasts cover all of the guided examples—plus some other topics of interest.

To make screencasts as accessible as possible, we've embedded QR codes ("quick response" codes) in the text. With a QR reading app, you can simply point your smartphone camera at a screencast link and that tutorial video will play automatically. These smartphone apps can be downloaded for free and they are built in on some web browsers. We encourage you to watch screencast videos as you practice new skills on your computer. If you want to watch a screencast on your computer, you can find and view all of our screencast tutorials on the book's website: **edge.sagepub .com/pollock**.

1

Introduction to SPSS

 Watch screencasts of the guided examples in this chapter. **edge.sagepub.com/pollock**

Procedures Covered

File ▶ Open ▶ Data
Edit ▶ Options
Utilities ▶ Variables
Analyze ▶ Descriptive Statistics ▶ Frequencies
File ▶ Print
File ▶ Open ▶ Output
Format ▶ TableLooks (in Table Editing window)
File ▶ New ▶ Syntax

In this chapter, we take readers on a quick tour of the SPSS program. We describe the main windows that students will encounter: the welcome screen, the data editor, and the viewer (equivalent to the console in other statistical analysis programs). For maximum benefit, practice the steps and procedures we discuss here on your own computer.

THE DATA EDITOR

Open the General Social Survey dataset, GSS.sav, to get acquainted with SPSS's Data Editor. To open this dataset, locate the GSS.sav file in the folder where you saved it and double-click it. If you already have SPSS running, select File ▶ Open ▶ Data and find the GSS.sav file.

Recent versions of SPSS will open several windows at once. You may see a welcome screen (Figure 1-1). You can skip the welcome screen in the future by checking the "Don't show this dialog in the future" option in the lower left corner of the window.[1] Click the "Close" button to close the welcome screen.

SPSS opens the data file and displays the Data Editor (Figure 1-2).

Screencast
Introduction to SPSS

---

[1] SPSS uses the welcome screen to promote some extensions you can add on to the program along with support resources. We won't delve into these extensions and resources, but they're worth exploring on your own.

FIGURE **1-1**   SPSS "Welcome Screen"

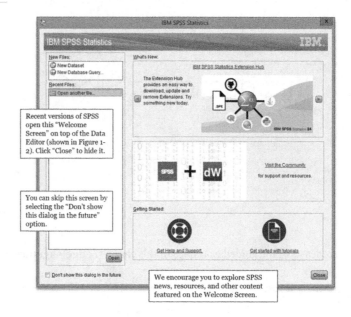

FIGURE **1-2**   SPSS Data Editor in Data View

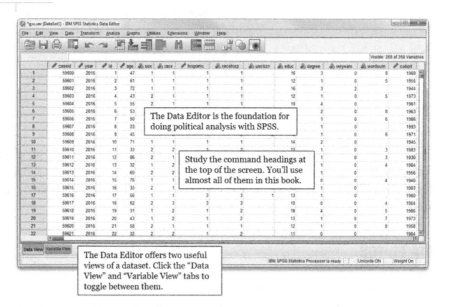

Notice the two tabs at the bottom of the Data Editor window: Data View and Variable View. The SPSS Data Editor offers two "views" of the dataset. Both views are useful. Select Data View or Variable View by clicking one of the tabs at the bottom of the Data Editor.

Turn your attention to the Data View. (Make sure the Data View tab is clicked.) The Data View shows how all the cases are organized for analysis. Information for each case occupies a separate row. When you're working with the GSS dataset, each row represents a person who participated in the survey. Numbers in the "id" column record each respondent's case identification number ("caseid"). The variables, given brief yet descriptive names, appear along the columns of the editor.

Scroll right to see information recorded from the first respondent. You can tell that the first respondent in the dataset is 47 years old (see the first value in the "age" column). You can also

FIGURE 1-3   SPSS Data Editor in Variable View

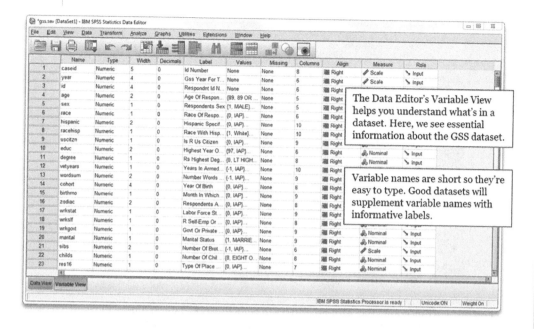

see that this respondent has a 1 in the "sex" column and a 1 in the "race" column. Storing information as numbers is efficient, but it's not immediately clear what these numbers really mean. To paint a more complete word portrait of this respondent, you need to see how all the variables are coded.

To see how the GSS variables are coded, click the Variable View tab (Figure 1-3). The Variable View, among other useful features, shows the word labels that the researcher has assigned to the numeric codes. This view shows complete information on the meaning and measurement of each variable in the dataset. (You can adjust the width of a column by clicking, holding, and dragging the column border.)

The most frequently used variable information is contained in Name, Label, Values, and Missing. Name is the brief descriptor recognized by SPSS when it does analysis. Names can be up to 64 characters in length, although they need to begin with a letter (not a number). Plus, names must not contain any special characters, such as dashes or commas, although underscores are okay.

Because variable names are short and often abbreviated, researchers will use labels, long descriptors (up to 256 characters are allowed), to provide more detailed information about variables. For example, when SPSS analyzes the GSS variable mobile16, it will look in the Variable View for a label. If it finds one, then it will label the results of its analysis by using Label instead of Name. So mobile16 shows up as "Geographic Mobility Since Age 16"—a bit more descriptive than "mobile16."

Just as Label permits a wordier description for Name, Values attaches descriptive labels to a variable's numeric values. We can examine the value labels for the sex and race variables to find out what it means when they're coded 1. To find out the value labels for the sex variable, find its row in the Variable View, click the mouse anywhere in the Values cell, and then click the gray button that appears. A Value Labels window opens, revealing the labels that SPSS will attach to the numeric codes of sex. Unless you instruct it to do otherwise, SPSS will apply these labels to its analysis of the sex variable. Repeat this process to find out what value 1 on the race variable signifies, or what the numeric codes of the "marital" variable mean (see Figure 1-4). You can see that respondents who have never been married are coded 5 on the variable marital. Click the Cancel button in the Value Labels window to return to the Variable View.

FIGURE 1-4   Value Labels of a Variable in the Data Editor

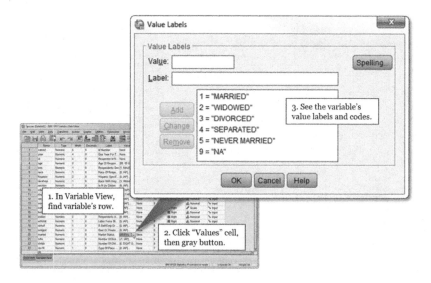

Finally, a word about the Missing column. Sometimes a dataset does not have complete information for all variables and observations. This happens for a variety of reasons; researchers may add or remove questions from the survey, some questions may not apply to everyone, or the response may not be clear. In coding the data, researchers typically give special numeric codes to missing values. In coding mobile16, for example, the GSS coders entered a value of 0 for respondents who were not asked the question ("IAP"), 8 for respondents did not know ("DK"), and 9 when the information was otherwise not available ("NA"). Because these numeric codes have been set to missing (and thus appear in the Missing column), SPSS does not recognize them as valid codes and will not include them in an analysis of mobile16. In many cases, the author has set most missing values in the datasets to *system-missing*, which SPSS automatically removes from the analysis. However, when you use an existing variable to create a new variable, SPSS may not automatically transfer missing values on the existing variable to missing values on the new variable. Later in this volume, we discuss how to handle such situations.

SETTING OPTIONS FOR VARIABLE LISTS

Now you have a feel for how data are organized and stored in SPSS. Before looking at how SPSS produces and handles output, you must do one more thing. To ensure that all the examples in this workbook correspond to what you see on your screen, you will need to follow the steps given in this section when you open each dataset for the first time.

DO THIS NOW: In the main menu bar of the Data Editor, select Edit ▶ Options. Make sure that the General tab is clicked (see Figure 1-5). If the Variables Lists options for Display names and Alphabetical are not already selected, select them (as in Figure 1-5). Click Apply and then OK, returning to the Data Editor. When you open a new dataset for the first time, go to Edit ▶ Options and ensure that Display names/ Alphabetical are selected and applied. This will help you find variables to analyze more efficiently. (If the radio button Display names *and* the radio button Alphabetical are already selected when you opened the Options menu, you are set to go and can click the Cancel button.)

FIGURE 1-5   Setting Options for Variable Lists

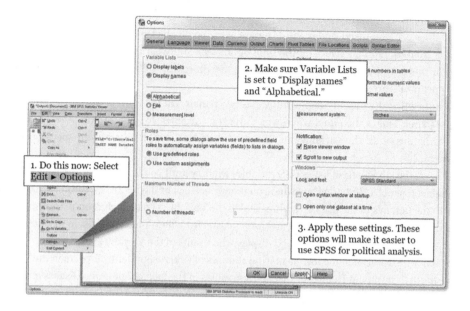

A CLOSER LOOK: VARIABLES UTILITY

Although the names of GSS variables are not terribly informative, SPSS makes it easy to view complete coding information. In the text, we show how you can access information about variables in the Data Editor's Variable View. You can also view detailed information about the variables in a dataset using Utilities ▶ Variables. This selection will yield the Variables window (Figure 1-6).

Suppose you want to view detailed information about the GSS variable marital to better understand how the dataset records respondents' marital statuses. Scroll through the alphabetical list of variables on the left side of the Variables window until you find "marital" and select it. You'll then see some essential information about the variable, like the text label associated with it ("Marital Status"), along with a breakdown of how different marital statuses are encoded.

FIGURE 1-6   Retrieving Coding Information

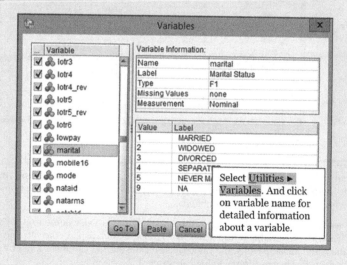

THE VIEWER

We will run through a brief example to show how SPSS analyzes variables and generates output. You execute most SPSS commands using a graphical user interface (GUI). SPSS's methods of analyzing variables are organized under the "Analyze" tab. You'll start most of your data analysis by clicking the Analyze tab and selecting the type of analysis you wish to perform from its menu of options. For this example, select Analyze ▶ Descriptive Statistics ▶ Frequencies. The Frequencies window appears (Figure 1-7).

You'll notice that the Frequencies window has two panels. On the right is the (currently empty) Variable(s) panel. This is the panel where you enter the variables you want to analyze. On the left you see the names of all the variables in GSS in alphabetical order, just as you specified in the Options menu.[2]

Scroll down the alphabetized list of GSS variables window until you find marital and add "marital" to the Variable(s) panel. (*Hint*: Click anywhere on the variable list and type "m" on the keyboard. SPSS will jump to the first m's in the list.) To add marital to the Variable(s) panel, click on marital and then click the arrow between the panels or drag and drop marital from the alphabetical list to the Variable(s) panel.[3] Click OK. SPSS runs the analysis and displays the results in the Viewer (Figure 1-8).

A frequency distribution table for the marital statuses of GSS respondents appears in the Viewer. We'll have more to say about frequency distribution tables in the next chapter and discuss many different types of tables in this book. In the future, we'll focus on the tables SPSS generates and won't show the entire Viewer as we do in Figure 1-8.

When you execute a procedure using the GUI, SPSS temporarily stores the information you inputted so you can return to the same window and adjust your selections. This is particularly useful

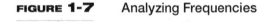

FIGURE 1-7   Analyzing Frequencies

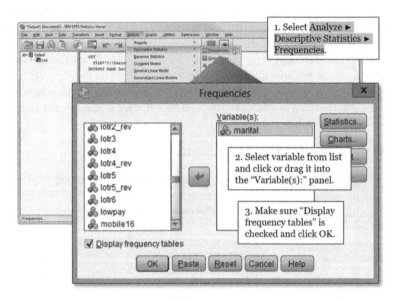

---

[2] If you don't see an alphabetized list of variable names in the Frequencies window, follow the DO THIS NOW instructions in the "Setting Options for Variable Lists" section above. Setting correct options for variable lists will make it easier for you to execute SPSS commands.

[3] You can also access variable information within this dialog. Put the mouse pointer on the variable, marital, and right-click. Then click on Variable Information. SPSS retrieves and displays the variable's name (marital), label (Marital Status), and, most usefully, the value labels for the marital variable's numeric codes. (To see all the codes, click the drop-down arrow in the Value Labels box.)

FIGURE 1-8   Sample Table Output in the SPSS Viewer

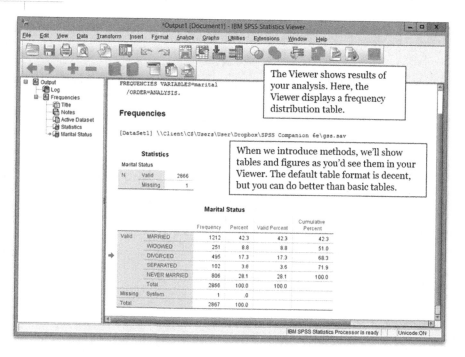

The Viewer shows results of your analysis. Here, the Viewer displays a frequency distribution table.

When we introduce methods, we'll show tables and figures as you'd see them in your Viewer. The default table format is decent, but you can do better than basic tables.

when you're executing complex commands for the first time, making graphics, or performing the same operation repeatedly on different variables. After running the frequency analysis illustrated in Figures 1-7 and 1-8, for example, you could select Analyze ▶ Descriptive Statistics ▶ Frequencies again and find marital still on the variables list, making it easy to change the command settings or analyze a different variable.

A CLOSER LOOK: KEYBOARD SHORTCUTS

Some SPSS users may find navigating the GUI cumbersome after a while. Those who prefer the keyboard to the mouse will be happy to know that there is an easy way to navigate the GUI using keyboard shortcuts. To get to the Frequencies window, hold down the "Alt" key and press "A", "E", then "F" (you don't need to capitalize the letters or use quotation marks). You can navigate the SPSS menu by pressing Alt followed by the letter(s) corresponding to different branches of the menu. If you look closely at the command notations above, you'll see that we've underlined the letters A, e, and F to show the keyboard shortcuts and we follow this convention throughout the book when we introduce new procedures.

Notice that the SPSS Viewer has two panes. In the Outline pane, SPSS keeps a running list of the analyses you are performing. The Outline pane references each element in the Contents pane, which reports the results of your analyses. In this book we are interested exclusively in the Contents pane.

You can minimize the Viewer's Outline pane by first placing the cursor on the Pane divider. Click and hold the left button of the mouse and then move the Pane divider over to the left-hand border of the Viewer. The Viewer should now look like Figure 1-9. The Contents pane shows you the frequency distribution of the marital variable with value codes labeled. In Chapter 2 we discuss frequency analysis in more detail. Our immediate purpose is to become familiar with SPSS output.

FIGURE 1-9   SPSS Viewer with the Outline Pane Minimized

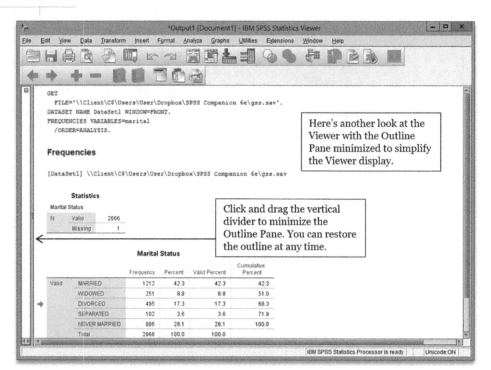

Here are some key points about the Viewer to keep in mind:

- The Viewer is a separate file, created by you during your analysis of the data. The Viewer file, a log of your analysis and output, is completely distinct from the data file. Whereas SPSS data files all have the file extension *.sav, Viewer files have the file extension *.spv. The output can be saved, under a name that you choose, and then reopened later in SPSS. You can't open a *.spv file in another program, like a word processor (e.g., Microsoft Word); if you want to use SPSS output in a document, follow the directions below for exporting graphics and copying tables.

- Output from each succeeding analysis does not overwrite the Viewer's *.spv file. Rather, it appends new results to the Viewer file. If you were to run another analysis for a different variable, SPSS would dump the results in the Viewer below the analysis you just performed.

- The quickest way to return to the Data Editor is to click the starred icon on the menu bar, as shown in Figure 1-8. And, of course, Windows accumulates icons for all open files along the bottom Taskbar.

- The "Analyze" tab appears at the top of the Viewer and the Data Editor so you can start your data analysis from either SPSS window. In fact, all tabs in the Data Editor window appear in the Viewer window (along with two tabs that appear only in the Viewer: Insert and Format). Because the results of your analysis appear in the Viewer, it makes sense to start your analysis there, but you can get the same results starting from the Data Editor.

As we discuss in the next two sections, you may select any part of the output file, format it, print it, or copy and paste it into a word processing program.

SELECTING, PRINTING, AND SAVING OUTPUT

Many of the exercises in this workbook will ask you to print the results of your SPSS analyses, so let's cover the print procedure. We'll also address a routine necessity: saving output.

Printing desired results requires, first, that you select the output or portion of output you want to print. A quick and easy way to select a single table or chart is to place the cursor anywhere on the desired object and click once. For example, if you want to print the marital frequency distribution table produced in the preceding section, place the cursor on the frequency table and click. A red arrow appears in the left-hand margin next to the table (Figure 1-10). Click the Printer icon on the Viewer menu bar or select File ▶ Print. The Print window opens. In the window's Print Range panel, the radio button next to "Selected output" should already be clicked. Clicking OK would send the frequency table to the printer.

To select more than one table or graph, hold down the Control key (Ctrl) while selecting the desired output with the mouse. Thus, if you wanted to print the frequency table and the statistics table, first click on one of the desired tables. While holding down the Ctrl key, click on the other table. SPSS will select both tables.

To copy your Viewer output to your computer's clipboard to paste into another document, simply select the table(s) you want to copy, right-click, and select the "Copy" option (see Figure 1-10). Recent versions of SPSS have greatly improved table formatting over prior versions and the table copied from the Viewer now looks decent in a document.

To save your Viewer output, simply click the familiar Save icon on the Viewer menu bar (refer to Figure 1-10 again). Browse for an appropriate location. Invent a file name (but preserve the ".spv" extension), such as "chap1.spv," and click Save. SPSS saves all of the information in the Viewer to the file chap1.spv. Saving your output protects your work. Plus, the output file can always be reopened later. Suppose you are in the middle of a series of SPSS analyses and you want to stop and return later. You can save the Viewer file, as described here, and exit SPSS. When you return, you start SPSS and load a data file (like GSS.dta) into the Data Editor. In the main menu bar of the Data Editor, you select File ▶ Open ▶ Output, find your .spv file, and open it. Then you can pick up where you left off.

FIGURE 1-10   Selecting, Printing, and Saving Output

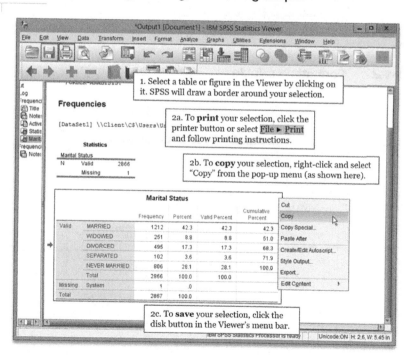

If you want to save a table or graphic that appears in the Viewer but don't want to save all of your Viewer output, select the Viewer object you want to save and right-click it. Select "Export . . . " from the pop-up dialog window (see Figure 1-11). If you've selected a table, you can export it to a variety of document types, such as a .pdf document. If you've selected a graphic, you can create a variety of different types of image files.

HOW TO FORMAT AN SPSS TABLE

When you analyze political science data, you'll create a lot of tables of results. You want the tables you create to communicate the results of your analysis effectively. No one wants to try to decipher results from a mess of numbers. Fortunately, SPSS offers some easy-to-use options for formatting tables.

FIGURE 1-11   Exporting Viewer Output

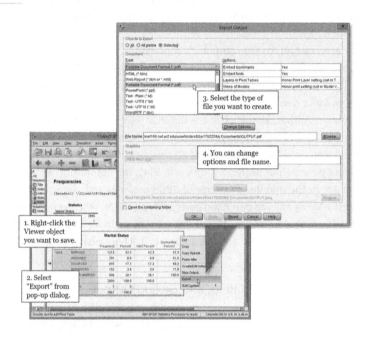

FIGURE 1-12   Formatting a Table

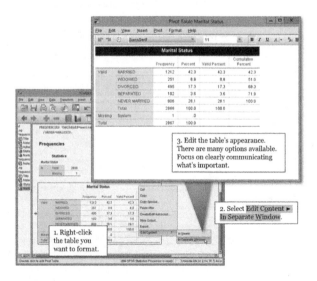

To access the table formatting tools, select the table you want to format and right-click it (like you would to copy or export it). Now, select the "Edit Content ▶ In Separate Window" option. You'll see your table in a new, separate window with formatting tools (see Figure 1-12). This table editing window allows you to change the look and feel of your table; you can change the colors, shading, fonts, alignments, and more. For example, you can widen the far-right column of the marital status frequency distribution table so the heading "Cumulative Percent" stays on one line. Keep in mind what you're attempting to communicate. If you're conducting serious analysis for an academic paper, a tropical color theme isn't the best choice.

Here's a suggestion to help you quickly create professional-style tables. The Academic-style tables are particularly good. In the separate table editing window, select Format ▶ TableLooks (this procedure is only available in the table editing window). TableLooks are a pre-defined set of table styles. There are many styles to choose from, but the "Academic" style is a solid choice for most of your political analysis. Select "Academic" from the list of TableLook files and click OK.

You'll see your table with your TableLook selection applied in the separate table editing window. You can close the separate table editing window by clicking the X button in the upper-right corner. Now you should see your freshly formatted table in the Viewer. If you selected the Academic look for the marital variable's frequency distribution table, your table should look like this:

Marital Status

		Frequency	Percent	Valid Percent	Cumulative Percent
Valid	MARRIED	1212	42.3	42.3	42.3
	WIDOWED	251	8.8	8.8	51.0
	DIVORCED	495	17.3	17.3	68.3
	SEPARATED	102	3.6	3.6	71.9
	NEVER MARRIED	806	28.1	28.1	100.0
	Total	2866	100.0	100.0	
Missing	System	1	.0		
Total		2867	100.0		

FIGURE 1-13   Creating Academic-style Tables

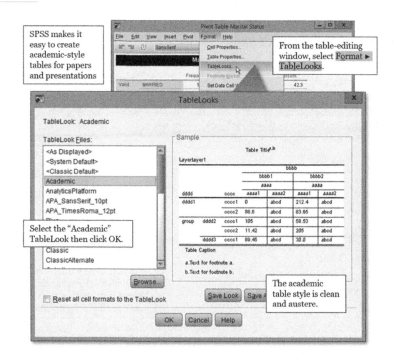

In this book, we'll show tables in the SPSS default style to make it easier to follow our examples, but you can make the Academic-style table your default format by selecting Edit ▶ Options and then the Pivot Tables tab, select Academic from the TableLook options, and then click OK. Tables in this pre-defined SPSS table format look a lot like the tables one sees in top political science journals. It's a good look for your political analysis.

SAVING COMMANDS IN SYNTAX FILES

In this book, we show how to implement essential political science research methods using SPSS's graphical user interface. SPSS's GUI offers a straightforward and consistent framework for analyzing data. In some situations, however, you may want to document your data analysis to enable others to see what you did and replicate your analysis. These situations call for making a syntax file.

A syntax file is a text document with the *.sps file extension that records the series of commands used to perform some data analysis. The procedures you execute using SPSS's GUI can also be stated as text commands. If you look closely at Figure 1-9, you'll see that SPSS displays the text equivalent of the frequency analysis of the marital variable in the Viewer:

FREQUENCIES VARIABLES=marital
/ORDER=ANALYSIS.

This text-command equivalent of the frequency analysis demonstrated above, executed from a syntax file, would yield the same results as using the GUI, enabling someone else to replicate the analysis.

This book demonstrates the essentials of political analysis without using the esoteric SPSS command language. For most data analysis tasks, the GUI works fine and will allow you to start applying core concepts much sooner than encoding commands. Thankfully, SPSS makes it easy for users to "reverse engineer" a syntax file for replication purposes.

To create a syntax file, select File ▶ New ▶ Syntax. This selection will call up a new window, the Syntax Editor (see Figure 1-14, which shows commands executed in this chapter). As we've seen, SPSS prints the text-command equivalent of procedures implemented through its GUI in the Viewer. You can copy and paste these text-equivalent commands into a syntax file. To create a complete

FIGURE 1-14   The Syntax Editor

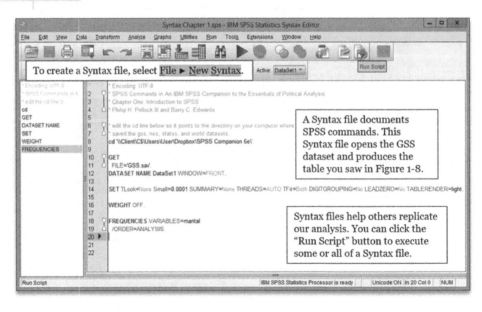

syntax file, you can also copy and paste the commands to get the GSS dataset, set viewing options, and execute the analysis. The grayed-out lines that start with * are comments (lines in the syntax file to be read by human users rather than executed by SPSS).

Another way to save your commands in a syntax file is the "Paste" button that appears in GUI windows that execute commands. Take another look at Figure 1-7, the procedure we used to generate a frequency distribution table for the marital variable. Next to the OK button, you'll see the Paste button. If you press this button, SPSS will paste the syntax for the procedure at the end of your syntax file (if you don't have a syntax file open, SPSS will open a new one). For completeness, you may want to add the commands to open the dataset and some user-friendly comments, but it's a very convenient feature for generating syntax files that replicate your analysis.

GETTING HELP

To view the formal how-to manual for any SPSS procedure, you can click the "Help" button from the GUI window that executes that procedure. For example, if you want to see detailed instructions on the frequency analysis procedure you used earlier in this chapter, you could click the Help button in the Frequencies window (see Figure 1-7). SPSS retrieves the technical manual information and displays it in a web browser (Figure 1-15).

You can also get help by watching screencasts the authors of this book produced to show students how to execute the procedures discussed in this book. We've included links to these screencasts throughout this book. You can find a complete list of screencasts on the SAGE Edge website for this book: **edge.sagepub.com/pollock**.

FIGURE 1-15   SPSS Help Manual

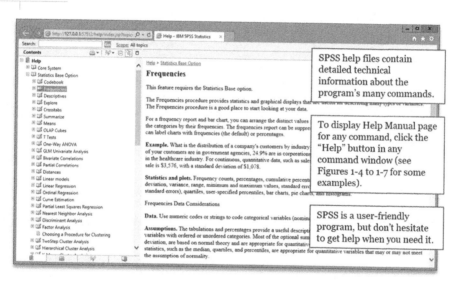

Name: Anna Jeffries   Date: 9/8/22

E-mail: anna.jeffries@spartans.ut.edu   Section: _____

CHAPTER 1 EXERCISES

1. (Dataset: gss.sav. Variables: income16, attend.) In this chapter, we spent some time using the Data View and the Variable View to describe the first respondent in the GSS dataset. In this exercise, you will use your familiarity with the Data Editor to find out this respondent's income (income16) and how often this respondent attends religious services (attend).

    A. With the GSS dataset open, go to the Data View. What numeric code does the first respondent have on income16? A code of (fill in the blank) ____26____. Go to the Variable View. Just as you did earlier in this chapter, find income16 and click in the Values cell. What is this respondent's income? (circle one)

    $25,000 to $29,999 $60,000 to $74,999

    $170,000 or over

    B. Return to the Data View. What is this respondent's code on the variable attend? A code of (fill in the blank) ____0____. Go to the Variable View. How often does this respondent attend religious services? (circle one)

    Never   Once a year   2–3 times a month

2. Suppose that you have just opened the World, States, or NES dataset for the first time. The first thing you do is select Edit ▶ Options and consider the Variable Lists panel of the General tab. You must make sure that which two choices are selected and applied? (check two)

    *   Display labels
    *   Display names
    *   Alphabetical
    *   File
    *   Measurement level

3. The GSS dataset contains the variable happy, which asks respondents how happy they are. Find the variable happy in the Data Editor's Variable View and answer the following questions.

    A. What is the descriptive label for the variable happy? General Happiness

    B. Respondents who say they are "very happy" have which numeric code? (circle one)

    1   2   3

4. Generate a frequency distribution table for the variable happy in the GSS dataset using the Analyze ▶ Descriptive Statistics ▶ Frequencies procedure.

    A. Print the table.

    B. Copy/paste the table into a blank document. Edit the table for appearance and readability, and then print it.

5. SPSS works with different types of files to analyze data and produce results. These file types include datasets that record information about sample observations, output files of SPSS results, and syntax files used to replicate SPSS commands. Each of these different file types has a unique, three-character file name extension. Complete the table below to help you remember the file name extension for each file type.

SPSS File Type	File Name Extension	
Dataset	.sav	?
Output	.spv	?
Syntax	.sps	?

6. A political scientist wants to analyze civic culture in the United States. Civic culture is an important concept but is difficult to measure empirically. The researcher could consider several different variables.

    A. Which variable in the States dataset records the number of years of social studies that states require students to take to graduate high school? ns_yrs_ss

    B. Which variable in the States dataset records the percentage of the voting age population that turned out to vote in the most recent federal election (for which data are available)? trnout00

    C. Which variable in the States dataset records the percentage of state residents who frequently attend religious services? attend_pct

D. Which variable in the States dataset records the percentage of state residents who do voluntary community service? **volunteer_rate**

7. Chapter 1 showed you how to view detailed information about a variable named marital in the GSS dataset. This variable identifies the survey respondents' marital statuses with numeric codes and assigns a label to each numeric value. The NES dataset contains a similar variable, also named marital, that records the marital statuses of its respondents. The numeric coding for marital in the NES is a little different than its GSS counterpart, however. It's important to pay close attention to how variables are coded. Fill in the following table to identify the labels that correspond to numeric codes of the NES marital variable.

NES Variable "marital"	
Numeric Code	Value Label
1	married: spouse present
2	married: spouse absent
3	widowed ?
4	divorced ?
5	separated ?
6	never married.

8. A political scientist wants to study health outcomes in countries around the world. Good government may improve health outcomes; a healthy country may also be more politically stable. To study the health-politics relationship, the researcher could consider several variables in the World dataset that measure health in countries around the world. For each variable, briefly describe what it measures in your own words.

A. fertility — this measures the number of children per woman; if there is a high fertility level the population will grow

B. hiv_percent — percentage of population aged 19-49 with HIV; high levels of HIV in young people shows bad health

C. infant_mortality — number of infants dying before age one

D. spendhealth — public spending on health care

E. unnoncom — death rates from non-communicable diseases

2

Descriptive Statistics

 Watch screencasts of the guided examples in this chapter. **edge.sagepub.com/pollock**

Procedures Covered

Analyze ▶ Descriptive Statistics ▶ Frequencies
Data ▶ Weight Cases
Graphs ▶ Legacy Dialogs ▶ Histogram
Analyze ▶ Reports ▶ Case Summaries

A nalyzing descriptive statistics is the most basic—and sometimes the most informative—form of analysis you will do. Descriptive statistics reveal two attributes of a variable: its typical value (central tendency) and its spread (degree of dispersion or variation). The precision with which you can describe central tendency for any given variable depends on the variable's level of measurement. For nominal-level variables you can identify the *mode*, the most common value of the variable. For ordinal-level variables, those whose categories can be ranked, you can find the mode and the *median*—the value of the variable that divides the cases into two equal-size groups. For interval-level variables you can obtain the mode, median, and arithmetic *mean*, the sum of all values divided by the number of cases.

In this chapter you will use the Analyze ▶ Descriptive Statistics ▶ Frequencies procedure to obtain appropriate measures of central tendency, and you will learn to make informed judgments about variation. With the correct prompts, the Frequencies procedure also provides valuable graphic support—bar charts and (for interval variables) histograms. These tools are essential for distilling useful information from datasets having hundreds of anonymous cases, such as the American National Election Study (NES) or the General Social Survey (GSS). For smaller datasets with aggregated units, such as the States and World datasets, SPSS offers an additional procedure: Analyze ▶ Reports ▶ Case Summaries. Case Summaries lets you see firsthand how specific cases are distributed across a variable that you find especially interesting.

HOW SPSS STORES INFORMATION ABOUT VARIABLES

Suppose you were hired by a telephone-polling firm to interview a large number of respondents. Your job is to find out and record three characteristics of each person you interview: their age, political ideology, and newspaper reading habits. The natural human tendency would be to record these attributes in words. For example, you might describe a respondent this way: "The respondent is 22 years old, ideologically moderate, and reads the newspaper about once a week." This would be a good thumbnail description, easily interpreted by another person. To SPSS, though, these words would not make sense.

Whereas people excel at recognizing and manipulating words, SPSS excels at recognizing and manipulating numbers. This is why researchers devise a *coding system*, a set of numeric identifiers for the different values of a variable. For one of the above variables, age, a coding scheme would be straightforward: Simply record the respondent's age in number of years, 22. To record information about political ideology and newspaper reading habits for data analysis, however, a different set of rules is needed. For example, the GSS applies the following coding schemes for political ideology (polviews) and newspaper reading habits (news):

Variable Name (GSS)	Response in Words	Numeric Code
Political ideology (polviews)	Extremely liberal	1
	Liberal	2
	Slightly liberal	3
	Moderate	4
	Slightly conservative	5
	Conservative	6
	Extremely conservative	7
Newspaper reading habits (news)	Every day	1
	A few times a week	2
	Once a week	3
	Less than once a week	4
	Never	5

Thus, the narrative profile "the respondent is 22 years old, is politically moderate, and reads the newspaper about once a week" becomes "22 4 3" to SPSS. SPSS doesn't really care what the numbers stand for. As long as SPSS has numeric data, it will crunch the numbers—telling you the mean age of all respondents or the modal level of newspaper reading. It is important, therefore, to provide SPSS with labels for each code so that the software's analytic work makes sense to the user.

INTERPRETING MEASURES OF CENTRAL TENDENCY AND VARIATION

Finding a variable's central tendency is ordinarily a straightforward exercise. Simply read the computer output and report the numbers. Describing a variable's degree of dispersion or variation, however, often requires informed judgment.[1] Here is a general rule that applies to any variable at any level of measurement: A variable has no dispersion if all the cases—states, countries, people, or whatever—fall into the same value of the variable. A variable has maximum dispersion if the cases are spread evenly across all values of the variable. In other words, the number of cases in one category equals the number of cases in every other category.

Central tendency and variation work together in providing a complete description of any variable. Some variables have an easily identified typical value and show little dispersion. For example, suppose you were to ask a large number of U.S. citizens what sort of political system they believe to be the best: democracy, dictatorship, or anarchy. What would be the modal response, or the economic system preferred by most people? Democracy. Would there be a great deal of dispersion, with large numbers of people choosing the alternatives, dictatorship or anarchy? Probably not.

---

[1] In this chapter we use the terms *dispersion*, *variation*, and *spread* interchangeably.

In other instances, however, you may find that one value of a variable has a more tenuous grasp on the label *typical*. And the variable may exhibit more dispersion, with the cases spread out more evenly across the variable's other values. For example, suppose a large sample of voting-age adults were asked, in the weeks preceding a presidential election, how interested they are in the campaign: very interested, somewhat interested, or not very interested. Among your own acquaintances you probably know a number of people who fit into each category. So even if one category, such as "somewhat interested," is the median, many people will likely be found at the extremes of "very interested" and "not very interested." In this instance, the amount of dispersion in a variable—its degree of spread—is essential to understanding and describing it.

We can describe the central tendency and dispersion of any variable, but the tools and terminology used to describe a variable depend on the variable's level of measure. The lower the level of measure, the more limited our toolkit for describing central tendency and dispersion. These and other points are best understood by working through some guided examples. In the next section, we'll show you how to use SPSS to describe a nominal-level variable (the lowest level of measurement).

DESCRIBING NOMINAL VARIABLES

For this and the next few analyses, you will use the GSS dataset. Open the GSS dataset by double-clicking the GSS.sav file or, if you already have SPSS running, select File ▶ Open ▶ Data and locate GSS.sav. Before you start analyzing this dataset, select Edit ▶ Options in the Data Editor and then click on the General tab. Just as you did when analyzing a dataset in Chapter 1, make sure that the radio buttons in the Variable Lists area are set for "Display names" and "Alphabetical." (If these options are already set, click Cancel. If they are not set, select them, click Apply, and then click OK. Now you are ready to go.)

First, you will obtain a frequency distribution table and bar chart for a nominal-level variable in the GSS dataset, zodiac, which records respondents' astrological signs. Select Analyze ▶ Descriptive Statistics ▶ Frequencies. Scroll down to the bottom of the left-hand list until you find zodiac. Click zodiac into the Variable(s) panel. To the right of the Variable(s) panel, click the Charts button

Screencast

Analyze a Variable with Dispersion

FIGURE **2-1**   Obtaining Frequencies and a Bar Chart (nominal variable)

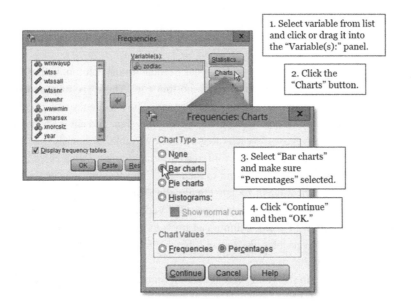

(Figure 2-1). The Frequencies: Charts dialog appears. In Chart Type, select "Bar charts." In Chart Values, be sure to select "Percentages." Click Continue, which returns you to the main Frequencies window. Make sure "Display frequency tables" is checked in the Frequencies window. Click OK. SPSS runs the analysis.

SPSS has produced two items of interest in the Viewer: a frequency distribution table of respondents' astrological signs and a bar chart of the same information. (The small "Statistics" table isn't of much interest to us but we include it here so you'll see what's in this book in your Viewer.) First, examine the frequency distribution table.

Statistics

Respondents Astrological Sign

N	Valid	2777
	Missing	90

Respondents' Astrological Sign

		Frequency	Percent	Valid Percent	Cumulative Percent
Valid	ARIES	237	8.3	8.5	8.5
	TAURUS	242	8.4	8.7	17.3
	GEMINI	232	8.1	8.4	25.6
	CANCER	267	9.3	9.6	35.3
	LEO	225	7.9	8.1	43.4
	VIRGO	262	9.2	9.4	52.8
	LIBRA	227	7.9	8.2	61.0
	SCORPIO	216	7.5	7.8	68.8
	SAGITTARIUS	216	7.5	7.8	76.6
	CAPRICORN	192	6.7	6.9	83.5
	AQUARIUS	225	7.9	8.1	91.6
	PISCES	233	8.1	8.4	100.0
	Total	2777	96.9	100.0	
Missing	System	90	3.1		
Total		2867	100.0		

The value labels for each astrological code appear in the leftmost column, with Aries occupying the top row of numbers and Pisces occupying the bottom row. There are four numeric columns: Frequency, Percent, Valid Percent, and Cumulative Percent. The Frequency column shows raw frequencies, the actual number of respondents having each zodiac sign. Percent is the percentage of *all* respondents, including missing cases, in each category of the variable. Ordinarily the Percent column can be ignored, because we generally are not interested in including missing cases in our description of a variable. Valid Percent is the column to focus on. Valid Percent tells us the percentage of non-missing responses in each value of zodiac. Finally, the Cumulative Percent column reports the percentage of cases that fall in *or below* each value of the variable. For ordinal or interval variables, as you will see, the Cumulative Percent column can provide valuable clues about how a variable is distributed. But for nominal variables like zodiac, which cannot be ranked, the Cumulative Percent column provides no information of value.

Now consider the values in the Valid Percent column more closely. Scroll between the frequency distribution table and the bar chart, which depicts the zodiac variable in graphic form (Figure 2-2).

FIGURE 2-2   Bar Chart of a Nominal-level Variable

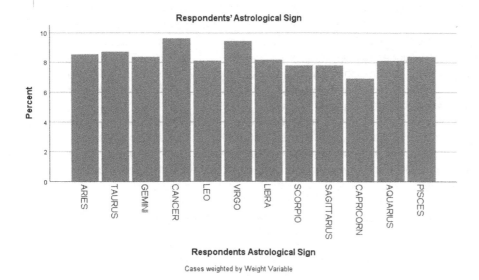

What is the mode, the most common astrological sign? For nominal variables, the answer to this question is (almost) always an easy call: Simply find the value with the highest percentage of responses. Virgo is the mode. When it comes to describing the central tendency of nominal-level variables like zodiac, our toolkit is limited to identifying the variable's mode.

Does the zodiac variable have little dispersion or a lot of dispersion? Again, study the Valid Percent column and the bar chart. Apply the following rule: *A variable has no dispersion if the cases are concentrated in one value of the variable; a variable has maximum dispersion if the cases are spread evenly across all values of the variable.* Are most of the cases concentrated in Virgo, or are there many cases in each sign of zodiac? Because respondents are spread out—all astrological signs are about equally represented—you would conclude that zodiac has a high level of dispersion. Looking at the bar chart of zodiac in Figure 2-3, it may be tempting to say the distribution is highest in the middle, but remember that the order of nominal-level values is essentially arbitrary; Virgo is not the middle zodiac sign, so the peak that appears to be in the middle of the bar chart is not a true feature of zodiac's dispersion.

A CLOSER LOOK: WEIGHTING THE GSS AND NES DATASETS

Many of this book's guided examples and exercises use the two survey datasets: the General Social Survey (GSS) and the American National Election Survey (NES). Before proceeding, you need to learn about a feature of these datasets that will require special treatment throughout the book.

In raw form, the GSS and NES datasets are not completely representative of all groups in the population. This lack of representativeness may be intentional (e.g., the American National Election Study purposely oversampled Latino respondents so that researchers could gain insights into the attitudes of this group) or unintentional (e.g., some income groups are more likely to respond to surveys than are other groups). For some SPSS commands, this lack of representativeness does not matter. For most SPSS commands, however, raw survey data produce incorrect results.

(Continued)

(Continued)

Fortunately, survey designers included the necessary corrective in the NES and GSS dataset: a weight variable. A *weight variable* adjusts for the distorting effect of sampling bias and calculates results that accurately reflect the makeup of the population. If a certain type of respondent is underrepresented in a sample, like young people in a survey conducted by dialing random landline phone numbers, that group's responses are weighted more heavily to make up for being underrepresented. If a certain type of respondent is oversampled, that group's responses are weighted less heavily.

To obtain correct results, *you must specify the weight variable whenever you analyze the GSS or NES datasets.* Otherwise, your analysis will be biased. To weight observations in these datasets to produce nationally representative results, select Data ▶ Weight Cases. When analyzing the GSS, you will specify the weight variable, *wtss* (Figure 2-3). For the NES dataset, the weight variable is *nesw*.

FIGURE 2-3   Weighting Observations in a Dataset

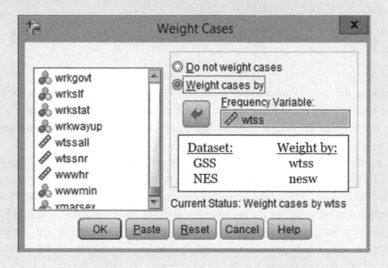

DESCRIBING ORDINAL VARIABLES

In this section, you will analyze and describe two ordinal-level variables in the GSS dataset, one of which has little variation and the other of which is more spread out. These ordinal-level variables examine public opinion on two social policy issues. Opinions on both questions are recorded on 5-point ordinal scales. We will use the same function we did to describe the nominal-level variable zodiac, so click the Analyze tab on the top menu bar of the Viewer and select Analyze ▶ Descriptive Statistics ▶ Frequencies.

SPSS remembers the preceding analysis, so the zodiac variable may still appear in the Variable(s) list. To begin a new descriptive analysis, click zodiac back into the left-hand list.

With your Frequencies dialog window cleared, scroll through the GSS dataset variable list until you find the variable "helppoor" and click on it so it is added to the Variable(s) list. The helppoor variable asks respondents to place themselves on a scale between 1 ("The government should take action to help poor people") and 5 ("People should help themselves"). SPSS should retain your earlier settings for Charts, so accompanying bar charts will appear in the Viewer.[2] Click OK.

---

[2] If you pressed the Reset button to clear zodiac from the Variable(s) list, you'll need to click the Charts button again to have SPSS produce a bar chart with values specified as percentages.

SPSS produces descriptive statistics for the helppoor variable. To better understand how people responded to the helppoor question, we'll look at the variable's frequency distribution table and bar chart (Figure 2-4).

Statistics

Should Govt Improve Standard of Living?

N	Valid	1882
	Missing	985

Should Govt Improve Standard of Living?

		Frequency	Percent	Valid Percent	Cumulative Percent
Valid	GOVT ACTION	339	11.8	18.0	18.0
	2	268	9.4	14.2	32.3
	AGREE WITH BOTH	807	28.2	42.9	75.1
	4	296	10.3	15.7	90.9
	PEOPLE HELP SELVES	172	6.0	9.1	100.0
	Total	1882	65.7	100.0	
Missing	System	985	34.3		
Total		2867	100.0		

Because helppoor is an ordinal variable, you can use both its mode and its median to describe central tendency. Its mode, clearly enough, is the response "Agree with both," which contains 42.9 percent of the cases. (If you get a different percentage in this category, make sure you've weighted observations properly.) What about the median? This is where the Cumulative Percent column of the frequency distribution comes into play. *The median for any ordinal (or interval) variable is the*

FIGURE 2-4   Bar Chart of an Ordinal Variable with Low Dispersion

Should Govt Improve Standard of Living?

Should Govt Improve Standard of Living?

Cases weighted by Weight Variable

category below which 50 percent of the cases lie. Is the first category, "Govt action," the median? No, this category contains fewer than half of the cases. How about the next higher category? No, again. The Cumulative Percent column still has not reached 50 percent. The median occurs in the "Agree with both" category (cumulative percentage, 75.1).

Now consider the question of whether helppoor has a high degree of dispersion or a low degree of dispersion. If helppoor had a high level of variation, then the percentages of respondents in each response category would be roughly equal, much like the zodiac variable that you analyzed earlier. So, roughly one-fifth of the cases would fall into each of the five response categories: 20 percent in "Gov't action," 20 percent in response category "2," 20 percent in "Agree with both," 20 percent in response category "4," and 20 percent in "People help selves." If helppoor had no dispersion, then all the cases would fall into one value. That is, one value would have 100 percent of the cases, and each of the other categories would have 0 percent. Which of these two scenarios comes closest to describing the actual distribution of respondents across the values of helppoor: the equal-percentages-in-each-category, high variation scenario, or the 100-percent-in-one-category, low variation scenario? It seems clear that helppoor is a variable with a relatively low degree of dispersion. "Agree with both," with 42.9 percent of the responses, contains nearly three times as many cases as its nearest rival ("Gov't action") and more than three times as many cases as any of the other response categories.

Now contrast helppoor's distribution with the distribution of the helpsick variable. The "helpsick" variable, using a similar 5-point scale, asks respondents about government responsibility or individual responsibility for medical care. You can produce a frequency distribution table and bar chart for helpsick (Figure 2-5) the same way we did to generate descriptive statistics for the helppoor variable. Review the preceding paragraphs as necessary to do this analysis.

Should Govt Help Pay for Medical Care?

		Frequency	Percent	Valid Percent	Cumulative Percent
Valid	GOVT SHOULD HELP	579	20.2	30.6	30.6
	2	358	12.5	18.9	49.5
	AGREE WITH BOTH	599	20.9	31.7	81.2
	4	206	7.2	10.9	92.1
	PEOPLE HELP SELVES	150	5.2	7.9	100.0
	Total	1893	66.0	100.0	
Missing	System	974	34.0		
Total		2867	100.0		

Interestingly, helpsick has the same mode as helppoor ("Agree with both," with 31.7 percent of the cases), and the same median (again, "Agree with both," where the cumulative percentage exceeds 50.0). Yet with helppoor it seemed reasonable to say that "Agree with both" was the typical response. Would it be reasonable to say that "Agree with both" is helppoor's typical response? No, it would not. Notice that, unlike helppoor, respondents' values on helpsick are more spread out, with sizable numbers of responses falling in the first value ("Gov't action," with 30.6 percent), making it a close rival to "Agree with both" for the distinction of being the modal opinion on this issue. Clearly, the public is more divided—more widely dispersed—on the question of medical assistance than on the question of assistance to the poor.

FIGURE 2-5   Bar Chart of an Ordinal Variable with High Dispersion

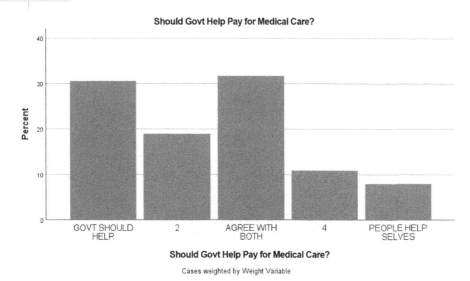

A CLOSER LOOK: ANALYZING TWO VARIABLES AT ONCE

In the preceding section, we demonstrated how to describe two ordinal-level variables, helppoor and helpsick, using frequency distribution tables and bar charts. We analyzed one variable at a time to keep things simple as you learn a new skill and to draw your attention to the differences between these two variables. In the future, if you are describing the distributions of two or more variables, you may prefer to analyze multiple variables at once to work more efficiently. Watch the "Analyze Two Variables" screencast to learn how to analyze two (or more) variables at once.

Watch Screencast

Analyze Two Variables

USING THE CHART EDITOR TO MODIFY GRAPHICS

SPSS permits the user to modify the content and appearance of any graphic object it produces in the Viewer using the Chart Editor. The user invokes the Editor by double-clicking on graphical output in the Viewer, edits the graphic using the Chart Editor tool, and closes the Chart Editor to return to the Viewer. Changes made to a graphic in the Chart Editor are recorded automatically in the Viewer.

In this section, we show how you can use the Chart Editor to edit the bar chart you just created to show the distribution of public opinion on paying for medical care for sick people. We'll show how to change labels on the chart and also change the style and color of the bars. (The default style and color is rather uninspired, and it doesn't print well.)

In the Viewer, place the cursor anywhere on the bar chart and double-click. SPSS opens the Chart Editor (Figure 2-6).

The Chart Editor recognizes the elements that make up the bar chart. It recognizes some elements as text. These elements include the axis titles and the value labels for the categories of helpsick. It recognizes other elements as graphic, such as the bars in the bar chart. First, we'll edit a text element, the title on the vertical axis. Then we will modify a graphic element, the color of the bars.

Place the cursor anywhere on the main title "Should Govt Help Pay For Medical Care?" and single-click it. SPSS selects the chart title. With the cursor still placed on the title, single-click again. SPSS moves the text into editing mode inside the chart (see the left side of Figure 2-7). The default

FIGURE 2-6   The Chart Editor

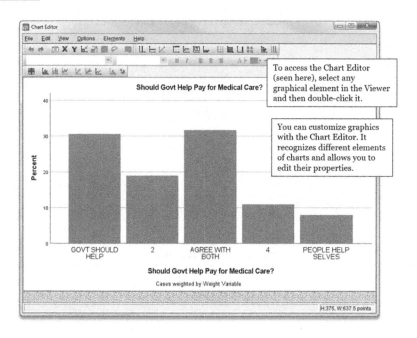

title is fine for understanding the distribution of this variable, but we could improve it to present the information to others. Edit the title so it reads "Should the Government Help People Pay for Medical Care?" We want the bar chart to communicate its information as clearly as possible. While you're using the Chart Editor to edit chart text, you can delete the redundant x-axis label and provide more descriptive x-axis labels in place of the numbers "2" and "4."

FIGURE 2-7   Editing the Bar Chart Title

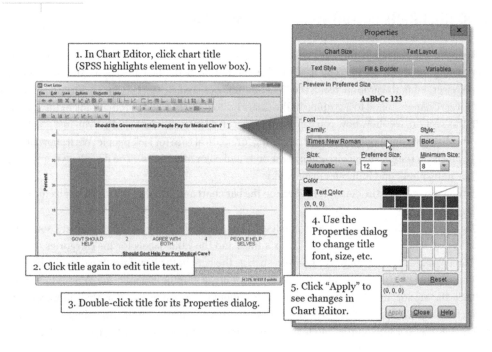

You can also use the Text Style menu in the Properties window that pops up automatically when you double-click a graphic element in the Chart Editor (see the right side of Figure 2-7) to change the font style of the main title and *x*-axis labels from the plain, default sans serif font to something more stylish. If you're going to use an SPSS graphic in a paper or presentation, you may want to match the font used in the graphic with the font used in the paper or presentation. When you change the font of a text element, change the font of all the other text elements to match so your graphic doesn't become a hodgepodge of text styles. Apply your changes to the chart text.

Now click on one of the vertical bars. The editor selects all the bars. As before, you can double-click an element in the Chart Editor to summon the associated Properties dialog window. Alternatively, you can select the element and press the "Show Properties Window" button located near the upper-left corner of the Chart Editor window as we show in Figure 2-8. This opens the Properties window, the most powerful editing tool in the Chart Editor's arsenal. (*Special note:* If you plan to do a lot of editing, it is a good idea to open the Properties window soon after you enter the Chart Editor. Each time you select a different text or graphic element with the mouse, the Properties window changes, displaying the editable properties of the selected element.)

The options for editing graphical elements like the bars in a bar chart are plentiful. You can change their color, adjust their order, and make them bigger or smaller. The "Depth & Angle" tab of the bar properties provides an option that dramatically transforms the humble bar chart into a visually interesting graphic: a 3-D effect. Select the 3-D option (see Figure 2-8) and apply it to the bar chart. You'll see the difference this option makes in the Chart Editor. If you close the Chart Editor, the finished product appears in the Viewer (Figure 2-9).

DESCRIBING INTERVAL VARIABLES

Let's now turn to the descriptive analysis of interval-level variables. An interval-level variable represents the most precise level of measurement. Unlike nominal variables, whose values stand for categories, and ordinal variables, whose values can be ranked, the values of an interval variable *tell you the exact quantity of the characteristic being measured*. For example, age qualifies as an interval-level variable because its values impart each respondent's age in years.

Screencast

Frequency Analysis with an Interval Variable

FIGURE **2-8**   Using the Properties Window to Edit Bars in a Bar Chart

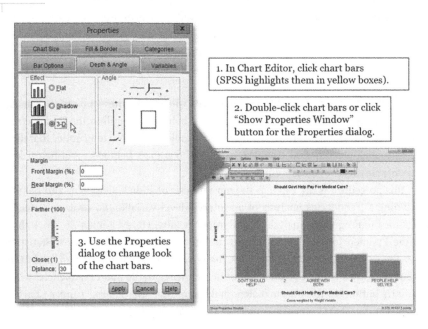

FIGURE 2-9   Edited Bar Chart in the Viewer

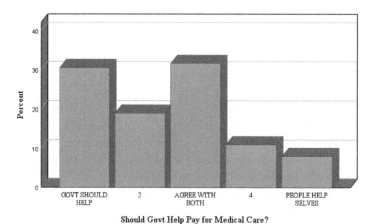

Should the Government Help People Pay for Medical Care?

Should Govt Help Pay for Medical Care?

Cases weighted by Weight Variable

Because interval variables have the most precision, they can be described more completely than can nominal or ordinal variables; we have a relatively large toolkit available for describing variables measured at the interval level. For any interval-level variable, you can report its mode, median, and arithmetic average, or *mean*. In addition to these measures of central tendency, you can make more sophisticated judgments about variation. Specifically, you can determine if an interval-level distribution is *skewed*.

Skewness refers to the symmetry of a distribution. If a distribution is not skewed, the cases tend to cluster symmetrically around the mean of the distribution, and they taper off evenly for values above and below the mean. If a distribution is skewed, by contrast, one tail of the distribution is longer and skinnier than the other tail. Distributions in which some cases occupy the higher values of an interval variable—distributions with a skinnier right-hand tail—have a *positive skew*. By the same token, if the distribution has some cases at the extreme lower end—the distribution has a skinnier left-hand tail—then the distribution has a *negative skew*. Skewness affects the mean of the distribution. A positive skew tends to "pull" the mean upward; a negative skew pulls it downward. However, skewness has less effect on the median. Because the median reports the middlemost value of a distribution, it is not tugged upward or downward by extreme values. *For badly skewed distributions, it is a good practice to use the median instead of the mean in describing central tendency.*

A step-by-step analysis of a GSS variable, age, will clarify these points. Select Analyze ▶ Descriptive Statistics ▶ Frequencies. If helppoor and helpsick are still in the Variable(s) list, click them back into the left-hand list. Click age into the Variable(s) list. You may notice that the icon next to the age variable looks different from the icon next to zodiac, helppoor, and helpsick; the icons signify the variable's level of measurement.

So far, this procedure is the same as in your analysis of zodiac, helppoor, and helpsick. When you are running a frequencies analysis of an interval-level variable, however, you need to adjust the settings for the Frequency analysis to get proper results. Here's a must-do: Click the Statistics button in the Frequencies window, as shown in Figure 2-10. The Frequencies: Statistics window appears. In the Central Tendency panel, click the boxes next to Mean, Median, and Mode. In the Distribution panel, click Skewness. Click Continue, returning to the main Frequencies window. Now click the Charts button. In the Charts dialog, make sure that "Bar charts" (under Chart Type) and "Percentages" (under Chart Values) are selected. Click Continue.

FIGURE 2-10 Requesting Statistics for an Interval Variable

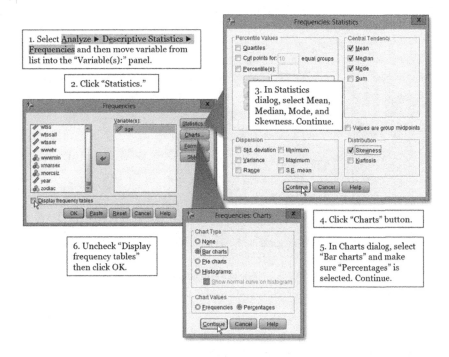

While you're in the main Frequencies window, here's something you may want to do before you execute the analysis: *Uncheck* the box next to "Display frequency tables," appearing at the foot of the left-hand list.[3] For interval-level variables, like age, that have many categories, a frequency distribution table can run several output pages and is not very informative. Unchecking the "Display frequency tables" box suppresses the frequency distribution. Click OK.

SPSS analyzes the age variable and outputs the requested statistics and bar chart (Figure 2-11) into the Viewer. Most of the entries in the Statistics table are familiar to you: valid number of cases; number of missing cases; and mean, median, and mode. In addition, SPSS reports values for skewness and a statistic called standard error of skewness. When a distribution is perfectly symmetrical—no skew—it has skewness equal to 0. If the distribution has a skinnier right-hand tail—positive skew—then skewness will be a positive number. A skinnier left-hand tail, logically enough, returns a negative number for skewness.

Statistics

Age of Respondent

N	Valid	2855
	Missing	12
Mean		47.56
Median		47.00
Mode		57
Skewness		.233
Std. Error of Skewness		.046

---

[3] A general guide: If the interval-level variable you are analyzing has 15 or fewer categories, go ahead and obtain the frequency distribution. If it has more than 15 categories, suppress the frequency distribution.

FIGURE 2-11   Bar Chart of the Interval-level Age Variable

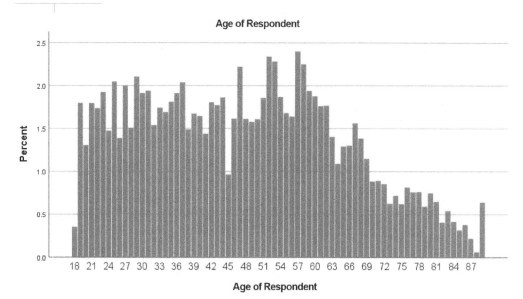

Cases weighted by Weight Variable

For the age variable, the skewness statistic is positive (.233). This suggests that the distribution has a skinnier right-hand tail—a feature that is confirmed by the shape of the bar chart. Note also that the mean (47.56 years) is slightly higher than the median (47 years), a situation that often—although not always—indicates a positive skew.[4] Even so, the mean and median are less than 1 year apart. You have to exercise judgment, but in this case, it would not be a distortion of reality to use the mean instead of the median to describe the central tendency of the distribution.[5]

All the guided examples thus far have used bar charts for graphic support. For nominal and ordinal variables, a bar chart should always be your choice. For interval variables, however, you may want to ask SPSS to produce a histogram instead. What is the difference between a bar chart and a histogram? A bar chart displays each value of a variable and shows you the percentage (alternatively, the raw number) of cases that fall into each category. A histogram is similar to a bar chart, but instead of displaying each discrete value, it collapses categories into ranges (called bins), resulting in a compact display. Histograms are sometimes more readable and elegant than bar charts. Most of the time a histogram will work just as well as a bar chart in summarizing an interval-level variable. For interval variables with many unique values, a histogram is the graphic of choice. (Remember: For nominal or ordinal variables, you always want a bar chart.)

So that you can become familiar with histograms, run the analysis of age once again—only this time ask SPSS to produce a histogram instead of a bar chart. Select Analyze ▶ Descriptive Statistics ▶ Frequencies. Make sure age is still in the Variable(s) list. Click Statistics, and then *uncheck* all the boxes: Mean, Median, Mode, and Skewness. Click Continue. Click Charts, and then select the Histograms radio button in Chart Type. Click Continue. For this analysis, we do not

---

[4] Paul T. von Hippel, "Mean, Median, and Skew: Correcting a Textbook Rule," *Journal of Statistics Education* 13, no. 2 (2005). "Many textbooks teach a rule of thumb stating that the mean is right of the median under right skew, and left of the median under left skew. This rule fails with surprising frequency." See http://www.amstat.org/publications/jse/v13n2/vonhippel.html.

[5] For demographic variables that are skewed, median values rather than means are often used to give a clearer picture of central tendency. One hears or reads reports, for example, of median family income or the median price of homes in an area.

FIGURE **2-12**   Creating a Histogram of an Interval Variable

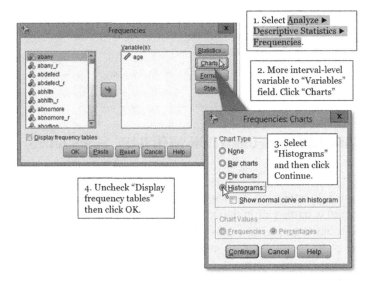

need a frequency distribution table. In the Frequencies window, uncheck the "Display frequency tables" box. (Refer to Figure 2-12.) Click OK.[6]

This is a bare-bones run. SPSS reports its obligatory count of valid and missing cases, plus a histogram for age (Figure 2-13). On the histogram's horizontal axis, notice the tick marks, which are spaced at 20-year intervals. SPSS has compressed the data so that each bar represents about 2

FIGURE **2-13**   Histogram of the Interval-level Age Variable

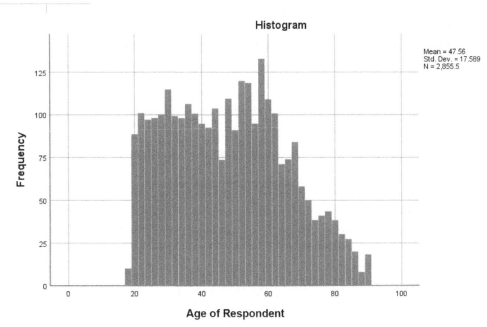

Cases weighted by Weight Variable

---

[6] Alternatively, you can select Graphs ▶ Legacy Dialogs ▶ Histogram to produce a histogram. Move age into the Variable field and click OK. This procedure should produce the same output as the method described in the text.

years of age rather than 1 year of age. Now scroll up the Viewer to the bar chart of age, which you produced in the preceding analysis. Notice that the histogram has smoothed out the choppiness of the bar chart, though it still captures the essential qualities of the age variable.

Statistics

Age of Respondent

N	Valid	2855
	Missing	12

OBTAINING CASE-LEVEL INFORMATION WITH CASE SUMMARIES

When you analyze a large survey dataset, as you have just done, you generally are not interested in how respondent X or respondent Y answered a particular question; they're just some random people who happened to participate in the survey. Rather, you want to know how the entire sample of respondents distributed themselves across the response categories of a variable (for this purpose, their randomness is vitally important). Sometimes, however, you gather data on particular cases because the cases are themselves inherently important.

Screencast

Analyze Case Summaries

When you work with the States dataset (states.sav) and the World dataset (world.sav), you may want to describe cases beyond the relative anonymity of Frequencies analysis and find out where particular states or countries "are" on an interesting variable. To obtain case-level information, select Analyze ▶ Reports ▶ Case Summaries. This SPSS procedure is readymade for such elemental insights.

Suppose you are interested in identifying states that have the most/fewest laws restricting access to abortions. To begin this guided example, close the GSS dataset and open the States dataset. The States dataset contains a variable named abortlaw17. This variable records the number of legal restrictions on abortion access in each state in 2017 (out of 14 possible restrictions). Exactly which states impose the most restrictions? Which states impose the fewest restrictions? Where does your state fall on the list? Case Summaries can quickly answer questions like these. SPSS will sort states based on a "grouping variable" (in this example, abortlaw17) and then produce a report telling you which states are in each group.

With the States dataset open, click Analyze ▶ Reports ▶ Case Summaries.

To conduct the desired analysis, you need to do three things in the Summarize Cases window (see Figure 2-14):

1. Click the variable containing the cases' identities into the Variables window. In the States dataset, this variable is named state, which is simply the name of each state.

2. Click the variable you are interested in analyzing, abortlaw17, into the Grouping Variable(s) window.

3. Uncheck the "Limit cases to first. . ." option. This won't affect the analysis of state abortion laws because there are fewer than 100 states, but if this box is left checked when you analyze the World dataset, SPSS will limit the analysis to the first 100 countries and produce an incomplete analysis.

Click OK and consider the output. SPSS sorts the cases on the grouping variable, abortlaw17, and tells us which state is associated with each value of abortlaw17. For example, Vermont, with 0 legal restrictions on abortion access, is the state with the fewest restrictions on access to abortions. Which states impose the most restrictions? Scroll to the bottom of the tabular output. With 13 restrictions, Kansas and Oklahoma are tied for imposing the most restrictions.

FIGURE 2-14   Obtaining Case Summaries

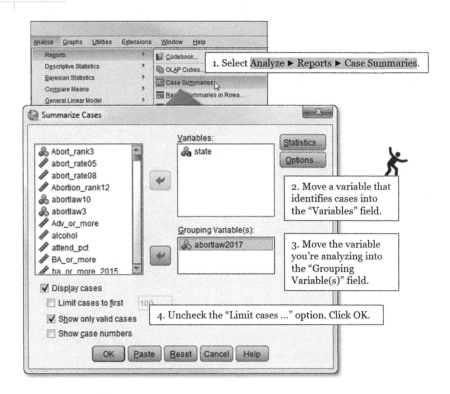

1. Select Analyze ▶ Reports ▶ Case Summaries.

2. Move a variable that identifies cases into the "Variables" field.

3. Move the variable you're analyzing into the "Grouping Variable(s)" field.

4. Uncheck the "Limit cases ..." option. Click OK.

Case Processing Summary

	Cases					
	Included		Excluded		Total	
	N	Percent	N	Percent	N	Percent
State Name * Number of restrictions on abortion	50	100.0%	0	0.0%	50	100.0%

Case Summaries

				State Name
Number of restrictions on abortion	0	1		Vermont
		Total	N	1
	2	1		Colorado
		2		New Hampshire
		3		Oregon
		Total	N	3
	3	1		California
		2		Connecticut
		3		New York
		4		Washington
		Total	N	4
	4	1		Hawaii
		2		New Jersey
		3		New Mexico
		4		Rhode Island
		5		West Virginia
		Total	N	5
	5	1		Alaska
		2		Illinois
		3		Maine
		4		Maryland
		5		Massachusetts
		6		Montana
		Total	N	6
	6	1		Delaware
		2		Nevada
		3		Wyoming
		Total	N	3
	7	1		Alabama

[Output omitted]

		4		Wisconsin
		Total	N	4
	9	1		Florida
		2		Georgia
		3		Kentucky
		4		Mississippi
		5		Nebraska
		6		North Dakota
		7		Pennsylvania
		Total	N	7
	10	1		Arizona
		2		Arkansas
		3		Michigan
		4		Ohio
		5		South Carolina
		6		South Dakota
		7		Tennessee
		8		Texas
		9		Utah
		10		Virginia
		Total	N	10
	11	1		Louisiana
		2		Missouri
		Total	N	2
	12	1		Indiana
		Total	N	1
	13	1		Kansas
		2		Oklahoma
		Total	N	2
Total		N		50

Note: The state names have been edited for spacing.

Name: **Anna Jeffries**   Date: **9/15/20**

E-mail: **anna.jeffries@spartans.ut.edu**   Section: _____

CHAPTER 2 EXERCISES

1. (Data set: GSS. Variables: science_quiz, wtss.) The late Carl Sagan once lamented, "We live in a society exquisitely dependent on science and technology, in which hardly anyone knows anything about science and technology." This is a rather pessimistic assessment of the scientific acumen of ordinary Americans. Sagan seemed to be suggesting that the average level of scientific knowledge is quite low and that most people would fail even the simplest test of scientific facts.

The GSS dataset contains science_quiz, which was created from ten true-false questions testing respondents' knowledge of basic scientific facts. Values on science_quiz range from 0 (the respondent did not answer any of the questions correctly) to 10 (the respondent correctly answered all ten).[7]

A. Obtain a frequency distribution table of science_quiz. Fill in the table that follows. Be sure to weight observations with the wtss variable.

science_quiz Score	Frequency*	Percent	Cumulative Percent
0	2	.4 ?	.4 ?
1	9	2.0 ?	2.4 ?
2	13	2.9 ?	5.3 ?
3	38	8.2 ?	13.4 ?
4	54	11.6 ?	25.1 ?
5	66	14.2 ?	39.2 ?
6	80	17.1 ?	56.3 ?
7	78	16.8 ?	73.1 ?
8	60	12.9 ?	86.0 ?

science_quiz Score	Frequency*	Percent	Cumulative Percent
9	45	9.6 ?	95.6 ?
10	21	4.4 ?	100.00%
Total	465	100.00%	

*Weighted frequencies.

B. When you use the Analyze ▸ Descriptive Statistics ▸ Frequencies procedure, click the Statistics button and ask SPSS to report the mean, median, and skewness of the science_quiz variable. The science_quiz variable has a mean equal to **6.03**, a median equal to **6.00**, and a skewness equal to **-.229**.

C. Create a bar chart for science_quiz by clicking the Charts button and requesting a bar chart. Print the bar chart. (Alternatively, you can create a histogram, but there is no need to group observations into binned values of science_quiz values.)

D. Exercise your judgment. What would be the more accurate measure of science_quiz's central tendency: the mean or the median? (circle one)

mean   (median)

E. Briefly explain your choice in D.

I think this would make more sense because the quiz is only going to be scored in whole numbers so the median (6) would better show the average score

F. According to conventional academic standards, any science_quiz score of 5 or lower would be an F, a failing grade. A score of 6 would be a grade of D, a 7 would be a C, an 8 a B, and scores of 9 or 10 would be an A. Based on these standards, about what percentage of people got passing grades on science_quiz? (circle one)

About 30 percent   About 40 percent
About 50 percent   About 60 percent

What percentage got an A on science_quiz? (circle one)

About 5 percent   About 10 percent
About 15 percent   About 20 percent

---

[7] The science_quiz variable was created by summing the number of correct responses to the following questions (all are in true-false format, except for earthsun): The center of the Earth is very hot (General Social Survey variable, hotcore); it is the father's gene that decides whether the baby is a boy or a girl (boyorgrl); electrons are smaller than atoms (electron); the universe began with a huge explosion (bigbang); the continents on which we live have been moving their locations for millions of years and will continue to move in the future (condrift); human beings, as we know them today, developed from earlier species of animals (evolved); does the Earth go around the sun, or does the sun go around the Earth (earthsun); all radioactivity is manmade (radioact); lasers work by focusing sound waves (lasers); and antibiotics kill viruses as well as bacteria (viruses).

2. (Dataset: World. Variables: women13, country.) What percentage of members of the U.S. House of Representatives are women? In 2013 the number was 17.8 percent, according to the Inter-Parliamentary Union, an international organization of parliaments.[8] How does the United States compare to other democratic countries? Is 17.8 percent comparatively low, comparatively high, or average for a typical national legislature?

   A. The World dataset contains women13, the percentage of women in the lower house of the legislature in each of ninety democracies. Obtain summary statistics for the women13 variable. Fill in the table that follows.

Statistics for women13 Variable		
Mean	21.1044	?
Median	20.8000	?
Skewness	.478	?

   B. Examine the results of the summary analysis. Recall that 17.8 percent of U.S. House members are women. Now, consider the following statement: "The percentage of women in the U.S. House is about average for a democratic country." Is this statement accurate? Answer yes or no, and explain your reasoning.

   The US is a little below average so this statement is somewhat accurate.

   C. Suppose a women's advocacy organization vows to support female congressional candidates so that the U.S. House might someday "be ranked among the top 10 percent of democracies in the percentage of female members." According to the percentiles column of the summary analysis, to meet this goal women would need to constitute about what percentage of the House? (circle one)

      About 25 percent   About 40 percent
      About 50 percent

   D. Create a histogram of women13. Print the histogram.

   E. Run Analyze ▶ Reports ▶ Case Summaries. Click Country into the Variables box and women13 into the Grouping Variable(s) box. Make sure to uncheck the box next to "Limit cases to first 100." Examine the output.

The five countries with the *lowest percentages* of women legislators are
   1. Papua New Guinea
   2. Comoros
   3. Sri Lanka
   4. Nigeria
   5. Japan

The five countries with the *highest percentages* of women legislators are
   1. Sweden
   2. Senegal
   3. Finland
   4. Nicaragua
   5. Iceland

3. (Dataset: GSS. Variables: femrole, wtss.) Two pundits are arguing about the general public's views on the role of women in the home and in politics.

   Pundit 1: "Our society has a minority of traditionally minded individuals who think that the proper 'place' for women is taking care of the home and caring for children. This small but vocal group of traditionalists aside, the typical adult supports the idea that women belong in work and in politics."

   Pundit 2: "Poppycock! It's just the opposite. The extremist feminist crowd has distorted the overall picture. The typical view among most citizens is that women should be in the home, not in work and politics."

   A. Dataset GSS (file name: gss.sav) contains femrole, an interval-level variable that measures respondents' attitudes toward women in society and politics. Scores can range from 0 (women belong in the home) to 9 (women belong in work and politics).

   If Pundit 1 is correct, femrole will have (circle one)

      a negative skew.   no skew.   a positive skew.

   If Pundit 2 is correct, femrole will have (circle one)

      a negative skew.   no skew.   a positive skew.

   If Pundit 1 is correct, femrole's mean will be (circle one)

      lower than its median   the same as its median.
      higher than its median.

   If Pundit 2 is correct, femrole's mean will be (circle one)

      lower than its median.   the same as its median.
      higher than its median.

   B. Perform a frequencies analysis of femrole. Obtain the mean, median, and mode, as well as skewness. Obtain a bar chart with percentages. Fill in the table that follows.

Statistics for femrole Variable	
Mean	5.87 ?
Median	6.00 ?
Mode	6 ?
Skewness	-.289 ?

C. Create a bar chart of femrole. Be sure to use sample weights so the distribution is nationally representative. Override the default bar fill color with a color of your choice. Print the bar chart.

D. Consider the evidence you obtained in parts B and C. Based on your analysis, whose assessment is more accurate? (circle one)

    [Pundit 1's]   Pundit 2's

Citing *specific evidence* obtained in parts B and C, explain your reasoning.

The histogram skews negatively, as was predicted if Pundit #2 was correct, meaning people generally think women belong at work.

4. (Dataset: GSS. Variables: attend, wtss.) The GSS dataset (file name: gss.sav) provides a rich array of variables that permit scholars to study religiosity in the adult population. The GSS dataset contains attend, a 9-point ordinal scale that measures how often respondents attend religious services. Values can range from 1 ("Never") to 9 ("More than once a week").

A. The shell of a bar chart is given below. The categories of attend appear along the horizontal axis. What would a bar chart of attend look like if this variable had maximum dispersion? Sketch inside the axes a bar chart that would depict maximum dispersion.

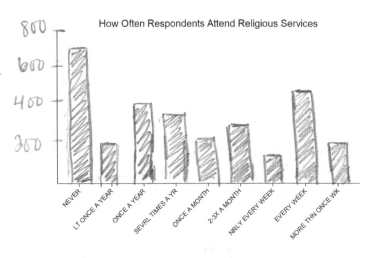

How Often Respondents Attend Religious Services

B. What would a bar chart of attend look like if this variable had no dispersion? Sketch inside the axes a bar chart that would depict no dispersion.

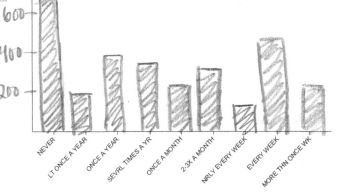

How Often Respondents Attend Religious Services

C. Obtain frequencies output and a bar chart for attend. In the main Frequencies window, make sure that the "Display frequencies table" box is checked. In Statistics, see that all the boxes are unchecked. In Charts, request a bar chart with percentages. Based on your results, complete the following table.

attend Value	Frequency*	Percent	Cumulative Percent
Never	711.33	25.0 ?	25.0 ?
Less than once a year	167.88	5.9 ?	30.8 ?
Once a year	377.98	13.3 ?	44.1 ?
Several times a year	316.54	11.1 ?	55.2 ?
Once a month	198.52	7.0 ?	62.2 ?
2 to 3 times a month	249.13	8.7 ?	70.9 ?
Nearly every week	126.56	4.4 ?	75.4 ?
Every week	498.02	17.5 ?	92.8 ?
More than once a week	204.03	7.2 ?	100.00%
Total	2,850	100.00%	

*Weighted frequencies rounded to two decimal places

D. Print the bar chart you obtained for the last part of this exercise.

E. Based on your examination of the frequency distribution,

the mode of attend is ___0, never___.

the median of attend is ___3, several times a yr.___

F. Based on your examination of the frequency distribution and bar chart, you would conclude that attend has (circle one)

low dispersion.   high dispersion.

5. (Dataset: NES. Variables: immig_chldrn, grass, pres_job, nesw.) We frequently describe public opinion by referring to how citizens distribute themselves on a political issue. *Consensus* is a situation in which a large majority, 60–70 percent of the public, holds the same position, or very similar positions, on an issue. *Dissensus* is a situation in which opinion is spread out evenly across all positions on an issue. *Polarization* refers to a configuration of opinion in which people are split between two extreme poles of an issue, with only a few individuals populating the more moderate, middle-of-the-road positions.

In this exercise you will decide whether consensus, dissensus, or polarization best describes public opinion, as measured by three NES variables: opinions about allowing people brought to this country illegally as children to stay in the United States (immig_chldrn), opinions on whether marijuana should be legalized (grass), and opinions about how well the president is performing his job (pres_job). The question regarding children brought illegally is measured on a 6-point scale, from "Should send back—favor a great deal" (point 1) to "Should allow to stay—favor a great deal" (point 6). The marijuana legalization question uses a 3-point scale: "Favor" (point 1), "Neither favor nor oppose" (point 2), and "Oppose" (point 3). Presidential job approval is measured on a 4-point scale, from "Approve strongly" (point 1) to "Disapprove strongly" (point 4).[9]

A. Obtain frequency distributions and bar charts for immig_chldrn, grass, and pres_job. Remember to weight the analyses using nesw. In the tables that follow, write the appropriate percentage next to each question mark.

Send back children brought to U.S. illegally?	Percentage
1. Should send back—favor a great deal	7.9 ?
2. Should send back—favor a moderate amount	8.9 ?
3. Should send back—favor a little	2.7 ?
4. Should allow to stay—favor a little	9.9 ?

[9] Keep in mind this question was asked in 2016 when Barack Obama was president.

Send back children brought to U.S. illegally?	Percentage
5. Should allow to stay—favor a moderate amount	33.9 ?
6. Should allow to stay—favor a great deal	37.3 ?
Total	100.00%

Should marijuana be legal?	Percentage
Favor	49.3 ?
Neither favor nor oppose	21.8 29.8
Oppose	28.9 ?
Total	100.00%

Presidential Approval Scale	Percentage
Approve strongly	36.0 ?
Approve	17.2 ?
Disapprove	9.7 ?
Disapprove strongly	37.1 ?
Total	100.00%

B. Examine the percentages you entered in the tables above. Of the three issues, which one *most closely* approximates consensus? (check one)

☑ Sending back children brought to U.S. illegally

❏ Legalization of marijuana

❏ Presidential approval

Briefly explain your reasoning.

The overwhelming majority 81.1% are favorable of letting children brought illegally stay wheras there is only a small group that opposes it

C. Of the three issues, which one *most closely* approximates dissensus? (circle one)

❏ Sending back children brought to U.S. illegally

☑ Legalization of marijuana

❏ Presidential approval

Briefly explain your reasoning.

The opinions are spread relatively evenly across viewpoints with favorably, the most popular position, only being 49.3% of the population.

D. Of the three issues, which one *most closely approximates* polarization? (circle one)

- ❏ Sending back children brought to U.S. illegally
- ❏ Legalization of marijuana
- ☑ Presidential approval

Briefly explain your reasoning.

This is the most dramatically split with large portions of the population disapproving strongly approving and a smaller group in the middle.

E. Print the bar chart of the variable you chose in part D.

6. (Dataset: NES. Variables: cong_approve, cong_incumb_approve, nesw.) Pedantic pontificator claims he has discovered how voters evaluate the performance of House incumbents: "I call it my 'guilt by association' theory. When voters disapprove of the way Congress has been handling its job, they transfer that negative evaluation to their House incumbent. My theory is eminently plausible and surely correct. The distribution of opinions about House incumbents will be very similar to the distribution of opinions about the whole Congress."

The NES dataset contains cong_approve, which gauges respondent approval or disapproval of "the way the U.S. Congress has been handling its job." The dataset also has cong_incumb_approve, which measures approval or disapproval of the way each respondent's House incumbent "has been handling his or her job."

A. To test pedantic pontificator's theory, perform a frequencies analysis of cong_approve and cong_incumb_approve. Obtain bar charts with percentages. Refer to the Valid Percent column of the frequency distributions. In the table that follows, write the appropriate percentages next to each question mark.

	U.S. Congress	My House Incumbent
Approve strongly	7.2 ?	29.4 ?
Approve	18.0 ?	44.9 ?
Disapprove	20.0 ?	18.4 ?
Disapprove strongly	54.6 ?	11.3 ?
Total	100.00%	100.00%

B. Consider the evidence. Does pedantic pontificator's theory appear to be correct or incorrect? (circle one)

correct   **incorrect**

Explain your reasoning.

While most respondents strongly disapprove of Congress as a whole, they majority approve of their incumbent.

7. (Dataset: States. Variables: defexpen, state.) Here is some conventional political wisdom: Well-positioned members of Congress from a handful of states are successful in getting the federal government to spend revenue in their states—defense-related expenditures, for example. The typical state, by contrast, receives far fewer defense budget dollars.

A. Suppose you measured the amount of defense-related expenditures in each state. The conventional wisdom says that when you look at the amount of defense-related expenditures in the United States, a few states would have a high amount of defense spending. Most states, however, would have lower values on this variable.

If the conventional wisdom is correct, the distribution of defense-related expenditures will have (circle one)

a negative skew.   no skew.   **a positive skew.**

If the conventional wisdom is correct, the *mean* of defense-related expenditures will be (circle one)

lower than its median.   the same as its median.   **higher than its median.**

B. The States dataset contains the variable defexpen, defense expenditures per capita for each of the fifty states. Perform a frequencies analysis of defexpen. In Statistics, obtain the mean and median, as well as skewness. (You do not need to obtain the mode for this exercise.) In the main Frequencies window, uncheck the "Display frequency tables" box. In Charts, request a histogram. Examine the results. Examine the histogram. Record the mean, median, and skewness next to the question marks in the table that follows.

Statistics for defexpen Variable	
Mean	1093.74 ?
Median	931.90 ?
Skewness	2.293 ?

C. Which is the better measure of central tendency? (circle one)

mean   **median**

Briefly explain your answer.

Because there is a skew, the median is a better measure of central tendency as it is unaffected by the skew.

D. Print the histogram you produced in part B.

E. Based on your analysis, would you say that the conventional wisdom is accurate or inaccurate? (check one)

☑ The conventional wisdom is accurate.

❑ The conventional wisdom is inaccurate.

F. Use the Analyze ▸ Reports ▸ Case Summaries procedure to obtain a ranked list of states, from lowest per capita defense spending to highest per capita defense spending. The state with the lowest per capita defense spending is Virginia, with $4485 per capita. The state with the highest per capita defense spending is West Virginia, with $282 per capita.

8. (Dataset: States. Variables: blackpct_2016, hispanicpct_2016.) Two demographers are arguing over how best to describe the racial and ethnic composition of the "typical" state.

Demographer 1: "The typical state is 8.25 percent black and 8.20 percent Hispanic."

Demographer 2: "The typical state is 10.61 percent black and 11.26 percent Hispanic."

A. Run frequencies for blackpct_2016 (the percentage of each state's population that is African American) and hispanicpct_2016 (the percentage of each state's population that is Hispanic). Click the Statistics button to request the mean and median, as well as skewness. (You do not need to obtain the mode for this exercise.) In Charts, obtain histograms. In the main Frequencies window, uncheck the "Display frequency tables" box. Record the appropriate statistics for each variable in the table that follows.

	blackpct_2016	hispanicpct_2016
Mean	10.52 ?	$11.94 ?
Median	7.3 ?	9.09 ?
Skewness	1.162 ?	1.862 ?

B. Based on your analysis, which demographer is more accurate? (circle one)

Demographer 1 | Demographer 2

Write a few sentences explaining your reasoning.

The hispanic population is 11.54% which is closest to demographers 2's claim.

C. Use the Analyze ▸ Reports ▸ Case Summaries procedure to obtain information on the percentage of Hispanics in the fifty states.

Which five states have the *lowest percentages* of Hispanics?

1. West Virginia
2. Maine
3. Mississippi
4. Kentucky
5. New Hampshire
(2)North Dakota

Which five states have the *highest percentages* of Hispanics?

1. New Mexico
2. Texas
3. California
4. Arizona
5. Nevada

3

Transforming Variables

 Watch screencasts of the guided examples in this chapter. **edge.sagepub.com/pollock**

Procedures Covered

Transform ▸ Recode into Different Variables

Transform ▸ Create Dummy Variables

Transform ▸ Visual Binning

Transform ▸ Compute Variable

Analyze ▸ Descriptive Statistics ▸ Descriptives (standardize variable)

Political researchers sometimes must modify the variables they want to analyze. Generally speaking, such *variable transformations* become necessary or desirable in two common situations. Often a researcher wants to collapse a variable, combining its values or codes into a smaller number of useful categories. The researcher can do so using SPSS's Recode procedure or its Visual Binning procedure. In other situations, a dataset may contain several variables that provide similar measures of the same concept. In these instances, the researcher may want to use SPSS's Compute procedure to combine the values of different variables to create a new and more precise measure. Whether the researcher is simplifying a measurement or enhancing the level of detail, variable transformations allow researchers to use datasets creatively.

In this chapter you will learn how to use the Recode, Visual Binning, and Compute commands to transform variables. The variables you modify or create in this chapter (and in this chapter's exercises) should become permanent variables in the datasets. You can use variables you create to do your own political analysis. We'll work with transformed variables a number of times in this book.

The variable transformation procedures discussed in this chapter allow you to transform a variable at any level of measurement—nominal, ordinal, or interval. These methods are extremely useful and frequently used, but you should exercise vigilance and care when using them. When you transform data, be sure to follow these guidelines:

1. Before transforming a variable, examine a frequency distribution table (or other descriptive statistics) of the variable you intend to manipulate. If the variable coding isn't self-evident, read the dataset's codebook to learn exactly how researchers encoded the variable.

2. Properly label the new variable and its values. Give variables you create new names so you can distinguish them from the original variables they are derived from. Don't overwrite or delete the original variables.

3. After creating a new variable, use descriptive statistics to check your work.

4. After you complete each guided example (and chapter exercise), be sure to save the dataset.

CREATING INDICATOR VARIABLES

Screencast

Transforming a Categorical Variable Using Recode

An indicator variable is a variable used to distinguish observations that possess some characteristic from those that don't possess the characteristic. Observations that possess the named quality are coded as 1s and observations that don't possess the named quality are coded as 0s. Indicator variables are extremely useful. Researchers are often interested in what effect the indicated value has, or what causes observations to have this value, so being able to create indicator variables is a great skill to learn.

Open the States dataset, states.sav, and we will work through the first example. The States dataset contains a variable named judge_selection. This variable identifies the methods used by states to select appellate court judges. Across the United States, there are five different methods used to select appellate court judges: appointment by a commission (code 1), appointment by the governor (code 2), appointment by the legislature (code 3), nonpartisan elections (code 4), and partisan elections (code 5). Appellate court judges play an important role in the American judicial system so it's important to select good judges, but there is a lot of debate over which selection methods work best.

Following the first rule of data transformations, we will first run the Analyze ▶ Descriptive Statistics ▶ Frequencies procedure on the existing judge_selection variable to produce a frequency distribution table that will help us clearly understand its values and frequencies. A Frequencies analysis of judge_selection produces the following result:

Statistics

Method used to select appellate court judges

N	Valid	50
	Missing	0

Method Used to Select Appellate Court Judges

		Frequency	Percent	Valid Percent	Cumulative Percent
Valid	Appointed by commission	21	42.0	42.0	42.0
	Appointed by governor	5	10.0	10.0	52.0
	Appointed by legislature	2	4.0	4.0	56.0
	Non-partisan election	15	30.0	30.0	86.0
	Partisan election	7	14.0	14.0	100.0
	Total	50	100.0	100.0	

According to the Cumulative Percent column, 56.0 percent of the states appoint judges; this is the cumulative percentage of states that appoint appellate judges by commission, governor, or legislature. This of course means that the rest of the sample, 44.0 percent, uses elections to select appellate court judges. The two numbers, 56.0 and 44.0, will help us verify that we performed the recode correctly. We're not going to weight observations in the States dataset; each state is weighted equally in this analysis.

Suppose we want to create a new variable that identifies states that elect appellate court judges. To make our intended variable transformation clear, we can write out the recoding protocol. The new variable, judges_elected, will have two codes: states that appoint judges will be coded 0 and states that elect judges will be coded 1. Plus, we need to make sure that any states that have missing values on judge_selection also have missing values on judges_elected. (This variable doesn't happen to be missing values, but that won't always be the case so it's important to get in the habit of properly coding missing values.) Our recoding protocol would look like this:

Judge Selection Method	Old Value (judge_selection)	New Value (judges_elected)
Appointed by commission	1	0
Appointed by governor	2	0
Appointed by legislature	3	0
Nonpartisan election	4	1
Partisan election	5	1
	Missing	Missing

SPSS's Recode procedure can implement this recoding protocol. On the main menu bar, click Transform and consider the array of choices (Figure 3-1). Notice that SPSS presents two recoding options: Recode into Same Variables and Recode into Different Variables. When you recode a variable into the *same* variable, SPSS replaces the original codes with the new codes. The original information is lost. When you recode a variable into a *different* variable, SPSS uses the original codes to create a new variable. The original variable is retained. In some situations, you will want to pick Recode into Same Variables. Most of the time, however, you should use the second option, Recode into Different Variables.

FIGURE 3-1   Transforming an Existing Variable into a Different Variable

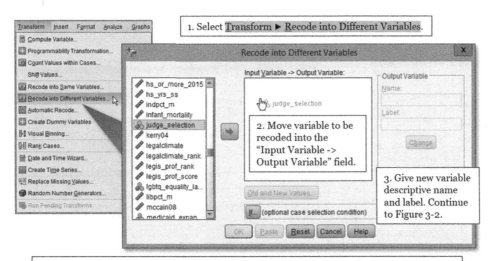

Note: We're not recoding or modifying the existing variable here. We're creating a new variable.

To create a new indicator variable in the States dataset, we'll recode the existing variable into a new variable. Select Transform ▶ Recode into Different Variables to open the Recode into Different Variables window (Figure 3-1).

Scroll down the left-hand variable list in the Recode into Different Variable dialog and find judge_selection. Click or drag judge_selection into the Input Variable → Output Variable field. SPSS puts judge_selection into the box, with this designation: "judge_selection →?" This is SPSS-speak for "What do you want to name the new variable you are creating from judge_selection?" Click in the Name box and type "judges_elected" (without quotation marks). When you recode an existing variable, you typically want to give your new variable a unique, descriptive name so you can identify your creation and don't alter the original variable.

Let's take this opportunity to give the new variable, judges_elected, a descriptive label. You may recall that a variable's label offers a longer description of the variable than its name and is printed on tables and graphs that use the variable. Click in the Label box and type "Does state elect judges?" Click the Change button. The Recode into Different Variables window should now look like Figure 3-2.

Once you've entered the name and label for the new, output variable, click the "Old and New Values" button in the Recode into Different Variables window. The Recode into Different Variables: Old and New Values window pops up (see Figure 3-3). There are two main panels in this window, which allow us to implement our recoding protocol. In the left-hand panel ("Old Value"), we will tell SPSS how to combine the original codes for judge_selection. In the right-hand panel ("New Value"), we will assign codes for the new variable, which we have named judges_elected.

By default, SPSS assumes that we want to recode each old value into each new value, one at a time. For example, we could recode value 1 of the old variable judge_selection as value 0 on the new variable judges_elected, judge_selection's old value 2 into judges_elected's new value 0, and so on. But notice that in the currently grayed-out area of the Old Value panel, SPSS will permit us to specify a *range* of old values to be recoded into a single new value. So that you can become comfortable with both approaches, we will use the range option to recode the judicial appointment codes (judge_selection's codes 1 through 3) and the one-value-at-a-time approach to recode the codes for judicial elections (judge_selection's codes 4 and 5).

FIGURE 3-2   Recoding a Categorical Variable

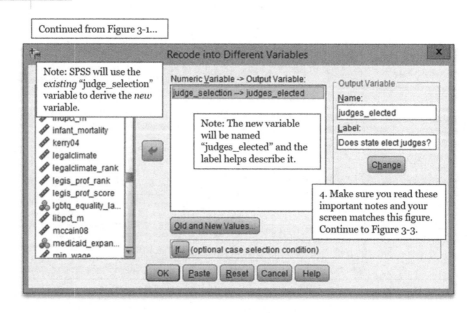

FIGURE 3-3 Recode into Different Variables: Old and New Values Window (default)

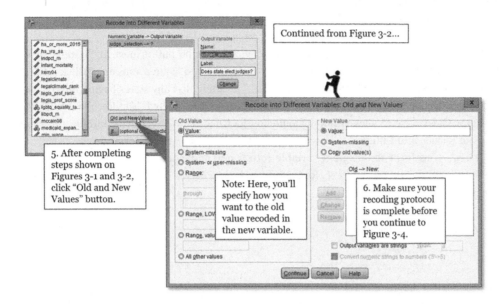

First, we'll enter instructions to recode judge_selection values 1 through 3. In the Old Value panel, select the uppermost Range button, the one simply labeled "Range." The two boxes beneath "Range" are activated. Type "3" in the upper Range box, and type "1" in the lower Range box. Move the cursor to the New Value panel and type "0" in the Value box. Click Add. SPSS responds, "1 thru 3 → 0," letting you know that states coded 1, 2, or 3 on judge_selection will be coded 0 on judges_elected (see Figure 3-4).

Next, we'll recode judge_selection values 4 and 5. In the Old Value, click the cursor in the box next to "Value" and type "4". Move the cursor directly across to the right-hand New Value panel and

FIGURE 3-4 Recoding a Categorical Variable to Create an Indicator Variable

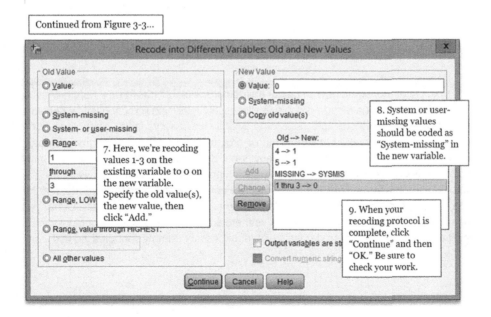

type "1" in the Value box. Click the Add button. In the Old → New box, SPSS records your instruction with "4 → 1," meaning "All states coded 4 on judge_selection will be coded 1 on judges_elected." Now return to the left-hand Old Value panel and type "5" in the Value box. Again move to the right-hand New Value panel and type "1" in the Value box. Click Add. SPSS responds, "5 → 1," meaning "All states coded 5 on judge_selection will be coded 1 on judges_elected."

One last loose end: In the Old Value panel, click the radio button next to "System- or user-missing." In the New Value panel, click the radio button next to "System-missing." Click Add. SPSS records your instruction as "MISSING → SYSMIS," meaning that any states having missing values on judge_selection will be assigned missing values on judges_elected. The Recode into Different Variables: Old and New Values window should now look like Figure 3-4. Click Continue, returning to the main Recode into Different Variables window. Click OK. SPSS runs the recode.

Did we transform the original variable into a new indicator correctly? This is where the check-your-work rule takes effect. Run Frequencies on judges_elected to ensure that you did things right:

Statistics

Does state elect judges?

N	Valid	50
	Missing	0

Does State Elect Judges?

		Frequency	Percent	Valid Percent	Cumulative Percent
Valid	.00	28	56.0	56.0	56.0
	1.00	22	44.0	44.0	100.0
	Total	50	100.0	100.0	

The frequency distribution table displays the label for the newly minted variable. More important, the valid percentages check out: 56.0 percent of states are coded 0 (do not elect judges) and 44.0 percent coded 1 (elect judges). The recode worked as planned.

A CLOSER LOOK: CREATING MULTIPLE DUMMY VARIABLES

In the text, we demonstrate how to create an indicator variable based on a nominal-level variable with multiple values. The recode procedure discussed in the text is most useful when you want to transform a variable with multiple values into a single indicator variable. When you want to create multiple dummy variables from a nominal or ordinal variable, the Transform ▶ Create Dummy Variables procedure may be more efficient. We'll demonstrate this procedure in Chapter 9 to create a series of dummy variables for regression analysis. For example, if we wanted a dummy variable for each method of selecting judges, we could use this procedure instead of the recode method that generates one new variable at a time. The Transform ▶ Create Dummy Variables procedure creates as many new variables as there are unique values of the original variable; however, it can quickly clutter your datasets with unnecessary dummy variables, so use it selectively.

FIGURE 3-5   Assigning Value Labels to a Recoded Variable

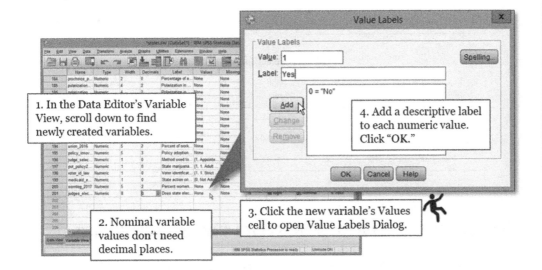

WORKING WITH VARIABLE LABELS

In the prior section, we created an indicator variable to identify states that elect appellate court judges. Creating this indicator variable could be the starting point for evaluating the practice of elect-ing judges and contributing to the ongoing debate over which judicial selection method works best. However, we still need to make sure that the indicator's numeric codes are labeled properly: "No" for numeric code 0 and "Yes" for numeric code 1. Properly labeling variable values helps us understand our analysis and communicate results effectively. So, one more step is required to complete this vari-able transformation.

In the Data Editor, make sure that the Variable View tab is clicked. Scroll down to the bot-tom of the Data Editor, where you will find judges_elected (Figure 3-5). (SPSS always puts newly created variables on the bottom row of the Variable View.) While we are doing the essential work of assigning value labels, we will also tidy up the formatting of the variable we just created. Click in the Decimals cell, which shows "2," and change this value to "0." Next, click in the Values cell (which currently says "None"), and then click on the button that appears. The Value Labels window presents itself. In the box next to "Value," type "0." In the box next to "Label," type "No." Click Add. Repeat the process for code 1, typing "1" in the Value box and "Yes" in the Label box. Click Add. Click OK.

A final Frequencies run will confirm that the labeling worked as planned (see Does State Elect Judges table on p. 54):

The procedure you use to label the new judges_elected indicator variable can also be used to edit the labels and value labels of existing variables. When you're doing political analysis with real data-sets, you'll often find that variables and their values aren't labeled as clearly or concisely as they could be. You may find that you need to edit existing variable labels so your tables and figures communicate results clearly and succinctly.

You have just invested your time in recoding an original variable into a new variable and, in the process, made the States dataset better and more usable. Before going on to the next example, make sure you save the dataset.

Statistics

Does state elect judges?

N	Valid	50
	Missing	0

Does State Elect Judges?

		Frequency	Percent	Valid Percent	Cumulative Percent
Valid	No	28	56.0	56.0	56.0
	Yes	22	44.0	44.0	100.0
	Total	50	100.0	100.0	

RECODING INTERVAL-LEVEL VARIABLES INTO SIMPLIFIED CATEGORIES

Collapsing the values of a categorical variable, as you have just done, is perhaps the most common use of the Recode transformation feature. The original variable may be nominal level, such as judge_ selection. Or it may be ordinal level. For example, it might make sense to collapse four response categories such as "strongly agree," "agree," "disagree," and "strongly disagree" into two, "agree" and "disagree." At other times the original variable is interval level, such as age in years or income in dollars. In such cases you could use Recode to create a new variable having, say, three or four ordinal-level categories. Sometimes, simplifying a measurement facilitates meaningful comparisons. Let's pursue this route.

The NES dataset, NES.sav, contains the variable ft_SCOTUS, which measures respondents' attitudes toward the Supreme Court of the United States. The ft_SCOTUS variable is one of the many "feeling thermometer" scales used by the American National Election Studies to record respondents' ratings of groups, political personalities, and other political objects. Scale scores can range from 0 (cold or negative feelings) to 100 (warm or positive feelings), with 50 being a neutral score. Consider a bar chart of ft_SCOTUS values (Figure 3-6).

For some analysis purposes, ft_SCOTUS may be too finely tuned; one may prefer to analyze support for the Supreme Court in broad terms rather than 1-degree increments. Suppose we want to use ft_SCOTUS to create a new variable, ft_SCOTUS_3cat, by classifying respondents into three ordinal categories—those who rated the Supreme Court at 30 degrees or lower, those giving ratings of 31 through 69, and those who rated the Court at 70 or higher. This simplified, three-category variable would allow us to broadly compare people who have negative, neutral, and positive attitudes about the nation's highest court. A frequency distribution table of ft_SCOTUS (not shown because it has over 100 rows) tells us that 8.5 percent of respondents will fall into the first category, and 65.5 percent will fall into the first *and* second categories of the transformed variable.

To recode this interval-level feeling thermometer into an ordinal-level variable, select Transform ▶ Recode into Different Variables. If SPSS shows some prior recoding settings, click Reset to clear the panels. Now, click ftgr_fedgov into the "Numeric Variable → Output Variable:" box. Type "ft_ SCOTUS_3cat" in the Name box. Type "Feeling therm: US Supreme Court, 3 Categories" in the Label box and click Change (Figure 3-7). Once you've named and labeled the new, ordinal-level variable you're creating, click the Old and New Values button.

In the Recode into Different Variables: Old and New Values window, we'll specify exactly how we want the ft_SCOTUS variable recoded to create the new, ordinal-level ft_SCOTUS_3cat variable. First, create the lowest category for ft_SCOTUS_3cat. In the Old Value panel, select the radio button next to "Range, LOWEST through value"; doing so activates the box. Type "30" in the box.

FIGURE **3-6**   Bar Chart of a SCOTUS Feeling Thermometer, an Interval-level
Variable

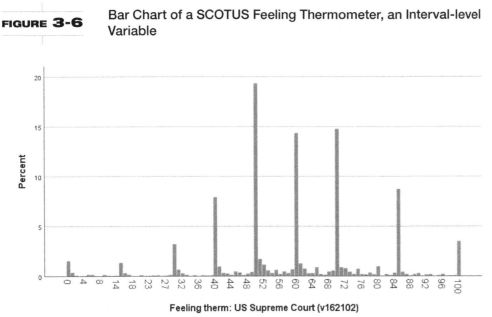

Feeling therm: US Supreme Court (v162102)

Cases weighted by Weight variable (v160102)

In the New Value panel, type "1" in the Value box and click Add. SPSS translates the instruction as "Lowest thru 30 → 1." This will lump respondents who reported scores for the Supreme Court between 0 (the lowest possible score) and 30 on ft_SCOTUS into category 1 of the new variable, ft_SCOTUS_3cat. Next, in the Old Value panel, select the "Range" button and type "31" in the upper box and "69" in the lower box. Type "2" in the Value box in the New Value panel and click Add. That's the middle category, now coded 2 on ft_SCOTUS_3cat. In the Old Value panel, select the radio button next to "Range, value through HIGHEST" and type "70" in the box. Type "3" in the Value box in the New Value panel and click Add. That puts the highest values of ft_SCOTUS into

FIGURE **3-7**   Recoding an Interval-level Variable

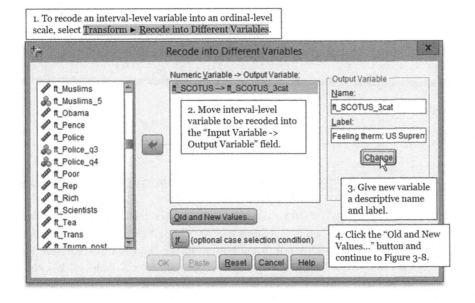

FIGURE 3-8   Recoding Settings to Collapse an Interval-level Variable into Categories

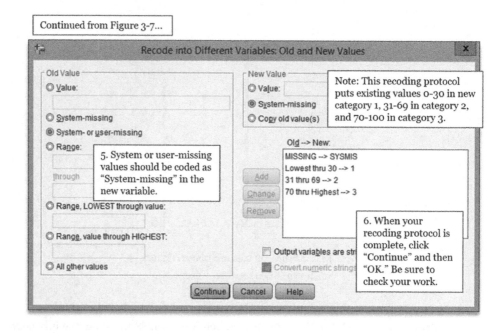

category 3 on ft_SCOTUS_3cat. Complete the recode by clicking the "System- or user-missing" button in the Old Value panel and the "System-missing" button in the New Value panel. Click Add. The Recode into Different Variables: Old and New Values window should now look like Figure 3-8. Click Continue.

If your Recode into Different Variables: Old and New Values dialog looked the same as the one shown in Figure 3-8, click the OK button in the Recode into Different Variables window (see Figure 3-7). Check your work by running Frequencies on ft_SCOTUS_3cat and examining the output.

Feeling Therm: US Supreme Court, 3 Categories

		Frequency	Percent	Valid Percent	Cumulative Percent
Valid	1.00	307	8.4	8.5	8.5
	2.00	2057	56.4	57.0	65.5
	3.00	1245	34.1	34.5	100.0
	Total	3608	98.9	100.0	
Missing	System	41	1.1		
Total		3649	100.0		

The cumulative percent markers, 8.5 percent and 65.5 percent, are just where they are supposed to be. Our new ft_SCOTUS_3cat variable checks out.

Before we save our newly created variable in the NES dataset, let's assign descriptive labels to the numeric categories 1, 2, and 3 to create a new bar chart. As we did before (to label values 0 and 1 of an indicator variable), scroll to the bottom of the Data Editor's Variable View and make two changes to ft_SCOTUS_3cat. First, change Decimals to 0. Second, click in the Values cell and label ft_SCOTUS_3cat's values with the following labels: 1, "Cold"; 2, "Neutral"; and

FIGURE 3-9   Bar Chart of a SCOTUS Feeling Thermometer, Three Categories

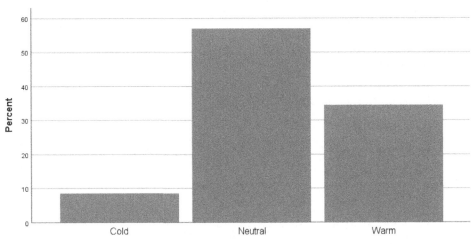

Feeling therm: US Supreme Court, 3 Categories

Cases weighted by Weight variable (v160102)

3, "Warm." Review Figure 3-5 as necessary to complete these tasks. Now, create a bar chart of ft_SCOTUS_3cat, admire this clear image of public support/indifference for the Supreme Court, and save the NES dataset.

SIMPLIFYING AN INTERVAL-LEVEL VARIABLE WITH VISUAL BINNING

For nominal and ordinal variables, the Recode procedure is fast and easy to use. However, for transforming interval variables, SPSS's more obscure Visual Binning procedure sometimes provides an attractive alternative to Recode. Like the Recode procedure, Visual Binning can be used to create variables, such as ft_SCOTUS_3cat, for which the researcher has selected theoretically meaningful cutpoints for defining the categories of the new variable. Visual Binning is more useful than Recode when you want to quickly collapse an interval-level variable into a handful of categories, each containing roughly equal numbers of cases, but aren't sure what cutpoints to use.

Screencast

Collapsing an Interval-level Variable with Visual Binning

To demonstrate Visual Binning, let's work through a guided example using NES's Income variable, a 28-level measure of each respondent's income. You will use Visual Binning to create a three-category ordinal, Income_3cat, which will break the original Income variable into thirds or terciles: the lowest tercile ("Low"), the middle tercile ("Middle"), and the highest tercile ("High").

An obligatory Frequencies analysis of the Income variable produces the following frequency distribution table (if your numbers aren't quite the same, make sure you're weighting observations to get nationally representative results; see Pre Income Summary table, p. 58):

If you were using Recode to collapse this variable into three equally sized groups, you could create the "Low" group by collapsing codes 1 through 12 (cumulative percent, 35.8), the "Middle" group by combining codes 13 through 21 (cumulative percent, 70.0), and the "High" group by collapsing codes 22 through 28. That's a relatively complex Recode order. Visual Binning will accomplish the same task with fewer clicks and less typing.

To start the Visual Binning procedure, select Transform ▶ Visual Binning to open the Visual Binning window. Scroll down the variable list, find Income, and click it into the "Variables to Bin:" panel as shown in Figure 3-10 and click Continue.

Pre Income Summary (v161361x)

		Frequency	Percent	Valid Percent	Cumulative Percent
Valid	01. Under $5,000	257	7.1	7.3	7.3
	02. $5,000-$9,999	70	1.9	2.0	9.3
	03. $10,000-$12,499	109	3.0	3.1	12.4
	04. $12,500-$14,999	25	.7	.7	13.1
	05. $15,000-$17,499	91	2.5	2.6	15.7
	06. $17,500-$19,999	59	1.6	1.7	17.4
	07. $20,000-$22,499	126	3.5	3.6	21.0
	08. $22,500-$24,999	48	1.3	1.4	22.3
	09. $25,000-$27,499	128	3.5	3.6	26.0
	10. $27,500-$29,999	21	.6	.6	26.6
	11. $30,000-$34,999	168	4.6	4.8	31.3
	12. $35,000-$39,999	158	4.3	4.5	35.8
	13. $40,000-$44,999	153	4.2	4.3	40.2
	14. $45,000-$49,999	116	3.2	3.3	43.5
	15. $50,000 -$54,999	178	4.9	5.1	48.5
	16. $55,000-$59,999	72	2.0	2.0	50.6
	17. $60,000-$64,999	166	4.6	4.7	55.3
	18. $65,000-$69,999	97	2.7	2.8	58.0
	19. $70,000-$74,999	115	3.2	3.3	61.3
	20. $75,000-$79,999	107	2.9	3.1	64.4
	21. $80,000-$89,999	198	5.4	5.6	70.0
	22. $90,000-$99,999	166	4.5	4.7	74.7
	23. $100,000-$109,999	167	4.6	4.7	79.4
	24. $110,000-$124,999	145	4.0	4.1	83.6
	25. $125,000-$149,999	152	4.2	4.3	87.9
	26. $150,000-$174,999	146	4.0	4.2	92.0
	27. $175,000-$249,999	160	4.4	4.5	96.6
	28. $250,000 or more	120	3.3	3.4	100.0
	Total	3519	96.4	100.0	
Missing System		130	3.6		
Total		3649	100.0		

The Visual Binning procedure continues to a second window (see Figure 3-11). If the right side of this window is grayed out and inactive, click on Income in the Scanned Variable List. You will see three sections to the right of the Scanned Variable List: a top section for variable names and labels, a graphic display of the selected variable in the middle, and a Grid of cutpoints at the bottom.

Starting in the top right-hand section, click in the field for the Name of the Binned Variable. This is where you provide a name for the variable you are about to create. Type "Income_3cat" (without the quotation marks). Click in the adjacent field for the Binned Variable's Label, where SPSS has supplied a wordy default name. Modify the Label field to read "Family Income,

3 categories" (also without the quotation marks). Later, you will attend to the Grid section, but first you need to create Income_3cat's categories. Now, click the Make Cutpoints button and consider the Make Cutpoints window (Figure 3-12).

Because you want equal-sized groups, select the radio button next to Equal Percentiles Based on Scanned Cases. And because you want three groups, click in the Number of Cutpoints box and type "2." Why 2? Here is the rule: If you wish to create a variable having k categories, then you must request $k - 1$ cutpoints. (Reassuringly, after you type "2," SPSS automatically puts "33.3" in the Width(%) box.) Click Apply, returning to the continuation window (Figure 3-13).

Now, notice the values "12.0," "21.0," and "HIGH" that SPSS has entered in the Grid panel. Earlier, when we inspected the frequency distribution of Income, we thought that these cutpoints would divide respondents into nearly equal groups.

Let's finish the job by adding descriptive labels in the Labels fields next to each cutpoint Value in the Grid section, as shown in Figure 3-13: "Low" next to "12.0," "Middle" next to "21.0," and "High" next to "HIGH."[1] Click OK. (Click OK again when SPSS issues the warning, "Binning specifications will create 1 variables.") Check your work by running Frequencies on Income_3cat; see Family Income, 3 Categories table here):

Family income, 3 Categories

		Frequency	Percent	Valid Percent	Cumulative Percent
Valid	Low	1261	34.6	35.8	35.8
	Middle	1202	32.9	34.2	70.0
	High	1056	29.0	30.0	100.0
	Total	3519	96.4	100.0	
Missing	System	130	3.6		
Total		3649	100.0		

FIGURE 3-10   Visual Binning Opening Window

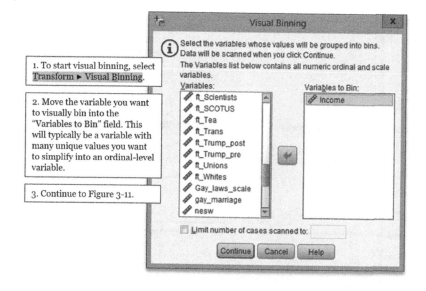

---

[1] The SPSS-supplied numbers in the Value cells of the Grid panel are not the numeric codes that SPSS assigns to the categories. The numeric codes are numbered sequentially, beginning with 1. So incgroup3 has numeric codes 1 ("Low"), 2 ("Middle"), and 3 ("High").

FIGURE 3-11 Visual Binning Continuation Window

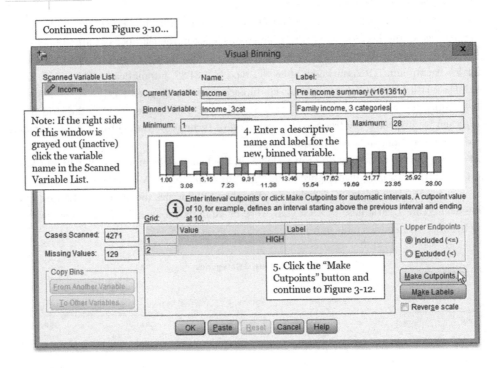

Continued from Figure 3-10...

Note: If the right side of this window is grayed out (inactive) click the variable name in the Scanned Variable List.

4. Enter a descriptive name and label for the new, binned variable.

5. Click the "Make Cutpoints" button and continue to Figure 3-12.

FIGURE 3-12 Visual Binning: Make Cutpoints Window

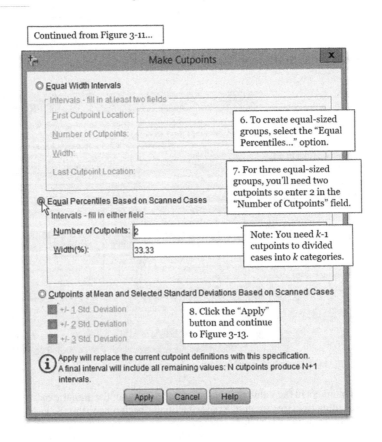

Continued from Figure 3-11...

6. To create equal-sized groups, select the "Equal Percentiles..." option.

7. For three equal-sized groups, you'll need two cutpoints so enter 2 in the "Number of Cutpoints" field.

Note: You need k-1 cutpoints to divided cases into k categories.

8. Click the "Apply" button and continue to Figure 3-13.

FIGURE 3-13   Labeling New Variable Values in the Visual Binning Continuation Window

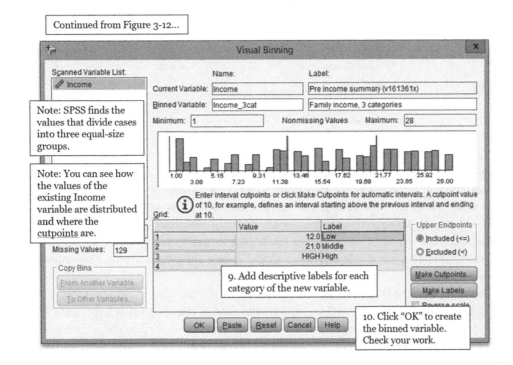

This is a nice-looking three-category ordinal. It could be used to analyze the relationship between income and politics in all sorts of interesting ways. Save the dataset, and let's move to the next topic.[2]

CENTERING OR STANDARDIZING A NUMERIC VARIABLE

In this section we'll illustrate two related methods used to simplify interval-level variables: centering and standardizing variables. These techniques are useful when we want to compare observations that have above-average or below-average values of a variable to those with average values.

To illustrate, let's consider the economic importance of foreign trade to countries around the world. This concept is measured by the trade_percent_gdp variable in the World dataset, world. sav. This variable divides the dollar value of a country's imports and exports by the country's gross domestic product. The larger the value, the more important foreign trade is to the national economy. In some countries, the dollar value of foreign trade is larger than the value of the domestic economy; so in these countries, the variable exceeds 100 percent. Use the Analyze ▶ Descriptive Statistics ▶ Frequencies procedure to calculate basic descriptive statistics for trade_percent_gdp, including its mean, standard deviation, minimum, and maximum.

---

[2] Suppose you wanted to collapse ft_SCOTUS into ft_SCOTUS_3cat using Visual Binning instead of Recode. You would follow these steps: (1) Click Transform ▶ Visual Binning and scan ft_SCOTUS. (2) In the Scanned Variable List of the continuation window, select ft_SCOTUS. (3) In the Name panel, supply the name "ft_SCOTUS_3cat" and the label "Ratings of US Supreme Court, 3 Categories." (4) In the Value cells of the Grid panel, type "30" in the topmost cell and "69" in the next lower cell. (SPSS automatically supplies the word "HIGH" in the lowest of the three cells.) (5) In the Label cells of the Grid panel, supply value labels for each value ("Cold" goes with "30," "Neutral" goes with "69," and "High" goes with "HIGH"). (6) Click OK. The ft_SCOTUS_3cat variable will be created and labeled correctly.

Statistics

International trade as percentage of GDP

N	Valid	162
	Missing	7
Mean		86.0090
Std. Deviation		51.94790
Minimum		21.12
Maximum		419.47

The output tells us that the mean trade as a percentage of GDP among 162 countries in the World dataset is 86.0090 and the standard deviation is 51.94790.[3]

Centering, or mean centering, transforms values of a variable by subtracting the variable's mean value from each observation. The mean-centered variable will have positive values for observations with above-average values, negative values for those with below-average values, and zero for those equal to the mean. (As you'll discover later, centering is a nice technique to use when estimating a multiple regression model so that the intercept term corresponds to a typical case.)

To center the variable measuring the importance of international trade, select Transform ▶ Compute Variable to bring up the Compute Variable window (Figure 3-14). A box labeled "Target Variable" is in the window's upper left-hand corner. This is where we name the new variable. You want to generate a new, mean-centered variable without disturbing the trade_percent_gdp variable, so type "trade_percent_centered" in the Computer Variable window's "Target Variable" field. The large box on the right side of the window, labeled "Numeric Expression," is where we tell SPSS which variables to use and how to combine them. We'll subtract trade_percent_gdp's mean (86.0090) from each observation of trade_percent_gdp by entering the expression "trade_percent_gdp – 86.0090." Replicate Figure 3-14 and click OK.

To confirm the results, summarize the new variable, trade_percent_centered, using the Analyze ▶ Descriptive Statistics ▶ Frequencies procedure. This new variable should have a mean of 0.00 and the same standard deviation as the original variable trade_percent_gdp. We transformed the trade_percent_gdp variable by a constant amount without changing how much observations vary from one another.

Statistics

trade_percent_centered

N	Valid	162
	Missing	7
Mean		0.0000
Std. Deviation		51.94790
Minimum		-64.89
Maximum		333.46

When you standardize a variable, you subtract its mean value from each observation and divide the result by the variable's standard deviation. Standardizing a variable is useful when one is concerned about relative differences but not the scale of measurement. Sticking with our measure of the

---

[3] If you're curious which countries have the minimum (21.12) and maximum (419.47) values, see the section on obtaining case-level information from a dataset in Chapter 2.

FIGURE 3-14   Creating a Mean-Centered Variable

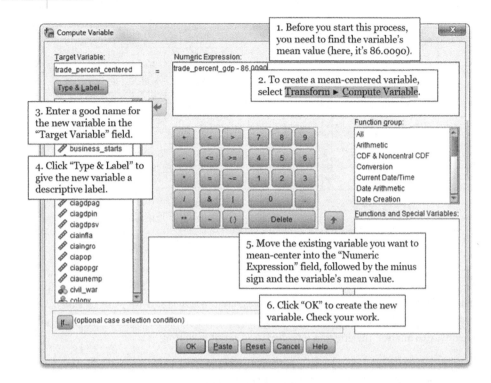

importance of foreign trade to national economies, let's create a new variable that equals the standardized value of trade_percent_gdp.

To standardize an interval-level variable, select Analyze ▸ Descriptive Statistics ▸ Descriptives to call up the Descriptives window (Figure 3-15). Find trade_percent_gdp on the left-hand variables list and click or drag it into the Variable(s) box. Check the "Save standardized values as variables" box. SPSS will add a standardized version of the trade_percent_gdp variable to the World dataset with the letter "Z" added to the beginning of its name (so this variable will be named Ztrade_percent_gdp).

Once again, to make sure the variable has been properly standardized, summarize the new variable, trade_percent_centered, using the Analyze ▸ Descriptive Statistics ▸ Frequencies procedure. This new variable should have a mean of 0.00 and a standard deviation of 1.00.

Statistics

Zscore: International trade as percentage of GDP

N	Valid	162
	Missing	7
Mean		0.0000000
Std. Deviation		1.00000000
Minimum		-1.24912
Maximum		6.41914

Notice now that the standard deviation of Ztrade_percent_gdp equals 1. Why is this? We divided each observation's deviation from the mean value by the standard deviation of trade_percent_gdp. Now, a country with a Ztrade_percent_gdp value equal to 1.00 has a trade_percent_gdp value one

FIGURE 3-15   Standardized Interval-level Variable

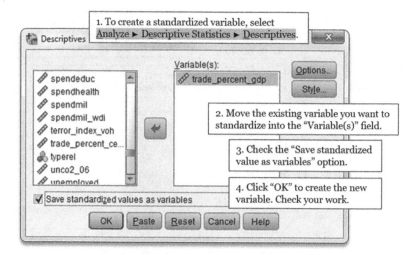

standard deviation higher than the mean value, and a country with a Ztrade_percent_gdp value of −1.00 has a trade value one standard deviation less than the mean. If we want to analyze how the importance of foreign trade to the national economy affects a country, Ztrade_percent_gdp gives us a great way to analyze the effect of a typical amount of variation.

USING COMPUTE TO CREATE AN ADDITIVE INDEX

Although SPSS permits the creation of new variables through a dizzying variety of complex transformations, the typical use of Compute is pretty straightforward. By and large, Compute is typically used to create a simple *additive index* from similarly coded variables.[4]

Additive indexes, a type of scaled measure, are an extremely useful way of transforming nominal- or ordinal-level measures into interval-level measures; this kind of transformation allows the researcher to apply more elegant methods to analyze the variable. We've created a number of scales in the companion datasets. In this section, we'll show you how we created the additive index of support for abortion access.

Consider measuring support for abortion access. Suppose you have seven variables, each of which measures a respondent's support for abortion access in different circumstances. In the GSS, respondents are asked whether they think a woman should be permitted to have an abortion in the following circumstances:

1. Strong chance of serious birth defect (abdefect)

2. Woman's health seriously endangered (abhlth)

3. Married woman wants no more children (abnomore)

4. Parents can't afford more children (abpoor)

5. Pregnant as a result of rape (abrape)

6. Mother not married (absingle)

7. If woman wants for any reason (abany)

Screencast

Using Compute

---

[4] For a detailed discussion of additive indexes, see Philip Pollock III, *The Essentials of Political Analysis*, 5th ed. (Thousand Oaks, CA: CQ Press, An Imprint of SAGE Publications, 2016), 27–29.

Now, each of these variables is interesting in its own right, but we are going to add these variables together to create an interval-level measure. Think about a respondent who does not support access to abortion under any circumstance. What would be his or her score on an additive index? People who did not support access under any condition would have a value of 0 on the new variable; those who supported access under just one condition, a code of 1; those who supported access under two conditions, a code of 2; and so on. Respondents who supported access under all listed circumstances would have a code of 7.

Here are some suggested guidelines to follow in using the "generate" command to create a simple additive index. First, before generating the new variable, make sure that each of the variables is identically coded. In the above illustration, if the "abdefect" variable were coded 1 for no and 2 for yes, and the other variables were coded 0 and 1, the resulting additive index would be incorrect. Second, make sure that the variables are all coded in the same *direction*. If the "abdefect" variable were coded 0 for yes and 1 for no, and the other variables were coded 0 for no and 1 for yes, the additive index would again be incorrect.[5] Third, after running "generate," obtain a frequency distribution of the newly created variable. Upon examining the frequency distribution, you may decide to run "recode" to collapse the new variable into more useful categories.

The seven GSS questions about abortion access weren't encoded with numeric value 0 corresponding to "No" responses, so we need to do some recoding before creating an additive index. We want each component variable to be coded such that a value of 1 corresponds to support for abortion access and 0 indicates opposition. The coding protocol in Table 3.1 helped us recode these variables correctly.

Having created seven new indicator variables, each coded the same way with 1 representing support for abortion access and 0 signifying opposition, we ask SPSS to compute a new variable,

TABLE 3.1   Coding Protocol for an Additive Index of Abortion Rights Support

GSS Variable	GSS Coding	New Variable	New Coding
abdefect	1 = "Yes" 2 = "No"	abdefect_r	1 = "Yes" 0 = "No"
abhlth	1 = "Yes" 2 = "No"	abhlth_r	1 = "Yes" 0 = "No"
abnomore	1 = "Yes" 2 = "No"	abnomore_r	1 = "Yes" 0 = "No"
abpoor	1 = "Yes" 2 = "No"	abpoor_r	1 = "Yes" 0 = "No"
abrape	1 = "Yes" 2 = "No"	abrape_r	1 = "Yes" 0 = "No"
absingle	1 = "Yes" 2 = "No"	absingle_r	1 = "Yes" 0 = "No"
abany	1 = "Yes" 2 = "No"	abany_r	1 = "Yes" 0 = "No"

[5] Survey datasets are notorious for "reverse coding." Survey designers do this so that respondents don't fall into response bias, or automatically give the same response to a series of questions. Although you may need to be on the lookout for reverse coding in your future research, none of the examples or exercises in this book will require that you "repair" the original coding of any variables.

which we named abortion, by summing the values of abdefect_r, abhlth_r, abnomore_r, abpoor_r, abrape_r, absingle_r, and abany_r.

To replicate the abortion scale, click Transform ▶ Compute Variable, invoking the Compute Variable window. Click in the Target Variable field and type "abortion_n7." Next, build the numeric expression by adding the components of the scale together. Click abany_r into the Numeric Expression box. Using the keyboard (or the calculator pad beneath the Numeric Expression box), type or click a plus sign (+) to the right of abany_r. Returning to the variable list, click abdefect_r into the Numeric Expression box. Repeat this process for the remaining variables until the Numeric Expression box reads "abany_r + abdefect_r + abhlth_r + abnomore_r + abpoor_r + abrape_r + absingle_r" (see Figure 3-16).

Before we create abortion_n7, let's give it a descriptive label. Click the Type & Label button, which opens the Compute Variable: Type and Label window, as shown in Figure 3-16. Type "Abortion access index" in the Label box and click Continue. You are ready to run the compute variable procedure. Click OK. SPSS does its work.

SPSS computes the abortion access index and deposits the new variable, abortion_n7, at the bottom of the Data Editor's Variable View.[6] What does the new variable look like? To find out, run Analyze ▶ Descriptive Statistics ▶ Frequencies on abortion_n7. Request a bar chart.

Statistics

Abortion access index

N	Valid	1662
	Missing	1205

Abortion Access Index

		Frequency	Percent	Valid Percent	Cumulative Percent
Valid	0.00	143	5.0	8.6	8.6
	1.00	142	4.9	8.5	17.1
	2.00	171	5.9	10.3	27.4
	3.00	310	10.8	18.6	46.0
	4.00	109	3.8	6.5	52.6
	5.00	70	2.4	4.2	56.8
	6.00	100	3.5	6.0	62.8
	7.00	619	21.6	37.2	100.0
	Total	1662	58.0	100.0	
Missing	System	1205	42.0		
Total		2867	100.0		

This is an interesting variable, well worth the effort of computing it. Although the strongest pro–abortion rights position (a value of 7) is the mode of the distribution (with nearly 40 percent of the cases), a substantial minority of respondents did not support any of the policies (a little less than 10 percent in value 0). Code 4—yes to four of the questions, no to three of the questions—is the median. Although abortion opinions are often cast in the binary terms pro-life and pro-choice, it appears that a substantial number of respondents take middle-ground positions on abortion rights.

Before proceeding with the exercises, be sure to save the dataset.

[6] In Data Editor's Variable View, perform the usual housekeeping tasks with abortion_n7. Change Decimals to 0. If you didn't label the variable when you created it, do so now.

FIGURE 3-16   Computing an Additive Index

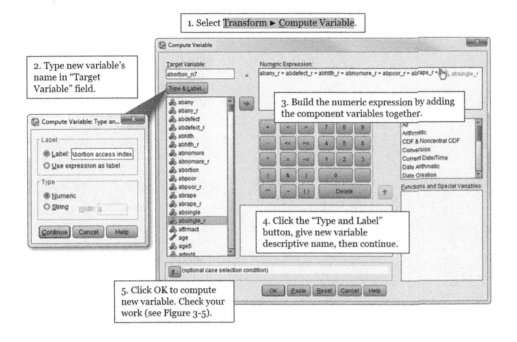

FIGURE 3-17   Bar Chart of the Abortion Access Additive Index

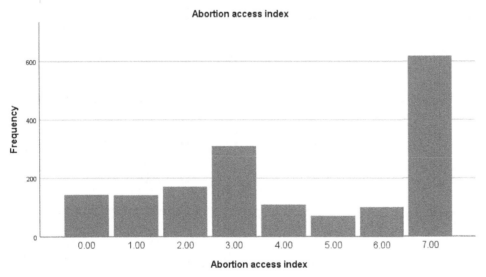

Name: Anna Jeffries   Date: 10/16/22

E-mail: _____   Section: _____

CHAPTER 3 EXERCISES

For the exercises in this chapter, you will use the GSS dataset (file name: gss.dta).

1. (Dataset: GSS. Variables: polviews, wtss.) The GSS dataset contains polviews, which measures political ideology—the extent to which individuals "think of themselves as liberal or conservative." Here is how polviews is coded (the labels are fully written out):

Numeric Code	Value Label
1	Extremely liberal
2	Liberal
3	Slightly liberal
4	Moderate
5	Slightly conservative
6	Conservative
7	Extremely conservative

A. Apply the Analyze ▶ Descriptive Statistics ▶ Frequencies procedure to polviews, making sure to weight the data using the wtss variable. Eyeball the percent column and make some rough-and-ready estimates.

The percentage of respondents who are either "extremely liberal," "liberal," or "slightly liberal" is (circle one)

about 18 percent. | about 28 percent |
about 38 percent.

The percentage of respondents who are either "slightly conservative," "conservative," or "extremely conservative" is (circle one)

about 10 percent. | about 20 percent. |
about 30 percent.

B. Use polviews and the Transform ▶ Recode into Different Variables procedure to create a new variable named polview3. Give polview3 this label: "Ideology: 3 categories." Collapse the three liberal codes into one category (coded 1 on polview3), put the moderates

into their own category (coded 2 on polview3), and collapse the three conservative codes into one category (coded 3 on polview3). Don't forget to recode missing values on polviews into missing values on polview3. Run Frequencies on polview3.

The percentage of respondents who are coded 1 on polview3 is (fill in the blank) 28.5 percent.

                                    MOD
The percentage of respondents who are coded 2 on polview3 is (fill in the blank) ~~37.2 37.2~~ percent.
                                    37.2

Make sure that the two percentages you wrote down in part B match the percentages you recorded in part A. The numbers may be slightly different and may still be considered a match. If the two sets of numbers match, proceed to part C. If they do not match, you performed the recode incorrectly. Review this chapter's discussion of the Recode procedure and try the recode again.

C. In the Variable View of the Data Editor, change Decimals to 0, and then click in the Values cell and supply the appropriate labels for the numeric codes of the new polview3 variable: "Liberal" for code 1, "Moderate" for code 2, and "Conservative" for code 3. Run the Analyze ▶ Descriptive Statistics ▶ Frequencies procedure on polview3. Use your results to fill in the table below.

Ideology: Three Categories	Frequency*	Percent	Cumulative Percent
Liberal	788 ?	28.5?	28.5 ?
Moderate	1026 ?	37.2?	65.7 ?
Conservative	947 ?	34.3?	100.00%
Total	2761 ?	100.00%	

*Round weighted frequencies to two decimal places.

2. (Dataset: GSS. Variables: colmslm, libmslm, spkmslm, wtss.) The GSS dataset contains three variables that gauge tolerance toward "anti-American Muslim clergymen"—whether they should be allowed to teach in college (colmslm), whether their books should be removed from the library (libmslm), and whether they should be allowed

to preach hatred of the United States (spkmslm). For each variable, respondents are given two choices: a less tolerant response and a more tolerant response. For this problem, you'll create and analyze an additive index of tolerance of anti-American Muslim clergymen.

A. Create indicator variables for colmslm, libmslm, and spkmslm by completing the coding protocol below. Be sure to give the three variables you create new, descriptive names so you don't overwrite the existing variables in the dataset. (Don't forget to recode missing values on the colmslm, libmslm, and spkmslm variables into missing values on your new indicator variables.)

Should anti-American Muslim clergymen be allowed to teach in college?	Existing Numeric Code for colmslm	Numeric Coding for New Variable Named _____
Yes, allowed	4	1
Not allowed	5	0

Should anti-American Muslim clergymen's books be removed from library?	Existing Numeric Code for libmslm	Numeric Coding for New Variable Named _____
Remove	1	0
Not remove	2	1

Should anti-American Muslim clergymen be allowed to preach hatred of the United States?	Existing Numeric Code for spkmslm	Numeric Coding for New Variable Named _____
Yes, allowed	1	1
Not allowed	2	0

B. Imagine creating an additive index from the three variables you created in part A. The additive index would have scores that range between ___0___ and ___3___.

C. Suppose a respondent takes the more tolerant position on two questions and the less tolerant position on the third question. This respondent would have a score of ___2___.

D. Use the Transform ▶ Compute Variable procedure to create an additive index from the three variables you created in part A. Name the new variable muslim_tol. Run Analyze ▶ Descriptive Statistics ▶ Frequencies on

muslim_tol. Referring to your output, fill in the table that follows.

The muslim_tol Scale		
Score on muslim_tol	Frequency*	Percentage
0 ?	795 ?	43.0 ?
1 ?	301 ?	16.3 ?
2 ?	259 ?	14.0 ?
3 ?	494 ?	26.7 ?
Total	1848 ?	100.00%

*Rounded frequencies.

EC.

3. (Dataset: GSS. Variables: rincom16, wtss.) In this chapter you learned to use Visual Binning to simplify a measure of respondents' income in the NES dataset into three roughly equal ordinal categories. In this exercise, you will use Visual Binning to collapse a very similar variable from the GSS dataset (rincom16) into rincom16_q3, a three-category ordinal measure of respondents' incomes.

Refer to this chapter's visual binning guided example and retrace the steps to create the new rincom16_q3 variable. Here is new information you will need:

Variable to bin	rincom16
Binned variable name	rincom16_q3
Binned variable label	Income tercile
Number of cutpoints	2
Labels for Value cells	Low, Middle, High

Run Analyze ▶ Descriptive Statistics ▶ Frequencies on your newly created variable rincom16_q3. Refer to your output to fill in the table that follows.

Three Quantiles of rincom16_q3	Frequency	Percent	Cumulative Percent
1	586 ?	34.5 ?	34.5 ?
2	550 ?	32.4 ?	67.0 ?
3	560 ?	33.0 ?	100.00%
Total	1695 ?	100.00%	

4. (Dataset: GSS. Variables: pornlaw, wtss.) In this chapter you learned to use the Transform ▶ Recode into Different

Variables procedure to create indicator variables. In this exercise, you will create indicator variables from pornlaw, which measures individuals' opinions about pornography. Respondents who think pornography should be "Illegal to all" are coded 1, those saying "Illegal under 18" are coded 2, and respondents who say "Legal (to all)" are coded 3. You will create an indicator variable coded 1 for individuals saying "Illegal to all," and coded 0 for any other response.

A. Run a Frequencies analysis on pornlaw. Make sure you're weighting the sample with wtss. Use your results to fill in the frequency distribution table below.

Pornography Law Opinion	Frequency	Percent	Cumulative Percent
Illegal to all	609 ?	31.3?	31.3?
Illegal under 18	1251 ?	64.8 ?	96.1 ?
Legal (to all)	76 ?	3.9 ?	100.00%
Total	1931 ?	100.00%	

B. Use the Transform ▶ Recode into Different Variables procedure to create a new indicator variable that identifies respondents who think pornography should be illegal for everyone. Name this variable "porn_ban." Run a Frequencies analysis on porn_ban and use your results to fill in the frequency distribution table below.

Value of porn_ban	Frequency	Percent	Cumulative Percent
0	1326 ?	68.7 ?	68.7 ?
1	609 ?	31.3?	100.00%
Total	1931 ?	100.00%	

By performing the exercises in this chapter, you have added four variables to the GSS dataset: polview3, muslim_tol, rincom16_q3, and porn_ban. Be sure to save the dataset.

4

Making Comparisons

 Watch screencasts of the guided examples in this chapter. **edge.sagepub.com/pollock**

Procedures Covered

Analyze ▶ Descriptive Statistics ▶ Crosstabs

Analyze ▶ Compare Means ▶ Means

Graphs ▶ Legacy Dialogs ▶ Line

Graphs ▶ Legacy Dialogs ▶ Bar

Graphs ▶ Legacy Dialogs ▶ Boxplot

All hypothesis testing in political research follows a common logic of comparison. The researcher separates observations according to values of the independent variable and then compares the values of the dependent variable in these subgroups. For example, suppose you think that gender (independent variable) affects opinions about gun control (dependent variable) and that women are more likely than men to favor gun control. You would divide subjects into two groups on the basis of gender, women and men, and then compare the percentage of women who favor gun control with the percentage of men who favor gun control. Similarly, if you hypothesize that Republicans have higher incomes than do Democrats, you would divide subjects into partisanship groups (independent variable), Republicans and Democrats, and compare the average income (dependent variable) of Republicans with that of Democrats.

Screencast

Cross-tabulation Analysis and Mean Comparison Analysis

Although the logic of comparison is always the same, the appropriate method for making comparisons depends on the level of measurement of the independent and dependent variables. In this chapter you will learn to make comparisons in two common hypothesis-testing situations: those in which both the independent and the dependent variables are categorical (nominal or ordinal) and those in which the independent variable is categorical and the dependent variable is interval level. You will also learn to add visual support to your comparisons by creating and editing bar charts and line charts.

CROSS-TABULATION ANALYSIS

Cross-tabulations are the workhorse vehicles for making comparisons with categorical variables. Cross-tabulations are similar to frequency distribution tables we've produced in prior chapters, but they have multiple columns that allow us to compare the distribution of responses across different values of an independent variable. When setting up a cross-tabulation, you must observe the following three rules:

1. Put the independent variable on the columns and the dependent variable on the rows.

2. Always obtain column percentages, not row percentages.

3. Test the hypothesis by comparing the percentages of subjects who fall into the same category of the dependent variable.

Consider this hypothesis: In a comparison of individuals, people who have lower incomes will be more likely to identify with the Democratic Party than those who make higher incomes. The NES dataset contains the variable partyid3, which measures respondents' partisanship in three categories: Democrat ("Dem"), Independent ("Ind"), and Republican ("Rep"). This will serve as the dependent variable. The dataset also contains the variable income3, which classifies individuals by terciles of income: the lowest one-third ("Low"), the middle third ("Middle"), and the highest one-third ("High"). This income measure will serve as the independent variable.

Before we use SPSS to analyze the relationship between income and Democratic Party identification, try making your own predictions. In Table 4-1, below, you'll see nine blank cells. In these cells, make your best guess regarding the partisan identification of those with low, medium, and high incomes. To help you out, we've provided the row and column percentage totals.

Before checking your predictions, make sure you understand the rules for setting up a cross-tabulation. Do your column totals add up to 100 percent? They should because respondents, regardless of their income level, identify as either Democrat, Independent, or Republican. Do the percentages you wrote in the row for Democrats average about 35.7 percent? The percentages in this row can't all be higher (or lower) than 35.7 percent because that would mean the population total must be higher (or lower) than 35.7 percent. Do the percentages identifying as Democrat decrease from left to right? That was our hypothesis. (If the independent variable has no effect on the dependent variable, the percentages in every column will look like the row total percentages.)

To create a cross-tabulation of party identification and incomes, select Analyze ▶ Descriptive Statistics ▶ Crosstabs in the Data Editor. The Crosstabs window appears (see Figure 4-1), sporting four panels. For now, focus on the two upper right-hand panels: Row(s) and Column(s). This is where we apply the first rule for a properly constructed cross-tabulation: The independent variable defines the columns, and the dependent variable defines the rows. Because partyid3 is the dependent variable, click it into the Row(s) panel, as shown in Figure 4-1. Find income3 in the left-hand variable list and click it into the Column(s) panel.

Now for the second rule of cross-tab construction: Always obtain column percentages. On the right-hand side of the Crosstabs window, click the Cells button (refer to Figure 4-1). SPSS displays the available options for Counts, Percentages, and Residuals. Left to its own defaults, SPSS will produce a cross-tabulation showing only the number of cases ("observed" counts) in each cell of the table. That's fine. But to follow the second rule, we also want column percentages—the percentage

TABLE 4-1   Predicted Partisan Identification by Income Level

	Low Income	Medium Income	High Income	Total
% Democrat	?	?	?	35.7%
% Independent	?	?	?	36.4%
% Republican	?	?	?	27.9%
Total	100%	100%	100%	100%

FIGURE **4-1**   Creating a Cross-tabulation

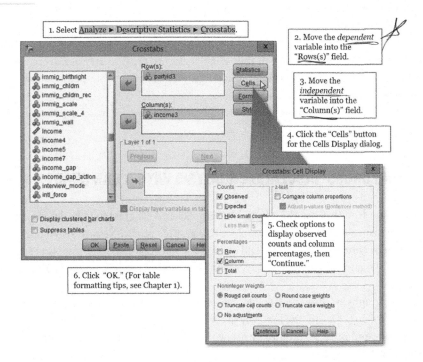

of each category of the independent variable falling into each category of the dependent variable. Check the Column box in the Percentages panel. Click Continue, which returns you to the Crosstabs window.[1] Click OK.

SPSS runs the analysis and displays the results in the Viewer—a case-processing summary followed by the requested cross-tabulation:

Party ID (v161158x) * Income (v161361x) Crosstabulation

			Income (v161361x)			
			1	2	3	Total
Party ID (v161158x)	Dem	Count	493	404	351	1248
		% within Income (v161361x)	39.7%	33.6%	33.3%	35.7%
	Indep	Count	505	418	352	1275
		% within Income (v161361x)	40.7%	34.8%	33.4%	36.4%
	Rep	Count	244	380	352	976
		% within Income (v161361x)	19.6%	31.6%	33.4%	27.9%
Total		Count	1242	1202	1055	3499
		% within Income (v161361x)	100.0%	100.0%	100.0%	100.0%

When SPSS runs Crosstabs, it produces a set of side-by-side frequency distributions of the dependent variable—one for each category of the independent variable—plus an overall frequency distribution for all analyzed cases. Accordingly, this cross-tabulation table has four columns of numbers: one for low-income individuals, one for those in the middle-income tercile, one for those in the highest income group, and a total column showing the distribution of all cases across the dependent variable. And, as requested, each cell shows the number (count) and column percentage. (If your numbers are a little different, make sure you're weighting observations appropriately.)

---

[1]The oddly labeled "Layer 1 of 1" panel comes into play in Chapter 5.

What do you think? Does the cross-tabulation fit the hypothesis? The third rule of cross-tabulation analysis is easily applied to a properly constructed cross-tabulation. Focusing on the "Dem" value of the dependent variable, we see a pattern in the hypothesized direction. A comparison of respondents in the "Low" column with those in the "Middle" column reveals a decline from 39.7 to 33.6 in the percentage who are Democrats, a drop of about 6 percentage points. Moving from the "Middle" column to the "High" column, we find another decrease, from 33.6 percent to 33.3 percent, a relatively mild change. Are lower-income people more likely to be Democrats than middle-income and higher-income people? Yes. Across the full range of the independent variable, from "Low" to "High" income, the percentage of Democrats declines by about 6.5 percentage points.[2]

VISUALIZING CROSS-TABULATION ANALYSIS WITH A BAR CHART

Screencast

Bar Charts

We have already seen that bar charts and histograms can be a great help in describing the central tendency and dispersion of a *single* variable. SPSS graphic procedures are also handy for illustrating relationships *between* variables. It will come as no surprise that SPSS supports a large array of graphic styles. To get a taste of this variety, select Graphs ▶ Legacy Dialogs and consider the choices (Figure 4-2).

The legacy graphs, as the name implies, use interfaces developed in earlier releases of SPSS. Even so, the Legacy Dialogs are still the best way to create graphics in SPSS. In this chapter you will learn to use Bar, Line, and Boxplot. (You will work with Error Bar in Chapter 6, and you will use Scatter/Dot in Chapter 8.)

A bar chart is useful for summarizing the relationship between two categorical variables. In this guided example, you will obtain a bar chart of the relationship you analyzed earlier between party

FIGURE 4-2   Graphs Drop-down Menu

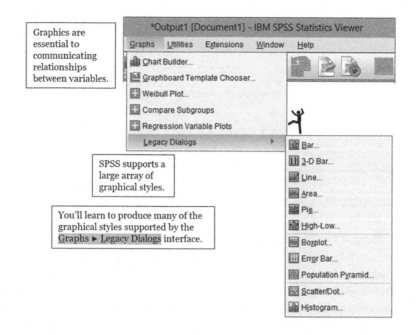

---

[2] In Chapter 7, we'll use the chi-square test to evaluate whether the differences we observe when making comparisons with a cross-tabulation could be the result of random sampling error rather than a systematic relationship between the variables.

identification (the dependent variable partyid3) and income (the independent variable income3). To get started, select Graphs ▸ Legacy Dialogs ▸ Bar. The Bar Charts window gives you a set of choices: Simple, Clustered, and Stacked (see Figure 4-3). To get a handle on using bar charts to visualize cross-tabulation analysis, we'll demonstrate both simple and clustered bar charts, starting with a clustered bar chart because it's directly analogous to the cross-tabulation and a bit easier to create.[3]

Click the button for Clustered bar chart and make sure the "Summaries for groups of cases" option is selected in the "Data in Chart Are" section. With these basic settings in place, click the Define button. The Define Clustered Bar window opens.

The terminology used in the Defined Clustered Bar Chart dialog doesn't correspond to our familiar dependent and independent variable distinction. For this graph, the dependent variable, partyid3, goes in the "Category Axis" field and the independent variable, income3, goes in the "Define Clusters by" field. Next, in the "Bars Represent" section, select the "% of cases" option because we want to visualize the column percentages reported in the cross-tabulation produced in the prior

FIGURE 4-3   Creating a Bar Chart to Visualize Cross-tabulation Results

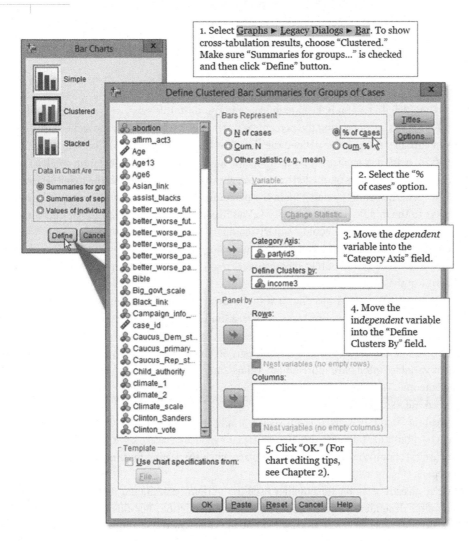

---

[3] The bar chart generated by clicking the "Display clustered bar chart" option in the Crosstabs window (see bottom-right of Figure 4-1) produces a misleading impression of the income3-partyid3 relationship. This option will produce a clustered bar chart based on the cell counts, not column percentages, which is misleading when the column total counts vary.

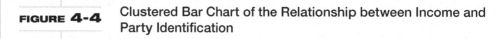

FIGURE 4-4   Clustered Bar Chart of the Relationship between Income and Party Identification

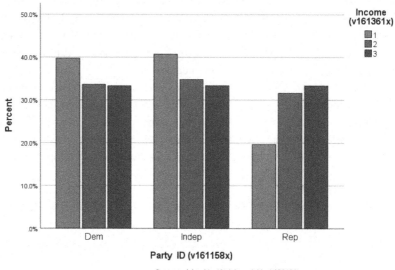

section. When defining a graph, keep its purpose in mind. In this case, we want a graph that helps us interpret results by comparing the percentages of subjects who fall into the same category of the dependent variable. After you've defined the clustered bar chart, click the OK button.

Figure 4-4 helps us visualize the pattern we first detected using cross-tabulation results. Focusing on the cluster of "Dem" bars on the left side of the graph, we see a pattern in the hypothesized direction. We see a decline from 39.7 to 33.6 in the percentage who are Democrats from the low income category (1) to the middle income category (2) and relatively mild decrease to 33.3 percent in the high income category (3). We could similarly compare the percentages of respondents who identify as Independents by level of income, which is analogous to reading the second row of the cross-tabulation, and we see that Republican percentages rise with income, which can also be gleaned from the third row of the cross-tabulation.

The clustered bar chart is nice, but it will not always be the ideal vehicle for making comparisons. In the preceding section, our hypothesis was limited to the relationship between income and Democratic Party identification, so plotting the results for Independents and Republicans may be too much information. The dependent variable partyid3 has only three unique values, but categorical dependent variables often have more unique values that we don't want to plot if we are interested in only one outcome. To focus on the relationship between income and Democratic Party identification, we'll now create a simple bar chart.

To create a simple bar chart, again select Graphs ▶ Legacy Dialogs ▶ Bar but now click the "Simple" chart button. Make sure the "Summaries for groups of cases" option is selected in the "Data in Chart Are" section. With these settings in place, click the Define button. The Define Simple Bar window opens (Figure 4-5).

As we've already seen, the terminology used in the Define Simple Bar dialog doesn't correspond to our familiar dependent and independent variable distinction. For this graph, the *independent* variable, income3, goes in the "Category Axis" field. Values of the income3 variable will define the *x*-axis. There's no need to further define bars by clusters, because we're focused on only one dependent variable in a simple bar chart.

At this point, however, the peculiarities of Bar Chart require that we refamiliarize ourselves with specific coding information about the dependent variable, partyid3. Why so? As a substantive matter, we want to depict the percentage of respondents in each category of income3 who are Democrats.

FIGURE 4-5   Creating a Simple Bar Chart

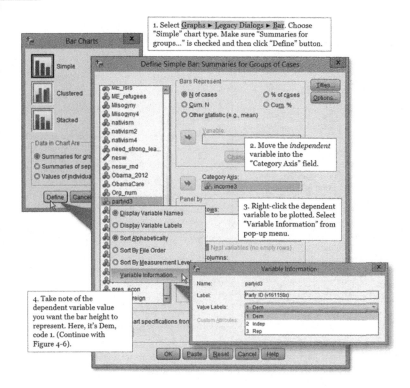

To accomplish this, Bar Chart will need specific coding information. Find partyid3 in the left-hand variable list, place the cursor pointer on it, and then *right*-click. Click on Variable Information and review the numeric codes. Respondents who are Democrats are coded 1, Independents are coded 2, and Republicans are coded 3. Commit this fact to short-term memory: Democrats are coded 1 on the dependent variable, partyid3.

Keeping in mind information about the numeric values of partyid3, return to the "Bars Represent" panel of the Define Simple Bar dialog. Click the radio button for the "Other statistic" option, and click partyid3 into the Variable box. The designation "MEAN(pid_3)" appears in the Variable field by default; this is fine for mean comparisons, but it won't do in this case. Click the "Change Statistic" button.[4] The Statistic dialog presents itself (Figure 4-6).

The radio button for the default, "Mean of values," is selected when we open the Statistic dialog. However, we are interested in obtaining the percentage of cases in code 1 ("Democrat") on partyid3. How do we get SPSS to display the percentages of Democrats? Click the radio button at the bottom on the left, the one labeled "Percentage inside," as shown in Figure 4-6. The two boxes, one labeled "Low" and the other labeled "High," are now active. Our request is specific and restrictive: We want the percentage of respondents in code 1 only. Expressed in terms that SPSS can understand, we want the percentage of cases "inside" a coded value of 1 on the low side and a coded value of 1 on the high side. Click the cursor in the Low box and type a "1." Click the cursor in the High box and type a "1." The Statistic window should now look like Figure 4-6. Click Continue, returning to the Define Simple Bar window. We have defined the simple bar chart we want to see. Click OK.

Our special instructions have paid off. SPSS displays a bar chart of the relationship between income and Democratic Party identification (Figure 4-7).

---

[4] The Change Statistic button will not be available unless the variable in the Variable box is highlighted. A variable is highlighted automatically when you click it into the Variable box. If you are experimenting and lose the highlighting, simply click directly on the variable in the Variable box. This restores the highlighting.

FIGURE 4-6   Define Simple Bar and Change Statistic Windows

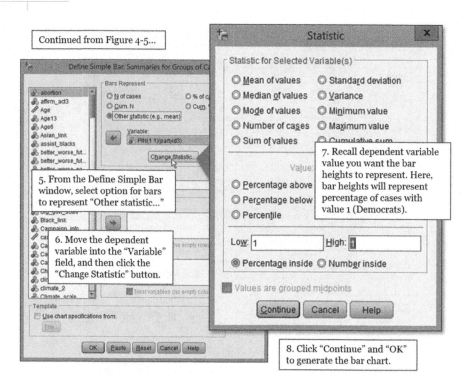

Continued from Figure 4-5...

5. From the Define Simple Bar window, select option for bars to represent "Other statistic..."

6. Move the dependent variable into the "Variable" field, and then click the "Change Statistic" button.

7. Recall dependent variable value you want the bar heights to represent. Here, bar heights will represent percentage of cases with value 1 (Democrats).

8. Click "Continue" and "OK" to generate the bar chart.

FIGURE 4-7   Bar Chart of the Relationship between Income and Democratic Party Identification

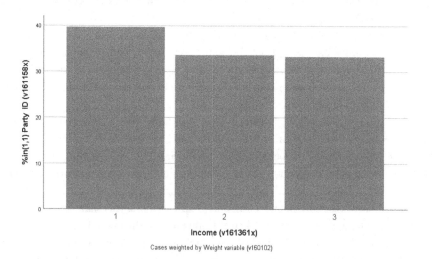

The heights of the bars clearly depict this pattern: As incomes increase from low to high, the percentage of Democrats declines. At least *we* know what the bars represent, because we did the analysis. An interested observer, however, might do a double-take at the title on the vertical axis, "%in(1,1) Party ID (v161158x)." SPSS is relentlessly literal. We asked it to graph the percentages of people between code 1 and code 1 on partyid3, so that is how SPSS has titled the axis. It would help to give the vertical axis a more descriptive title, and perhaps make other appearance-enhancing changes. Simple graphs are great, but they don't have to be boring. To enhance the appearance and content of the charts you create, use SPSS's Chart Editor, which we discussed in Chapter 2. When you edit graphs, keep the essential purpose of the graph in mind.[5]

MEAN COMPARISON ANALYSIS

We now turn to another common hypothesis-testing situation: when the independent variable is categorical and the dependent variable is interval level. The logic of comparison still applies—divide cases according to values of the independent variable and compare values of the dependent variable—but the method used to make this kind of comparison is different from that used when the dependent variable is categorical. Instead of comparing percentages, we now compare means.

To illustrate, let's say that you are interested in explaining this dependent variable: attitudes toward President Donald Trump. Why do some people have positive feelings toward him, whereas others harbor negative feelings? Here is a plausible (if not self-evident) idea: Partisanship (independent variable) will have a strong effect on attitudes toward President Trump (dependent variable). The hypothesis: In a comparison of individuals, Democrats will have less favorable attitudes toward Trump than will Republicans.

FIGURE 4-8   Conducting Mean Comparison Analysis

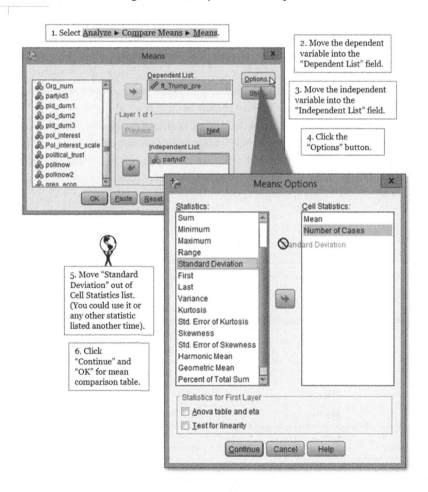

---

[5] Don't needlessly decorate a graphic to make it more visually interesting. For example, it may be tempting to give each bar in Figure 4-7 a different color, but doing so would imply that the bars measure different values when we've defined them to represent only the percentage of respondents who identify as Democrats.

The NES dataset contains a variable named ft_Trump_pre, a 100-point feeling thermometer (conducted before the 2016 election). In the survey, each respondent was asked to rate candidate Trump on this scale, from 0 (cold or negative) to 100 (warm or positive). This is the dependent variable. The dataset also has partyid7, which measures partisanship in seven ordinal categories, from Strong Democrat (coded 1) to Strong Republican (coded 7). (The intervening codes capture gradations between these poles: Weak Democrat, Independent-Democrat, Independent, Independent-Republican, and Weak Republican). This is the independent variable.

If the hypothesis is correct, we should find that Strong Democrats have the lowest mean scores on ft_Trump_pre and that mean scores increase systematically across categories of partyid7, hitting a high point among respondents who are Strong Republicans. Do the data support this hypothesis?

To do mean comparison analysis, select Analyze ▶ Compare Means ▶ Means. The Means window pops into view. Scroll down the left-hand variable list until you find ft_Trump_pre, and then move it into the Dependent List field, as shown in Figure 4-8. Now find partyid7 in the variable list and move it into the field labeled "Layer 1 of 1" (this is our independent variable). Once you've entered the dependent and independent variables in the appropriate fields, click the Options button in the Means window.

The Means: Options window (also shown in Figure 4-8) permits you to select desired statistics from the left-hand Statistics panel and click them into the right-hand Cell Statistics panel. Alternatively, you can remove statistics from Cell Statistics by clicking them back into the left-hand panel. Unless instructed otherwise, SPSS will always report the mean, number of cases, and standard deviation of the dependent variable for each category of the independent variable. Because at present we are not interested in obtaining the standard deviation, select it with the mouse and move it back into the left-hand Statistics panel. Our mean comparison table will report only the mean value of ft_Trump_pre and the number of cases for each category of partyid7. Click Continue, returning to the Means window. Click OK.

Compared with cross-tabulations, mean comparison tables are models of minimalism. The independent variable, partyid7, defines the leftmost column, which shows all seven categories, from Strong Democrat at the top to Strong Republican at the bottom. Beside each category, SPSS has calculated the mean of ft_Trump_pre and reported the number of respondents falling into each value of partisanship. Because the dependent variable is measured at the interval level, we can calculate its mean and don't have to report percentages across all its values. The bottom row, "Total," gives the mean for the whole sample. (If you get slightly different numbers, remember to apply sample weights.)

Report

Feeling therm: Donald Trump (pre, v161087)

Party ID (v161158x)	Mean	N
StrngDem	7.68	768
WkDem	21.24	498
IndDem	18.13	401
Indep	35.30	491
IndRep	57.46	416
WkRep	53.81	435
StrngRep	73.05	577
Total	36.41	3586

Among Strong Democrats, the mean Trump rating is quite frosty—about 8 degrees. Do Trump ratings warm up as attachment to the Democratic Party weakens and identification with the Republican Party strengthens? Notice that the mean more than doubles moving from Strong Democrats to Weak Democrats (who average about 21 degrees), then declines slightly among Independent-Democratic

Leaners (about 18). The mean rating increases to about 35 among Independents, increases again among Independent-Democratic Leaners (57), and then (interestingly) dips somewhat among Weak Republicans (about 54 degrees) before ending at a balmy 73 degrees among Strong Republicans. Interesting hiccups aside, we can see that, on the whole, this mean comparison analysis supports the hypothesis.

VISUALIZING MEAN COMPARISON ANALYSIS WITH A LINE CHART

Screencast

Line Charts

SPSS supports several methods of visualizing mean comparison analysis. In this section, we'll continue our analysis of the relationship between partisan identification and attitudes about President Trump and show how to create a line chart that depicts that relationship. A line chart adds clarity to the relationship between an ordinal-level independent variable and an interval-level dependent variable. Line charts are elegant and parsimonious, and they can be used to display the relationship between an ordinal-level independent variable and a categorical dependent variable as well.

To create a line chart, select Graphs ▶ Legacy Dialogs ▶ Line to open the Line Charts window (the left side of Figure 4-9). Make sure that the icon next to "Simple" is clicked and that the radio button next to "Summaries for groups of cases" is selected.[6] Click the Define button to call up the Define Simple Line window (see the right side of Figure 4-9).

FIGURE 4-9   Creating a Line Chart of the Relationship between Trump Ratings and Party Identification

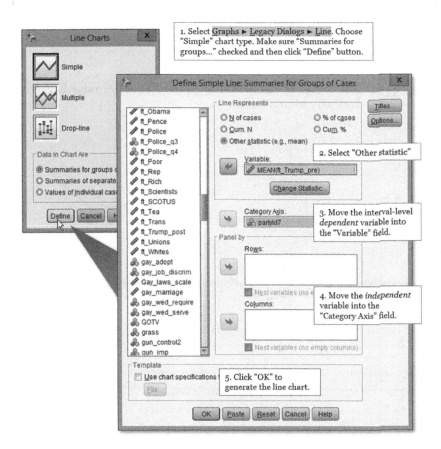

_____

[6] Because we are graphing one relationship, we want a single line. And because we are comparing groups of partisans, we want SPSS to display a summary measure, the mean, for each group.

We'll use the Define Simple Line window to tailor the line chart to our specifications. We want to graph the mean values of ft_Trump_pre for each category of partyid7. First, let's specify our independent variable. In SPSS idiom, "category axis" means *x*-axis or horizontal axis—the axis that represents values of the independent variable. Because partyid7 is the independent variable in the current example, scroll down to partyid7 and click it into the Category Axis field.

Next, let's specify our dependent variable, ft_Trump_pre. To do this, SPSS requires instruction.[7] In the Line Represents panel, select the "Other statistic" radio button, as shown in Figure 4-7. The Variable box is activated. Now scroll the left-hand variable list until you find ft_Trump_pre, and then click ft_Trump_pre into the Variable field. SPSS moves ft_Trump_pre into the Variable box and gives it the designation "MEAN(ft_Trump_pre)." In Line Chart, whenever you request "Other statistic" and click a variable into the Variable box (as we have just done), SPSS assumes that you want to graph the mean values of the requested variable (as we do in this case).[8] So this default serves our current needs. Click OK. (There are two additional boxes in the "Panel by" area, one labeled "Rows" and one labeled "Columns," as shown in Figure 4-9. For our purposes in this book, these boxes may be safely ignored.)

A line chart of the Trump sentiment–party identification relationship appears in the Viewer (Figure 4-10).

The horizontal axis, called the *category axis*, displays values of the independent variable, party identification. Each partisanship category is represented by a hash mark, from Strong Democrat on the left to Strong Republican on the right. The vertical axis, called the *summary axis*, represents mean values of the dependent variable, Donald Trump thermometer ratings. The line chart should show us the results we read in the mean comparison table in the last section. Among Strong Democrats, the mean Trump rating is quite cold, about 8 degrees, but Trump ratings tend to warm up as respondents identify more and more with the Republican Party (with some interesting kinks in the line), culminating with very warm feelings reported by Strong Republicans.

FIGURE 4-10   Line Chart of Mean Trump Feeling Thermometer Scores by Party Identification

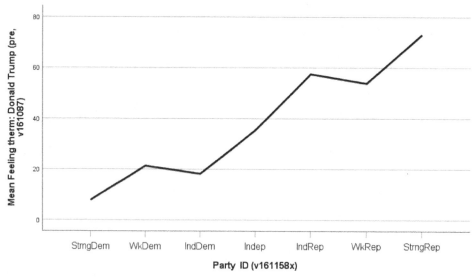

Cases weighted by Weight variable (v160102)

---

[7] Unless we modify the Line Represents panel to suit our analysis, SPSS will produce a line chart for the number of cases (*N* of cases) in each category of partyid7.

[8] Of course, you will encounter situations in which you do not want mean values. Later in this chapter we review the procedure for Change Statistic.

FIGURE **4-11**   How to Read a Box Plot

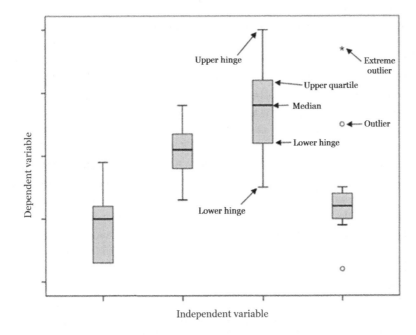

CREATING A BOX PLOT TO MAKE COMPARISONS

We have seen that a line chart, which plots the mean of a dependent variable across the values of an independent variable, is aimed squarely at visualizing mean comparisons by re-expressing them in graphic form. A box plot (also called a box-and-whiskers plot) can also be used to compare values of an interval-level dependent variable across values of an independent variable. Box plots describe an interval-level variable by graphing a five-number summary: minimum, lower quartile, median, upper quartile, and maximum.

Why would one use a box plot to help make comparisons instead of creating a line chart? Both graphs are essential in the political analyst's toolkit. Here are some factors to consider in picking the right graphing method:

Screencast

Box Plots

- A box plot favors the display of dispersion over central tendency.

- Box plots display the median value of the dependent variable, not its mean value. If the dependent variable has a skewed distribution, its median may be a better measure of central tendency than its mean.

- Box plots reveal outliers.[9]

- When the independent variable is measured at the nominal level, plotting a line between means may be misleading because the value order is arbitrary; in a box plot, the boxes are not connected to one another.

- Box plots are particularly useful for graphing relationships in small-*N* datasets with intrinsically interesting cases, such as states in the United States or countries in the world.

---

[9] Robert I. Kabacoff, *R in Action: Data Analysis and Graphics with R* (Shelter Island, NY: Manning Publications, 2011), 133. Box plots may also be used to describe ordinal-level variables that have many discrete values.

Consider Figure 4-11, a stylized box plot of the relationship between an independent variable that divides observations into four different categories (displayed along the horizontal axis) and an interval-level dependent variable (displayed on the vertical axis).

Each box communicates three values: the lower quartile (the value below which 25 percent of the cases fall), the median (the value that splits the cases into two equal-size groups), and the upper quartile (the value below which 75 percent of the cases fall). Thus, the distance between the bottom and the top of the box defines the interquartile range (IQR), the range of a variable that encompasses the "middle half" of a distribution. The lower and upper hinges of each box connect the minimum and maximum values, as long as those values fall in the interval between one and a half IQRs above the upper quartile and one and a half IQRs below the lower quartile. Outliers are defined as cases that fall outside those boundaries.

SPSS distinguishes two species of outlier. If an outlier falls in the interval between one and a half IQRs and three IQRs above the upper quartile (or below the lower quartile), it is symbolized by a small circle. If the outlier is "extreme"—if it lies beyond three IQRs above the upper quartile (or below the lower quartile)—it is symbolized by a star. By default, SPSS uses case numbers to identify outliers.

To learn how to create box plots, we will work through an example from the States dataset, states. sav. Open the States dataset. Let's analyze regional variation in labor force unionization using a box plot. For this analysis, the independent variable is named region and the dependent variable is named union_2016 (the percentage of a state's workforce that belonged to a labor union in 2016).

To create a box plot, select Graphs ▸ Legacy Dialogs ▸ Boxplot, opening the Boxplot dialog (left side of Figure 4-12). Click Define and consider the Define Simple Boxplot window (right side of Figure 4-12).

As with the other charts you have produced, the independent variable (in the example, region) goes in the Category Axis field, and the dependent variable (union_2016) goes in the Variable field. The "Label Cases by" box allows you to identify outliers with text labels (rather than numeric codes). In the States dataset, there are two choices: the variable state (the state's full name) and StateID (the two-letter state abbreviation). Click state into the "Label Cases by" box and click OK. The box plot appears in the Viewer (Figure 4-13).

FIGURE 4-12   Creating a Box Plot

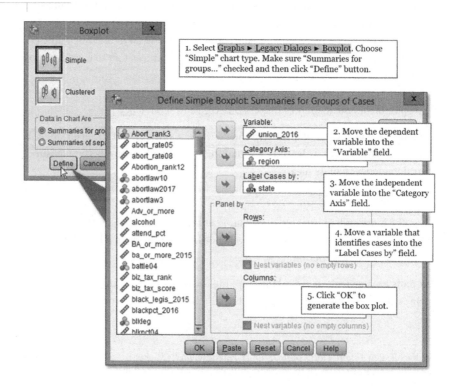

FIGURE 4-13   Box Plot with Outliers Identified

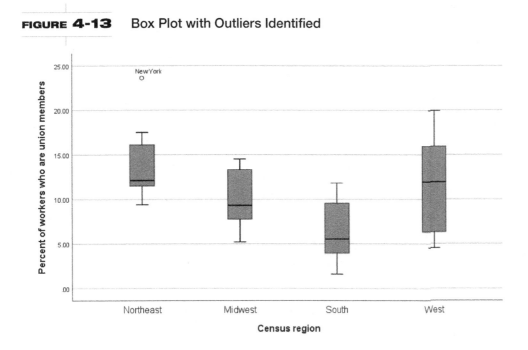

This box plot tells us a lot about regional variation in labor force unionization. Median unioniza-tion is highest in the West and Northeast, lower in the Midwest, and lowest in the South. The upper hinge for unionization in the South region is no greater than median unionization in the Northeast or West regions. Also notice how spread out Western states are. Unionization percentages in the West are far more varied than those in the Northeast, even though these regions have comparable median unionization percentages. Among all states, New York is the outlier; labor force unionization in New York is much higher than it is in other states in the Northeast.

Name: Anna Jeffries   Date: 10/27/22

E-mail: _____   Section: _____

CHAPTER 4 EXERCISES

1. (Dataset: NES. Variables: Who_2016, better_worse_past_econ, nesw.) What factors determine how people vote in presidential elections? Political scientists have investigated and debated this question for many years. A particularly powerful and elegant perspective emphasizes voters' *retrospective* evaluations. According to this view, for example, voters who think the country's economy has gotten better during the year preceding the election are likely to reward the candidate of the incumbent party. Voters who believe the economy has worsened, by contrast, are likely to punish the incumbent party by voting for the candidate of the party not currently in power. As political scientist V. O. Key once famously put it, the electorate plays the role of "rational god of vengeance and reward."[10] Does Key's idea help explain how people voted in the 2016 election?

A. Test this hypothesis: In a comparison of individuals, those who thought the economy had improved during the year preceding the 2016 election were more likely to vote for the candidate of the incumbent party, Hillary Clinton, than were individuals who thought the economy had not improved. Apply the Analyze ▶ Descriptive Statistics ▶ Crosstabs procedure to obtain a cross-tabulation of the relationship between these two variables from the NES dataset: Who_2016 (dependent variable) and better_worse_past_econ (independent variable). Be sure to weight observations using nesw (weight variable) and request column percentages in the cross-tab cells. Record the percentages voting for Clinton and Trump in the table that follows.

Respondent's vote, 2016	Did the economy get better/worse in the last year?					
	Much Better	Somewhat Better	About Same	Somewhat Worse 29.5	Much Worse	Total
Hillary Clinton	95.9% ?	84.8% ?	?	?	9.3% ?	92.7% ?
Donald Trump	35.4% ?	19.2% ?	?	?	90.7% ?	47.3% ?
Total	100.00%	100.00%	100.00%	100.00%	100.00%	100.00%

49.1   74.5

B. What do you think? Are the data consistent with V. O. Key's *retrospective* evaluation hypothesis? Write a paragraph explaining your reasoning.

This is consistent because those who thought the economy was worse, supported Trump who was the opposite party.

C. *Loss aversion* is an interesting psychological phenomenon that can shape the choices people make.[11] One idea behind loss aversion is that losses loom larger than commensurate gains. According to this theory, for example, the psychological pain felt from losing $100 is greater than the pleasure felt from gaining $100. Applied to retrospective voting, loss aversion might suggest that the "vengeance" impulse is stronger than the "reward" impulse—that the anti-incumbent party motivation among those who say the economy has worsened will be stronger than the pro-incumbent party motivation among those who think it has improved.

With this idea in mind, examine the percentages in the table in part A. What do you think? Do the data suggest that Key's rational god of vengeance is stronger than his rational god of reward? Answer yes or no, and write a few sentences explaining your reasoning.

I don't think so because then the percent supporting Trump and thinking the economy worsend should be much higher than support for Hillary.

[10] V. O. Key, *Politics, Parties, and Pressure Groups*, 5th ed. (New York: Crowell, 1964), 568.

[11] George A. Quattrone and Amos Tversky, "Contrasting Rational and Psychological Analyses of Political Choice," *American Political Science Review* 82, no. 3 (Sept. 1988), 719–736.

2. (Dataset: NES. Variables: libcon7_Dem, libcon7_Rep, partyid7, nesw.) Partisan polarization can create some interesting perceptual distortions. Do partisans tend to view themselves as more moderate than they view the opposing party? For example, do Democrats think Republicans are ideologically extreme, yet see themselves as more moderate? By the same token, do Republicans perceive Democrats as liberal extremists, but perceive themselves as purveyors of middle-of-the-road politics? Where do Independents place Democrats and Republicans on the left-right continuum? A Pew survey found this thought-provoking asymmetry: All partisans—Democrats, Independents, and Republicans—placed the Republicans at practically the same conservative position on the liberal-conservative scale. However, the placement of the Democrats varied widely: Republicans placed Democrats well toward the liberal side, Independents saw Democrats as somewhat left of center, and Democrats placed themselves squarely at the moderate position.[12] In this exercise, you will see if you can replicate the Pew report's findings using the NES dataset.

The NES variable, libcon7_Dem, measures respondents' perceptions of the ideological position of the Democratic Party using the standard 7-point scale: 1 ("Extremely liberal"), 2 ("Liberal"), 3 ("Slightly liberal"), 4 ("Moderate"), 5 ("Slightly conservative"), 6 ("Conservative"), and 7 ("Extremely conservative"). Another variable, libcon7_Rep, asks respondents to place the Republican Party along the same 7-point metric. For the purposes of this exercise, you will treat these two measures as interval-level variables. Thus, lower mean values denote higher perceived liberalism, values around 4 denote perceived moderation, and higher mean values denote higher levels of perceived conservatism. For this exercise, libcon7_Dem and libcon7_Rep are the dependent variables. Our old reliable variable, partyid7, is the independent variable. If the Pew results are correct, you should find that all partisan groups, from Strong Democrats to Strong Republicans, share very similar conservative perceptions of the Republican Party—but hold very different perceptions of the Democratic Party.

A. Use the Analyze ▶ Compare Means ▶ Means procedure to run two mean comparison analyses: one for the relationship between libcon7_Dem and partyid7 relationship, and one for the relationship between libcon7_Rep and partyid7. Fill in the means in the following table.

Respondent's Party ID	Mean Ideological Placement of Democrats		Mean Ideological Placement of Republicans	
Strong Democrat	3.36	?	5.38	?
Weak Democrat	3.09	?	5.31	?
Independent-Democrat	3.06	?	5.59	?
Independent	3.37	?	4.76	?
Independent-Republican	2.12	?	5.10	?
Weak Republican	2.5	?	5.19	?
Strong Republican	1.69	?	5.42	?

B. Examine your findings. Are the Pew findings borne out by the NES data? Explain your reasoning.

They are consistent because the means of republicans are all very similar and the means of democrats are more varied.

3. (Dataset: GSS. Variables: polviews, femrole, wtss.) Why do some people hold more traditional views about the role of women in society and politics, whereas others take a less traditional stance? General ideological orientations, liberalism versus conservatism, may play an important role in shaping individuals' opinions on this cultural question. Thus, it seems plausible to suggest that ideology (independent variable) will affect opinions about appropriate female roles (dependent variable). The hypothesis: In a comparison of individuals, liberals will be more likely than conservatives to approve of non-traditional female roles.

The GSS dataset (file name: gss.sav) contains femrole, a scale that measures opinions about the appropriate role of women. The numeric values of femrole range from 0 (women belong in traditional roles) to 9 (women belong in non-traditional roles). That is, higher scores denote less traditional beliefs. This is the dependent variable. The dataset has another familiar variable, polviews, a 7-point ordinal scale measuring ideology. Scores on polviews can range from 1 (extremely liberal) to 7 (extremely conservative). This is the independent variable.

A. According to the hypothesis, as the values of polviews increase, from 1 through 7, mean values of femrole should (circle one)

decrease.   neither decrease nor increase.   increase.

polviews (handwritten)
indep (handwritten)

B. Use the Analyze ▶ Compare Means ▶ Means procedure to obtain mean values of femrole across values of polviews. Use your results to fill in the table that follows.

dep. fem. (handwritten)

Summary of Female Role by Respondent's Ideological Self-Placement

Respondent's Ideological Self-Placement	Mean	Frequency*
Extremely liberal	6.96 ?	87 ?
Liberal	6.49 ?	228 ?
Slightly liberal	6.02 ?	206 ?
Moderate	5.91 ?	662 ?
Slightly conservative	5.75 ?	264 ?
Conservative	5.27 ?	270 ?
Extremely conservative	4.86 ?	65 ?
Total	5.88 ?	1782 ?

*Report weighted frequencies.

C. Do the results support the hypothesis? Write a few sentences explaining your reasoning. Yes, because as it gets more conservative the mean gets lower denoting a more traditional view on gender roles.

D. Use the Graphs ▶ Legacy Dialogs ▶ Line procedure to create and print a line chart showing mean values of femrole (y-axis) over values of polviews (x-axis). Add descriptive titles to the axis labels. For assistance, refer to this chapter's examples. Print the chart.

4. (Dataset: NES. Variables: egalit_3, educ4, nesw.) Pedantic pontificator is offering a group of students his thoughts about the relationship between educational attainment and egalitarianism, the belief that government should do more to make sure resources are more equitably distributed in society: "Educated people have a humanistic world view that is sorely lacking among the self-seeking, less-educated classes. They see inequality. . . and want to rectify it! Plus, most colleges and universities are populated with liberal faculty, who indoctrinate their students into left-wing ideologies at every opportunity. Thus, it's really quite simple: As education goes up, egalitarianism increases." *dep* (handwritten)

The NES dataset contains egalit_3, which measures egalitarian beliefs in three categories: "Low," "Medium," and "High." The NES dataset also has educ4, which records educational attainment in four categories: high school or less ("HS or less"), some college or associate's degree ("SmColl/Assoc"), bachelor's degree ("BA"), and graduate degree ("Grad").

A. Use the Analyze ▶ Descriptive Statistics ▶ Crosstabs procedure to conduct a cross-tabulation analysis that tests pedantic pontificator's idea about the relationship between education and egalitarianism. Obtain column percentages. Be sure to use the nesw sample weights variable to produce nationally representative results. Use your results to fill in the missing percentages in the table below.

	High School or Less	Some College or Associate's Degree	Bachelor's Degree	Graduate Degree	Total
Low egalitarianism	32.5 ?	31.5 ?	30.5 ?	29.5 ?	30.9 ?
Medium egalitarianism	34.7 ?	32.1 ?	30.5 ?	22.3 ?	31.5 ?
High egalitarianism	32.8 ?	36.4 ?	39.0 ?	52.2 ?	37.6 ?
Total	100.00%	100.00%	100.00%	100.00%	100.00%

B. Create a bar chart of the relationship between education and egalitarianism. *Hint*: You might decide to graph, for each value of the independent variable, the percentage of respondents falling into the "Low" category of the dependent variable (coded 1 on egalit_3). Alternatively, you could graph the percentage of respondents falling into the "High" category of the dependent variable (coded 3 on egalit_3). In the Graph Editor, give the vertical axis a more descriptive label. Edit the chart for appearance. Print the chart.

C. Based on your analysis, would it appear that pedantic pontificator is correct? Answer yes or no, and explain. There is a weak relationship, the only time there is a significant amount more egalitarian is for graduate degree. Otherwise little difference.

5. (Dataset: GSS. Variables: intsex, fepol, fefam, wtss.) Untruthful answers by survey respondents can create big headaches for public opinion researchers. Why might a respondent not tell

an interviewer the truth? Certain types of questions, combined with particular characteristics of the interviewer, can trigger a phenomenon called preference falsification: "the act of misrepresenting one's genuine wants under perceived social pressures."[13] For example, consider the difficulty in gauging opinions on the role of women in society. One might reasonably expect people questioned by a female interviewer to express greater support for feminist views than those questioned by a male pollster. Someone who supports traditional gender roles, not wanting to appear insensitive to a female questioner, might instead offer a false pro-feminist opinion.[14]

The GSS dataset contains intsex, *intep.* which is coded 1 and labeled "Male" for respondents questioned by a male interviewer and coded 2 and labeled "Female" for those questioned by a female interviewer. This is the independent variable that will allow you to test two preference falsification hypotheses:

Hypothesis 1: In a comparison of individuals, those questioned by a female interviewer will be more likely to disagree with the proposition that women are unsuited for politics than will those questioned by a male interviewer. (The dependent variable is fepol, *dep.* coded 1 for "Agree" and 2 for "Disagree.")

Hypothesis 2: In a comparison of individuals, those questioned by a female interviewer will be more likely to disagree with the statement that it's better for men to work and women to tend home than will those questioned by a male interviewer. (The dependent variable is fefam, which is coded 1 for "Strongly Agree," 2 for "Agree," 3 for "Disagree," and 4 for "Strongly Disagree".)

A. Run a cross-tabulation analysis analyzing the relationship between intsex and fepol. Make sure to request column percentages and use weights. Complete the cross-tabulations that follow.

Statement: Women are not suited for politics.	Interviewer's Gender		
	Male	Female	Total
Percentage who "Agree"	31.1?	26?	26.9?
Percentage who "Disagree"	69.3?	74?	73.1?
Total	100.00%	100.00%	100.00%

26.4 18.2 19.0
73.6 81.8 81.0

[13] Timur Kuran, *Private Truths, Public Lies: The Social Consequences of Preference Falsification* (Cambridge, MA: Harvard University Press, 1995), 3.

[14] It may have occurred to you that this effect might be greater for white respondents than for black respondents, with white subjects more likely to hide their true preferences in the presence of a black interviewer. An exercise in Chapter 5 will give you a chance to investigate this possibility.

These findings (circle one)

[support Hypothesis 1.] | do not support Hypothesis 1.

Briefly explain your reasoning.

The disagreement is higher with the female interviewer though not by much.

B. Run a cross-tabulation analysis analyzing the relationship between intsex and fefam. Make sure to request column percentages and use weights. Complete the cross-tabulations that follow.

Statement: It's better for men to work and women to tend home.	Interviewer's Gender		
	Male	Female	Total
Percentage who "Strongly Agree"	10.6?	9.1?	5.7?
Percentage who "Agree"	24.1?	20.9?	21.2?
Percentage who "Disagree"	40.2?	46.9?	46.2?
Percentage who "Strongly Disagree"	25.1?	27.1?	26.9?
Total	100.00%	100.00%	100.00%

These findings (circle one)

[support Hypothesis 2.] | do not support Hypothesis 2.

Briefly explain your reasoning.

The percent that disagree are higher with a female interviewer, though not by much.

C. Create and print a nicely optioned bar chart of the relationship between interviewer gender and opinions about whether women are suited for politics (the relationship you analyzed in part A). Be sure to provide clear axis titles.

6. (Dataset: States. Variables: ProLife, region, state.) In this exercise, you will (i) create and print a box plot of the relationship between ProLife (the percentage of the public *dep.* holding a "pro-life" position on abortion) and region, *indep.* (ii) identify outliers within regions, and (iii) use the box plot to determine if two hypothetical claims are correct.

A. Obtain and print a box plot of the relationship between ProLife and region. You will want to apply the options discussed in this chapter. To identify outliers, click the alphabetic variable, state, into the "Label Cases by" box.

B. The box plot you produced in part A identifies one outlier in the Northeast and two outliers in the West. (Fill in the blanks that follow.) Which state is the outlier in the Northeast? **Pennsylvania**. Which two states are outliers in the West? **Utah** and **Idaho**.

C. Consider this claim: "As measured by the interquartile range, Southern states are less spread out—that is, have less variation in pro-life opinions—than states in the Midwest." Is this claim correct? Answer yes or no, and briefly explain.

This is false because the box and lower hinge are larger, showing more diversity of opinions.

D. Consider this claim: "Ignoring their outliers, the Northeastern states are more cohesive in their pro-life opinions than are the Western states." Is this claim correct? Answer yes or no, and briefly explain.

Yes because the box and hinges are smaller than that of the west.

7. (Dataset: States. Variables: suicide_rate, Gun_rank3.) Two policy researchers are debating whether gun control can prevent suicides:

Policy Researcher 1: "People who are determined to commit suicide will find a way to do it. Restricting access to guns will have no effect on suicide rates."

Policy Researcher 2: "Look, any behavior that's made more difficult will tend to decrease. If state governments want to discourage suicides, then restricting access to guns will certainly have the desired effect. More restrictions mean fewer suicides."

Imagine a bar chart of the relationship between restrictions on guns and suicide rates. The horizontal axis measures access to guns in three categories, from more restrictive on the left to less restrictive on the right. The vertical axis records the suicide rate per 100,000 population. Below are two graphic shells, A and B. In shell A, you will sketch a bar chart depicting what the relationship would look like if Policy Researcher 1 is correct. In shell B, you will sketch a bar chart depicting what the relationship would look like if Policy Researcher 2 is correct.

A. If Policy Researcher 1 were correct, what would the bar chart look like? Sketch three bars inside the graphic space, depicting the relationship proposed by Policy Researcher 1.

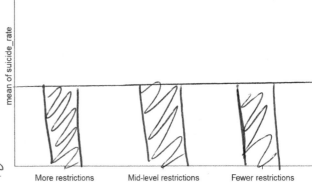

B. If Policy Researcher 2 were correct, what would the bar chart look like? Sketch three bars inside the graphic space, depicting the relationship proposed by Policy Researcher

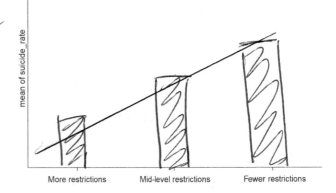

C. The States dataset contains the variables suicide_rate and Gun_rank3. Run a mean comparison analysis using the Analyze ▸ Compare Means ▸ Means procedure with suicide_rate as the dependent variable and Gun_rank3 as the independent variable. Record your results in the table that follows.

Access to guns	Suicide Rate per 100,000 Population	
	Mean	Frequency
More restrictions	12.56 ?	15 ?
Middle restrictions	15.0429 ?	14 ?
Fewer restrictions	17.7283	21 ?
Total	15.43	50

D. Create and print a nicely optioned bar chart of the relationship you just analyzed. Be sure to include descriptive axis titles.

E. Examine the mean comparison table and the line chart. Which policy researcher is more correct? (check one)

☐ Policy Researcher 1 is more correct.

☑ Policy Researcher 2 is more correct.

F. Write a paragraph explaining your reasoning in part E.

The more restrictions, the lower the suicide rate so researcher 2 is correct.

8. (Dataset: World. Variables: regime_type3, durable.) Three comparative politics scholars are trying to figure out what sort of institutional arrangement produces the longest-lasting, most stable political system.

Scholar 1: "Presidential democracies, like the United States, are going to be more stable than are any other type of system. In presidential democracies, the executive and the legislature have separate electoral constituencies and separate but overlapping domains of responsibility. The people's political interests are represented both by the president's national constituency and by legislators' or parliament members' more localized constituencies. If one branch does something that's unpopular, it can be blocked by the other branch. The result: political stability."

Scholar 2: "Parliamentary democracies are by far more stable than presidential democracies. In presidential systems, the executive and legislature can be controlled by different political parties, a situation that produces deadlock. Since the leaders of parliament can't remove the president and install a more compliant or agreeable executive, they are liable to resort to a coup, toppling the whole system. Parliamentary democracies avoid these pitfalls. In parliamentary democracies, all legitimacy and accountability resides with the legislature. The parliament organizes the government and chooses the executive (the prime minister) from among its own leaders. The prime minister and members of parliament have strong incentives to cooperate and keep things running smoothly and efficiently. The result: political stability."

Scholar 3: "You two have made such compelling—if incorrect—arguments that I almost hesitate to point this out: Democracies of any species, presidential or parliamentary, are inherently unstable. Any system that permits the clamor of competing parties or dissident viewpoints is surely bound

to fail. If it's stability that you value above all else, then dictatorships will deliver. Strong executives, feckless or nonexistent legislatures, powerful armies, social control. The result: political stability."

dep

The World dataset contains the variable durable, which measures the number of years since the last regime transition. The more years that have passed since the system last failed (higher values on durable), the more stable a country's political system. The variable regime_type3 captures system type: dictatorship, parliamentary democracy, or presidential democracy.

A. Use the Analyze ▸ Compare Means ▸ Means procedure to perform a mean comparison analysis of the relationship between durable and regime_type3. Based on a comparison of means, which is the apparently correct ranking of regime types, from most stable to least stable?

☑ Parliamentary democracies (most stable), presidential democracies, dictatorships (least stable)

☐ Parliamentary democracies (most stable), dictatorships, presidential democracies (least stable)

☐ Dictatorships (most stable), presidential democracies, parliamentary democracies (least stable)

B. Create a box plot of the relationship between durable (*y*-axis) and regime_type3 (*x*-axis). Closely examine the box plot. In what way does the graphic evidence support the ranking you chose in part A?

The box plot shows parlimentary as the most stable, but presidential which ranked third is actually less stable than dictatorship it just has some very stable outliers.

C. In what way does the graphic evidence NOT support the ranking you chose in part A?

D. Print the box plot you created in part B.

9. (Dataset: World. Variables: enpp3_democ, district_size3, frac_eth3.) Two scholars of comparative politics are discussing possible reasons why some democracies have many political parties and other democracies have only a few.

Scholar 1: "It all has to do with the rules of the election game. Some countries, such as the United Kingdom, have single-member electoral districts. Voters in each district elect only one representative. This militates in favor of fewer and larger parties, since small parties have less chance of winning enough votes to gain the seat. Other countries, like Switzerland, have multimember districts. Because voters choose more than one representative per district, a larger number of smaller parties have a chance to win representation. It doesn't surprise me in the least, then, that the UK has fewer political parties than Switzerland."

Scholar 2: "I notice that your explanation fails to mention the single most important determinant of the number of political parties: social structural heterogeneity. Homogeneous societies, those with few linguistic or religious differences, have fewer conflicts and thus fewer parties. Heterogeneous polities, by the same logic, are more contentious and will produce more parties. By the way, the examples you picked to support your case also support mine: The UK is relatively homogeneous and Switzerland relatively heterogeneous. It doesn't surprise me in the least, then, that the UK has fewer political parties than Switzerland."

A. Scholar 1's hypothesis: In a comparison of democracies, those having single-member districts will have (circle one)

(**fewer political parties** /   more political parties)

than democracies electing multiple members from each district.

[handwritten margin notes: high → lots PP; low → no PP]

B. State Scholar 2's hypothesis:

Homogeneous societies like the UK will have less political parties than heterogeneous societies, like Switzerland.

The World dataset variable enpp3_democ measures, for each democracy, the number of effective parliamentary parties: "1–3 parties," "4–5 parties," or "6–11 parties." Use enpp3_democ (an ordinal-level variable) as the dependent variable to test each hypothesis. For independent variables, test Scholar 1's hypothesis using district_size3, which measures, for each democracy, the number of members per district: "single-member" districts, more than one but fewer

than six members (">1 to 5"), and countries with "6 or more members" per district. Test Scholar 2's hypothesis using frac_eth3, which classifies each country's level of ethnic/linguistic fractionalization as "Low," "Medium," or "High."

C. In the table that follows, record the percentages of cases falling into the lowest code of the dependent variable, 1–3 parties. You should find these values on one row of each of your cross-tabulations.

	Average Number of Members per District		
	Single Member	2 to 5 Members	6 or More Members
Percentage having 1–3 parties	*68.2?*	*37.5?*	*13.8?*

	Level of Ethnic Fractionalization		
	Low	Medium	High
Percentage having 1–3 parties	*35.3?*	*33.3?*	*42.9?*

D. Which of the following statements best summarizes your findings? (check one)

☑ Scholar 1's hypothesis is supported by the analysis, but Scholar 2's hypothesis is not supported by the analysis.

☐ Scholar 2's hypothesis is supported by the analysis, but Scholar 1's hypothesis is not supported by the analysis.

☐ Both hypotheses are supported by the analysis.

☐ Neither hypothesis is supported by the analysis.

E. Making specific reference to your findings, write a paragraph explaining your choice in part D.

The first analysis has the ~~highest percent~~ of most countries with 1–3 political parties in countries with single member districts. The second has high levels of fractionalization in countries with 1–3 political parties, which should be the opposite if scholar 2 was correct.

CHAPTER

5

Making Controlled Comparisons

 Watch screencasts of the guided examples in this chapter. **edge.sagepub.com/pollock**

Procedures Covered

Analyze ▶ Descriptive Statistics ▶ Crosstabs
(with Layers)

Analyze ▶ Compare Means ▶ Means (with Layers)

Graphs ▶ Legacy Dialogs ▶ Line (Multiple)

Graphs ▶ Legacy Dialogs ▶ Bar (Clustered)

Political analysis often begins by making simple comparisons using cross-tabulation analysis or mean comparison analysis. Simple comparisons allow the researcher to examine the relationship between an independent variable, X, and a dependent variable, Y. However, there is always the possibility that alternative causes—rival explanations—are at work, affecting the observed relationship between X and Y. An alternative cause is symbolized by the letter Z. If the researcher does not control for Z, then he or she may misinterpret the relationship between X and Y.

CROSS-TABULATION ANALYSIS WITH A CONTROL VARIABLE

To demonstrate how to use SPSS Crosstabs to produce control tables, we will work through an example with the GSS dataset, GSS.sav. Open the GSS dataset.

Consider this hypothesis: In a comparison of individuals, those who attend religious services less frequently will be more likely to favor the legalization of marijuana than will those who attend religious services more frequently. In this hypothesis, attend3, which categorizes respondents' church attendance as "Low," "Moderate," or "High," is the independent variable. The GSS variable grass records respondents' opinions on the legalization of marijuana. (Code 1 is "Legal," and code 2 is "Not legal.")

To stay acquainted with cross-tabulation analysis, we will start by looking at the uncontrolled relationship between attend3 and grass. In addition to considering whether the hypothesis has merit, we will note the tendency of the relationship and we will apply a non-statistical measure of the relationship's strength. By determining tendency and gauging strength, you are better able to interpret relationships involving control variables. To produce an uncontrolled, zero-order cross-tabulation, follow the steps detailed in Chapter 4. Recall that you start by selecting Analyze ▶ Descriptive Statistics ▶ Crosstabs (refer to Figure 4-1 as necessary).

Screencast

Cross-tabulation Analysis with a Control Variable, Additive relationship

In the Crosstabs window, find the dependent variable, grass, in the left-hand variable list and click it into the Row(s) panel. Find the independent variable, attend3, and click it into the Column(s) panel. Click the Cells button and select the box next to "Column" in the Percentages panel. Click Continue, and then click OK. SPSS reports the results:

Should Marijuana Be Made Legal * How Often R Attends Religious Services, 3 Categories Crosstabulation

			How Often R Attends Religious Services, 3 Categories			
			Low	Moderate	High	Total
Should Marijuana Be Made Legal	LEGAL	Count	609	295	194	1098
		% within How Often R Attends Religious Services, 3 Categories	74.5%	60.1%	37.2%	60.0%
	NOT LEGAL	Count	208	196	327	731
		% within How Often R Attends Religious Services, 3 Categories	25.5%	39.9%	62.8%	40.0%
Total		Count	817	491	521	1829
		% within How Often R Attends Religious Services, 3 Categories	100.0%	100.0%	100.0%	100.0%

Clearly the hypothesis has merit. Of the low attenders, 74.5 percent favor legalization, compared with 60.1 percent of moderate attenders and 37.2 percent of the highly observant.[1] And note that given the way attend3 is coded—increasing values denote increasing church attendance—a negative relationship exists between religiosity and the percentage favoring legalization. As attendance increases, the percentage favoring legalization declines. (If you interpret the cross-tabulation by examining the "Not legal" row, then the tendency is positive. As attendance increases, the percentage opposing legalization increases.)

How strong is the relationship between church attendance and marijuana legalization opinions? You can arrive at a quick and easy measure of strength by figuring out the percentage-point change in the dependent variable across the full range of the independent variable. At one pole, 74.5 percent of low attenders favor legalization. At the other pole, 37.2 percent of frequent attenders are in favor. Therefore, the percentage favoring legalization drops by 74.5 − 37.2 = 37.3, or about 37 percentage points. By this rudimentary measure, the relationship's strength is 37 percentage points. (In Chapter 7, we consider statistical measures of strength.)

What other factors, besides church attendance, might account for differing opinions on marijuana legalization? Here's a plausible answer: whether the respondent has children. Regardless of religiosity, people with children may be less inclined to endorse the legalization of marijuana than are people who do not have children. And here is an interesting (if complicating) fact: People who attend church regularly are substantially more likely to have children than are

[1] If you get somewhat different numbers, don't forget to weight observations using the wtss variable.

people who rarely or never attend.[2] Thus, when we compare the marijuana opinions of "High" and "Low" attenders, as we have just done, we are also comparing people who are more likely to have children ("High") with people who are less likely to have children ("Low"). It could be that secular individuals are more inclined to favor legalization, not because they are less religious but because they are less likely to have children. By the same token, those who go to church more often might oppose legalization for reasons unrelated to their religiosity: They're more likely to have children.

The only way to estimate the effect of church attendance on marijuana opinions, free from the confounding effect of having children, is to compare low attenders who do not have children with high attenders who do not have children, and to compare low attenders who have children with high attenders who have children. In other words, we need to control for the effect of having children by holding it constant. Crosstabs with layers will perform the controlled comparison we are after.

Let's run the grass–attend3 analysis again, this time adding kids as a control variable. To produce a controlled cross-tabulation, again select Analyze ▸ Descriptive Statistics ▸ Crosstabs, returning to the Crosstabs window. You should find the dependent variable, grass, and the independent variable, attend3, in the Crosstabs window just where you left them. To obtain a controlled comparison—the relationship between grass and attend3, controlling for kids—scroll down the variable list until you find "kids" and move it into the box labeled "Layer 1 of 1," as shown in Figure 5-1. The GSS variable kids classifies respondents into one of two categories:

FIGURE 5-1 Generating a Crosstabs with a Control Variable (Layer)

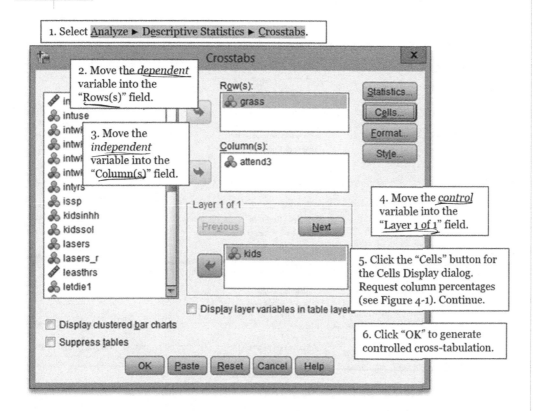

---

[2] According to the GSS dataset, 80.1 percent of "High" attenders have children, compared with 65.1 percent of "Low" attenders—a 15-percentage-point difference.

those with children (coded 1 and labeled "Yes" on kids) or those without (coded 0 and labeled "No" on kids). Click OK.

SPSS will run a separate cross-tabulation analysis for each value of the variable that appears in the Layer box. And that is precisely what we want: a cross-tabulation of grass and attend3 for respondents without children and a separate analysis for those with children. SPSS returns its version of a control table:

Should Marijuana Be Made Legal * How Often R Attends Religious Services, 3 Categories * Does R H ave Children? Crosstabulation

Does R Have Children?				How Often R Attends Religious Services, 3 Categories			
				Low	Moderate	High	Total
No	Should Marijuana Be Made Legal	LEGAL	Count	257	98	44	399
			% within How Often R Attends Religious Services, 3 Categories	84.3%	72.1%	38.6%	71.9%
		NOT LEGAL	Count	48	38	70	156
			% within How Often R Attends Religious Services, 3 Categories	15.7%	27.9%	61.4%	28.1%
	Total		Count	305	136	114	555
			% within How Often R Attends Religious Services, 3 Categories	100.0%	100.0%	100.0%	100.0%
Yes	Should Marijuana Be Made Legal	LEGAL	Count	351	196	150	697
			% within How Often R Attends Religious Services, 3 Categories	68.7%	55.4%	37.0%	54.9%
		NOT LEGAL	Count	160	158	255	573
			% within How Often R Attends Religious Services, 3 Categories	31.3%	44.6%	63.0%	45.1%
	Total		Count	511	354	405	1270
			% within How Often R Attends Religious Services, 3 Categories	100.0%	100.0%	100.0%	100.0%
Total	Should Marijuana Be Made Legal	LEGAL	Count	608	294	194	1096
			% within How Often R Attends Religious Services, 3 Categories	74.5%	60.0%	37.4%	60.1%
		NOT LEGAL	Count	208	196	325	729
			% within How Often R Attends Religious Services, 3 Categories	25.5%	40.0%	62.6%	39.9%
	Total		Count	816	490	519	1825
			% within How Often R Attends Religious Services, 3 Categories	100.0%	100.0%	100.0%	100.0%

Crosstabs output with layers can be a bit confusing at first, so let's closely consider what SPSS has produced. There are three cross-tabulations, appearing as one table.[3] To the left-hand side of the table you will see the label of the control variable, kids: "Does R Have Children?" The first value of kids (0), labeled "No," appears beneath that heading. So the top cross-tabulation shows the grass–attend3 relationship for people who do not have children. The next cross-tabulation shows the relationship for respondents with children, respondents with the value "Yes" on the control variable. Finally, the bottom cross-tabulation, labeled "Total," shows the overall relationship between grass and attend3.

First, assess the tendency and strength of the relationship between church attendance and support for marijuana legalization among respondents who do not have children. Among people without children, the tendency is negative. As the values of attend3 increase from low to high, support for legalization declines: 84.3 percent of the low attenders favor legalization, compared with 72.1 percent of the middle group and 38.6 percent of the high attenders. How large is the drop? Across the full range of religious attendance, the percentage favoring legalization declines from 84.3 to 38.6—an "attendance effect" of about 46 percentage points!

Next, assess tendency and strength among respondents who have children, the middle section of the controlled cross-tabulation. Note that the tendency, once again, is negative: 68.7 percent of the low attenders favor legalization, compared with 55.4 percent of moderate attenders and 37.0 percent of high attenders. Note also that the strength of the relationship is also very strong for people who have children. Among respondents with kids, the percentage who favor legalization drops from 68.7 among low attenders to 37.0 among high attenders—an "attendance effect" of about 32 percentage points.

To help you make correct interpretations of controlled comparisons, it is a good idea to evaluate the relationship between the control variable and the dependent variable, within each value of the independent variable. In the current example, we would determine the tendency and strength of the relationship between the control variable, kids, and marijuana attitudes, controlling for church attendance. This is accomplished by jumping between the "No" cross-tabulation and the "Yes" cross-tabulation, comparing marijuana opinions of people who share the same level of attendance but who differ on the control variable, kids. Among low attenders, those without kids are more likely to favor legalization than those with kids. When the control variable switches from "No" to "Yes," the percentage of marijuana supporters drops from 84.3 percent to 68.7 percent—a "kid effect" of about 16 percentage points. How about moderate attenders? As with low attenders, the kid effect is negative: 72.1 percent compared with 55.4 percent—about 17 points. Among high attenders, the effect is in the same direction but not as strong: 38.6 percent versus 37.0 percent—a kid effect of about 2 percentage points.

How would you characterize this set of relationships? Does a spurious relationship exist between grass and attend3? Or are these additive relationships, with attend3 explaining legalization opinions and kids adding to the explanation? Or is interaction going on? If the grass–attend3 relationship were spurious, then the relationship would weaken or disappear after controlling for kids. Among respondents without children, low, moderate, and high attenders would all hold the same opinion about marijuana legalization. Ditto for people with children: Attendance would not play a role in explaining the dependent variable. Because the relationship persists after controlling for kids, we can rule out spuriousness.

Now, it is sometimes difficult to distinguish between additive relationships and interaction relationships. In additive relationships, the effect of the independent variable on the dependent variable is the same or quite similar for each value of the control variable. In interaction

Screencast

Cross-tabulation Analysis with a Control Variable, Interactive relationship

---

[3] If you don't like the look of SPSS's default cross-tabulation, remember you can easily edit an SPSS table. See the section on "How to Format an SPSS Table" in Chapter 1.

relationships, by contrast, the effect of the independent variable on the dependent variable varies in tendency or strength for different values of the control variable. In this example, we found that the "attendance effect" for non-parents was a whopping 46 percentage points, compared to a 32-percentage-point difference for parents. Similarly, the "kid effect" was about the same for low and moderate attenders (16 and 17 percentage points, respectively) but just 2 percentage points for those who attend church frequently. So, the grass–attend3 relationship is interactive with parent status.

Let's do one more controlled cross-tabulation to see an example of an additive relationship. Rather than looking at the effect of church attendance on opinions about marijuana legalization, let's consider individuals' employment status. The wrkslf variable in the GSS dataset distinguishes between people who are self-employed and those who work for someone else. Those who are self-employed face fewer consequences from workplace drug testing and probably value individual choice more highly than those who work for others, which may increase their support for marijuana legalization.

To analyze the relationship between employment status and marijuana opinions, controlling for having children, again select Analyze ▶ Descriptive Statistics ▶ Crosstabs, returning to the Crosstabs window. You should find the variables grass, attend3, and kids in the Crosstabs window just where you left them. Move the old column variable, attend3, back to the variable list and replace it with wrkslf (Figure 5-2). Assuming you've requested column percentages in the cells, click the OK button.

Now, if someone were to ask, "What is the effect of employer status on marijuana opinions?" we would not be misrepresenting the results to reply, "People who work for themselves are about 8 percentage points more likely to favor legalization than those who work for someone else." (This corresponds to the average of effects of employer status for parents, 9.4 percentage points, and non-parents, 7.4 percentage points.) If asked about the role of children, we would be well

FIGURE 5-2   Controlled Cross-tabulation of an Additive Relationship

Refer to instructions on Figure 5-1.

This example generates a controlled cross-tabulation with an additive relationship among variables.

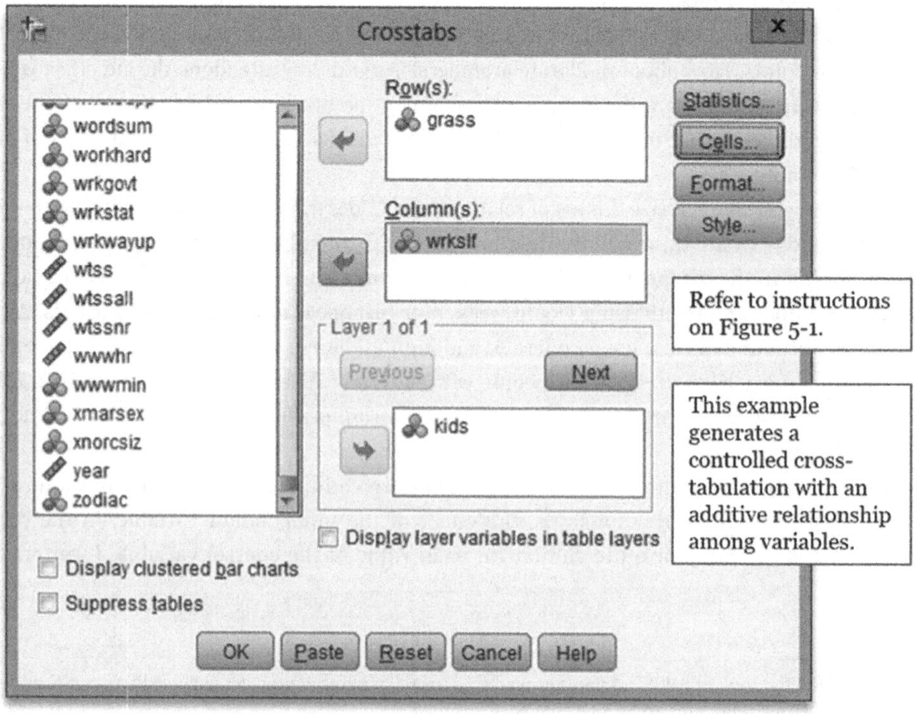

Should Marijuana Be Made Legal * R Self-Emp Or Works For Somebody * Does R Have Children? Crosstabulation

Does R Have Children?				R Self-Emp Or Works For Somebody		
				SELF-EMPLOYED	SOMEONE ELSE	Total
No	Should Marijuana Be Made Legal	LEGAL	Count	30	342	372
			% within R Self-Emp Or Works For Somebody	78.9%	71.5%	72.1%
		NOT LEGAL	Count	8	136	144
			% within R Self-Emp Or Works For Somebody	21.1%	28.5%	27.9%
	Total		Count	38	478	516
			% within R Self-Emp Or Works For Somebody	100.0%	100.0%	100.0%
Yes	Should Marijuana Be Made Legal	LEGAL	Count	87	611	698
			% within R Self-Emp Or Works For Somebody	64.0%	54.6%	55.6%
		NOT LEGAL	Count	49	509	558
			% within R Self-Emp Or Works For Somebody	36.0%	45.4%	44.4%
	Total		Count	136	1120	1256
			% within R Self-Emp Or Works For Somebody	100.0%	100.0%	100.0%
Total	Should Marijuana Be Made Legal	LEGAL	Count	117	953	1070
			% within R Self-Emp Or Works For Somebody	67.2%	59.6%	60.4%
		NOT LEGAL	Count	57	645	702
			% within R Self-Emp Or Works For Somebody	32.8%	40.4%	39.6%
	Total		Count	174	1598	1772
			% within R Self-Emp Or Works For Somebody	100.0%	100.0%	100.0%

within the boundaries of the data to say, "People without kids are about 16 percentage points more likely to favor legalization than are people who have children." (This corresponds to the average of effects of kids for those self-employed, 14.9 percentage points, and those who work for others, 16.9 percentage points.) All additive relationships share this straightforward simplicity: same tendency, same or similar strengths, at all values of the control variable.

GRAPHING CONTROLLED COMPARISONS WITH CATEGORICAL DEPENDENT VARIABLES

In Chapter 4 you learned how to create bar charts and line charts to show the relationship between a categorical independent variable and a dependent variable. Building on these methods, you can use SPSS to produce two types of graphs for controlled comparisons: clustered bar charts and multiple line charts.

For clarifying controlled comparisons, multiple line charts are preferred, particularly when the independent variable is measured at the ordinal level. Compared with bar charts, line charts are simpler and more elegant, and they have a more favorable data/ink ratio, defined as "the proportion of a graphic's ink devoted to the non-redundant display of data-information."[4] In other words, if one were to "add up" all the ink used in a graph, line charts tend to devote a larger proportion of the total ink to the essential communication of the data.[5]

Screencast

Multiple Line Chart, Additive

In the following guided example, we produce a multiple line chart for the additive relationship analyzed at the beginning of the chapter, the relationship between grass and attend3 (an ordinal independent variable), controlling for kids. To create this multiple line chart, select Graphs ▶ Legacy Dialogs ▶ Line. When the Line Charts dialog opens, click Multiple and make sure that the Summaries for Groups of Cases radio button is selected (the default). Click Define. The Define Multiple Line: Summaries for Groups of Cases window appears (Figure 5-3).

What do we want the line chart to depict? We want to see the percentage of respondents who think marijuana should be legal (code 1 on grass) for each value of the independent variable (attend3). Furthermore, we want to see the grass–attend3 relationship separately for each value of the control variable, kids. In all SPSS charts, the values of the independent variable appear along the axis labeled "Category Axis." Move the independent variable, attend3, into the Category Axis field, as shown in Figure 5-3. For this controlled comparison, we want to see the attend3–grass relationship for each value of the control variable, kids. In a multiple line chart, the values of the control variable "define" the lines. The variable named "kids" is the control variable, so click kids into the "Define Lines by" field.

Now we need to make sure that the lines will represent the percentages of respondents saying "legal." In the Lines Represent panel, select the "Other statistic" radio button, which activates the Variable box. Find grass in the variable list and then move it into the Variable box. By default, SPSS will display the mean value of grass, "MEAN(grass)," which does not suit our purpose so we'll click the Change Statistic button. In the Statistic window, click the "Percentage inside" radio button. Type "1" in the Low box and "1" in the High box. As in Figure 5-3, these instructions tell SPSS to display the percentage of respondents in one category of the dependent variable, the percentage coded 1 on grass. Click Continue, returning to the Define Multiple Line window. The Variable box should now read "PIN(1 1)(grass)," meaning "The lines will display the percentages of respondents inside the value of 1 on grass at the low end and the value of 1 on grass at the high end." Once, you've defined the right multiple line chart settings, click OK.

The multiple line chart, constructed to our specifications, appears in the Viewer (Figure 5-4).

This multiple line chart greatly facilitates interpretation of the controlled comparison. The upper line shows the relationship between grass and attend3 for people without children, and the lower line depicts the relationship for people with children. Trace the effect of the independent variable by moving from left to right along each line, across the values of attend3. As we learned from the controlled cross-tabulation, the "attendance effect" is more pronounced for respondents without kids than it is for those with kids. Viewed another way, as the vertical distance between lines,

---

[4] Edward R. Tufte, *The Visual Display of Quantitative Information*, 2nd ed. (Cheshire, Conn.: Graphics Press, 2001), 93.

[5] The Graphs ▶ Legacy Dialogs ▶ Bar (Clustered) interface is comparable to the multiple line chart interface, except the control variable is used to define the category axis (rather than lines) and the independent variable is used to define clustered. The chart should separate observations according to values of the control variable and then facilitate controlled comparisons. If you prefer clustered bar charts, which may be more appropriate for nominal-level independent variables, you can directly apply the skills you will learn in this chapter.

FIGURE 5-3   Creating a Multiple Line Chart

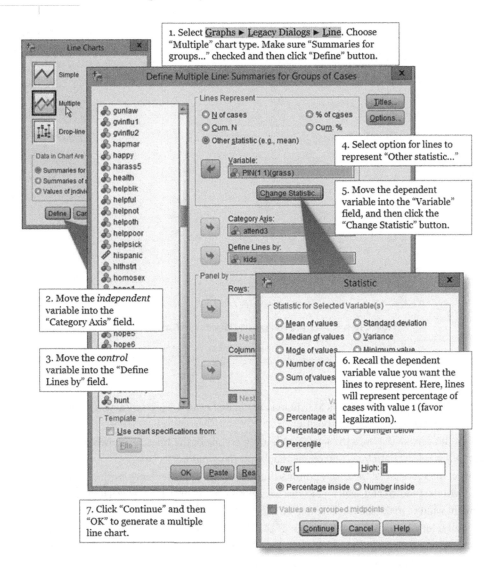

1. Select Graphs ▸ Legacy Dialogs ▸ Line. Choose "Multiple" chart type. Make sure "Summaries for groups..." checked and then click "Define" button.

2. Move the *independent* variable into the "Category Axis" field.

3. Move the *control* variable into the "Define Lines by" field.

4. Select option for lines to represent "Other statistic..."

5. Move the dependent variable into the "Variable" field, and then click the "Change Statistic" button.

6. Recall the dependent variable value you want the lines to represent. Here, lines will represent percentage of cases with value 1 (favor legalization).

7. Click "Continue" and then "OK" to generate a multiple line chart.

we see that the "kid effect" is quite similar for low and moderate attenders but is relatively minor among those with high church attendance. This is a very informative graphic. Before moving on, let's spruce up this multiple line chart using the Chart Editor.

We will make three changes to the chart: First, we will change the title on the *y*-axis. Second, we will make the lines thicker. Finally, we will change the style of one of the lines, so that the legend clearly communicates the categories of the control variable, kids. (If you print graphics in black and white, as we do in this book, it is sometimes difficult to distinguish subtle differences in the colors of the lines.)

Recall how to start SPSS's Chart Editor. Either double-click the chart in the Viewer or right-click it and select "Edit Content ▸ In Separate Window." You'll see the multiple line chart in the Chart Editor.

To change the title on the *y*-axis, single-click the axis title. SPSS will highlight the *y*-axis title. After the title is highlighted, single-click it again. (It's like a slow-motion double-click.) You'll see the original title displayed in a text box, ready for editing (see Figure 5-5). Replace the current title with

FIGURE 5-4   Multiple Line Chart of an Interactive Relationship

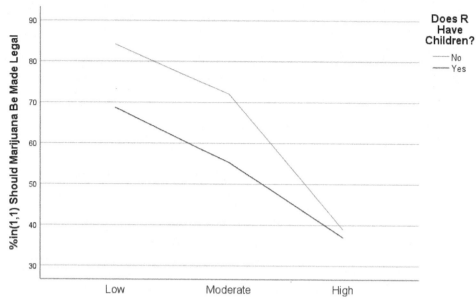

Cases weighted by Weight Variable

this new title: "Percent Who Think Marijuana Should Be Legal." (Clicking anywhere else on the chart returns the axis title to its proper position.)

Next, let's make the lines thicker. Double-click on one of the lines, as shown in Figure 5-6. The Chart Editor selects both lines and opens the Properties window.

Select the Lines tab of the Chart Editor's Properties dialog. In the Lines section of this panel, click the Weight drop-down and select a heavier weight such as 1.5 or 2. (If you're using SPSS Version 25, you might want to make the lines lighter.) Click Apply. The Editor makes both lines thicker.

Finally, let's change the style of one of the lines to make it easier to tell them apart. To edit the properties of a single line, single-click on the line. SPSS highlights both lines. Now single-click the line again (another slow-motion double-click). The Chart Editor will select/highlight only that line. Now double-click the one highlighted line to call up the Properties dialog again (see Figure 5-7).

To edit the line's style, click the Style drop-down from the Lines tab and choose from among the many dashed patterns. When you click Apply, the Editor modifies the line's style and makes a corresponding change in the legend. Close the Properties window and exit the Chart Editor. A newly edited multiple line chart appears in the Viewer (Figure 5-8).

MEAN COMPARISON ANALYSIS WITH A CONTROL VARIABLE

Mean comparison analysis is used when the dependent variable is interval level and the independent variable and the control variable are nominal or ordinal level. In most ways, the procedure for using Compare Means with layers to obtain controlled comparisons is similar to that for using Crosstabs. However, the two procedures differ in one important way. We will work through two guided examples using the NES dataset (NES.sav). The first example shows an interesting pattern of interaction. The second example gives you a chance to identify a set of additive relationships. Open the NES dataset and let's begin the first guided example.

Screencast

Mean Comparison Analysis with a Control Variable

FIGURE 5-5   Changing the y-Axis Title with the Chart Editor

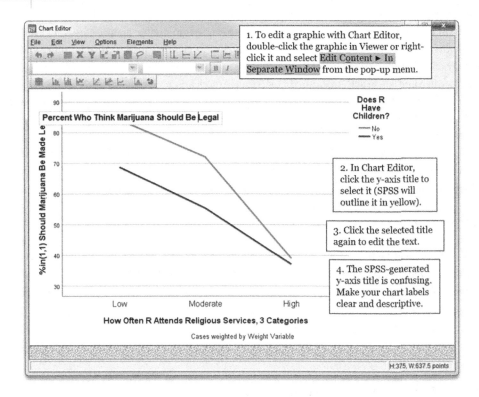

FIGURE 5-6   Changing Line Weights with the Chart Editor

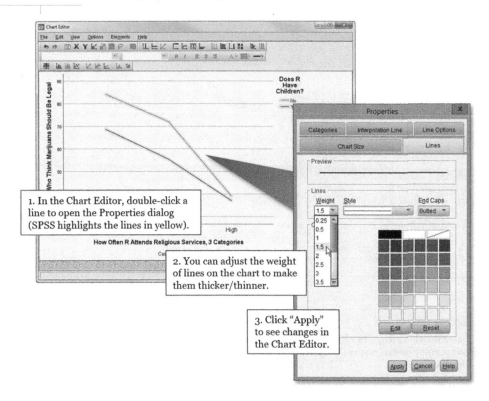

Example of an Interaction Relationship

In Chapter 4, we looked at the relationship between party identification and feeling thermometer ratings of President Donald Trump. We found, not too surprisingly, that individuals who identify more strongly with the Republican Party give Trump higher mean scores than do those who identify less strongly with the Republican Party. In this chapter, we'll control for other variables that may explain the partisan difference in mean Trump ratings.

It has become an article of faith that African Americans are more strongly attracted to the Democratic Party than whites are. Indeed, on NES's Democratic Party feeling thermometer (ft_Dem), African Americans' mean rating is over 30 degrees warmer than whites' mean rating: 74 degrees versus 43 degrees. It may be the case, then, that the partisan differences we observed initially are, to some extent, the result of racial differences in partisan identification. To compare party differences independent of racial differences, let's investigate the relationship between party identification and Trump ratings, controlling for race (NES variable Race2).

As you know, the NES dataset contains many feeling thermometer variables, which record respondents' ratings of different political groups and personalities on a scale from 0 (cold or negative) to 100 (warm or positive). The ft_Trump_pre variable, which gauges feelings toward President Donald Trump, will be the dependent variable in the current example. The independent variable is partyid7, a seven-category ordinal measure. For the control variable we will use Race2.[6] We will use Analyze ▶ Compare Means ▶ Means to produce mean values of ft_Trump_pre for each value of partyid7, controlling for race.

FIGURE 5-7   Changing a Line Style with the Chart Editor

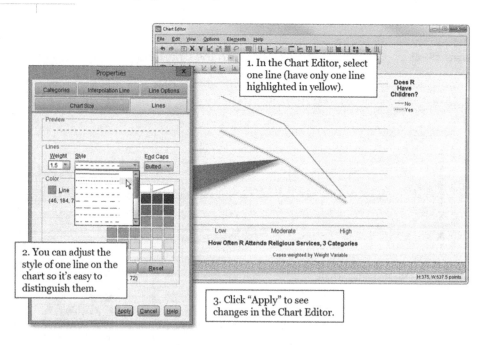

----

[6] The Race2 variable identifies white and black respondents. It makes for a simpler demonstration of controlled mean comparison analysis, but you are welcome to work with the Race3 variable, which also identifies Hispanics, if you prefer.

FIGURE 5-8   Edited Multiple Line Chart of an Interactive Relationship

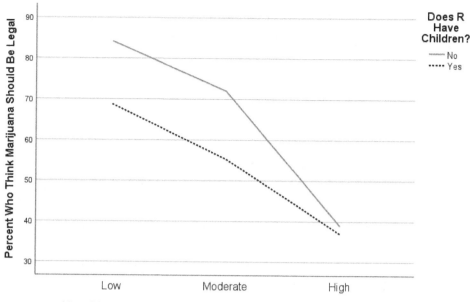

Cases weighted by Weight Variable

To conduct a controlled mean comparison analysis with SPSS, select Analyze ▸ Compare Means ▸ Means. Find ft_Trump_pre in the variable list and click it into the Dependent List box. Now we want SPSS to proceed as follows. First, we want it to separate respondents into two groups, whites and African Americans, based on the control variable, Race2. Second, we want SPSS to calculate mean values of ft_Trump_pre for each category of the independent variable, partyid7. SPSS handles mean comparisons by first separating cases on the variable named in the first Layer field. It then calculates means of the dependent variable for variables named in the subsequent Layer field. For this reason, it is best to put the control variable in the first layer and to put the independent variable in the second layer. Because Race2 is the control variable, locate it in the variable list and move it into the "Layer 1 of 1" box (Figure 5-9). Click Next.

The next Layer field, labeled "Layer 2 of 2," opens. The independent variable, partyid7, goes in this field. Move partyid7 into the "Layer 2 of 2" field (Figure 5-9). One last thing: Click Options. In Cell Statistics, click Standard Deviation back into the left-hand Statistics box, and then click Continue. You are ready to go. Click OK.

The following controlled mean comparison table appears in the Viewer.

The values of the control variable, Race2, appear along the left-hand side of the table. The topmost set of mean comparisons shows the mean Trump thermometer ratings for white respondents, the next set is for black respondents, and the bottom set (labeled "Total") shows the uncontrolled relationship between ft_Trump_pre and partyid7—for white and black respondents combined. This is a compact table, yet it contains a wealth of information. From the "Total" table, we can retrieve the overall relationship between party ID and the feeling thermometer: 8.16 for Strong Democrats all the way to 74.07 for Strong Republicans, about a 66-point swing. (The "Total" row of the "Total" table tells us the overall mean for the entire sample: 39.02 degrees.) Notice, too, that we have obtained the overall means for white (42.93) and black (13.84) respondents—a nearly 30-point divide.

FIGURE 5-9 Procedure for Controlled Mean Comparison Analysis

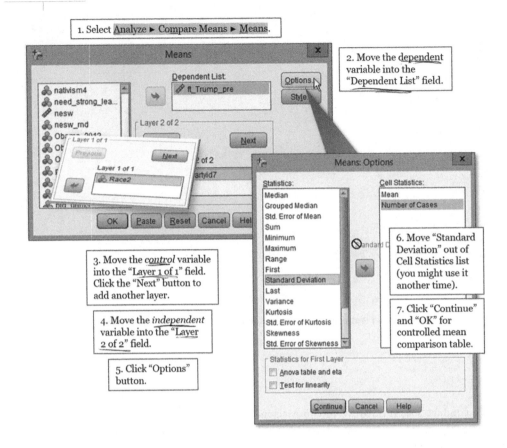

Now, to evaluate the controlled effect of the independent variable, partyid7, on Trump ratings, we would compare the mean ratings of Trump at varying party identifications separated by race. What do these comparisons reveal? Consider white respondents. The mean Trump rating among white Strong Democrats is 8.83. This mean warms all the way to 75.02 among Strong Republicans. So, for white respondents, the thermometer gets 66 degrees warmer as we move across the party ID scale. Now shift your attention to African American respondents. The mean Trump rating among black Strong Democrats is 6.74. This mean warms up to 40.06 among Strong Republicans. So, for black respondents, the thermometer gets 33 degrees warmer as we move across the party ID scale (half the amount of warming observed among whites).

Does the partyid7–Trump thermometer relationship have the same tendency/direction at both values of the control? Yes, for both white and black respondents, those who identify more strongly with the Republican Party have more positive feelings about Trump than do those with weaker Republican identifications. Do the relationships have the same (or similar) strengths at both values of the control? No, the relationship between party ID and Trump ratings is stronger among whites than it is among blacks; the swing from one end of the party scale to the other is about twice as large among whites than it is among blacks. Again, a situation such as this—same tendency, different strengths—is one form of interaction.

Confirm the interaction interpretation by determining how the control variable, Race2, affects Trump ratings for each value of party identification. For Strong Democrats, for instance, there is a difference of about 2 degrees: 8.83 for white Strong Democrats compared with 6.74 for black Strong Democrats. Among Weak Democrats, the white-black difference is about 13 degrees, however; for Independent Democrats, 5 degrees; Independents, 18 degrees; Independent-Republicans,

Report

Feeling therm: Donald Trump (pre, v161087)

White/Black (v161310x)	Party ID (v161158x)	Mean	N
White	StrngDem	8.83	412
	WkDem	26.67	290
	IndDem	18.75	264
	Indep	39.82	321
	IndRep	59.22	344
	WkRep	55.11	360
	StrngRep	75.02	505
	Total	42.93	2496
Black	StrngDem	6.74	197
	WkDem	13.56	74
	IndDem	16.88	41
	Indep	22.20	47
	IndRep	67.28	5
	WkRep	40.74	11
	StrngRep	40.06	14
	Total	13.84	388
Total	StrngDem	8.16	609
	WkDem	24.00	364
	IndDem	18.50	306
	Indep	37.59	368
	IndRep	59.33	348
	WkRep	54.70	371
	StrngRep	74.07	519
	Total	39.02	2884

−8 degrees; Weak Republicans, 14 degrees; and Strong Republicans, 35 degrees.[7] Again, the relationship has the same tendency (whites tend to rate Trump higher than do blacks), but different strengths (the race difference is substantially larger among Republican identifiers than it is among other party identifications).

Example of an Additive Relationship

Compared with the protean complexity of interaction, additive relationships are the soul of symmetry. In a set of additive relationships, both the independent and the control variables help to explain the dependent variable. More than this, the effect of the independent variable is the same or very similar—same tendency, same strength—for all values of the control variable. Interaction relationships assume several forms. Additive relationships assume only one.

To demonstrate, we'll stick with our familiar comparison of mean Trump ratings for varying party identifications. This time, however, we'll control for gun ownership, suspecting that gun

---

[7] The exceptional 67.28 mean Trump rating among African American Independent-Republicans should be read with caution, as it is based on only five respondents.

ownership is correlated with both Trump ratings and party identification. To compare party differences independent of differences in gun ownership, let's investigate the relationship between party identification and Trump ratings, controlling for gun ownership (NES variable gun_own). Start by selecting Analyze ▶ Compare Means ▶ Means.

If settings from our ft_Trump_pre–partyid7–Race2 analysis are still in place, you can simply move gun_own into the "Layer 1 of 2" field (in place of Race2). If you're starting with a reset Means window, move ft_Trump_pre into the Dependent list. Click the control variable, gun_own, into the first Layer box. Click Next. Click the independent variable, partyid7, into the second Layer box. Click Options and remove the Standard Deviation from Cell Statistics. Click OK (refer to Figure 5-9, keeping in mind we're using gun_own in place of Race2 in this analysis). Another information-rich table is at hand:

Report

Feeling therm: Donald Trump (pre, v161087)

Does R own a gun? (v161496)	Party ID (v161158x)	Mean	N
No	StrngDem	6.55	564
	WkDem	20.02	358
	IndDem	16.91	287
	Indep	33.95	313
	IndRep	57.17	212
	WkRep	52.84	221
	StrngRep	71.67	275
	Total	31.32	2229
Yes	StrngDem	10.71	187
	WkDem	22.93	129
	IndDem	21.71	102
	Indep	37.18	159
	IndRep	57.39	159
	WkRep	54.95	193
	StrngRep	73.47	249
	Total	43.39	1178
Total	StrngDem	7.59	751
	WkDem	20.79	487
	IndDem	18.17	390
	Indep	35.04	472
	IndRep	57.26	371
	WkRep	53.82	413
	StrngRep	72.53	524
	Total	35.49	3407

Does gun ownership add to our explanation of varying Trump feeling thermometer scores? Yes. For both non-gun owners and gun owners, mean values of ft_Trump_pre ascend as we move from "Strong Democrat" to "Independent" to "Strong Republican." Indeed, the magnitude of the end-to-end increase is virtually identical for both groups: 65 degrees for non-gun owners (71.67 − 6.55) and 63 degrees for gun owners (73.47 − 10.71). And notice the consistent effects of gun ownership.

At each value of the independent variable, gun owners rate Trump a few degrees warmer than do non-gun owners: 4 degrees separate the Strong Democrats, 3 degrees separate the Weak Democrats, and so forth. (The Independent-Republican category is a bit of a hiccup in the analysis.) Thus, regardless of party identification, the "gun ownership effect" is about 3 degrees. And, controlling for gun ownership, the "party effect" is about 64 degrees.

VISUALIZING CONTROLLED MEAN COMPARISONS

There are a few different ways to graphically depict controlled mean comparisons. If the independent variable is measured at the ordinal level, a line chart is often the best choice. In this section, we will show how to make a line chart of mean Trump sentiment with an ordinal measure of party identification serving as the independent variable. If you make a controlled mean comparison with a nominal-level independent variable, connecting mean values with a sloping line is misleading because the order of *x*-axis values is arbitrary; in this situation, consider producing a clustered bar chart with bar height representing the mean dependent value in each category defined by the independent and control variables.[8]

Screencast

Multiple Line Chart, Interaction

A line chart can illuminate the interactive and additive relationships we identified in the previous section. The steps for obtaining a multiple line chart for an interval-level dependent variable are the same steps you learned earlier, with one labor-saving exception.

To create a line chart that compares mean Trump feeling thermometer ratings by party ID, controlling for race, complete the following steps:

1. Select Graphs ▶ Legacy Dialogs ▶ Line. This opens the Line Charts window.

2. In the Line Charts window, click Multiple, and then click Define. Keep the default summaries for groups of cases option selected. This opens the Define Multiple Line window.

3. Click the independent variable, partyid7, into the Category Axis box.

4. Click the control variable, Race2, into the "Define Lines by" box.

5. In the Lines Represent panel of the Define Multiple Line window, select the "Other statistic" radio button. This activates the Variable box.

6. Click the dependent variable, ft_Trump_pre, into the Variable box. SPSS moves ft_Trump_pre into the Variable box with its default designation, "MEAN(ft_Trump_pre)." For an interval-level dependent variable, this default is precisely what you want. (There is no need to change the statistic now.)

7. Click OK.

We now have a tailor-made line chart of the partyid7–ft_Trump_pre relationship, controlling for race (Figure 5-10).

You can see why line charts are essential for correctly interpreting controlled comparisons. By tracing along each line, from Strong Democrat to Strong Republican, you can see the effect of party ID on Trump thermometer ratings. Among white respondents, the line slopes up sharply; there is a huge difference in mean Trump ratings from one end of the political spectrum to the other. Among black respondents, by contrast, the line rises less sharply. (The high mean score for African American

---

[8] For example, if we were comparing mean Trump sentiment between gun owners and non-gun owners (instead of party identification) controlling for race, we would suggest a clustered bar chart instead of a line chart. See Figure 7-7 for an example of a clustered bar chart that depicts a controlled comparison with a nominal-level independent variable. The bar height in that graph represents the proportion of cases with a specific dependent variable value, rather than the mean of the dependent variable in each subcategory, but the general idea is the same.

FIGURE **5-10**   Multiple Line Chart of Interaction Relationships

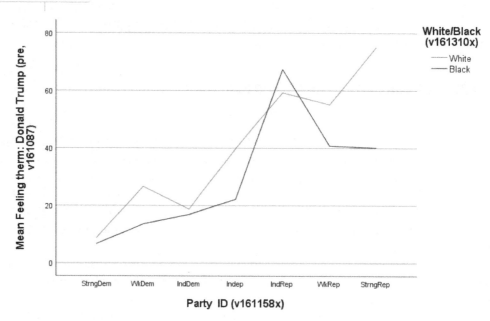

Cases weighted by Weight variable (v160102)

Independent-Republicans throws things off, but remember that is based on only five respondents.) Notice, too, that the relationship between race and the dependent variable varies from one side of the graph to the other: although the mean for whites is higher, the gap is wider on the right than it is on the left.

The relationship between the independent and dependent variables has the same tendency for both values of the control variable, but the relationship is stronger for one value than for the other value. Interaction can assume other forms, too. Interaction has two field marks, though, that will give it away. First, when you examine the relationship between the independent variable and the dependent variable at different values of the control variable, you may find that the relationship varies in tendency or direction, perhaps positive for one value of the control variable or zero or negative for other control values. Second, the relationship may have the same tendency for all control values but differ in strength, such as negative-weak versus negative-strong or positive-weak versus positive-strong. In identifying interaction, practice makes perfect. And, believe it or not, statistics can help (see Chapter 9).

Let's create a multiple line chart of the partyid7–ft_Trump_pre relationship, controlling for gun ownership. By now, creating this graph should be a straightforward exercise. Follow the seven steps outlined above, but specify a different control variable in step 4:

1 – 3.   Same as above.

4.   Click the control variable, gun_own, into the "Define Lines by" box.

5 – 7.   Same as above.

You can see how this line chart (Figure 5-11) communicates the additive relationship.

Moving from left to right, from strong identification with the Democratic Party to strong identification with the Republican Party, each line rises by about 64 units. That's the effect of the independent variable in this analysis, partyid7. The effect of gun ownership is conveyed by

FIGURE **5-11**   Multiple Line Chart of Additive Relationships with Positive Tendency

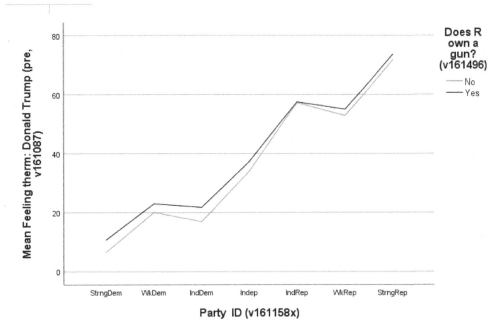

Cases weighted by Weight variable (v160102)

the vertical distance between the two lines. Despite a narrowing in the Independent-Republican category, the difference between gun owners and non-gun owners is quite consistent.

Now, you might encounter additive relationships in which the lines slope downward, imparting a negative relationship between the independent and dependent variables. And the lines might "float" closer together, suggesting a consistent but weaker effect of the control variable on the dependent variable, controlling for the independent variable. But you will always see symmetry in the relationships. The effect of the independent variable on the dependent variable will be the same or very similar for all values of the control variable, and the effect of the control variable on the dependent variable will be the same or very similar for all values of the independent variable.

The multiple line charts produced from default settings (like Figures 5-10 and 5-11) leave plenty of room for improvement. Invoke the Chart Editor and make some improvements to this multiple line chart. Experiment with the Chart Editor. Ask the Properties window to do new things. Figure 5-12 may serve as an example. (We'll demonstrate more chart editing techniques in Chapter 8.)

FIGURE 5-12   Multiple Line Charts Edited with the Chart Editor

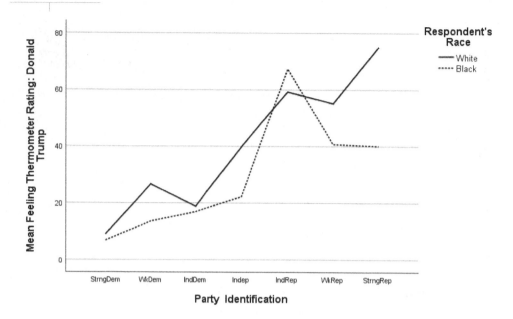

Cases weighted by Weight variable (nesw)

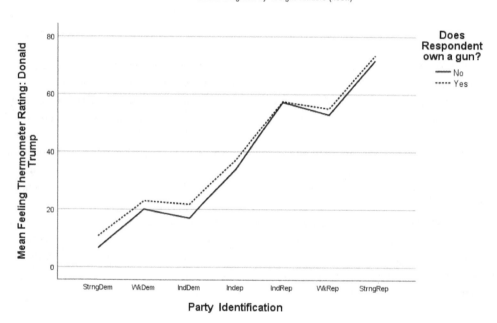

Cases weighted by Weight variable (nesw)

Name: _anna.jefferies@spartans.ut.edu_

E-mail: _____

Date: _10/3/22_

Section: _____

CHAPTER 5 EXERCISES

1. (Dataset: NES. Variables: polknow2, political_trust, ft_Tea, nesw.) Given the Tea Party movement's deep skepticism of government activism, it seems plausible to hypothesize that individuals who distrust the government would have warmer feelings toward the Tea Party than would those who trust the government to do what's right. Of course, persons would need to be reasonably well informed about politics to make the connection between their assessment of government and their evaluation of the Tea Party. When we control for political knowledge (control variable), we may find that the relationship between Tea Party ratings (dependent variable) and trust of government (independent variable) gets stronger as knowledge increases. In other words, interaction could be occurring in this set of relationships. Consider two propositions and an ancillary hypothesis.

   Proposition 1: At all levels of political knowledge (NES variable, polknow2), individuals who distrust the government (political_trust) will give the Tea Party higher ratings (ft_Tea) than will people who trust the government.

   Proposition 2: The relationship between political trust and Tea Party ratings will be weaker for lower-knowledge respondents than for those with higher knowledge.

   Ancillary hypothesis: In a comparison of individuals, those with higher levels of political knowledge are more likely to trust the government than are those with lower levels of political knowledge.

   The dependent variable is the Tea Party feeling thermometer (ft_Tea), which runs from 0 (cold or negative feelings) to 100 (warm or positive feelings). The independent variable is political_trust, which captures how often respondents trust in government to do what's right, with five ordinal values—never, some, about half, most, or always.

   A. Use the Analyze ▶ Compare Means ▶ Means procedure (with layers) to do a controlled mean comparison analysis of ft_Tea for each combination of political_trust and polknow2. Record the means next to the question marks in the following table. Use weights so your results are nationally representative.

How often can you trust federal government to do what's right?	Political Knowledge		
	Low	High	Total
Never	48.67?	55.16?	51.37?
Some	47.66?	41.29?	45.01?
About half	46.96?	37.30?	43.09?
Most	47.40?	28.67?	39.94?
Always	51.77?	34.66?	49.89?
Total	47.69?	40.41?	44.73?

   B. Create a presentation-quality multiple line chart of the relationship between the Tea Party thermometer and political_trust, controlling for polknow2. There should be one line for high-knowledge respondents and another for low-knowledge respondents. Print the chart.

   C. Consider the numeric table and the graph. Do the results support Proposition 1? Answer yes or no, and explain.

   This is not supported because those with low political knowledge have consistently lukewarm feelings toward the tea party.

   D. Do the results support Proposition 2? Answer yes or no, and explain.

   Yes because the relationship is strong between those with high political knowlege, but nonexistent with people with low political knowledge.

   E. Test the ancillary hypothesis by producing a cross-tabulation with political_trust as the dependent variable and polknow2 as the independent variable.

Obtain column percentages. Do the results support the hypothesis? Answer yes or no, and explain, making specific reference to the cross-tabulation percentages.

No, trust in the government is relatively consistent regardless of political knowledge.

2. (Dataset: World. Variables: women13, womyear2, pr_sys.) In the Chapter 2 exercises, you analyzed the distribution of the variable women13, the percentage of women in the lower house of the legislatures in a number of countries. In this exercise you will analyze the relationship between women13 and two variables that could have an impact on the number of women serving in national legislatures.

First, consider the role of the type of electoral system. Many democracies have proportional representation (PR) systems. PR systems foster multiple parties having diverse ideological positions—and, perhaps, having diverse demographic compositions as well. Non-PR systems, like the system used in U.S. elections, militate in favor of fewer and more homogeneous parties. Thus, you might expect that non-PR countries will have fewer women in their national legislatures than will countries with PR-based electoral systems.

Next, consider the role of history and tradition. In some countries, women have had a long history of political empowerment. New Zealand, for example, gave women the right to vote in 1893. In other countries, such as Switzerland (where women were not enfranchised until 1971), women have had less experience in the electoral arena. Thus, it seems reasonable to hypothesize that countries with longer histories of women's suffrage (say, that enfranchised women before 1944) will have higher percentages of women in their national legislatures than will countries in which women's suffrage is a more recent development (since 1944). In this exercise you will isolate the effect of the type of electoral system on the percentage of women in parliament, controlling for the timing of women's suffrage. However, before you run any analyses, you will graphically depict different possible scenarios for the relationships you might discover.

Parts A and B contain graphic shells showing the percentage of women in parliament along the vertical axis and the type of electoral system along the horizontal axis. Countries without PR systems are represented by "No," and countries with PR systems by "Yes." For each shell, you will draw four bars within the graphic space: a bar for "1944 or before" countries without PR systems ("No"),

a bar for "1944 or before" countries with PR systems ("Yes"), a bar for "After 1944" countries without PR systems ("No"), and a bar for "After 1944" countries with PR systems ("Yes").

A. Draw an *additive* relationship fitting this description: Countries with PR systems have higher percentages of women in parliament than do countries with non-PR systems, and countries with a longer history of women's suffrage have higher percentages of women in parliament than do countries with a shorter history of women's suffrage. (*Hint:* In additive relationships, the strength and tendency of the relationship is the same or very similar for all values of the control variable.)

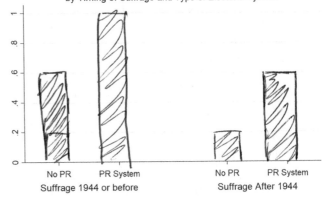

Percentage of Women in Parliament
by Timing of Suffrage and Type of Electoral System

B. Draw a set of *interaction* relationships fitting this description: For countries with a longer history of women's suffrage, those with PR systems have higher percentages of women in parliament than do countries with non-PR systems. For countries with a shorter history of women's suffrage, the type of electoral system has no effect on the percentage of women in parliament.

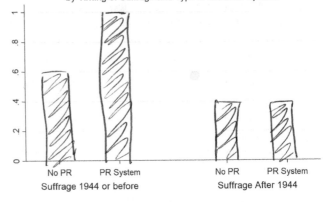

Percentage of Women in Parliament
by Timing of Suffrage and Type of Electoral System

In addition to the dependent variable, women13, the World dataset contains pr_sys, labeled "No" and coded 0 for countries with non-PR systems and labeled "Yes" and coded 1 for those having PR systems. Use pr_sys as the independent variable. World also contains womyear2, which measures the timing of women's suffrage by two values: "1944 or before" (coded 0) and "After 1944" (coded 1). Use womyear2 as the control variable.

C. Use the Analyze ▶ Compare Means ▶ Means procedure (with layers) to produce a controlled mean comparison table showing mean values of women13 for each value of pr_sys, controlling for womyear2. In the table below, record the mean values of women13 next to each question mark.

PR system?	Women's Suffrage		Total
	1944 or before	After 1944	
No	19.369 ?	16.280 ?	17.8825
Yes	29.9741 ?	20.799 ?	23.7286
Total	22.9319 ?	18.6453	20.9090

D. Produce a clustered bar chart of the relationship between women13 and pr_sys, controlling for womyear2. Make desired changes to enhance appearance and readability. Print the chart you created.

E. Examine the numeric data (part C) and the chart (part D). Consider the women13–pr_sys relationship for countries that enfranchised women in 1944 or before. Examine the difference between the means for non-PR countries and PR countries. This difference shows that the mean for PR countries is _____ points (circle one)

lower than   (higher than)
the mean for non-PR countries.

Now consider the women13–pr_sys relationship for countries that enfranchised women after 1944. Examine the difference between the means for non-PR countries and PR countries. This difference shows that the mean for PR countries is _____ points (circle one)

lower than (higher than)
the mean for non-PR countries.

F. Which of the following best characterizes the women13–pr_sys relationship, controlling for womyear2? (check one)

☑ The women13–pr_sys relationships have the same tendency and very similar strengths at both values of womyear2.

❏ The women13–pr_sys relationships have the same tendency but very different strengths at each value of womyear2.

❏ The women13–pr_sys relationships have different tendencies at each value of womyear2.

G. Review your artistic work in parts A and B. Examine the table (part C) and the chart (part D) as well as your conclusions in parts E and F. Which possible scenario—the bar chart you drew in part A or B—resembles more closely the pattern shown in the data? (circle one)

(The chart in part A)   The chart in part B

3. (Dataset: NES. Variables: ft_Rep, region, Race2, nesw.) Two political analysts are discussing reputed partisan differences between southern and non-southern states.

Political Analyst 1: "Media pundits and confused academics tend to exaggerate the South's reputation as a stronghold of Republican sentiment. In fact, people who live outside the South and people who live in the South don't differ that much in their ratings of the Republican Party. Look at my latest SPSS analysis. I found this: Non-southerners rated the Republicans at 40.85 on the feeling thermometer; this compared with a slightly warmer 46.05 for southerners. That's a paltry 5-point difference on the 100-point scale!"

Political Analyst 2: "Hmmm. . . that's interesting. But did you control for race? I wonder what happens to the relationship between region and Republican ratings after you take race into account. After all, blacks are less strongly attracted to the Republicans than are whites. And since southern states have a higher proportion of blacks than do non-southern states, racial differences in Republican ratings could affect regional differences in Republican ratings."

A. According to Political Analyst 2, why did Political Analyst 1's analysis find a relatively small difference between the Republican ratings of non-southerners and the Republican ratings of southerners? (check two)

❏ Because southern respondents are more likely to be white than are non-southern respondents

☑ Because southern respondents are more likely to be black than are non-southern respondents

☑ Because blacks give the Republican Party lower ratings than do whites

❏ Because blacks give the Republican Party higher ratings than do whites

B. Create a dummy variable to identify NES respondents from the South. You can use the Transform ▶ Recode into Different Variables procedure to generate a

[Handwritten margin notes: 1 = NE, 2 = MW, 3 = S, 4 = W]

new dummy variable based on the existing region variable. Check your work by running the <u>Analyze</u> ▶ <u>Descriptive Statistics</u> ▶ <u>Frequencies</u> procedure on your new dummy variable. According to this analysis, *[handwritten: 37.6]* percent of respondents are from the South and *[handwritten: 62.9]* percent of respondents are not from the South. (Make sure you weight observations and your two entries sum to 100.)

C. Obtain a breakdown table showing mean thermometer ratings of the Republican Party (ft_Rep) by non-southern/southern region of residence (the dummy variable you created in part B), controlling for race (Race2). The independent variable is the South region dummy variable. Use Race2 as the control variable: "White" is coded 1, and "Black" is coded 2. Fill in the mean values (Mean) and weighted frequencies (rounded to two decimal places) next to each question mark in the table below.

Means and frequencies of feeling thermometer: Republican Party	Race of Respondent		
	White	Black	Total[9]
Non-South mean	?	?	41.68
Non-South weighted frequency	1,627	159	1,786
South mean	?	?	46.91
South weighted frequency	853	236	1,089
Total mean	?	?	43.66
Total weighted frequency	2,480	395	2,874.46

D. Now figure out if the group of southern respondents has proportionately more blacks than the group of non-southern respondents. According to the table in part C, there are about 1,089 southern respondents in the data set. About what percentage of these 1,089 southern respondents are black? (circle one)

    about 20 percent   about 30 percent
        about 40 percent

About what percentage of the 1,786 non-southern respondents are black? (circle one)

    about 10 percent   about 20 percent
        about 30 percent

---

[9] The totals reported here are a little different than those stated by Political Analyst 1 because not all respondents have values white or black on the Race2 variable.

E. Evaluate the relationship between ft_Rep and the South/Non-South, controlling for race. When you compare southern whites with non-southern whites, you find that southern whites are _____ points (circle one)

       cooler   warmer

toward the Republican Party than are non-southern whites.

When you compare southern blacks with non-southern blacks, you find that southern blacks are _____ points (circle one)

       cooler   warmer

toward the Republican Party than are non-southern blacks.

F. Use the <u>Graphs</u> ▶ <u>Legacy Dialogs</u> ▶ <u>Bar</u> (Clustered) procedure to obtain a presentation-quality clustered bar chart of the relationship between ft_Rep and south, controlling for Race2. The category axis for this graphic should be the dummy variable you created to identify southern respondents and the clusters should be defined by Race2. Print the chart.

G. Consider all of the evidence you have obtained in this exercise. How would you characterize this set of relationships? (circle one)

    spurious   additive   interaction

Explain your reasoning:

_____

_____

_____

_____

_____

4. (Dataset: GSS. Variables: fepol, natchld, natenvir, intsex, sex, wtss.) For an exercise in Chapter 4, you tested for the presence of *preference falsification*, the tendency for respondents to offer false opinions that they nonetheless believe to be socially desirable under the circumstances. You evaluated the hypothesis that respondents are more likely to express support for feminist viewpoints when questioned by a female interviewer than when questioned by a male interviewer. But you did not control for the respondent's gender. That is, you did not look to see whether men are more (or less) likely than women to misrepresent their support for feminist viewpoints, depending on the gender of the interviewer.

Furthermore, it may be that men, and perhaps women as well, will engage in the same preference-falsifying behavior for policies that do not explicitly reference race but that may *symbolize* gendered issues, such as "government spending for child care." Although "child care" does not mention "women," it may be that respondents see "child care" through a gendered lens and will respond *as if* the question refers to a gendered issue. Of course, some policies, such as "government spending for improving and protecting the environment," do not evoke such symbolic connections. Questions about these gender-neutral policies should not show the same gender-of-interviewer effects as questions that make explicit—or implicit—reference to gender.

In this exercise you will extend your Chapter 4 analysis in two ways. First, you will analyze the relationship between interviewer gender (intsex, the independent variable) and three dependent variables: opinions on an explicitly gendered issue (fepol, which asks if females are suited for politics), a symbolically gendered policy (natchld, opinions on spending for child care), and a gender-neutral policy (natenvir, spending for improving and protecting the environment). Second, you will perform these analyses while controlling for respondents' gender (sex).

Based on previous research in this area, what might you expect to find? Here are two plausible expectations:

Expectation 1: For both male and female respondents, the gender-of-interviewer effect will be strongest for the explicitly gendered issue (fepol), weaker for the symbolically gendered policy (natchld), and weakest for the gender-neutral policy (natenvir).

Expectation 2: For the explicitly gendered issue (fepol) and for the symbolically gendered policy (natchld), the gender-of-interviewer effect will be greater for male respondents than for female respondents. For the gender-neutral policy (natenvir), the gender-of-interviewer effect will be the same (or close to 0) for both male respondents and female respondents (see Expectation 1).

A. Use the Analyze ▶ Descriptive Statistics ▶ Crosstabs procedure (with layers) to conduct the appropriate controlled cross-tabulation analyses. You will need to execute this procedure at least three times (one time per dependent variable). In the table that follows, record the *percentages* of respondents who express the following liberal opinions: disagree with statement women unsuited for politics (fepol), believe that national government spends too little on childcare (natfare), and think that national government spends too little on improving and protecting the environment (natenvir).

	Gender of Respondent				
	Male		Female		Total
	Gender of Interviewer		Gender of Interviewer		
	Male	Female	Male	Female	
Disagree with statement women unsuited for politics	76.9? ~~78~~ ~~106~~	83.2? ~~84.8~~	? 71.2	? 80.6	80.97%
Government spends too little on childcare	? 52.8	? 59.5	? 64.6	? 58.7	57.66%
Government spends too little on improving and protecting the environment	? 59.3	? 60.6	? 62.2	? 65.2	63.28%

B. Examine the data closely. Among male respondents, would you say that Expectation 1 is or is not supported by the evidence? (circle one)

~~Expectation 1 is not supported.~~
Expectation 1 is supported.

Explain your reasoning.

Yes, because they are ~~less likely to support~~ effect is strongest in the first answer (fepol) and then weaker in the rest.

Among female respondents, would you say that Expectation 1 is or is not supported by the evidence? (circle one)

Expectation 1 is not supported.
~~Expectation 1 is supported.~~

Explain your reasoning.

Women are definitely affected by the interviewer but it is conflicting between the first two variables.

C. Now compare the gender-of-interviewer effects between respondents of different genders. That is, compare the gender-of-interviewer effect on fepol among male respondents with the gender-of-interviewer effect on fepol among female respondents. Do the same for natchld and natenvir. Generally speaking, would you say that Expectation 2 is supported or is not supported by the evidence? (circle one)

Expectation 2 is not supported.
Expectation 2 is supported.

Explain your reasoning.

The effect is stronger on women respondents than on men But across all three variables.

D. Use the Graphs ▶ Legacy Dialogs ▶ Bar (Clustered) procedure to obtain a presentation-quality clustered bar chart of the relationship between natchld and intsex, controlling for sex. The category axis for this graphic should be the respondents' gender (sex) and the clusters should be defined by the interviewers' gender (intsex). Print the chart.

5. (Dataset: World. Variables: world.dta, democ, gdpcap08_2, frac_eth3.) Some countries have democratic regimes, and other countries do not. What factors help to explain this difference? One idea is that the type of government is shaped by the ethnic and religious diversity in a country's population. Countries that are relatively homogeneous, with most people sharing the same language and religious beliefs, are more likely to develop democratic systems than are countries having more linguistic conflicts and religious differences. Consider the ethnic heterogeneity hypothesis: In a comparison of countries, countries with lower levels of ethnic heterogeneity will be more likely to be democracies than will countries with higher levels of ethnic heterogeneity.

A. According to the ethnic heterogeneity hypothesis, if you were to compare countries having lower heterogeneity with countries having higher heterogeneity, you should find (check one)

❑ a lower percentage of democracies among countries having lower heterogeneity.

❑ a higher percentage of democracies among countries having lower heterogeneity.

❑ no difference between the percentage of democracies among countries having lower heterogeneity and the percentage of democracies among countries with higher heterogeneity.

B. The World dataset contains the variable democ ("Democracy?"), which classifies each country as a democracy ("Yes," coded 2) or a dictatorship ("No," coded 1). The variable democ is the dependent variable in this analysis. The dataset also contains frac_eth3, which classifies countries according to their level of ethnic heterogeneity: "Low" (coded 1), "Medium" (coded 2), or "High" (coded 3). This is the independent variable. Use the Analyze ▶ Descriptive Statistics ▶ Crosstabs procedure to test the ethnic heterogeneity hypothesis. Fill in the percentages of democracies in the following table.

	Ethnic Heterogeneity			
	Low	Medium	High	Total
Democracy	?	?	?	59.3%
Not democracy	?	?	?	40.7%
Total	?	?	?	100.0%

C. Based on these results, you could say that (check one)

❑ as ethnic heterogeneity increases, the percentage of democracies increases.

❑ as ethnic heterogeneity increases, the percentage of democracies decreases.

❑ as ethnic heterogeneity increases, there is little change in the percentage of democracies.

D. A country's level of economic development also might be linked to its type of government. According to this perspective, countries with higher levels of economic development will be more likely to be democracies than will countries with lower levels. The World dataset contains the variable gdpcap08_2. This variable, based on gross domestic product per capita, is an indicator of economic development. Countries are classified as "Low" (coded 0) or "High" (coded 1). Use the Analyze ▶ Descriptive Statistics ▶ Crosstabs procedure (with layers) to obtain a cross-tabulation analysis of the democ–frac_eth3 relationship, controlling for gdpcap08_2. Fill in the percentages of democracies in the table.

	Economic Development in Country						
	Low GDP per capita			High GDP per capita			
	Ethnic Heterogeneity			Ethnic Heterogeneity			
	Low	Medium	High	Low	Medium	High	Total
Democracy	?	?	?	?	?	?	59.33%
Not democracy	?	?	?	?	?	?	40.67%
Total	?	?	?	?	?	?	100.00%

E. Examine the relationship between ethnic heterogeneity and democracy in high-GDP countries and low-GDP countries.

Consider the democ–frac_eth3 relationship for low-GDP countries. Are ethnic heterogeneity and democracy related? Answer yes or no and briefly explain.

_____

_____

_____

_____

_____

Now consider the democ_regime–frac_eth3 relationship for high-GDP countries. Are ethnic heterogeneity and democracy related? Answer yes or no and briefly explain.

_____

_____

_____

_____

_____

F. Obtain and print a presentation-quality multiple line chart of the democ–frac_eth3 relationship, controlling for gdpcap08_2. (Remember that democracies are coded 1 on democ.) In the Chart Editor, give the scale axis this new title: "Percentage of Democracies." Edit the line weights. Change the style of one of the lines. Make other desired changes to enhance appearance and readability. Print the chart you created.

G. Think about the set of relationships you just analyzed. Consider all the numeric and graphic evidence. How would you describe the relationship between ethnolinguistic heterogeneity and democracy, controlling for GDP per capita? (circle one)

spurious   additive   interaction

Explain your reasoning.

_____

_____

_____

_____

_____

That concludes the exercises for this chapter. Before exiting SPSS, be sure to save your datasets.

CHAPTER

6

Making Inferences about Sample Means

 Watch screencasts of the guided examples in this chapter. **edge.sagepub.com/pollock**

Procedures Covered

Analyze ▶ Descriptive Statistics ▶ Descriptives (standard error)

Analyze ▶ Compare Means ▶ One-Sample T Test

Analyze ▶ Compare Means ▶ Independent-Samples T Test

Graphs ▶ Legacy Dialogs ▶ Error Bar

Analyze ▶ Descriptive Statistics ▶ Crosstabs (with z-test option)

Political research has much to do with observing patterns, creating explanations, framing hypotheses, and analyzing relationships. In interpreting their findings, however, researchers often operate in an environment of uncertainty. This uncertainty arises, in large measure, from the complexity of the political world. As we have seen, when we infer a causal connection between an independent variable and a dependent variable, it is hard to know for sure whether the independent variable is causing the dependent variable. Other, uncontrolled variables might be affecting the relationship, too. Yet uncertainty arises, as well, from the simple fact that research findings are often based on random samples.

In an ideal world, we could observe and measure the characteristics of every element in the population of interest—every voting-age adult, every student enrolled at a university, every bill introduced in every state legislature, and so on. In such an ideal situation, we would enjoy a high degree of certainty that the variables we have described and the relationships we have analyzed mirror what is really going on in the population. But, of course, we often do not have access to every member of a population. Instead we rely on a sample, a subset drawn at random from the population. By taking a random sample, we introduce random sampling error. In using a sample to draw inferences about a population, therefore, we never use the word *certainty*. Rather, we talk about *confidence* or *probability*. We know that the measurements we make on the sample will reflect the characteristics of the population, within the boundaries of random sampling error.

What are the boundaries of estimates we make from samples? If we calculate the mean income of a random sample of adults, for example, how confident can we be that the mean income we observe in our sample is the same as the mean income in the population? The answer depends on the standard error of the sample mean, the extent to which the mean income of the sample departs by chance from the mean income of the population. If we use a sample to calculate a mean income for women and a mean income for men, how confident can we be that the difference between the means of these two samples reflects the true income difference between women and men in the population? Again, the answer depends on the standard error—in this case, the standard error of the *difference* between the sample means, the extent to which the difference in the sample departs from the difference in the population.

In this chapter you will use a variety of SPSS procedures to explore and apply inferential statistics. First, you will learn to use the Analyze ▶ Descriptive Statistics ▶ Descriptives procedure to obtain basic information about interval-level variables. Second, using the One-Sample T Test procedure, you will obtain the 95 percent confidence interval (95% CI) for a sample mean. The 95% CI will tell you the boundaries within which there is a .95 probability that the true population mean falls. Third, using the Independent-Samples T Test procedure, you will test for statistically significant differences between two sample means. Finally, you will apply SPSS procedures to make inferences regarding proportions.

FINDING THE 95% CONFIDENCE INTERVAL OF A SAMPLE MEAN

Screencast

One-Sample T Test

To gain insight into the properties and application of inferential statistics, we will work through an example using the World dataset, world.sav. We begin by looking at the Analyze ▶ Descriptive Statistics ▶ Descriptives procedure, which yields basic information about interval-level variables. We then demonstrate the fundamentals of inference using the One-Sample T Test procedure.

To demonstrate the procedures used to make inferences about means, we'll examine global environmental data. The World dataset contains the variable carbon_footprint. This is an interval-level measure of carbon emissions by different countries on a per capita basis produced by the Global Footprint Network. There are many ways of quantifying carbon emissions; the carbon_footprint variable is roughly equivalent to the number of soccer-field-sized forests needed to offset a country's

FIGURE 6-1   Descriptive Statistics with Standard Error of Mean

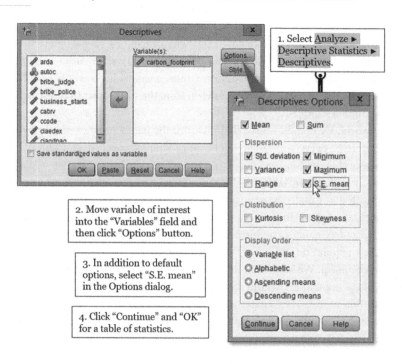

per capita carbon emissions. The larger the number, the greater the country's per capita carbon emissions. We can use Descriptives to obtain summary information about carbon_footprint. Open the World dataset. Select <u>A</u>nalyze ▶ <u>D</u>escriptive Statistics ▶ <u>D</u>escriptives.

In the main Descriptives window, scroll down the left-hand variable list until you find carbon_footprint. Move carbon_footprint into the Variable(s) list (Figure 6-1). Click the Options button. Now you can specify which descriptive statistics you would like SPSS to produce. These defaults should already be checked: mean, standard deviation, minimum, and maximum. That's fine. Also check the box beside "S.E. mean," which stands for "standard error of the mean," as shown in Figure 6-1. Click Continue, and then click OK.

Descriptive Statistics

	N	Minimum	Maximum	Mean		Std. Deviation
	Statistic	Statistic	Statistic	Statistic	Std. Error	Statistic
Carbon footprint	159	.01	12.65	1.7574	.15414	1.94364
Valid N (listwise)	159					

SPSS reports the requested statistics for carbon_footprint: number of cases analyzed (N), minimum and maximum observed values for carbon_footprint, mean value of carbon_footprint, standard error of the mean, and standard deviation. Among the 159 countries analyzed, scores on carbon_footprint range from .01 to 12.65. The mean value of carbon_footprint is 1.76. Countries' carbon footprints have a standard deviation of 1.94.[1]

How closely does the mean of 1.76 reflect the true mean in the population from which this sample was drawn? The answer depends on the standard error of the sample mean. The standard error of a sample mean is based on the standard deviation and the size of the sample. SPSS determines the standard error just as you would—by dividing the standard deviation by the square root of the sample size. The standard error of the carbon_footprint mean is equal to the standard deviation, 1.94, divided by the square root of 159.

$$\text{Standard Error of Sample Mean} = \frac{\text{Standard Deviation}}{\sqrt{\text{Sample Size}}}$$

A CLOSER LOOK: TREATING CENSUS AS A SAMPLE

In the running example involving carbon emission statistics, we are not analyzing a random sample since we have information on nearly all the countries in the world. Nevertheless, we are using inferential statistics created to analyze relatively small samples drawn from large populations. This is common practice, but it raises some interesting philosophical questions to think about. Perhaps we think that many countries could exist (if, for example, Franz Ferdinand had just stayed home on June 28, 1914) and we are observing a sample of them. Our estimates of conflict and democracy around the world would probably vary in repeated samples as well from random measurement errors. In the running example, we assume, for illustrative purposes, that we have just analyzed a random sample and have estimated carbon emissions from that sample.

---

[1] Be careful not to confuse the standard deviation of many carbon footprint values in the sample with the standard *error* of the mean carbon footprint estimate from the sample.

FIGURE 6-2   One-Sample T Test Procedure

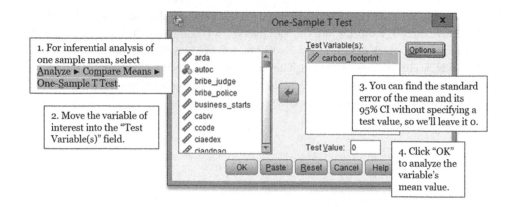

1. For inferential analysis of one sample mean, select Analyze ▶ Compare Means ▶ One-Sample T Test.

2. Move the variable of interest into the "Test Variable(s)" field.

3. You can find the standard error of the mean and its 95% CI without specifying a test value, so we'll leave it 0.

4. Click "OK" to analyze the variable's mean value.

This number, .15, tells us the extent to which the sample mean of 1.76 departs by chance from the population mean.[2] The standard error is the essential ingredient for making inferences about the population mean. But let's get SPSS to help us make these inferences.

We will use SPSS's One-Sample T Test procedure to do two things: find the 95% CI of the mean and use the confidence interval to test a hypothetical claim about the population mean. Select Analyze ▶ Compare Means ▶ One-Sample T Test to open the One-Sample T Test window (Figure 6-2).

To generate inferential statistics about means using the One-Sample T Test procedure, we supply SPSS with information in two places: the Test Variable(s) panel and the Test Value box, which currently contains the default value of 0. Now, One-Sample T Test is not naturally designed to report the 95% CI for a mean. Rather, it is set up to compare the mean of a variable in the Test Variable(s) panel with a hypothetical mean (provided by the user in the Test Value box) and to see if random error could account for the difference. (We will discuss this calculation below.) However, if you run One-Sample T Test on its defaults, it will provide the 95% CI. Simply click the variable into the Test Variable(s) panel, as shown in Figure 6-2, and click OK.

One-Sample Statistics

	N	Mean	Std. Deviation	Std. Error Mean
Carbon footprint	159	1.7574	1.94364	.15414

One-Sample Test

Test Value = 0

	t	df	Sig. (2-tailed)	Mean Difference	95% Confidence Interval of the Difference	
					Lower	Upper
Carbon footprint	11.401	158	.000	1.75736	1.4529	2.0618

[2] For simplicity, we've rounded the standard error to two decimal places. SPSS calculates the standard error with greater precision as .15414.

The output for One-Sample T Test includes two tables. In the One-Sample Statistics table, SPSS reports summary information about carbon_footprint. This information is similar to the Descriptives output discussed earlier. Again, we can see that carbon_footprint has a mean of 1.76, a standard deviation of 1.94, and a standard error of .15 (which, reassuringly, is the same number we calculated using the standard error of mean formula). We are interested mainly in the second table, the One-Sample Test table. In fact, when using One-Sample T Test to obtain confidence intervals, you may safely ignore all the information in the One-Sample Test table except for the rightmost cells. (We'll apply the "test value" and interpret the test statistic shortly.) The values appearing under the label "95% Confidence Interval of the Difference," 1.45 and 2.06, define the lower and upper boundaries of the 95% CI.

It is an established statistical rule that 95 percent of all possible population means will fall in this interval:

$$\text{Sample Mean} \pm \text{Margin of Error}$$

The margin of error in this equation is the product of the standard error (in this case, .15) and the t-score for 95% confidence. The t-score for 95% confidence is based on a t-distribution. The t-distribution has a bell curve shape like a normal distribution, but its shape depends on sample size. With 159 observations (158 degrees of freedom), the t-score for 95% confidence is 1.98.[3] The margin of error, therefore, is 1.98 × .15 = .30. Given our estimate of the carbon_footprint mean and its margin of error, the lower boundary is 1.76 − .30 = 1.46 and the upper boundary is 1.76 + .30 = 2.06. (SPSS reports slightly different values because we've rounded to two decimal places.) There is a high probability, a 95 percent probability, that the true population mean lies in the region between 1.46 at the low end and 2.06 at the high end. Notice that our point estimate of the carbon footprint mean, 1.76, is exactly the midpoint of the 95% CI. 1.76 is our best estimate of the carbon_footprint mean based on this sample, but given the inherent randomness of sampling, we wouldn't be too surprised if the true mean of carbon_footprint is as low as 1.46 or as high as 2.06.

The statistical intricacies of the t-test can be confusing. Here's a good rule of thumb: the margin of error is two times the standard error.[4] This means that the 95% CI is the sample mean ± 2 standard errors.

Figure 6-3 graphically depicts the One-Sample T Test results. The observed sample mean, 1.76, is represented by a dot. The two horizontal "whiskers" define the 95% CI, which lies between 1.47 and 2.05. The 95% CI is the foundation for the .05 level of statistical significance, the basic standard of hypothesis testing using inferential statistics. Any hypothetical claim stating that the true population mean is less than the lower boundary, or greater than the upper boundary, can be rejected as statistically unlikely. There is a probability of .05 or less (≤.05) that the population mean is below the lower boundary (one-half of .05 is equal to .025) or above the upper boundary (the remaining half of .05, equal to .025). By the same token, any hypothetical claim that the true population mean is anywhere within the 95% CI must be accepted as statistically

---

[3] You can find the t-score for 95 percent confidence with a given number of degrees of freedom in statistical tables. For example, see Philip H. Pollock, *The Essential of Political Analysis*, 5th ed. (Thousand Oaks, CA: CQ Press, An Imprint of SAGE Publications, 2016), p. 148, Table 6-4. The comparable z-score (based on a standard normal distribution) is 1.96. SPSS automatically computes the relevant t-score to conduct the t-test.

[4] The exact t-score for 95% confidence depends on the t-distribution's degrees of freedom (which is related to sample size), but in practice it will usually be less than 2 so the rule of thumb suggested in the text is a conservative approximation. With very small samples, like a mean calculated from a class of thirty students, the rule of thumb can be misleading.

FIGURE 6-3   Error Bar Chart (One Sample Mean)

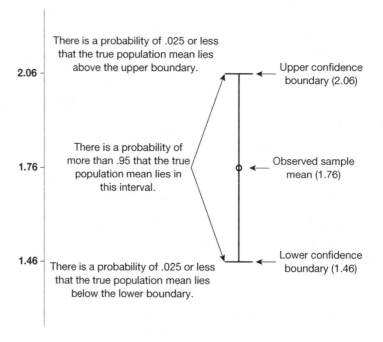

likely—*likely* being defined as an event that would occur more frequently than 5 times out of 100 (>.05). Of course, not all hypothetical claims within the 95% CI are equally probable. Proposed population means that are closer to the observed sample mean (in our example, around 1.76) are much more likely than population means farther out, on the frontier near the upper or lower boundaries.

TESTING A HYPOTHETICAL CLAIM ABOUT THE POPULATION MEAN

The 95% CI—and the .05 standard—also comes into play when making inferences about the difference between a sample mean and a hypothetical population mean. Suppose an environmental protection organization sets 2.00 as a goal for reducing the mean carbon footprint of countries around the world. The organization's goal will serve as the hypothesized mean value against which we'll compare our sample data. The null hypothesis would be that the population mean equals 2.00; the alternative hypothesis, the population mean does not equal 2.00. Based on our data, have countries around the world met this hypothetical carbon emissions benchmark?

Even though we estimated the mean of carbon_footprint to be 1.76, the proposed mean of 2.00 falls between the lower and upper boundaries of the 95% CI, 1.47 and 2.05. Thus, there is a probability of greater than .05 that the true mean is not below 2.00, and so we cannot confidently rule out the possibility that the true carbon_footprint is greater than 2.00. Now, the fact that the hypothetical mean falls within the 95% CI directly implies that the *difference* between the observed mean (1.76) and the proposed mean (2.00) is not statistically significant; that is, it would occur by chance more than 5 times out of 100. Framed in the same language used earlier to describe the 95% CI of a single sample mean, we can say that 95 percent of all possible *differences* between an observed sample mean and a hypothetical population mean will fall in this interval:

$$(\text{Sample Mean} - \text{Hypothesized Mean}) \pm (\text{Margin of Error})$$

If 0 falls within the 95% CI of the difference between the sample and hypothesized means, then we must infer that the difference between the sample and hypothesized means is statistically indistinguishable from zero. Logically enough, if this 95% CI does not include 0, then we conclude that the difference between the sample and hypothesized means is statistically significant.

Applying the rule above to the running example, the lower boundary for 95% CI for the difference of means equals $(1.76 - 2.00) - (1.98 \times .15) = -.24 - .30 = -.54$. The upper boundary equals $(1.76 - 2.00) + (1.98 \times .15) = -.24 + .30 = .06$. Figure 6-4 displays the 95% CI for this example. Notice that the 95% CI includes 0. Thus, even though the sample and hypothesized means, 1.76 and 2.00, may appear different, from a statistical standpoint they are not different at all. We estimated the difference between sample and hypothesized means to be $-.24$, but given the inherent randomness of sampling, we wouldn't be too surprised if the actual difference is as low as $-.54$ or as high as .06.

The 95% CI is a simple, yet effective, inferential tool. But it is blunt. It can tell us whether there is a probability greater than .05 that the population mean—or the difference between two means—lies outside the interval's lower and upper limits or if there's more than a .95 probability that the population mean—or the difference between two means—lies within the interval.

A more precise inferential method, the *P*-value approach, allows the researcher to determine the exact probability associated with a hypothetical claim about the population mean. For example, our confidence interval analysis of the hypothetical global carbon_footprint mean of 2.00 revealed that a random sample would yield sample means like 1.76 more than 5 times out of 100. But how many times, *exactly*? Six times? Twenty-six times? Thirty-six times? Put differently, we know that the probability is greater than .05 that 1.76 and 2.00 come from the same distribution of population means. What, precisely, is that probability?

To conduct a One-Sample T Test on the carbon_footprint variable to determine the *P*-value associated with the hypothetical mean of 2.00, select Analyze ▶ Compare Means ▶ One-Sample T Test. The carbon_footprint variable should still be in the Test Variable(s) panel. Now click in the Test Value box and type "2" (Figure 6-5). SPSS will calculate the difference between the mean of the test variable, carbon_footprint, and the test value, 2.00. SPSS will then report the

FIGURE 6-4   Error Bar Chart (Difference between Sample Mean and Hypothesized Mean)

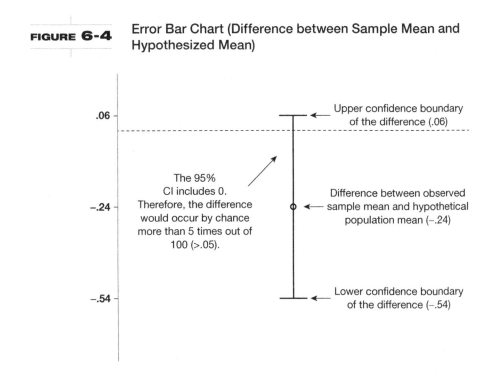

FIGURE 6-5   Testing a Hypothetical Claim about a Sample Mean

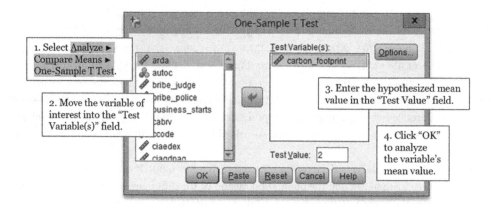

probability that the test value, 2.00, could have come from the same population as did the sample mean of the variable carbon_footprint. Click OK. Again, we have One-Sample T Test output.

One-Sample Statistics

	N	Mean	Std. Deviation	Std. Error Mean
Carbon footprint	159	1.7574	1.94364	.15414

One-Sample Test

Test Value = 2

	t	df	Sig. (2-tailed)	Mean Difference	95% Confidence Interval of the Difference Lower	Upper
Carbon footprint	-1.574	158	.117	-.24264	-.5471	.0618

Notice that the numbers from our earlier analysis appear in the "Mean Difference" column and "95% Confidence Interval of the Difference" column (with some slight differences due to rounding). Now, however, we are after the exact probability that 1.76 and 2.00 reside in the same distribution of possible population means. To address this inferential issue, SPSS calculates a Student's t-test statistic, or t-ratio. A t-statistic is calculated using the following formula:

$$t\text{-Statistic} = \frac{(\text{Sample Mean} - \text{Hypothesized Mean})}{\text{Standard Error of Sample Mean}}$$

$$= \frac{(1.76 - 2.00)}{.15} = \frac{-.24}{.15} = -1.60$$

This t-statistic value, −1.60, appears in the leftmost cell of the One-Sample Test table.[5] Thus, the sample mean of carbon_footprint falls 1.60 standard errors below the hypothetical mean of 2.00.

---

[5] SPSS performs this calculation at 32-decimal precision. So if you were to check SPSS's math using the mean difference and standard error that appear in the SPSS Viewer, you may arrive at a slightly different t-ratio than the value of t reported in the One-Sample Test table.

Turn your attention to the cell labeled "Sig. (2-tailed)," which contains the number .117. This is the *P*-value associated with the *t*-statistic, and it may be interpreted this way: There is a probability of .117 that the sample mean and the hypothetical mean were drawn from the same distribution of means. A less intuitive, but technically more proper, interpretation is as follows: If the difference between the two means is assumed to be 0, then random sampling error would produce an observed difference like this one 11.7 percent of the time, by chance. So, the no-difference hypothesis holds up. From the 95% CI, we already knew that 1.76 and 2.00 were not significantly different. The *P*-value approach puts a finer point on this inference.[6]

INFERENCES ABOUT THE DIFFERENCE BETWEEN TWO SAMPLE MEANS

Screencast

Independent-Samples T Test

We now turn to a common hypothesis-testing situation: comparing the sample means of a dependent variable in two different groups. In this section, we'll use the NES dataset, NES.sav. Someone investigating the gender gap, for example, might test the hypothesis that women are more egalitarian than men. Egalitarianism is a political philosophy that emphasizes equality among people. This philosophy usually means more than equality of opportunity; it is also important to have equality in wealth and income. The gender difference hypothesis asserts that, in the unobserved population of individuals, women and men form distinct subpopulations. The true mean of the egalitarianism scale is higher for women than it is for men.

The researcher always tests his or her hypotheses against a skeptical foil, the *null hypothesis*. The null hypothesis claims that, regardless of any differences a researcher observes between groups in a random sample, no group differences exist in the population from which the sample was drawn. Thus, the null hypothesis states that distinct subpopulation means do not exist, that the mean for women and the mean for men were drawn from the same population. How does the null hypothesis explain systematic patterns that might turn up in a sample, such as a mean difference between women and men on the egalitarianism scale? Random sampling error. In essence, the null hypothesis says, "You observed such and such a difference between two groups in your random sample. But, in reality, no difference exists in the population. When you took the sample, you introduced random sampling error. Thus, random sampling error accounts for the difference you observed."

For the hypothesis of gender difference on the egalitarianism scale, the null hypothesis says that there is no real difference between men and women in the population—that men do not score lower than women on the egalitarianism scale. The null hypothesis further asserts that any observed differences in the sample can be accounted for by random sampling error.

The null hypothesis, abbreviated H_0, is so central to the methodology of statistical inference that we always begin by assuming it to be correct. We then set a fairly high standard for rejecting it. The researcher's hypothesis is considered the alternative hypothesis, abbreviated H_A. In the current case, H_A is the hypothesis that women are more egalitarian than men.

The Independent-Samples T Test procedure permits us to test each alternative hypothesis against the null hypothesis and to decide whether the observed differences between males and females are too large to have occurred by random chance when the sample was drawn. For each

---

[6] SPSS returns two-tailed *P*-values (labeled "Sig."), not one-tailed values. Two-tailed values report the probability associated with the absolute value of *t*, or |*t*|. For the current example, even though SPSS puts a negative sign on the *t*-ratio, −1.60, the accompanying significance value, .117, combines *P*-values for the region of the Student's *t*-distribution below *t* = −1.60 *and* above *t* = +1.60. Because most hypotheses are directional—for example, we would properly hypothesize that mean carbon_footprint is *less than* 2.00, not that mean carbon_footprint is *different* than 2.00—two-tailed *P*-values are equivalent to a stringent .025 one-tailed test of statistical significance. However, such stringency is statistically acceptable, because it biases inference in favor of Type II error. Moreover, the two-tailed standard is widely used in political research, and so it is followed in this book.

mean comparison, the Independent-Samples T Test procedure will give us a *P*-value: the probability of obtaining the sample difference under the working assumption that the null hypothesis is true.

To reject the null hypothesis, we must be confident that the mean difference could not occur by chance more than 5 times out of 100. Thus, for *P*-values less than or equal to .05 (≤.05), reject H_0. For *P*-values greater than .05 (>.05), do not reject H_0. This probabilistic decision rule may strike you as decidedly out of sync with ordinary life experiences. If you were planning an outdoor activity and the weather forecast called for a 10 percent chance of rain, you would not change your plans—.10 is a low probability. Indeed, a 25 percent chance of rain (a probability equal to .25) may not even cause you to carry an umbrella. When it comes to testing H_0, however, the definition of a "high" probability is much more stringent. Suppose we have every expectation that our analysis will confirm our hypothesis, H_A. Suppose further that we obtain a set of results telling us that random sampling error, H_0's favorite process, would produce our results 6 times out of 100. Now, a probability of .06 seems quite low. But it is not low enough to reject the null hypothesis. The idea behind the decision rule is to minimize the probability of rejecting the null hypothesis when, in the population from which our sample was randomly drawn, the null hypothesis is in fact true. This is called Type I error. If we are going to get it wrong, we want to accept the null hypothesis when, in fact, it is false. This is called Type II error, and the inferential rule is freighted toward committing Type II error and away from committing Type I error.

With these principles in mind, let's ask SPSS to test the gender gap hypothesis. With the NES dataset open, select Analyze ▶ Compare Means ▶ Independent-Samples T Test. The Independent-Samples T Test window appears (Figure 6-6). SPSS wants to know two things: the name or names of the test variable(s) and the name of the grouping variable. SPSS will calculate the mean values of the variables named in the Test Variable(s) panel for each category of the variable named in the Grouping Variable box. It will then test to see if the differences between the means are significantly different from 0.

We want to compare the means for men and women on the egalitarianism scale. The egalitarianism variable is a measure of egalitarian beliefs that ranges from 0 (low egalitarianism) to 16 (high egalitarianism). Find egalitarianism in the variable list and move it into the Test Variable(s) panel (see Figure 6-6). Because you want the means of these variables to be calculated separately for each

FIGURE 6-6   Conducting an Independent-Samples T Test

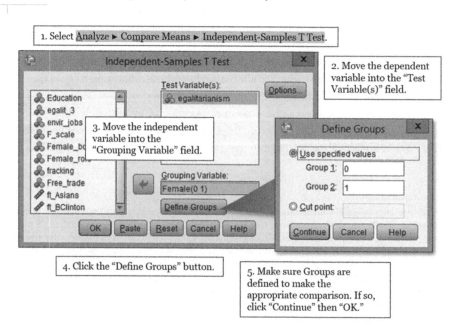

sex, Female is the grouping variable. When you click Female into the Grouping Variable box, SPSS moves it into the box with the initial designation "Female(? ?)" and the Define Groups button is activated. SPSS needs more information. It needs to know the codes of the two groups you wish to compare. Click the Define Groups button.

In the Define Groups dialog, we specify the groups we're comparing: men and women. There are two ways to define the groups you want to compare: "Use specified values" (the default) and "Cut point." The choice depends on the situation. If you opt for "Use specified values," then SPSS will divide the cases into two groups based on the codes you supply for Group 1 and Group 2. If the grouping variable has more than two categories, then you may wish to use "Cut point." SPSS will divide the cases into two groups based on the code entered in the Cut point box—one group for all cases having codes equal to or greater than the Cut point code and one group having codes less than the Cut point code. Because the Female variable has two codes—0 for males and 1 for females—we will go with the "Use specified values" option in this example. (How do we know this? Recall that by right-clicking on a variable you can reacquaint yourself with that variable's codes.) Click in the Group 1 box and type "0," and then click in the Group 2 box and type "1." Click Continue. Notice that SPSS has replaced the question marks next to gender with the numeric codes for males and females (see Figure 6-6). Click OK.

SPSS performs the mean comparison and reports the result in the Viewer. The top table, labeled "Group Statistics," shows descriptive information about the means of egalitarianism by gender. The bottom table, "Independent Samples Test," tests for statistically significant differences between men and women on the dependent variable.

Group Statistics

	Is R female? (v161342)	N	Mean	Std. Deviation	Std. Error Mean
Egalitarianism scale	Male	1723	10.09	3.401	.082
(v162243-v162246)	Female	1850	10.81	3.335	.078

Independent Samples Test

		Levene's Test for Equality of Variances		t-test for Equality of Means					95% Confidence Interval of the Difference	
		F	Sig.	t	df	Sig. (2-tailed)	Mean Difference	Std. Error Difference	Lower	Upper
Egalitarianism scale (v162243-v162246)	Equal variances assumed	.009	.923	-6.398	3571	.000	-.721	.113	-.942	-.500
	Equal variances not assumed			-6.394	3541.736	.000	-.721	.113	-.942	-.500

From the Group Statistics table we can see that males, on average, scored 10.09 on the egalitarianism scale, whereas females had a higher mean, 10.81. Our alternative hypothesis appears to have merit. The difference between these two means is 10.09 minus 10.81, or −.72. (SPSS always calculates the difference by subtracting the Group 2 mean from the Group 1 mean. This value appears in the "Mean Difference" column of the Independent-Samples Test table.) The null hypothesis claims that this difference is the result of random sampling error and, therefore, that the true male–female difference in the population is equal to 0. Using the information in the Independent Samples Test table, we test the null hypothesis (H_0) against the alternative hypothesis (H_A) that the male mean is lower than the female mean.

Notice that there are two rows of numbers for each dependent variable. One row is labeled "Equal variances assumed" and the other is "Equal variances not assumed." The statistics along "Equal variances not assumed" are generally more conservative, so it is a safer bet to use them.[7]

In comparing two sample means, SPSS calculates a t-statistic using the following formula[8]:

$$t\text{-Statistic}=\frac{(\text{Group}1\,\text{Mean}-\text{Group}2\,\text{Mean})}{\sqrt{(\text{SE of Sample Mean}_{\text{Group}1})^2+(\text{SE of Sample Mean}_{\text{Group}2})^2}}$$

$$=\frac{(10.09-10.81)}{\sqrt{.08^2+.08^2}}=\frac{-.72}{\sqrt{.0064+.0064}}=-6.36$$

For the gender difference in egalitarianism hypothesis, SPSS returns an extreme t-statistic, -6.39 (we calculated a slightly different t-statistic due to rounding error). If you happened to glance at the boundaries of the 95% CI—from $-.94$ at the low end to $-.50$ at the high end—you already knew that the results would be bad news for the null hypothesis. It comes as no surprise, then, that SPSS reports a P-value of .000. It's important to note here that the P-value is not equal to 0, it just looks that way rounded to three decimal places; it's better to think of the P-value as $<.001$.[9] Is a value $<.001$ equal to or less than .05? Yes, it is. Safe conclusion: Under the assumption that the null hypothesis is correct, random sampling error would yield an observed mean difference of $-.72$ very nearly 0 percent of the time. Reject the null hypothesis.

VISUALIZING MEAN COMPARISONS WITH ERROR BARS

In the preceding sections, we tested the difference between a sample mean and a hypothesized value as well as the difference between two sample means. Inferential statistics help us determine how confident we should be about mean comparisons and are therefore an important part of comparing means. In some cases, due to large variation in the thing being measured or small sample size, we find that some seemingly large differences could be the product of random error and are not statistically significant. In other cases, when variation is limited and sample sizes are large, seemingly small differences are statistically significant. It can be helpful to visualize inferences about sample means by plotting point estimates and confidence intervals. We used error bar plots in Figures 6-3 and 6-4 to convey the general logic of testing hypotheses about means. In this section, we'll show you how to visualize inferences about sample means using the NES dataset.

---

[7] One of the statistical assumptions of mean comparisons is that the amount of variation in the dependent variable is the same for the groups being compared—for example, that the amount of variation in ftgr_gay is the same in the female subsample and the male subsample. If this assumption holds up, then it is safe to use the "Equal variances assumed" row. If it does not hold up, then the "Equal variances not assumed" row must be used. SPSS tests the equal-variances assumption by reporting statistics for Levene's test. Technically, if the significance value for Levene's test is greater than or equal to .05, you can use the "Equal variances assumed" row. If Levene's significance value is less than .05, then you must use the "Equal variances not assumed" row. As a practical matter, the two rows of numbers are never wildly different. But it is statistically prudent (and simpler) to assume that the variances are not equal.

[8] The bottom part (denominator) of this formula is the standard error of the difference of the mean, which SPSS automatically calculates and reports in the Viewer results. We write it out in long form in the text so you can see how this value is calculated.

[9] A P-value cannot exactly equal 0. There is always some chance, however remote, that random error produced the difference observed in the sample. Although the editing of SPSS tabular output is not covered in this book, it is possible to double-click on a table (SPSS refers to tabular objects as "pivot tables") to make appearance-enhancing changes or to look at the mind-numbingly precise numbers that SPSS rounds to produce the digits on display in the table. Double-clicking on the Independent-Samples T Test output shown in the text, and then double-clicking on the "Sig. (2-tailed)" value just discussed (the value .000), reveals this number: 1.8279E-10. That's scientific notation for .00000000018279, a number very close to, but not quite, 0.

FIGURE 6-7   Visualizing Inferences about the Difference of Sample Means

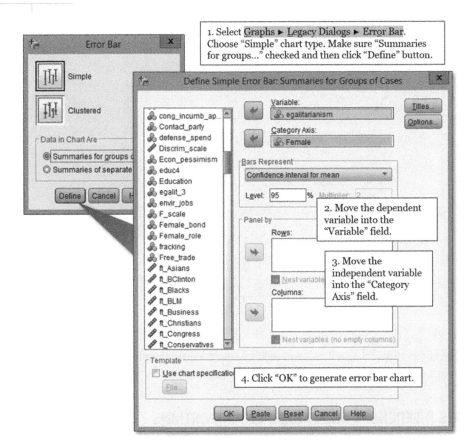

To visualize the comparison of two sample means, select Graphs ▸ Legacy Dialogs ▸ Error Bar to open the Error Bar dialog (Figure 6-7). We are going to create a simple error bar graphic to visualize the difference between male and female egalitarianism scores in the NES dataset. Make sure the "Simple" and "Summaries for groups of cases" options are selected and click the Define button.

We want to compare the mean egalitarianism scores we estimate for men and women, so find the egalitarianism variable in the list and move it into the Variable field. Find the Female variable and move it into the Category Axis field. The default setting for what the error bars represent is just what we want to see: the 95% confidence intervals for the means. Click OK.

In the Viewer, we find a graphical counterpart to our analysis of two samples in the preceding section. On the left side of the chart, we see the upper and lower bounds of the 95% CI of the egalitarianism scores for males with the point estimate at the midpoint of the error bar; on the right side, we see the comparable information for females. It's easy to see here that the mean for women is higher than the mean for men, even taking into account the uncertainty of each sample mean: the entire 95% CI for females is higher than it is for males.

Before moving on, make sure you understand the difference between what's shown in Figure 6-8 and what's displayed in a graphic like Figure 4-13 (a box-and-whiskers plot comparing values of a dependent variable across categories). In Chapter 4, we compared the distribution of dependent variable values in a sample across categories, using a graphic to show the variable's dispersion in the sample. This kind of graphic, or perhaps a histogram, could help us visualize the standard *deviation* of egalitarianism scores in the sample (3.40 for males and 3.34 for females). The graphic in Figure 6-8, in contrast, helps us visualize the standard *error* of the means we estimated from the sample. Standard errors are a mathematical property of statistics, not an empirical property

FIGURE 6-8   Error Bar Chart Comparing Two Sample Means

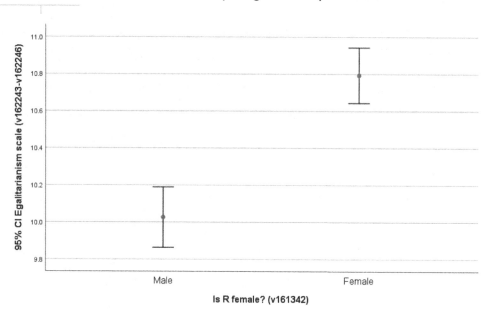

of sample observations; they tell us how much we would expect sample means to vary if we were to take not just one sample but many samples (.08 for males and .08 for females).

MAKING INFERENCES ABOUT SAMPLE PROPORTIONS

When we're analyzing a dependent variable that's measured at the nominal or ordinal level, we do not make inferences about its mean value, strictly speaking, because we only calculate a variable's mean when it's measured at the interval level (see "Describing Interval Variables" in Chapter 2). Instead, you might calculate the proportion of observations with a specific value of the dependent variable and make inferences about that proportion. Making inferences about sample proportions follows the same general logic as making inferences about means but requires us to make a few adjustments to the methods we use. SPSS does not have a built-in procedure for making inferences about proportions, but one can learn to navigate its limitations to make inferences regarding one- and two-sample proportions.

In this section, we'll analyze an ordinal-level variable in the GSS dataset, givinfusa, which measures public opinion about domestic spying programs. The GSS asked people if the U.S. federal government should collect information about U.S. citizens without their knowledge. Of those surveyed, 18.4 percent responded that the government definitely has the right to collect information on its citizens without their knowledge (numeric code 1); 30.8 percent responded that the government probably should have this right (numeric code 2); 25.1 percent responded the government probably should not have this right (numeric code 3); and 25.7 percent responded definitely not (coded 4). To simplify our analysis of proportions, let's start by following the Transform ▶ Recode into Different Variables procedure discussed in Chapter 3 to transform this ordinal-level measure with four possible responses into a binary variable reflecting two possible opinions on domestic spying: "support" (existing values 1 thru 2 → 1) and "oppose" (existing values 3 thru 4 → 0). Let's give the new variable the name "domestic_spying" and label its numeric values while we're at it.

Having recoded the givinfusa variable into a new variable, let's use the Analyze ▶ Descriptive Statistics ▶ Frequencies procedure to generate descriptive statistics for the new domestic_spying variable, see how opinions line up on this controversial issue, and make sure we have recoded the givinfusa variable correctly.

Support Domestic Spying?

		Frequency	Percent	Valid Percent	Cumulative Percent
Valid	Oppose	687	24.0	50.8	50.8
	Support	667	23.3	49.2	100.0
	Total	1354	47.2	100.0	
Missing	System	1513	52.8		
Total		2867	100.0		

According to the descriptive statistics, a slight majority of Americans oppose domestic spying (50.8 percent oppose compared to 49.2 percent in favor). Of course, these figures are based on a sample, not the entire population, so how much are these figures likely to vary if this sample were repeated? Should we be confident that a majority of Americans oppose domestic spying?

To find the standard error of the proportion who oppose domestic spying and the 95% CI of the estimated proportion, we can employ the following standard error of proportion formula:

$$SE_{proportion} = \sqrt{\frac{(\text{proportion}) \times (1 - \text{proportion})}{N}}$$

This result tells that we could expect the estimated proportion that oppose (or support) domestic spying to vary by .014 on average (equivalent to ±1.4%) if we conducted this sample of 1,354 opinions about domestic spying again.

When the responses of interest are coded as 0s and 1s, as they are with the domestic_spying variable, the proportion giving the response coded 1 will equal the mean of the variable and the standard error of the proportion can be approximated by the standard error of the mean using the Analyze ▶ Descriptive Statistics ▶ Descriptives procedure with the S.E. mean option selected (and the standard deviation option omitted).[10] See Figure 6-1 for assistance with this procedure.

Descriptive Statistics

	N	Minimum	Maximum	Mean*	
	Statistic	Statistic	Statistic	Statistic	Std. Error
domestic_spying	1354	.00	1.00	.4924	.01359
Valid N (listwise)	1354				

*Note: We are actually calculating a proportion here.

Having calculated the standard error of the proportion, we can find the 95% CI of the proportion of Americans who support domestic spying. The 95% CI of a proportion is analogous to the 95% CI of a mean, discussed above:

$$\text{Sample Proportion} \pm (1.96 \times SE \text{ of Sample Proportion})$$

By this rule, the lower boundary of the proportion of Americans who support domestic spying is .492 − (1.96 × .014) = .492 − .027 = .465. The upper boundary is .492 + (1.96 × .0.14) = .492 + .027 = .519.

---

[10] Applying SPSS's built-in procedure for calculating standard errors to a binary variable will generate larger standard errors than the standard error of proportion formula yields, but the difference is negligible in large samples. We've rounded the standard error of proportion to .014 in the text from 0.01358.

As was the case with finding the standard error of proportion, when the responses of interest are coded as 0s and 1s, we can use SPSS's built-in Analyze ▶ Compare Means ▶ One-Sample T Test procedure to approximate the 95% CI of the proportion who oppose domestic spying (see Figure 6-2). Applying SPSS's built-in procedure in this manner yields a slightly larger interval, but the difference is negligible in large samples.

One-Sample Test

Test Value = 0

	t	df	Sig. (2-tailed)	Mean Difference	95% Confidence Interval of the Difference	
					Lower	Upper
domestic_spying	36.230	1353	.000	.49238	.4657	.5190

The 95% CI for a proportion is analogous to the 95% CI for a mean as we discussed in preceding sections. In repeated samples, we would expect 95 percent of proportions estimated to oppose domestic spying to fall between the lower boundary, 0.466, and the upper boundary, 0.519.[11] The 95% CI for the oppose proportion overlaps 0.500 so we can't be confident from this sample that the majority of Americans oppose domestic spying.[12]

While it appears that Americans are evenly divided on the issue of the federal government's collecting information on citizens without their consent, one might wonder if different groups of Americans feel the same way. Do some groups support domestic spying more than other groups do? Let's analyze this question with respect to race.

To compare the support for domestic spying between groups or subsets of observations, select Analyze ▶ Descriptive Statistics ▶ Crosstabs. We have used this procedure to make comparisons with nominal- or ordinal-level dependent variables, so it should look familiar (see Figure 4-1 for additional reference). The dependent variable, domestic_spying, should define the rows and the independent variable should be moved into the Column(s) field. To test the differences of proportions, click the Cells button and select the "Compare column proportions" option in the z-test section of the Cell Display dialog (see Figure 6-9). Click Continue and OK.

Support Domestic Spying? * Race of Respondent Crosstabulation

% within Race of Respondent

		Race of Respondent			
		WHITE	BLACK	OTHER	Total
Support domestic spying?	Oppose	51.0%a, b	44.7%b	58.3%a	50.8%
	Support	49.0%a, b	55.3%b	41.7%a	49.2%
Total		100.0%	100.0%	100.0%	100.0%

Each subscript letter denotes a subset of Race Of Respondent categories whose column proportions do not differ significantly from each other at the .05 level.

The cross-tabulation of opinions about domestic spying and respondents' race should look familiar, except for the "a" and "b" subscripts on the column percentages. As SPSS rather cryptically notes, each letter identifies subsets of independent variable categories that do not differ significantly at the .05 level. Thus, groups with the "a" subscript do not differ from one another:

---

[11] The difference in the lower boundary we calculated using the formula is due to rounding error.

[12] The one-sample t-test can also be adapted to test the observed proportion of support for domestic spying against the hypothesized value .5, as we did to test the mean carbon_footprint of countries in the world against the hypothesized value 2 (see Figure 6-5).

FIGURE 6-9   Testing Differences of Proportions across Groups

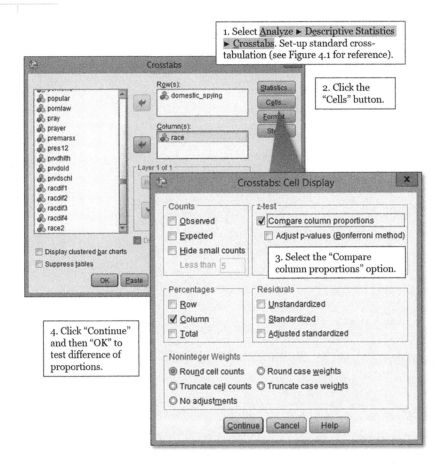

whites and other races/ethnicities do not have significantly different opinions on domestic spying. Likewise, groups with the "b" subscript do not differ from one another: whites and blacks do not have significantly different opinions on domestic spying. According to these results, blacks and other races/ethnicities do have significantly different opinions about domestic spying; support for domestic spying is higher among blacks (0.553) than it is among other races (0.417). While the SPSS procedure for testing differences of proportions across values of an independent variable is limited to detecting differences at the .05 level, it offers a convenient way of comparing several groups at once (rather than making a series of pairwise comparisons).

Name: _____   Date: _____

E-mail: _____   Section: _____

CHAPTER 6 EXERCISES

1. (Dataset: NES. Variables: spend8, nesw.) The NES dataset contains spend8, which records the number of government policy areas where respondents think spending should be increased. Scores range from 0 (the respondent does not want to increase spending on any of the policies) to 8 (the respondent wants to increase spending on all eight policies). The NES, of course, polls a random sample of U.S. adults. In this exercise you will analyze spend8 using the Analyze ▶ Compare Means ▶ One-Sample T Test procedure. You then will draw inferences about the population mean. Make sure you weight observations using the nesw variable so your results are nationally representative.

A. The spend8 variable has a sample mean of _____.

B. There is a probability of .95 that spend8's true population mean falls between a score of _____ at the low end and a score of _____ at the high end.

C. A researcher hypothesizes that political science majors will score significantly higher on spend8 than the typical adult. The researcher also hypothesizes that business majors will score significantly lower on spend8 than the average adult. Using the same questions asked in the NES, the researcher obtains scores on spend8 from a group of political science majors and a group of business majors. Here are the results: political science majors' mean, 4.53; business majors' mean, 4.05.

Using the confidence interval approach, you can infer that (check one)

❑ political science majors do not score significantly higher on spend8 than U.S. adults.

❑ political science majors score significantly higher on spend8 than U.S. adults.

Using the confidence interval approach, you can infer that (check one)

❑ business majors do not score significantly lower on spend8 than U.S. adults.

❑ business majors score significantly lower on spend8 than U.S. adults.

D. Use the Analyze ▶ Compare Means ▶ One-Sample T Test procedure to evaluate the difference between the NES spend8 mean and the business majors' mean. (For the purposes of this question, treat the business majors' mean, 4.05, as a hypothesized value for a one-sample test.) The mean difference is equal to _____. The t-ratio of the mean difference is equal to _____. The P-value is equal to _____.

E. Interpret the P-value you recorded in part D. Suppose someone hypothesized that the business majors' mean was drawn from the same population that produced the NES spend8 mean. Applying the .05 rule, you would (circle one)

reject   not reject

this claim because (fill in the blank) _____

_____

_____

2. (Dataset: NES. Variables: spend8, sex, nesw.) In discussing the gender gap, two scholars of public opinion observe that there are gender differences "on issues relating to jobs, education, income redistribution, and protection of the vulnerable in society."[13] In this exercise, you will analyze values of spend8 to test this idea. Recall that spend8 ranges from 0 (the respondent does not want to increase spending on any of eight government programs) to 8 (the respondent wants to increase spending on all eight programs). The NES dataset also contains the variable Female, with categories "Male" and "Female." Now, consider the following hypothesis: In a comparison of individuals, women will score significantly higher on spend8 than will men.

A. The null hypothesis for the relationship between Female and spend8 is as follows (fill in the blanks): In the population from which the sample is drawn, the difference between the mean value of spend8 for men and the mean value of spend8 for women is equal to _____. Any difference observed in the sample was produced by _____ when the sample was drawn.

_____

[13] Robert S. Erikson and Kent L. Tedin, *American Public Opinion: Its Origins, Content, and Impact*, 7th ed. (New York: Pearson Longman, 2005), 209.

B. Apply the Analyze ▶ Compare Means ▶ Independent-Samples T Test procedure to spend8 with Female as the grouping variable. Make sure you use sample weights so your results are nationally representative. Fill in the blanks:

Male mean: _____

Female mean: _____ .

Difference of means: _____

t-ratio: _____

P-value: _____

C. Which two of the following statements are supported by your findings? (check two)

❏ In the population, women probably do not score higher on spend8 than do men.

❏ The statistical evidence supports the alternative hypothesis.

❏ If the null hypothesis is correct, a random sample would produce the observed mean difference more than 5 percent of the time, by chance.

❏ Reject the null hypothesis.

3. (Dataset: GSS. Variables: authoritarianism, sibs, sex, relig, wtss.) Here are two bits of conventional wisdom, beliefs that are widely accepted as accurate descriptions of the world.

Conventional Wisdom 1: Catholics have bigger families than do Protestants.

Conventional Wisdom 2: Men have stronger authoritarian tendencies than do women.

In this exercise you will test these ideas and see how well they stand up to the statistical evidence.

A. Test Conventional Wisdom 1 by using the Analyze ▶ Compare Means ▶ Independent-Samples T Test procedure to compare the average number of siblings (GSS variable sibs) for Protestants and Catholics (relig). According to the GSS data, _____ is the mean number of siblings for Protestants and _____ is the mean number of siblings for Catholics. Make sure you use sample weights so your results are nationally representative.

The difference between the mean number siblings for Protestants and the mean number siblings for Catholics is _____. The t-ratio for this observed difference is _____, which has a corresponding P-value of _____.

Is Conventional Wisdom 1 supported by the data? (circle one)

Yes   No

B. Test Conventional Wisdom 2 by using the Analyze ▶ Compare Means ▶ Independent-Samples T Test procedure to compare mean authoritarianism scale scores (authoritarianism) for males and females (sex). The authoritarianism scale ranges from 0 (low authoritarianism) to 7 (high authoritarianism).

According to the GSS data, the mean authoritarianism scale score for males is _____ and the mean authoritarianism scale score for females is _____. Make sure you use sample weights so your results are nationally representative.

The difference between the mean authoritarianism scale score for males and the mean authoritarianism scale score for females is _____. The t-ratio for this observed difference is _____, which has a corresponding P-value of _____.

Is Conventional Wisdom 2 supported by the data? (circle one)

Yes   No

4. (Dataset: GSS. Variables: cappun, sex, wtss.) The GSS dataset includes the variable cappun, which gave respondents an opportunity to express whether they "favor" or "oppose" the death penalty for murder.

A. The sample proportion of Americans who favor the death penalty for murder is _____. Make sure you weight observations with the wtss variable so your results are nationally representative.

B. Use the following standard error of proportion formula to find the standard error for the estimated sample proportion of Americans who favor the death penalty for murder.

$$SE_{proportion} = \sqrt{\frac{(proportion) \times (1 - proportion)}{N}}$$

The standard error is _____.

C. There is a probability of .95 that the true proportion of Americans who favor capital punishment for murder falls between _____ at the low end and _____ at the high end.

D. Suppose someone hypothesized that the country is evenly divided on the use of capital punishment and that the sample proportion was drawn from a population with a .5 proportion in favor of the death penalty for murder. Based on the 95% confidence interval you identified in part C, you would (circle one)

reject   not reject

this claim because (fill in the blank) _____

_____

_____

E. Let's compare the proportions of males and females who favor the death penalty for murder. Use the Analyze ▶ Compare Means ▶ Independent-Samples T Test procedure to evaluate the difference of proportions between men and women.[14] The difference of proportions between males and females is _____ (observed difference).

F. The standard error of the difference of proportions is _____. This represents the amount of difference between men and women that could be attributed to random error rather than any systematic difference between the two groups. The test statistic (*t*-statistic) is _____ and its *P*-value is _____.

G. Suppose someone hypothesized that there is no difference between men and women in support for capital punishment. Based on the results of the test you performed and reported in parts E and F, you would (circle one)

               reject   not reject

this claim because (fill in the blank) _____

_____

_____

That concludes the exercises for this chapter.

---

[14] As noted in the text, we should be calculating the *z*-score rather than *t*-ratio, but given the large sample size, the substantive analysis is not affected.

7

Chi-square and Measures of Association

 Watch screencasts of the guided examples in this chapter. **edge.sagepub.com/pollock**

Procedures Covered

Analyze ▶ Descriptive Statistics ▶ Crosstabs (with Chi-Square statistic)

I n the preceding chapter you learned how to test for mean differences on an interval-level dependent variable. But what if you are not analyzing interval-level variables? What if you are doing cross-tabulation analysis and are trying to figure out whether an observed relationship between two nominal or ordinal variables mirrors the true relationship in the population? Just as with mean differences, the answer depends on the boundaries of random sampling error, the extent to which your observed results "happened by chance" when you took the sample. The Crosstabs procedure can provide the information needed to test the statistical significance of nominal or ordinal relationships, and it will yield appropriate measures of association.

You are familiar with the Crosstabs procedure. For analyzing datasets that contain a preponderance of categorical variables—variables measured by nominal or ordinal categories—cross-tabulation is by far the most common mode of analysis in political research. In this section we will revisit Crosstabs and use the Statistics subroutine to obtain the oldest and most widely applied test of statistical significance in cross-tabulation analysis, the chi-square test. With rare exceptions, chi-square can always be used to determine whether an observed cross-tabulation relationship departs significantly from the expectations of the null hypothesis. In the first guided example, you will be introduced to the logic behind chi-square, and you will learn how to interpret SPSS's chi-square output.

In this chapter you will also learn how to obtain measures of association for the relationships you are analyzing. If both are ordinal-level variables, then Somers' *d* is the appropriate measure of association. Somers' *d* is an *asymmetrical* measure. It reports different measures of the strength of a relationship, depending on whether the independent variable is used to predict the dependent variable or the dependent variable is used to predict the independent variable. Asymmetrical measures of association generally are preferred over *symmetrical* measures, which yield the same value, regardless of whether the independent variable is used to predict the dependent variable or the dependent variable is used to predict the independent variable.[1]

---

[1] Asymmetry is the essence of hypothetical relationships. Thus, one would hypothesize that income causes opinions on welfare policies, but one would not hypothesize that welfare opinions cause income. We would prefer a measure of association that tells us how well income (independent variable) predicts welfare opinions (dependent variable), not how well welfare opinions predict income. Or, to cite Warner's tongue-in-cheek example: "There are some situations where the ability to make predictions is asymmetrical; for example, consider a study about gender and pregnancy. If you know that an individual is pregnant, you can predict gender (the person must be female) perfectly. However, it you know that an individual is female, you cannot assume that she is pregnant." Rebecca M. Warner, *Applied Statistics* (Los Angeles: SAGE, 2008), 316.

Somers' *d* is a proportional reduction in error (PRE) measure of the strength of a relationship. A PRE measure tells you the extent to which the values of the independent variable predict the values of the dependent variable. A value close to 0 says that the independent variable provides little predictive leverage; the relationship is weak. Values close to the poles—to −1 for negative associations or to +1 for positive relationships—tell you that the independent variable provides a lot of help in predicting the dependent variable; the relationship is strong.[2]

For measuring the strength of nominal-level relationships, the choices are more limited. A nominal-level PRE measure, lambda, is sometimes used. Granted, PRE measures are generally preferred over measures that do not permit a PRE interpretation. Even so, lambda frequently underestimates the strength of relationships, a problem that is especially acute when one of the variables has low variation. Therefore, when you are analyzing a relationship in which one or both of the variables are nominal, you will request Cramer's *V*. Cramer's *V*, one of a variety of chi-square–based measures, does not measure strength by the PRE criterion. However, it is bounded by 0 (no relationship) and 1 (a perfect relationship). Cramer's *V* is particularly useful in evaluating controlled comparisons.

ANALYZING AN ORDINAL-LEVEL RELATIONSHIP

Analyzing an
Ordinal-Level
Relationship

We will begin by using the NES dataset, NES.sav, to analyze the relationship between two ordinal-level variables. Consider this hypothesis: In a comparison of individuals, those having higher levels of education will have less support for using force to solve international problems.

The NES dataset includes a variable named intl_force, an ordinal-level variable that measures the extent to which respondents support the use of military force to solve international problems. Responses are classified into five possible categories: extremely willing, very willing, moderately willing, a little willing, and not at all willing. This is the dependent variable. The NES variable educ4 is the independent variable. This ordinal-level variable has four different values: high school or less ("HS or less"), some college or an associate's degree ("SmColl/Assoc"), college degree ("BA"), or higher ("Grad").

First, we will compare support for using force across different categories of education by generating a cross-tabulation and comparing column percentages. This is the same type of analysis you conducted in Chapter 4 to make comparisons. For nationally representative results, we'll want to use survey weights. To generate this cross-tabulation and compare column percentages, select Analyze ▶ Descriptive Statistics ▶ Crosstabs. Remember to put the dependent variable, intl_force, on the rows and the independent variable, educ4, on the columns. Request column percentages. Run the analysis and consider the output.

Initial inspection of the cross-tabulation results appears to support the hypothesis that higher levels of education are correlated with reduced support for the use of force to solve international problems. Read across the first two rows. As education levels increase, the percentage of respondents extremely willing to use force tends to decrease: 6.7 percent, 4.0 percent, 2.2 percent, 3.6 percent. The percentage of respondents who state that they're very willing to use force to solve problems also decreases: 12.7 percent, 12.6 percent, 11.4 percent, 8.0 percent.

---

[2] Somers' *d* may be used for square tables (in which the independent and dependent variables have the same number of categories) and for non-square tables (in which the independent and dependent variables have different numbers of categories). Because of its other attractive properties, some methodologists prefer Somers' *d* to other measures, such as Gamma, Kendall's tau-b, or Kendall's tau-c. See George W. Bohrnstedt and David Knoke, *Statistics for Social Data Analysis*, 2nd ed. (Itasca, Ill.: Peacock Publishers, 1988), 325.

Willing to Use Force to Solve International Problems (v161154) *
Education (v161270 collapsed) Crosstabulation

			Education (v161270 collapsed)				
			HS or less	SmColl/Assoc	BA	Grad	Total
Willing to use force to solve international problems (v161154)	1. Extremely willing	Count	91	43	15	17	166
		% within Education (v161270 collapsed)	6.7%	4.0%	2.2%	3.6%	4.6%
	2. Very willing	Count	173	136	77	38	424
		% within Education (v161270 collapsed)	12.7%	12.6%	11.4%	8.0%	11.8%
	3. Moderately willing	Count	698	587	369	227	1881
		% within Education (v161270 collapsed)	51.1%	54.2%	54.6%	48.0%	52.3%
	4. A little willing	Count	297	252	186	166	901
		% within Education (v161270 collapsed)	21.8%	23.3%	27.5%	35.1%	25.0%
	5. Not at all willing	Count	106	65	29	25	225
		% within Education (v161270 collapsed)	7.8%	6.0%	4.3%	5.3%	6.3%
Total		Count	1365	1083	676	473	3597
		% within Education (v161270 collapsed)	100.0%	100.0%	100.0%	100.0%	100.0%

The hypothesis is off to a good start, but we should consider the possibility that the apparent relationship could result from random chance rather than a real relationship between these variables. Indeed, two political analysts might offer conflicting interpretations of these results. The first analyst might conclude that, yes, as education increases, support for using force to solve international problems decreases and support for diplomatic solutions increases. The other might declare the relationship too weak to support the hypothesis. Inferential statistics, of course, are designed to settle such arguments.

Let's evaluate the intl_force and educ4 cross-tabulation employing the chi-square test of statistical significance. The chi-square test compares frequencies we would expect to see in each cell when there is no relationship between the variables to the frequencies we observe in these cells to test whether the observed differences are likely to result from random variation. In the cross-tabulation above, you can see the frequencies observed in each cell. If the observed differences are relatively minor, one fails to reject the null hypothesis. If the observed differences are large, one rejects the null hypothesis.

Chi-square begins by looking at row totals, which report the overall distribution of support for the use of force. Reading down the "Total" column, we see that 4.6 percent of all respondents are extremely willing to use force, 11.8 percent are very willing, 52.3 percent are moderately willing, 25.0 percent are a little willing, and 6.3 percent are not at all willing. If the null hypothesis is correct, respondents' education level is not related to their support for the use of force, then a random sample of 1,365 people with high school education or less would produce the same distribution of opinions as the total distribution: 4.6 percent extremely, 11.8 percent very, 52.3 percent moderately, 25.0 percent a little, and 6.3 percent not at all willing to use force. By the same token, a random sample of 1,083 people with some college education or an associate's degree would yield a distribution that looks just like the total distribution; so would a random sample of 676 individuals with college degrees, or a random sample of 473 respondents with graduate education. Thus, if the null hypothesis is correct, then the distribution of cases down each column of the table will be the same as the distribution in the "Total" column. Of course, the null hypothesis asserts that any departures from these expected values are the result of random sampling error.

FIGURE 7-1   Chi-squared Test of the Relationship between Ordinal Variables

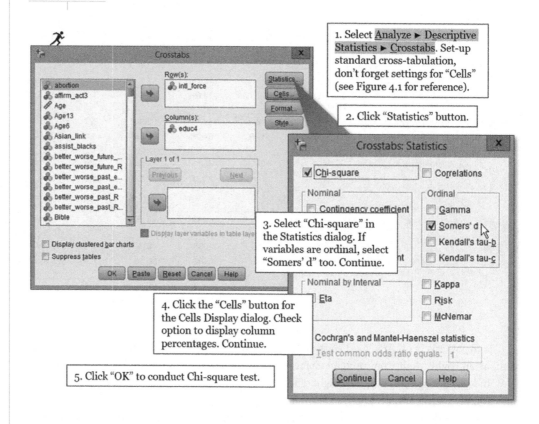

1. Select Analyze ► Descriptive Statistics ► Crosstabs. Set-up standard cross-tabulation, don't forget settings for "Cells" (see Figure 4.1 for reference).

2. Click "Statistics" button.

3. Select "Chi-square" in the Statistics dialog. If variables are ordinal, select "Somers' d" too. Continue.

4. Click the "Cells" button for the Cells Display dialog. Check option to display column percentages. Continue.

5. Click "OK" to conduct Chi-square test.

Now that we've seen the basic cross-tabulation and understand the intuition behind the chi-squared test, let's run the cross-tabulation procedure again, this time requesting additional inferential statistics. We will also obtain a measure of association for the relationship. Return to the Crosstabs window. Click Statistics. The Crosstabs: Statistics window pops up (Figure 7-1). There are many choices here, but we know what we want: We would like SPSS to perform a chi-square test on the table. Check the Chi-square box. We also know which measure of association to request. Because both intl_force and educ4 are ordinal-level variables, we will request Somers' *d*. Check the box next to "Somers' *d*." Click Continue, and then click OK.

SPSS runs the cross-tabulation analysis again, and this time it has produced two additional tables of statistics: Chi-Square Tests and Directional Measures. Given the parsimony of our requests, SPSS has been rather generous in its statistical output.

In the Chi-Square Tests table, focus exclusively on the row labeled "Pearson Chi-Square." The first column, labeled "Value," provides the chi-square test statistic. SPSS calculates this test statistic based on the magnitude of differences between the cell counts expected when the null hypothesis is true and the cell counts observed in the sample data. In general, the larger the test statistic, the less likely that the observed data can be explained by random sampling error. The smaller the test statistic, the more likely that the null's favorite process—random chance—accounts for the observed data. So, if the observed data perfectly fit the expectations of the null hypothesis, then the chi-square test statistic would be 0. As the observed data depart from the null's expectations, the test statistic increases, allowing the researcher to begin entertaining the idea of rejecting the null hypothesis.

For the intl_force and educ4 cross-tabulation, SPSS calculated a chi-square test statistic equal to 71.504. Is this number statistically different from 0, the value we would expect to obtain if the null

Chi-Square Tests

	Value	df	Asymptotic Significance (2-sided)
Pearson Chi-Square	71.504[a]	12	.000
Likelihood Ratio	71.187	12	.000
Linear-by-Linear Association	17.185	1	.000
N of Valid Cases	3597		

a. 0 cells (0.0%) have expected count less than 5. The minimum expected count is 21.83.

Directional Measures

		Value	Asymptotic Standard Error[a]	Approximate T[b]	Approximate Significance
Ordinal by Ordinal	Somers' d Symmetric	.061	.014	4.221	.000
	Willing to use force to solve international problems (v161154) Dependent	.058	.014	4.221	.000
	Education (v161270 collapsed) Dependent	.064	.015	4.221	.000

a. Not assuming the null hypothesis.

b. Using the asymptotic standard error assuming the null hypothesis.

hypothesis were true? Put another way: If the null hypothesis is correct, how often will we obtain a test statistic of 71.504 by chance? The answer is contained in the rightmost column of the Chi-Square Tests table, under the label "Asymp. Sig. (2-sided)." For the chi-square test of significance, this value is the *P*-value. In our example SPSS reports a *P*-value of .000. (The *P*-value is never 0 so better to report it as <.001.) If the null hypothesis is correct in its assertion that no relationship exists between the independent and dependent variables, then we will obtain a test statistic of 71.504, by chance, less than 1 time out of 1,000. Because <.001 is less than the .05 standard, we should reject the null hypothesis. From our initial comparison of percentages, we suspected that a relationship might exist between these two ordinal variables. The chi-square test supports that suspicion. Reject the null hypothesis.

Turn your attention to the Directional Measures table, which reports the requested measure of Somers' *d*. In fact, three Somers' *d* statistics are displayed. Because SPSS doesn't know how we framed the hypothesis, it provided values of Somers' *d* for every scenario: symmetric (no hypothetical expectations about the relationship), intl_force dependent (intl_force is the dependent variable and educ4 is the independent variable), and educ4 dependent (educ4 is the dependent variable and intl_force is the independent variable). Always use the dependent variable in your hypothesis to choose the correct value of Somers' *d*. Because intl_force is our dependent variable, we would report the Somers' *d* value, .058.

What does this value, .058, tell us about the relationship? If increasing codes of the independent variable are associated with increasing codes of the dependent variable, then Somers' *d* is a positive number. Here, increasing codes of the independent variable—from lower to higher levels of education—are associated with increasing codes of the dependent variable—from extremely willing to use force to not at all willing to use force. By being alert to how the variables are coded, you will know which sign is implied by your hypothesis, a positive sign or a negative sign.

What does the magnitude of Somers' *d*, .058, tell us about our ability to predict values of the dependent variable based on knowledge of the independent variable? Somers' *d* is a PRE measure of association. It tells us this: Compared with how well we can predict individuals' opinions about use of force without knowing their levels of education, knowledge of their education level improves our prediction by 6 percent.

A CLOSER LOOK: REPORTING AND INTERPRETING RESULTS

SPSS reports a chi-square test statistic, labeled "Pearson Chi-Square." This test statistic is calculated from the observed tabular data. Values close to 0 are within the domain of the null hypothesis. As chi-square increases in magnitude (the chi-square statistic cannot assume negative values), H_0's explanation for the observed data—"it all happened by chance"—becomes increasingly implausible.

The chi-square statistic is accompanied by a *P*-value, which appears beneath the label "Asymp. Sig. (2-sided)." Here is a template for writing an interpretation of the *P*-value:

If the null hypothesis is correct that, in the population from which the sample was drawn, there is no relationship between [independent variable] and [dependent variable], then random sampling error will produce the observed data [*P*-value] of the time.

Here's our example:

If the null hypothesis is correct that there is no relationship between education and attitudes about use of force, then random sampling error will produce the observed data less than 0.001 of the time.[3]

Use the .05 benchmark. If the *P*-value is less than or equal to .05, then reject the null hypothesis. If the *P*-value is greater than .05, accept the null hypothesis. If you find our template for interpreting results too rigid, don't get too caught up on using exact wording; focus on conveying the essential results in clear terms that you understand.

For ordinal-by-ordinal relationships, request Somers' *d*. Somers' *d* is a directional measure, ranging from –1 to +1. Somers' *d* has a PRE interpretation. Here is a template for writing an interpretation of Somers' *d* or, for that matter, any PRE measure:

Compared to how well we can predict [dependent variable] without knowing [independent variable], we can improve our prediction by [value of PRE measure] by knowing [independent variable].

Here's our example:

Compared to how well we can predict attitudes about use of force to solve international problems without knowing respondents' levels of education, we can improve our prediction by .058 by knowing respondents' education levels.[4]

Note that a negative sign on a PRE measure imparts the direction of the relationship, but it does not affect the PRE interpretation.

---

[3] Percentages may sound better here and our interpretation of the *P*-value could be written as ". . . will produce the observed data less than 0.1 percent of the time."

[4] We could also substitute a percentage here by saying ". . . we can improve our prediction by 5.8 percent by knowing respondents' education levels."

ANALYZING AN ORDINAL-LEVEL RELATIONSHIP WITH A CONTROL VARIABLE

In the preceding section we analyzed the relationship between individual opinions about the use of force to solve international problems and education levels. Based on a cross-tabulation and chi-squared test, we concluded that the data show a statistically significant relationship.

A sceptic might ask, having read Chapter 5 of this book, whether some variable other than education, like individual ideology, might explain different attitudes toward the use of force. We might want to analyze the relationship between opinions about the use of force and education levels controlling for individuals' partisan identification. The control variable is libcon3: liberal ("Lib," 1), moderate ("Mod," 2), and conservative ("Cons," 3). The dependent and independent variables remain intl_force and educ4.

For this analysis, we want SPSS to produce three ordinal-by-ordinal cross-tabulations—a cross-tabulation showing the intl_force–educ4 relationship for each value of libcon3. By this point in the book, cross-tabulation analysis has become routine. Return to the Crosstabs window. If you're starting with a reset window, move the intl_force variable into the Row(s) field and educ4 into the Column(s) field. Because libcon3 will be the control variable, move it into the "Layer 1 of 1" field (see Figure 7-2). The other necessary choices—column percentages in Cells, Chi-square, and Somers' *d* in Statistics—should still be in place from the previous analysis; if not, request them by clicking the Statistics and Cells buttons. Click OK.

SPSS outputs three cross-tabulations. One cross-tabulation reports the intl_force–educ4 relationship among individuals who identify as liberals; another reports the relationship among those who identify as moderates; finally, one reports the relationship among conservatives.

Within each category of political ideology, education plays a significant role in attitudes about use of force. Among liberals, the top cross-tabulation (with "Lib" in the far-left column), the chi-squared test statistic for the relationship between education and willingness to use force is 26.78, which corresponds to a *P*-value of .008. Among moderates, the chi-squared statistic equals 23.89,

FIGURE 7-2   Chi-squared Test with a Control Variable

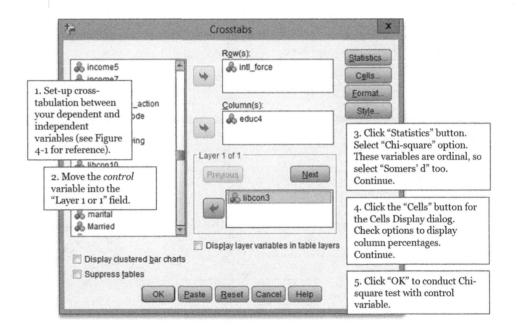

which has a *P*-value of .021. For conservatives, the relevant test statistic is 46.54, which has a *P*-value less than .001. Given these inferential statistics, it is extremely unlikely that the observed patterns were produced by random sampling error. The chi-square statistics invite us to reject the null hypothesis.

How strong is the relationship between education and willingness to use force for each ideological group? Refer to the Directional Measures table. Somers' *d* will provide a precise PRE measure of the strength of the intl_force–educ4 relationship at each value of libcon3. Remember, intl_force is the dependent variable in this analysis, so we'll focus on the direction measures where willingness

Willing to Use Force to Solve International Problems (v161154) * Education (v161270 collapsed) * Ideological Self-placement (v161126) Crosstabulation

	Ideological self-placement (v161126)		HS or less	SmColl/Assoc	BA	Grad
Lib	Willing to use force to solve international problems (v161154)	1. Extremely willing	8 / 2.3%	11 / 3.5%	3 / 1.3%	5 / 2.1%
		2. Very willing	51 / 14.5%	29 / 9.1%	19 / 7.9%	8 / 3.4%
		3. Moderately willing	151 / 42.9%	141 / 44.3%	112 / 46.9%	109 / 46.4%
		4. A little willing	121 / 34.4%	113 / 35.5%	89 / 37.2%	100 / 42.6%
		5. Not at all willing	21 / 6.0%	24 / 7.5%	16 / 6.7%	13 / 5.5%
	Total		352 / 100.0%	318 / 100.0%	239 / 100.0%	235 / 100.0%
Mod	Willing to use force to solve international problems (v161154)	1. Extremely willing	24 / 6.1%	10 / 3.8%	3 / 2.6%	1 / 1.4%
		2. Very willing	33 / 8.4%	22 / 8.3%	12 / 10.3%	3 / 4.1%
		3. Moderately willing	231 / 58.8%	154 / 58.1%	64 / 54.7%	37 / 50.0%
		4. A little willing	73 / 18.6%	58 / 21.9%	34 / 29.1%	28 / 37.8%
		5. Not at all willing	32 / 8.1%	21 / 7.9%	4 / 3.4%	5 / 6.8%
	Total		393 / 100.0%	265 / 100.0%	117 / 100.0%	74 / 100.0%
Cons	Willing to use force to solve international problems (v161154)	1. Extremely willing	58 / 9.8%	22 / 4.6%	9 / 2.8%	10 / 6.1%
		2. Very willing	84 / 14.3%	83 / 17.4%	46 / 14.6%	27 / 16.6%
		3. Moderately willing	305 / 51.8%	277 / 58.2%	190 / 60.1%	81 / 49.7%
		4. A little willing	94 / 16.0%	76 / 16.0%	63 / 19.9%	37 / 22.7%
		5. Not at all willing	48 / 8.1%	18 / 3.8%	8 / 2.5%	8 / 4.9%
	Total		589 / 100.0%	476 / 100.0%	316 / 100.0%	163 / 100.0%
Total	Willing to use force to solve international problems (v161154)	1. Extremely willing	90 / 6.7%	43 / 4.1%	15 / 2.2%	16 / 3.4%
		2. Very willing	168 / 12.6%	134 / 12.7%	77 / 11.5%	38 / 8.1%
		3. Moderately willing	687 / 51.5%	572 / 54.0%	366 / 54.5%	227 / 48.1%
		4. A little willing	288 / 21.6%	247 / 23.3%	186 / 27.7%	165 / 35.0%
		5. Not at all willing	101 / 7.6%	63 / 5.9%	28 / 4.2%	26 / 5.5%
	Total		1334 / 100.0%	1059 / 100.0%	672 / 100.0%	472 / 100.0%

Note: Table output edited to save space.

Chi-Square Tests

Ideological self-placement (v161126)		Value	df	Asymptotic Significance (2-sided)
Lib	Pearson Chi-Square	26.775[b]	12	.008
	Likelihood Ratio	28.230	12	.005
	Linear-by-Linear Association	7.932	1	.005
	N of Valid Cases	1144		
Mod	Pearson Chi-Square	23.893[c]	12	.021
	Likelihood Ratio	24.182	12	.019
	Linear-by-Linear Association	6.129	1	.013
	N of Valid Cases	849		
Cons	Pearson Chi-Square	46.536[d]	12	.000
	Likelihood Ratio	46.758	12	.000
	Linear-by-Linear Association	1.109	1	.292
	N of Valid Cases	1544		
Total	Pearson Chi-Square	70.572[a]	12	.000
	Likelihood Ratio	70.415	12	.000
	Linear-by-Linear Association	19.382	1	.000
	N of Valid Cases	3537		

a. 0 cells (0.0%) have expected count less than 5. The minimum expected count is 21.89.

b. 0 cells (0.0%) have expected count less than 5. The minimum expected count is 5.55.

c. 1 cells (5.0%) have expected count less than 5. The minimum expected count is 3.31.

d. 0 cells (0.0%) have expected count less than 5. The minimum expected count is 8.66.

to use force is the dependent variable. Note first that all the Somers' d statistics are positive numbers. At each education level, as the coded values of libcon3 increase from "Lib" to "Cons," intl_force numeric codes increase from 1 ("Extremely willing to use force") to 5 ("Not all at willing to use force"). Thus, the Somers' d statistics are consistent with the hypothesis that individuals with more education are less supportive of the use of force.

Now focus on the Somers' d magnitudes. Somers' d has a magnitude (absolute value) of .066 for the liberal group, .073 for the moderate group, and .022 for the conservative group. This tells us that the relationship between education and willingness to use force is strongest among moderates and weakest (although still significant) among conservatives. Plus, because Somers' d is a PRE measure, we can give a specific answer to the "how strong?" question. For liberal respondents we would say that, compared to how well we can predict their opinions on use of force without knowing their education level, we can improve our prediction by 6.6 percent by knowing their education level. The predictive leverage of the independent variable strengthens to 7.3 percent for the moderate group and decreases to 2.2 percent for those who identify themselves as conservatives.

Before we close the NES dataset, let's create a graphic that depicts the controlled cross-tabulation we have been discussing. In Chapter 5, we showed you how to create a multiple line chart to visualize a controlled cross-tabulation between variables measured at the interval level. We'll follow that procedure here. See Figure 7-3. Select Graphs ▶ Legacy Dialogs ▶ Line, click the Multiple icon, make sure "Summaries for groups of cases" is selected, and click the Define button. In the Define Multiple Line window, follow the standard procedure: move educ4 into the Category Axis field,

Directional Measures

Ideological self-placement (v161126)				Value	Asymptotic Standard Error[a]	Approximate T[b]	Approximate Significance
Lib	Ordinal by Ordinal	Somers' d	Symmetric	.070	.025	2.824	.005
			Willing to use force to solve international problems (v161154) Dependent	.066	.023	2.824	.005
			Education (v161270 collapsed) Dependent	.075	.027	2.824	.005
Mod	Ordinal by Ordinal	Somers' d	Symmetric	.076	.030	2.544	.011
			Willing to use force to solve international problems (v161154) Dependent	.073	.028	2.544	.011
			Education (v161270 collapsed) Dependent	.079	.031	2.544	.011
Cons	Ordinal by Ordinal	Somers' d	Symmetric	.024	.023	1.036	.300
			Willing to use force to solve international problems (v161154) Dependent	.022	.022	1.036	.300
			Education (v161270 collapsed) Dependent	.025	.024	1.036	.300
Total	Ordinal by Ordinal	Somers' d	Symmetric	.065	.015	4.446	.000
			Willing to use force to solve international problems (v161154) Dependent	.061	.014	4.446	.000
			Education (v161270 collapsed) Dependent	.068	.015	4.446	.000

a. Not assuming the null hypothesis.

b. Using the asymptotic standard error assuming the null hypothesis.

libcon3 into the "Define Lines by" field, click the "Lines Represent: Other statistic" option, move intl_force into the Variable field, and click the Change Statistic button.

We want the lines to represent the percentage of respondents opposed to the use of force to solve international problems. Recall that the variable intl_force uses numbers coded 1 to 5, with numbers 4 and 5 corresponding to little or no support for use of force to solve international problems. To communicate the essential features of the relationship, we'll define the y-axis statistic as the percentage of respondents with numeric codes over 3 on the intl_force variable. With these settings in place, click OK.

Figure 7-4 could use some refinement (we encourage you to experiment with the Chart Editor), but it helps us visualize the controlled cross-tabulations discussed above. For each ideological group, higher levels of education tend to increase opposition to the use of force to solve international problems, but it appears that political ideology also affects willingness to use force.

FIGURE 7-3   Creating a Multiple Line Chart for an Ordinal-level Relationship with a Control Variable

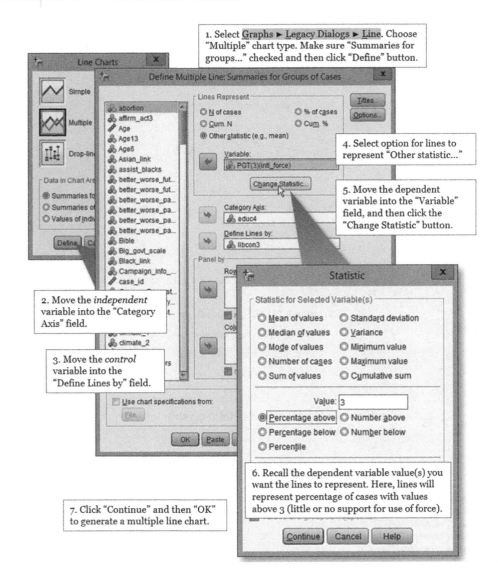

Do you notice that the line plotting the relationship for conservatives between education and willingness to use force isn't quite straight? Here, we can see why our measure of association, Somers' *d*, was highest for the moderate group (.073), lower for liberals (.066), and lowest for conservatives (.022).

ANALYZING A NOMINAL-LEVEL RELATIONSHIP

The variables analyzed in this chapter thus far have been ordinal level. Many social and political characteristics, however, are measured by nominal categories—gender, race, region, or religious denomination, to name a few. In this section, we'll analyze the relationship between a dependent variable and a nominal-level independent variable using a cross-tabulation, the chi-squared test, and Cramer's *V*.

Screencast

Analyzing a Nominal-level Relationship

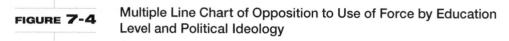

FIGURE **7-4**   Multiple Line Chart of Opposition to Use of Force by Education Level and Political Ideology

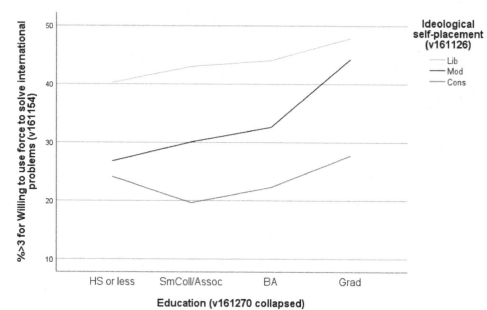

FIGURE **7-5**   Analyzing a Nominal-level Relationship with Chi-squared and Cramer's *V*

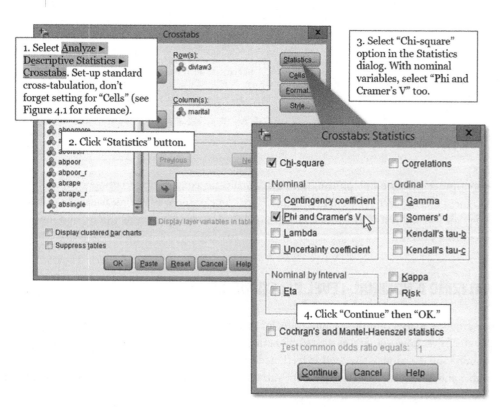

As a motivating example, we'll examine individual opinions about divorce laws. State laws regulating family life are politically controversial and affect many people. It stands to reason that someone's opinion about how difficult it should be to obtain a divorce depends on his or her marital status.

The GSS dataset, GSS.sav, contains a variable named marital, which records respondents' marital status. Marital status is a classic nominal-level variable with multiple values: married, widowed, divorced, separated, and never married. These values can't be ranked in order; they're just different marital statuses. A GSS variable named divlaw, the dependent variable in this analysis, records whether respondents think divorce should be made "Easier," "More difficult," or "Stay the same." To make our results easier to interpret, let's also recode the divlaw variable as divlaw3 so the intermediate "Stay the same" response comes between "Easier" and "More difficult."[5]

We'll begin our analysis with a cross-tabulation of marital–divlaw3. The familiar rules for organizing a cross-tabulation apply: values of the dependent variable divlaw3 define the rows and values of the independent variable marital define the columns. Let's go ahead and use the Statistics and Cells buttons to specify that we want column percentages, the chi-squared statistic, and a measure of association that's used with nominal-level relationships: Cramer's V (see Figure 7-5).

Opinion about Divorce Laws * Marital Status Crosstabulation

| | | | Marital Status | | | | | |
			MARRIED	WIDOWED	DIVORCED	SEPARATED	NEVER MARRIED	Total
Opinion about Divorce Laws	Easier	Count	264	41	116	44	242	707
		% within Marital Status	30.7%	36.6%	47.3%	71.0%	47.3%	39.5%
	Stay the same	Count	199	18	61	6	98	382
		% within Marital Status	23.1%	16.1%	24.9%	9.7%	19.1%	21.3%
	More difficult	Count	398	53	68	12	172	703
		% within Marital Status	46.2%	47.3%	27.8%	19.4%	33.6%	39.2%
Total		Count	861	112	245	62	512	1792
		% within Marital Status	100.0%	100.0%	100.0%	100.0%	100.0%	100.0%

Reading the cross-tabulation results, we find support for the hypothesis that marital status affects opinions about divorce laws. Consider the first row, the percentage of respondents who think it should be easier to get a divorce: 47.3 percent of divorced and never-married respondents and 71.0 percent of separated respondents expressed this opinion, while only 30.7 percent of married and 36.6 percent of widowed respondents shared this view.

Opinions seem to vary considerably depending on one's marital status, but we should confirm our impression of descriptive statistics by examining the chi-squared test results and the measure of association.

---

[5] In Chapter 3, we demonstrated how to recode a variable into a different variable. Start by selecting Transform ▶ Recode into Different Variables. To generate the new, recoded ordinal variable divlaw3, you can switch the numeric coding of divlaw categories 2 and 3: 2→3 and 3→2 so the neutral "stay the same" response is between "easier" and "more difficult." Don't forget to label the new variable's numeric values appropriately.

Chi-Square Tests

	Value	df	Asymptotic Significance (2-sided)
Pearson Chi-Square	85.015[a]	8	.000
Likelihood Ratio	85.687	8	.000
Linear-by-Linear Association	48.831	1	.000
N of Valid Cases	1792		

a. 0 cells (0.0%) have expected count less than 5. The minimum expected count is 13.22.

Symmetric Measures

		Value	Approximate Significance
Nominal by Nominal	Phi	.218	.000
	Cramer's V	.154	.000
N of Valid Cases		1792	

According to the Chi-Square Tests table, the marital–divlaw3 relationship defeats the null hypothesis (chi-square = 85.015, P-value <.001). While we can never rule out the possibility of observing a sample statistic by chance, this is about as close as it gets to no chance that the null hypothesis is true. Reject the null hypothesis. The relationship between marital status and opinions about divorce laws is statistically significant.

Let's see whether Cramer's V backs up our interpretation. Scroll down to the next table, Symmetric Measures. Cramer's V, a chi-square–based, nominal-level measure of strength, gives you an additional interpretive tool. Cramer's V does not have a PRE interpretation. However, it varies between 0 (weak relationship) and 1 (strong relationship). In this case, we get a Cramer's V of .154, which signifies a modestly strong relationship. Cramer's V is particularly useful for comparing the explanatory power of different independent variables and interpreting controlled comparisons, which we'll see in the last section of this chapter.

ANALYZING A NOMINAL-LEVEL RELATIONSHIP WITH A CONTROL VARIABLE

You may be thinking that marital status is the only factor that explains individual opinions about state regulation of marriage and divorce. You might want to examine the relationship between marital status and opinions about divorce law while controlling for other variables. The method used to produce a controlled cross-tabulation with a variable measured at the nominal level is the same as the method used earlier in this chapter to produce a controlled cross-tabulation with both variables measured at the ordinal level. We simply add the control variable as a "layer" in the cross-tabulation. Use the chi-squared statistic for each table to assess statistical significance and calculate Cramer's V to measure the association between variables.

Let's continue with our divlaw3–marital relationship example, controlling for whether the GSS respondents have children. You'll recall from Chapter 5 that having children seems to affect individual opinions about social regulations (in that chapter we compared opinions about marijuana legalization). To produce a controlled cross-tabulation with appropriate inferential statistics, follow the same procedure as the previous section (see Figure 7-5 for reference) but this time move the variable named kids into the "Layer 1 of 1" field of the Crosstabs window. Click OK.

Opinion about Divorce Laws * Marital Status * Does R Have Children?
Crosstabulation

Marital Status

Does R Have Children?			MARRIED	WIDOWED	DIVORCED	SEPARATED	NEVER MARRIED	Total
No	Opinion about Divorce Laws	Easier	34	3	15	4	169	225
			29.3%	30.0%	41.7%	80.0%	45.6%	41.8%
		Stay the same	34	2	10	1	77	124
			29.3%	20.0%	27.8%	20.0%	20.8%	23.0%
		More difficult	48	5	11	0	125	189
			41.4%	50.0%	30.6%	0.0%	33.7%	35.1%
	Total		116	10	36	5	371	538
			100.0%	100.0%	100.0%	100.0%	100.0%	100.0%
Yes	Opinion about Divorce Laws	Easier	230	39	101	40	73	483
			31.0%	38.2%	48.3%	71.4%	51.8%	38.6%
		Stay the same	165	16	51	5	21	258
			22.2%	15.7%	24.4%	8.9%	14.9%	20.6%
		More difficult	348	47	57	11	47	510
			46.8%	46.1%	27.3%	19.6%	33.3%	40.8%
	Total		743	102	209	56	141	1251
			100.0%	100.0%	100.0%	100.0%	100.0%	100.0%
Total	Opinion about Divorce Laws	Easier	264	42	116	44	242	708
			30.7%	37.5%	47.3%	72.1%	47.3%	39.6%
		Stay the same	199	18	61	6	98	382
			23.2%	16.1%	24.9%	9.8%	19.1%	21.4%
		More difficult	396	52	68	11	172	699
			46.1%	46.4%	27.8%	18.0%	33.6%	39.1%
	Total		859	112	245	61	512	1789
			100.0%	100.0%	100.0%	100.0%	100.0%	100.0%

Note: Table output edited to save space.

The results shown in the "Chi-Squared Tests" and "Symmetric Measures" tables for this controlled cross-tabulation are very interesting. For respondents without children, the relationship between marital status and opinions about divorce law has a chi-squared statistic of 14.992 with a P-value of .059. Strictly following the .05 standard, we would fail to reject the null hypothesis in this group because the P-value tells us there was more than a 5 percent chance the observed cell counts resulted from random error. For respondents with children, the chi-squared statistic is 72.650, which has a P-value less than .001, so we would reject the null hypothesis in the case of respondents with children. Comparing the Cramer's V values supports the conclusion that the relationship between marital status and divorce law opinions is more significant for respondents with kids (Cramer's V = .170) than it is for respondents without kids (Cramer's V = .118).

To create a figure that shows the relationship between marital status and opinion about divorce laws, see the section on graphing a categorical dependent variable in Chapter 4. If you continue this

Chi-Square Tests

Does R Have Children?		Value	df	Asymptotic Significance (2-sided)
No	Pearson Chi-Square	14.992[b]	8	.059
	Likelihood Ratio	16.613	8	.034
	Linear-by-Linear Association	6.818	1	.009
	N of Valid Cases	538		
Yes	Pearson Chi-Square	72.650[c]	8	.000
	Likelihood Ratio	73.077	8	.000
	Linear-by-Linear Association	45.754	1	.000
	N of Valid Cases	1251		
Total	Pearson Chi-Square	85.294[a]	8	.000
	Likelihood Ratio	86.017	8	.000
	Linear-by-Linear Association	48.291	1	.000
	N of Valid Cases	1789		

a. 0 cells (0.0%) have expected count less than 5. The minimum expected count is 13.03.

b. 6 cells (40.0%) have expected count less than 5. The minimum expected count is 1.15.

c. 0 cells (0.0%) have expected count less than 5. The minimum expected count is 11.55.

Symmetric Measures

Does R Have Children?			Value	Approximate Significance
No	Nominal by Nominal	Phi	.167	.059
		Cramer's V	.118	.059
	N of Valid Cases		538	
Yes	Nominal by Nominal	Phi	.241	.000
		Cramer's V	.170	.000
	N of Valid Cases		1251	
Total	Nominal by Nominal	Phi	.218	.000
		Cramer's V	.154	.000
	N of Valid Cases		1789	

analysis by controlling for another variable and want to visualize your results, see the section on making bar charts for controlled comparisons with categorical dependent variables in Chapter 5.

Before we conclude this discussion, let's create a graphic that depicts the relationship between marital status and opinions about divorce laws, controlling for whether someone has children. Because the independent variable, marital, is measured at the nominal level, the order of the marital statuses is arbitrary so drawing a sloped line from one category to the next may be misleading. So let's use a clustered bar chart instead. Select Graphs ▶ Legacy Dialogs ▶ Bar, click the Clustered icon, make sure "Summaries for groups of cases" is selected, and click the Define button. In the Define Clustered Bar window, move kids into the Category Axis field, marital into the "Define Clustered by" field, click the "Bars Represent: Other statistic" option, move divlaw3 into the Variable field, and click the Change Statistic button (Figure 7-6).

FIGURE 7-6   Creating a Clustered Bar Chart for a Nominal-level Relationship with a Control Variable

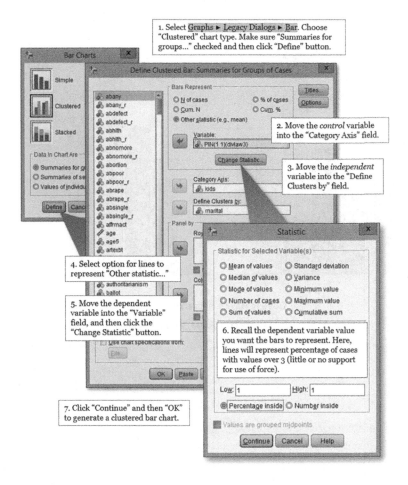

We want the bar heights to summarize opinions about divorce laws. Let's define bar height to be equal to the percentage of respondents saying it should be easier to get a divorce (numeric code 1); the clustered bar chart will then depict the top row of the cross-tabulation. With these settings in place, click OK.

Figure 7-7 could use additional refinement (we have only edited the *y*-axis label for clarity), but it helps us visualize the relationship between marital status and opinions about divorce laws, controlled for whether someone has children. Following the logic of control, the cases are separated by values of the control variable: those without kids are represented by the cluster of bars on the left and those with kids are represented by the cluster of bars on the right. We can examine each set to see how much opinions about divorce law vary by marital status. As we suspected, they seem to vary quite a bit. Which cluster of bars looks more varied to you? This graphic helps highlight an important point about substantive and statistical significance. The bars representing those without children may look more varied, implying a stronger relationship between marital status and opinions about divorce law in this group, but the inferential statistics for the controlled cross-tabulations indicated the relationship was significant only for respondents with kids, not among those without kids. How can this be? The random variation we can expect from a test statistic like chi-squared depends, in large part, on the sample size. Here, the number of GSS respondents with children is much larger than the number without children (1,251 to 538), so we can be more confident about our inferences about the relationship between marital status and opinions about divorce law among respondents with children.

FIGURE 7-7   Creating a Clustered Bar Chart for an Ordinal-level Relationship with a Control Variable

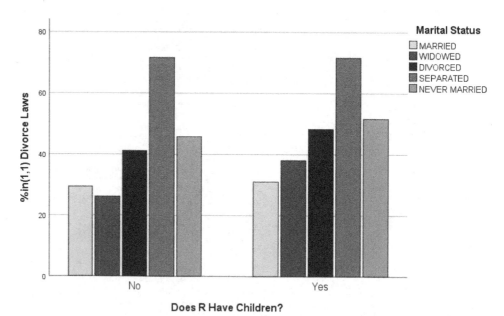

Cases weighted by Weight Variable

Name: Anna Jeffries   Date: 11/17

E-mail: anna.jeffries@spartans.ut.edu   Section: _____

CHAPTER 7 EXERCISES

1. (Dataset: GSS. Variables: abnomore, xmarsex, sex, wtss.) Interested Student has joined Pedantic Pontificator in a discussion of gender differences in U.S. politics.

Interested Student: "On what sorts of issues or opinions are men and women most likely to be at odds? What defines the gender gap, anyway?"

Pedantic Pontificator: "That's easy. A couple of points seem obvious, to me anyway. First, we know that the conflict over abortion rights is the defining gender issue of our time. Women will be more likely than men to take a strong pro-choice position on this issue. Second—and pay close attention here—on more mundane cultural questions, such as the morality of sex outside the confines of marriage, men and women will not differ at all."

A. Pedantic Pontificator has suggested the following two hypotheses about gender differences in U.S. politics: (check two)

- ☐ In a comparison of individuals, women will be less likely than men to think that abortion should be allowed.

- ☐ In a comparison of individuals, women and men will be equally likely to think that abortion should be allowed.

- ☑ In a comparison of individuals, women will be more likely than men to think that abortion should be allowed.

- ☐ In a comparison of individuals, women will be less likely than men to think that extramarital relations are wrong.

- ☑ In a comparison of individuals, women and men will be equally likely to think that extramarital relations are wrong.

- ☐ In a comparison of individuals, women will be more likely than men to think that extramarital relations are wrong.

B. Open the GSS data (file name: gss.sav). Use the Analyze ▶ Descriptive Statistics ▶ Crosstabs procedure (with chi-square statistic option) to produce two cross-tabulations to test Pedantic Pontificator's hypotheses. The GSS dataset contains two variables that will serve as dependent variables. The variable abnomore, which asks respondents whether an abortion should be allowed if a woman is married but doesn't want more children, is coded "Yes" and "No." The variable xmarsex, which measures attitudes toward sex with a person other than one's spouse, has four ordered values: always wrong, almost always wrong, sometimes wrong, and not wrong at all. The independent variable is sex, coded "Male" or "Female."

Complete the abnomore–sex cross-tabulation by filling in the missing percentages, chi-squared statistic, *P*-value, and Cramer's *V*. Be sure to weight observations using the wtss variable so your results are nationally representative. Sex is a nominal variable, so you should report Cramer's *V*.

Abortion permissible if woman is married but doesn't want more children?	Males	Females	Total
Yes	48.5 ?	43.1 ?	45.55%
No	51.9 ?	56.9 ?	54.45%
	100.00%	100.00%	100.00%
Chi-squared	5.309?		
P-value	.021 ?		
Cramer's *V*	.054 ?		

Complete the xmarsex–sex cross-tabulation by filling in the missing percentages, chi-squared statistic, *P*-value, and Cramer's *V*.

Is it wrong to have sex with person other than spouse?	Males	Females	Total
Always wrong	72.4 ?	78.7 ?	75.85%
Almost always wrong	15.4 ?	11.1 ?	13.07%
Sometimes wrong	9.3 ?	8.4 ?	8.80%
Not wrong at all	2.9 ?	1.8 ?	2.29%
	100.00%	100.00%	100.00%
Chi-squared	11.577?		
P-value	.009 ?		
Cramer's *V*	.079 ?		

(handwritten marginal note, left side, rotated): you will get the chi-squared statistic less frequently than 5 times out of 100. ①

C. Based on these results, you may conclude that (check all that apply)

❏ a statistically significant gender difference exists on abortion opinions.

☑ Pedantic Pontificator's hypothesis about the xmarsex–sex relationship is not supported by the analysis.

❏ under the assumption that the null hypothesis is correct, the abnomore–sex relationship could have occurred by chance more frequently than 5 times out of 100.

❏ Pedantic Pontificator's hypothesis about the abnomore–sex relationship is supported by the analysis.

☑ a higher percentage of females than males think that extramarital sex is always wrong.

D. The *P*-value of the chi-square statistic in the xmarsex–sex cross-tabulation tells you that, under the assumption that the null hypothesis is correct, (complete the sentence)

(handwritten): ~~there is~~ women are more likely to think that extramarital sex is wrong. The difference is somewhat statistically significant ①

2. (Dataset: NES. Variables: libcon3, Spend_Poor, gay_marriage, affirm_act3, nesw.) While having lunch together, three researchers are discussing what the terms *liberal*, *moderate*, and *conservative* mean to most people. Each researcher is touting a favorite independent variable that may explain the way survey respondents describe themselves ideologically.

Researcher 1: "When people are asked a question about their ideological views, they think about their attitudes toward *government spending*. If people think the government should spend more to help people in need, they will respond that they are 'liberal.' If they don't want too much spending, they will say that they are 'conservative.'"

Researcher 2: "Well, that's fine. But let's not forget about *social policies*, such as gay rights and family values. These issues must influence how people describe themselves ideologically. People with more progressive views on gay marriage will call themselves 'liberal.' People who favor more traditional family values will label themselves as 'conservative.'"

Researcher 3: "Okay, you both make good points. But you're ignoring the importance of *racial issues* in American politics. When asked whether they are liberal or conservative, people probably think about their opinions on racial policies, such

as affirmative action. Stronger proponents of racial equality will say they are 'liberal,' and weaker proponents will say they are 'conservative.'"

The NES dataset includes the variable libcon3, which is coded 1 for liberals, 2 for moderates, and 3 for conservatives. This is the dependent variable throughout this analysis.

A. Use the Analyze ▶ Descriptive Statistics ▶ Crosstabs procedure (with chi-square statistic option) to do a cross-tabulation analysis of the relationship between Researcher 1's favorite independent variable, Spend_Poor, and libcon3. *(handwritten: dep)* Spend_Poor is a three-category ordinal measure of attitudes toward government spending to help poor people. Spend_Poor is coded 1 ("increase" spending, liberal position), 2 ("keep same," middle position), or 3 ("decrease" spending, conservative position). Be sure to use the sample weights variable (nesw) so your results are nationally representative.

	Opinion on Government Spending on Aid to the Poor			
	Increase	Keep the Same	Decrease	Total
Liberals	47 ?	29.1 ?	11.4 ?	32.48%
Moderates	24.4 ?	29.2 ?	20.1 ?	23.98%
Conservatives	28.6 ?	49.7 ?	68.5 ?	43.54%
	100.00%	100.00%	100.00%	100.00%
Chi-squared	392.3 ?			
P-value	.001 ?			
Somers' d	< .001 ?			

B. Complete a cross-tabulation analysis of the relationship between Researcher 2's favorite independent variable, gay_marriage, and libcons3. This independent variable is a three-category ordinal measure of attitudes on gay marriage, coded 1 (the liberal view, gay couples should be allowed to marry), 2 (the moderate position, gay couples should be allowed to form civil unions), or 3 (the conservative view, gay couples should not be allowed to marry).

	Position on Gay Marriage			
	Should be Allowed	Civil Unions Only	Should Not Be Allowed	Total
Liberals	46.2 ?	14.6 ?	10.3 ?	32.53%
Moderates	29.6 ?	20.1 ?	23.2 ?	23.92%
Conservatives	28.2 ?	65.2 ?	66.5 ?	43.55%
	100.00%	100.00%	100.00%	100.00%
Chi-squared	578.8 ?			
P-value	< .001 ?			
Somers' d	< .001 ?			

C. Complete a cross-tabulation analysis of the relationship between Researcher 3's favorite independent variable, affirm_act3, and libcon3. The affirm_act3 variable is also a three-category ordinal variable. The affirm_act3 variable is coded 1 (favor affirmative action, most liberal position on racial policies), 2 (neutral, moderate position), or 3 (oppose affirmative action, most conservative position on racial policies).

	Opinion on Affirmative Action in Universities			
	Favor	Middle/ neutral	Oppose	Total
Liberals	98.5 ?	32.3 ?	27.4 ?	32.53%
Moderates	19.8 ?	33.9 ?	19.6 ?	24.09%
Conservatives	29.7 ?	33.9 ?	59.0 ?	43.38%
	100.00%	100.00%	100.00%	100.00%
Chi-squared	448.95			
P-value	< .001 ?			
Somers' d	.282 ? < .001			

D. Think about how SPSS calculates Somers' d. Assuming each researcher is correct, SPSS should report (check all that apply)

❏ a negative sign on Somers' d for the libcon3–Spend_Poor relationship.

❏ a positive sign on Somers' d for the libcon3–gay_marriage relationship.

❏ a negative sign on Somers' d for the libcon3–affirm_act3 relationship.

E. Consider the evidence you have assembled. Your analysis supports which of the following statements? (check all that apply)

☑ As numeric values of Spend_Poor increase, the percentage of respondents describing themselves as conservative decreases.

❏ As numeric values of gay_marriage increase, the percentage of respondents describing themselves as conservative increases.

❏ The relationship between affirm_act3 and libcon3 is not statistically significant.

☑ If the null hypothesis is correct, you will obtain the chi-squared statistic for the relationship between Spend_Poor and libcon3 *less frequently* than 5 times out of 100 by chance.

❏ If the null hypothesis is correct, you will obtain the chi-squared statistic for the relationship between Spend_poor and libcon3 *more frequently* than 5 times out of 100 by chance.

F. Somers' d for the relationship between libcon3 and gay_marriage is equal to (fill in the blank) _____. Thus, compared with how well we can predict libcon3 by not knowing (complete the sentence) _____
_____
_____
_____
_____
_____

G. The three researchers make a friendly wager. The researcher whose favorite independent variable does the *worst* job predicting values of the dependent variable has to buy lunch for the other two. Who pays for lunch? (circle one)

Researcher 1   Researcher 2   Researcher 3

3. (Dataset: World. Variables: protact3, gender_equal3, vi_rel3, pmat12_3.) Ronald Inglehart offers a particularly elegant and compelling idea about the future of economically advanced societies. According to Inglehart, the cultures of many post-industrial societies have been going through a value shift—the waning importance of materialist values and a growing pursuit of post-materialist values. In post-materialist societies, economically based conflicts—unions versus big business, rich versus poor—are increasingly supplanted by an emphasis on self-expression and social equality. Post-materialist societies also are marked by rising secularism and elite-challenging behaviors, such as boycotts and demonstrations. In this exercise you will investigate Inglehart's theory.[6]

The World dataset variable pmat12_3 *indep* measures the level of post-material values by a three-category ordinal measure: low post-materialism (coded 1), moderate post-materialism (coded 2), and high post-materialism (coded 3). Higher codes denote a greater prevalence of post-material values. Use pmat12_3 as the independent variable.

Here are three dependent variables, all of which are three-category ordinals: gender_equal3, which captures gender equality (1 = low equality, 2 = medium equality, 3 = high equality); protact3, which measures citizen participation in protests (1 = low, 2 = moderate, 3 = high); and vi_rel3, which gauges religiosity by the percentage of the public saying that religion is "very important" (1 = less than 20 percent, 2 = 20–50 percent, 3 = more than 50 percent).

---

[6] Ronald Inglehart has written extensively about cultural change in post-industrial societies. For example, see his *Culture Shift in Advanced Industrial Society* (Princeton: Princeton University Press, 1990).

Higher codes on the dependent variables denote greater gender equality (gender_equal3), more protest activity (protact3), and higher levels of religiosity (vi_rel3).

A. Using pmat12_3 as the independent variable, three post-materialist hypotheses can be framed:

Gender Equality Hypothesis (fill in the blanks): In a comparison of countries, those with higher levels of post-materialism will have _____ levels of gender equality than will countries having lower levels of post-materialism.

Protest Activity Hypothesis (fill in the blanks): In a comparison of countries, those with _____ levels of post-materialism will have _____ levels of protest activity than will countries having _____ levels of post-materialism.

Religiosity Hypothesis (complete the sentence): In a comparison of countries, those with _____ _____ _____

_____
_____
_____

B. Consider how the independent variable is coded and how each dependent variable is coded. In the way that SPSS calculates the Somers' *d*, which one of the three hypotheses implies a negative sign on the measure of association? (check one)

❑ The gender equality hypothesis

❑ The protest activity hypothesis

❑ The religiosity hypothesis

C. Use the <u>Analyze</u> ▶ <u>D</u>escriptive Statistics ▶ <u>C</u>rosstabs procedure (with chi-square statistic option) to test each hypothesis. Obtain chi-square ("chi2") and Somers' *d* statistics. The World dataset is not weighted. In the table that follows, record the percentages of countries falling into the highest category of each dependent variable. Also report chi-square statistics, *P*-values, and Somers' *d*.

Dependent Variable	Level of Post-materialism			Chi-square	P-value	Somers' d
	Low	Moderate	High			
Percentage of high gender equality	?	?	?	?	?	?
Percentage of high protest activity	?	?	?	?	?	?
Percentage of high religiosity	?	?	?	?	?	?

D. Which of the following inferences are supported by your analysis? (check all that apply)

❑ The gender equality hypothesis is supported.

❑ Compared with how well we can predict gender equality by not knowing the level of post-materialism, we can improve our prediction by 20.03 percent by knowing the level of post-materialism.

❑ The protest activity hypothesis is supported.

❑ If the null hypothesis is correct, the post-materialism–protest activity relationship would occur, by chance, less frequently than 5 times out of 100.

❑ The religiosity hypothesis is supported.

❑ If the null hypothesis is correct, the post-materialism–religiosity relationship would occur, by chance, less frequently than 5 times out of 100.

4. (Dataset: NES. Variables: partyid3, egalit_3, educ4.) Certainly, you would expect partisanship and egalitarian attitudes to be related: In a comparison of individuals, those with stronger egalitarian beliefs are more likely to be Democrats than those with weaker egalitarian beliefs. Yet it also seems reasonable to hypothesize that the relationship between egalitarianism (independent variable) and party identification (dependent variable) will not be the same for all education groups (control variable). It may be that, among people with less education, the party identification–egalitarianism relationship will be weaker than among those with higher levels of education. This idea suggests a set of interaction relationships: As education increases, the relationship between the independent variable and the dependent variable becomes stronger. In this exercise, you will test for this set of interaction relationships.

The NES dataset (file name: nes.sav) contains partyid3, which measures party identification: "Dem," "Indep," and "Rep." This is the dependent variable. (For this exercise, treat partyid3 as an ordinal-level variable, with higher codes denoting stronger Republican identification.) The independent variable is egalit_3: "Low," "Med," or "High" support for egalitarianism. The control variable is educ4: high school or less ("HS r less"), some college or an associate's degree ("SmColl/Assoc"), college degree ("BA"), or higher ("Grad").

Run the Analyze ▶ Descriptive Statistics ▶ Crosstabs procedure (with chi-square statistic option), using partyid_3 as the dependent variable, egalit_scale3

as the independent variable, and educ4 as the control variable (layer). Request the relevant statistics.

A. In the controlled comparison cross-tabulations, focus on the percentages of Democrats across the values of egalit_3. Fill in the table that follows.

| Egalitarian Scale | Democrat Identifiers | | | | Chi-square | P-value | Somers' d |
	HS or less	SmColl/ Assoc	BA	Grad			
Low	?	?	?	?	?	?	?
Medium	?	?	?	?	?	?	?
High	?	?	?	?	?	?	?
Total	100%	100%	100%	100%	?	?	?

B. Which of the following inferences are supported by your analysis? (check all that apply)

❑ At both levels of education, people with stronger egalitarian beliefs are more likely to be Democrats than are people with weaker egalitarian beliefs.

❑ For the less-educated group, random sampling error would produce the observed relationship between egalitarianism and partisanship less frequently than 5 times out of 100.

❑ The partisanship–egalitarianism relationship is stronger for the more-educated group than for the less-educated group.

C. Focus on the value of Somers' d for those who have a BA degree or more years of education. This value of Somers' d says that compared to how well you can predict (complete the sentence)

_____

_____

_____

_____

_____

D. Based on your analysis of these relationships, you can conclude that (check one)

❑ The partisanship–egalitarianism–education relationships are not a set of interaction relationships.

❑ The partisanship–egalitarianism–education relationships are a set of interaction relationships.

Explain your reasoning, making specific reference to the statistical evidence in part A.

_____

_____

_____

_____

_____

8

Correlation and Linear Regression

 Watch screencasts of the guided examples in this chapter. **edge.sagepub.com/pollock**

Procedures Covered

Analyze ▶ Correlate ▶ Bivariate

Analyze ▶ Regression ▶ Linear

Graphs ▶ Legacy Dialogs ▶ Scatter/Dot

File ▶ Save Chart Template (in Chart Editor)

File ▶ Apply Chart Template (in Chart Editor)

Correlation and regression are powerful and flexible techniques used to analyze interval-level relationships. Pearson's correlation coefficient (Pearson's r) measures the strength and direction of the relationship between two interval-level variables. Pearson's r is not a proportional reduction in error (PRE) measure, but it does gauge strength by an easily understood scale—from −1, a perfectly negative association between the variables, to +1, a perfectly positive relationship. A correlation of 0 indicates no relationship. Researchers often use correlation techniques in the beginning stages of analysis to get an overall picture of the relationships between interesting variables.

Regression analysis produces a statistic, the regression coefficient, that estimates the effect of an independent variable on a dependent variable. Regression also produces a PRE measure of association, R-square, which indicates how completely the independent variable (or variables) explains the dependent variable. In regression analysis the dependent variable is measured at the interval level, but the independent variable can be of any variety—nominal, ordinal, or interval. Regression is more specialized than correlation. Researchers use regression analysis to model causal relationships between one or more independent variables and a dependent variable.

In the first part of this chapter, you will learn to perform correlation analysis using the Correlate procedure, and you will learn to perform and interpret bivariate regression using the Analyze ▶ Regression ▶ Linear procedure. Bivariate regression uses one independent variable to predict a dependent variable. We will then turn to Scatter/Dot, an SPSS graphic routine that yields a scatterplot, a visual depiction of the relationship between two interval-level variables. With generous use of the Chart Editor, you will learn how to add a regression line to the scatterplot and how to edit the graph for elegance and clarity. Finally, you will use Analyze ▶ Regression ▶ Linear to perform multiple regression analysis. Multiple regression, which uses two or more independent variables to predict a dependent variable, is an essential tool for analyzing complex relationships.

Screencast

Correlation and Bivariate Regression

CORRELATION ANALYSIS

Suppose that a student of world politics is interested in peace and democracy around the world. On a global scale, one observes tremendous variation in how peaceful, democratic, and prosperous countries are. Why is there such variation in these fundamental variables? The student researcher begins to formulate explanations from the vast literature on these topics. Perhaps countries that are more democratic are more peaceful. And maybe economic conditions also play a role. Perhaps economically interdependent countries are more peaceful, as their prosperity depends on maintaining good relations with other countries.

At first, concepts like peace, democracy, and prosperity may seem too abstract and subjective for quantitative analysis, but this is not the case. Students interested in these topics benefit from many efforts to operationalize these concepts in measurable ways. Several organizations publish reports on the state of democratic development around the world that integrate many measurable characteristics of democratic governments into a numeric index.

In the World dataset, world.sav, there are multiple interval-level measures of how democratic countries are. Let's begin our analysis of peace and democracy around the world by taking a closer look at seven interval-level variables in the World dataset that measure how democratic countries are:

- dem_score14 from *The Economist*,

- democ11 from the United Nations (UN),

- polity from the Polity Project,

- fhrate08_rev from Freedom House,

- vdem_ldi from Varieties of Democracy,

- liberty_index_eiu from the Economist Intelligence Unit, and

- democ_fh_polity, which averages Freedom House and Polity Project scores.

FIGURE **8-1**   Analyzing Bivariate Correlations among Variables

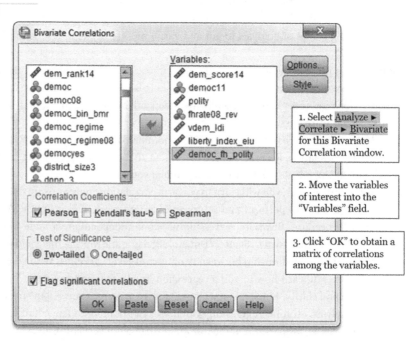

This variety of measures raises some interesting questions. Which one(s) should a researcher use to study world politics? Do any of the measures offer a significantly different picture of democracy around the world? Correlation analysis can help us answer these questions.

Correlation analysis would give this researcher an overview of the relationships among these interval-level variables. To begin this analysis, open the World dataset. Select Analyze ▶ Correlate ▶ Bivariate. The Bivariate Correlations window is a no-frills interface (Figure 8-1). We are interested in the suite of variables that measure democracy around the world: dem_score14, democ11, polity, fhrate08_rev, vdem_ldi, liberty_index_eiu, and democ_fh_polity. Click each of these variables into the Variables panel, as shown in Figure 8-1.

By default, SPSS will return Pearson correlation coefficients. So the Pearson box, which is already checked, suits our purpose. Click OK. SPSS reports the results in the Viewer.

Correlations

		Democracy score	Democracy score	Measure of democracy	FH rating of democracy	Liberal democracy index	Index of democracy	Scale measuring democracy
Democracy score	Pearson Correlation	1	0.851**	0.820**	0.914**	0.890**	0.947**	0.915**
	Sig. (2-tailed)		0.000	0.000	0.000	0.000	0.000	0.000
	N	165	144	144	152	161	165	165
Democracy score	Pearson Correlation	0.851**	1	0.969**	0.892**	0.812**	0.844**	0.954**
	Sig. (2-tailed)	0.000		0.000	0.000	0.000	0.000	0.000
	N	144	144	144	142	142	144	144
Measure of democracy	Pearson Correlation	0.820**	0.969**	1	0.858**	0.778**	0.824**	0.956**
	Sig. (2-tailed)	0.000	0.000		0.000	0.000	0.000	0.000
	N	144	144	144	142	142	144	144
Freedom House rating of democracy	Pearson Correlation	0.914**	0.892**	0.858**	1	0.895**	0.899**	0.934**
	Sig. (2-tailed)	0.000	0.000	0.000		0.000	0.000	0.000
	N	152	142	142	152	149	152	152
Liberal democracy index	Pearson Correlation	0.890**	0.812**	0.778**	0.895**	1	0.847**	0.877**
	Sig. (2-tailed)	0.000	0.000	0.000	0.000		0.000	0.000
	N	161	142	142	149	163	161	163
Index of democracy	Pearson Correlation	0.947**	0.844**	0.824**	0.899**	0.847**	1	0.909**
	Sig. (2-tailed)	0.000	0.000	0.000	0.000	0.000		0.000
	N	165	144	144	152	161	165	165
Scale measuring how democratic country is	Pearson Correlation	0.915**	0.954**	0.956**	0.934**	0.877**	0.909**	1
	Sig. (2-tailed)	0.000	0.000	0.000	0.000	0.000	0.000	
	N	165	144	144	152	163	165	167

**. Correlation is significant at the 0.01 level (2-tailed).

Note: Table column headings edited for size.

SPSS produces a table, called a correlation matrix, that shows the correlation of each variable with each of the other variables—it even shows the correlation between each variable and itself (by definition, perfect 1.000 correlation). Positive numbers signify positive correlation and the closer the numbers get to 1, the more strongly correlated the pair of variables. Because correlation is a symmetric measure, each of the correlations in which we are interested appears twice in the table: once above the upper-left-to-lower-right diagonal of 1's, and again below the diagonal.

Let's look at the correlation between some of the measures of democracy. According to the correlation matrix, the correlation between the dem_score14 variable (the first column/row) and the democ11 variable (the second column/row) is 0.851. How strong is the relationship? We know that Pearson's *r* is bracketed by −1 and +1, so we could say that this relationship is a very strong positive association. Reading down the first column, we see that the dem_score14 variable is strongly correlated with all seven other measures of democracy. The democ11 variable is strongly correlated with dem_score14 and, reading down the second column, we see it is also strongly correlated with all the other measures of democracy. There is strong positive correlation among all these measures; the lowest correlation among them, a 0.778 correlation between vdem_ldi and polity, is still a very strong positive correlation.

The high degree of correlation among these measures of democracy should assure researchers who use them that different organizations are measuring the concept in a consistent manner. The measures validate one another by showing there is a consensus among experts on which countries are more democratic than others are. We probably won't go wrong using any of them, but the democ_fh_polity variable appears to have the highest overall correlation with other variables and it also has the fewest missing observations among the contenders.[1] The democ_fh_polity variable ranges from 0 to 10, with higher values corresponding to higher levels of democracy.

Correlation analysis is a great tool for selecting variables and exploring datasets. In the next section, we'll use the democ_fh_polity variable as our independent variable to explore the effect of democracy on conflict.

BIVARIATE REGRESSION

Regression is more powerful than correlation, in part because it helps the researcher investigate causal relationships—relationships in which an independent variable is thought to affect a dependent variable. Regression analysis will (1) reveal the precise nature of the relationship between an independent and a dependent variable, (2) test the null hypothesis that the observed relationship occurred by chance, and (3) provide a PRE measure of the association between the independent variable and the dependent variable. Researchers will frequently go to great lengths to measure an outcome of interest at the interval level in order to use regression analysis.

To illustrate these and other points, we will estimate a bivariate regression model that explains the amount of conflict in countries as a function of how democratic they are. As a measure of conflict, we'll use the conflict_index variable in the World dataset, which is an interval-level measure of the level of domestic and international conflicts in countries around the world. The conflict_index variable ranges from 1 to 3.827, with higher values representing higher levels of violence in a country.[2]

For simple bivariate regression, select Analyze ▶ Regression ▶ Linear. The Linear Regression window appears (Figure 8-2). Click conflict_index into the Dependent box. Find democ_fh_polity in the variable list and click it into the Independent(s) box.[3] Click OK.

SPSS regression output includes four tables: Variables Entered/Removed, Model Summary, ANOVA (which stands for analysis of variance), and Coefficients. For the regression analyses you

[1] The democ_fh_polity variable's high correlations make sense because it is an average of democracy ratings by two other organizations: Freedom House and Polity. We evaluated missing observations using the Analyze ▶ Descriptive Statistics ▶ Frequencies procedure discussed in Chapter 2.

[2] If you're interested in seeing which countries are rated the most and least violent in the world, refer to the procedure discussed in the section on "Obtaining Case-level Information with Case Summaries" in Chapter 2.

[3] For this analysis, we are treating World dataset observations as if they were a sample. See the "A Closer Look: Treating Census as a Sample" discussion in Chapter 6.

FIGURE 8-2   Estimating Linear Regression with One Independent Variable

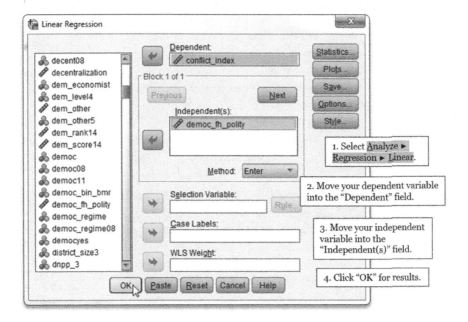

will perform in this book, the Model Summary table and the Coefficients table contain the most important information. Let's examine them.

First, consider the Coefficients table. The leftmost column, under the heading "Model," contains the names of the key elements in the regression equation. "Constant" is the y-intercept of the regression line, and "Scale measuring how democratic country is" is the label of the independent variable. The numbers along the "Constant" row report statistics about the y-intercept, and the numbers along the "Scale measuring how democratic country is" row report statistics about the independent variable. Now look at the first column of numbers, which shows the regression coefficient for each parameter. According to these values, the y-intercept is equal to 2.396 and the regression coefficient is −.106. According to these coefficients, the regression equation for estimating the effect of democracy on conflict is as follows:

$$\text{Conflict Index} = 2.396 - 0.106 \times \text{Democracy Scale}$$

The constant, 2.396, is the estimated value of the conflict index when the democracy scale measure equals 0. If you were using this equation to estimate the level of conflict in a country, you would start with 2.396 on the conflict index and then subtract 0.106 for each point the country earns on the democracy scale. So your estimate for a country with, say, a 6-point rating on the democracy scale (close to the global mean of 6.409) would be $2.396 - 0.106 \times 6 = 2.396 - 0.636 = 1.760$ on the conflict index. The main statistic of interest, then, is the regression coefficient, −0.106, which estimates the average change in the dependent variable for each unit change in the independent variable. A regression coefficient of −0.106 tells us that for each one-unit increase in a country's democratic rating, one expects a 0.106-point drop in the country's conflict index score.[4]

What would the null hypothesis have to say about all this? The null hypothesis would say what it always says: In the population from which the sample was drawn, there is no relationship between the independent variable (in this case, the degree of democracy in a country) and the dependent variable (the level of violence in a country). In the population, the true regression coefficient is equal to 0. Furthermore, the null hypothesis asserts that the regression coefficient that we obtained, −0.106, occurred by chance.

Variables Entered/Removed[a]

Model	Variables Entered	Variables Removed	Method
1	Scale measuring how democratic country is[b]	.	Enter

a. Dependent Variable: Extent of ongoing domestic and international conflict

b. All requested variables entered.

Model Summary

Model	R	R Square	Adjusted R Square	Std. Error of the Estimate
1	0.493[a]	0.243	0.238	0.57851

a. Predictors: (Constant), Scale measuring how democratic country is

ANOVA[a]

Model		Sum of Squares	df	Mean Square	F	Sig.
1	Regression	17.056	1	17.056	50.964	0.000[b]
	Residual	53.213	159	0.335		
	Total	70.270	160			

a. Dependent Variable: Extent of ongoing domestic and international conflict

b. Predictors: (Constant), Scale measuring how democratic country is

Coefficients[a]

Model		Unstandardized Coefficients		Standardized Coefficients	t	Sig.
		B	Std. Error	Beta		
1	(Constant)	2.396	0.105		22.844	0.000
	Scale measuring how democratic country is	-0.106	0.015	-0.493	-7.139	0.000

a. Dependent Variable: Extent of ongoing domestic and international conflict

In SPSS regression results, you test the null hypothesis by examining two columns in the Coefficients table—the column labeled "t," which reports t-ratios, and the column labeled "Sig.," which reports P-values. Informally, to safely reject the null hypothesis, you generally look for t-ratios with magnitudes (absolute values) of 2 or greater. According to the results of our analysis, the regression coefficient for conflict_index has a t-ratio of −7.139, well above the informal 2-or-greater rule.

A P-value, which tells you the probability of obtaining the results if the null hypothesis is correct, helps you to make more precise inferences about the relationship between the independent variable and the dependent variable. If "Sig." is greater than .05, then the observed results would occur too frequently by chance, and you should *not reject* the null hypothesis. By contrast, if "Sig." is equal to or less than .05, then the null hypothesis represents an unlikely occurrence and may be rejected.

---

[4] Regression analysis on variables measured on constructed indexes like these can be confusing. Always stay focused on the exact units of measurement. The substantive interpretation of these results can be supplemented using graphics and referencing specific countries as examples.

The *t*-ratio for conflict_index has a corresponding *P*-value of less than .001.[5] If the null is correct, then random sampling error would have produced the observed results less than one time in a thousand. Reject the null hypothesis. It depends on the research problem at hand, of course, but for most applications you can ignore the *t*-ratio and *P*-value for the constant.[6]

How strong is the relationship between democ_fh_polity and conflict_index, the variables we are using to measure democracy and conflict around the world? The answer is provided by the *R*-square statistics, which appear in the Model Summary table. SPSS reports two values, one labeled "R Square" and one labeled "Adjusted R Square." Which one should you use? Most research articles report the adjusted value, so let's rely on adjusted *R*-squared to provide the best overall measure of the strength of the relationship. See "*R*-Squared and Adjusted *R*-Squared: What's the Difference?" for a closer look at the difference between these two statistics. Adjusted *R*-squared is equal to .238. What does this mean? *R*-squared communicates the proportion of the variation in the dependent variable that is explained by the independent variable. Like any proportion, *R*-squared can assume any value between 0 and 1. Thus, of all the variation in conflict intensity in countries around the world, .238, or 23.8 percent, is explained by how democratic countries are. The rest of the variation in conflict_index, 76.2 percent, remains unexplained by the independent variable.

A CLOSER LOOK: *R*-SQUARED AND ADJUSTED *R*-SQUARED: WHAT'S THE DIFFERENCE?

Most data analysis programs, SPSS included, provide two values of *R*-squared—a plain version, which SPSS labels "R Square," and an adjusted version, "Adjusted R Square." Adjusted *R*-squared is often about the same as (but is always less than) plain *R*-squared. What is the difference? Just like a sample mean, which provides an estimate of the unseen population mean, a sample *R*-squared provides an estimate of the true value of *R*-squared in the population. And just like a sample mean, the sample *R*-squared is equal to the population *R*-squared, give or take random sampling error. However, unlike the random error associated with a sample mean, *R*-squared's errors can assume only positive values—squaring any negative error, after all, produces a positive number—introducing upward bias into the estimated value of *R*-squared. This problem, which is more troublesome for small samples and for models with many independent variables, can be corrected by adjusting plain *R*-squared "downward." We use the following formula for a sample of size *N* and a regression model with *k* predictors:

$$\text{Adjusted } R\text{-squared} = 1 - \left[\frac{(N-1)}{(N-k-1)} (1 - R\text{-squared}) \right]$$

The $(N-1)/(N-k-1)$ term in the adjusted *R*-squared formula tells us how much the *R*-squared should be adjusted downward. The numerator of this term, $N-1$, is always greater than the denominator, $N-k-1$, so its value is greater than 1. The larger this "penalty" term, the more *R*-squared is reduced to arrive at adjusted *R*-squared; because the term is, by definition, greater

(Continued)

---

[5] Remember, *P*-values never equal exactly 0. There is always some chance that the results we observe occurred by chance, but there is not always room to print enough zeros after the decimal place to show just how small the *P*-value is.

[6] The *t*-ratio for the *y*-intercept permits you to test the null hypothesis that, in the population, the *y*-intercept is 0. In this case we have no interest in testing the hypothesis that countries rating 0 on the democracy scale score 0 on the conflict index.

(Continued)

than 1, there is always some downward adjustment of *R*-squared. The difference between *R*-squared and adjusted *R*-squared is minimal when you are analyzing large datasets, like the GSS or NES, with relatively few independent variables. The difference is more noticeable when you work with datasets with fewer observations (*N*), such as the States or World datasets, and estimate multiple regression models with numerous independent variables (*k*).[7]

CREATING SCATTERPLOTS FOR BIVARIATE REGRESSION ANALYSIS

Screencast

Scatterplots

An SPSS graphic routine, Scatter/Dot, adds a visual dimension to correlation and regression and thus can help you paint a richer portrait of a relationship. Consider Figure 8-3, created using the Graphs ▶ Legacy Dialogs ▶ Scatter/Dot procedure and edited in the Chart Editor.

This graph, generically referred to as a scatterplot, displays the cases in a two-dimensional space according to their values on the two variables. The horizontal axis (*x*-axis) is defined by the independent variable and the vertical axis (*y*-axis) is defined by the dependent variable. We know from our regression analysis that there is a statistically significant negative relationship between democracy and conflict (that is, *higher* levels of democracy correspond to *lower* levels of conflict). We can now see what this relationship "looks like."

Consider Figure 8-3, which overlays two graphic forms: a scatterplot and a linear prediction or linear fit line. The scatterplot displays countries in a two-dimensional space according to their values on the two variables. The horizontal axis is defined by the independent variable, democ_fh_polity, and the vertical axis is defined by the dependent variable, conflict_index. Based on the figure, more democratic countries tend to be less violent. As you move from left to right along the *x*-axis, values on the *y*-axis generally decrease, just as the negative partial regression coefficient suggested. Notice the cluster of countries in the bottom-right corner of the plot that score 10 on the democracy scale and have very low conflict index scores; those observations have a lot of influence on our regression analysis.

The dots have been overlaid by the linear prediction line obtained from the analysis we just performed: Conflict Index = 2.396 − 0.106 × Democracy Scale. Thanks to this visual depiction, one can see that the linear summary of the relationship, while reasonably coherent, is far from perfect. Quite a few countries are more violent than their level of democratic development would suggest. Obviously, this graph adds depth and interest to our description of the relationship.

Notice the sparse clarity of the graph. The dots are solid, but the background is white, both inside and outside the data space. The two key data elements—the dots representing each case and the regression line summarizing the relationship—do not compete for our attention with any other lines, colors, or text. The scatterplot in Figure 8-3 comes close to what Edward R. Tufte calls an "erased" graph, a graph in which non-essential elements have been deleted.[8] Let's recreate this graphic step by step.

---

[7] See Barbara G. Tabachnick and Linda S. Fidell, *Using Multivariate Statistics*, 3rd ed. (New York: HarperCollins, 1996), 164–165.

[8] In Chapter 5, we touched on Tufte's definition of the data/ink ratio, the proportion of a graph's total ink devoted to depicting the information contained in the data. Tufte, a leading expert on the visual communication of quantitative information, recommends that the greatest share of a graph's elements should be devoted to data ink—graphic features that convey the essence of the relationship. Edward R. Tufte, *The Visual Display of Quantitative Information*, 2nd ed. (Cheshire, Conn.: Graphics Press, 2001). Tufte's work has inspired other excellent treatments of visual communication. For example, see Stephen Few, *Show Me the Numbers: Designing Tables and Graphs to Enlighten* (Oakland, Calif.: Analytics Press, 2004); and Howard Wainer, *Graphic Discovery: A Trout in the Milk and Other Visual Adventures* (Princeton: Princeton University Press, 2005).

FIGURE 8-3   Scatterplot with a Regression Line

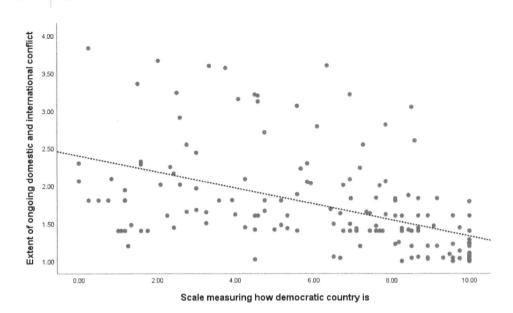

To create a scatterplot with SPSS, select <u>Graphs</u> ▸ <u>Legacy Dialogs</u> ▸ <u>Scatter/Dot</u>. In the Scatter/Dot window, select Simple Scatter and click Define, opening the Simple Scatterplot dialog (Figure 8-4). Click the independent variable (democ_fh_polity) into the X Axis box, click the dependent variable (conflict_index) into the Y Axis box, and click OK.

Based on this simple definition, SPSS applies the default settings and generates a basic scatterplot (Figure 8-5).

This is a good start, but improvement is always possible. Let's use the Chart Editor to make a couple of helpful changes. First, we will add a prominent linear regression line. Second, we'll remove some unnecessary elements: the grid of horizontal and vertical lines SPSS draws by default from the x- and y-axis tick marks and the margin note regarding the R-squared statistics; these elements don't show essential information about the relationship between democracy and conflict.

To make changes to a graphic, double-click on the image in the Viewer, opening the Chart Editor. To add the regression line, click the Add Fit Line at Total button. SPSS superimposes the line, selects it, and automatically opens the Properties window (see Figure 8-6).

The Fit Line tab (the opening tab) should have the Fit Method: Linear option selected; do not change this but uncheck the "Attach label to line" option.[9] Click the Apply button, but be sure to keep the Properties window open.[10] Next, click the Lines tab. The default gray line is difficult to distinguish from the axes, so change its color to black using the color palette and increase the line weight to 1.5. In its solid-black attire, the regression line looks more like a sure thing than a probabilistic estimate, so click the Style drop-down and pick one of the dashed-line options. Click Apply again and then close the Fit Line Properties dialog box. The revised scatterplot appears in the Chart Editor.

---

[9] Other fit method options may produce more interesting lines, but they won't depict linear regression analysis. Simpler empirical models are often more useful than more complicated ones. We remove the line equation label because we report the numerical results in a table.

[10] You will want to keep the Properties window open for your entire excursion into the Chart Editor. Each time you select a different part of the graph for editing, SPSS automatically adjusts the Properties window to reflect the editable features of the graphic element you have selected. Naturally, you can open the Properties window upon entering the Chart Editor by clicking the Properties button.

FIGURE 8-4   Defining a Simple Scatter/Dot Graphic

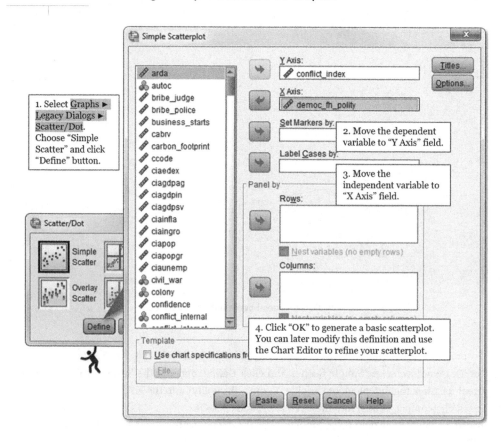

1. Select Graphs ▶ Legacy Dialogs ▶ Scatter/Dot. Choose "Simple Scatter" and click "Define" button.

2. Move the dependent variable to "Y Axis" field.

3. Move the independent variable to "X Axis" field.

4. Click "OK" to generate a basic scatterplot. You can later modify this definition and use the Chart Editor to refine your scatterplot.

FIGURE 8-5   Unedited Simple Scatterplot

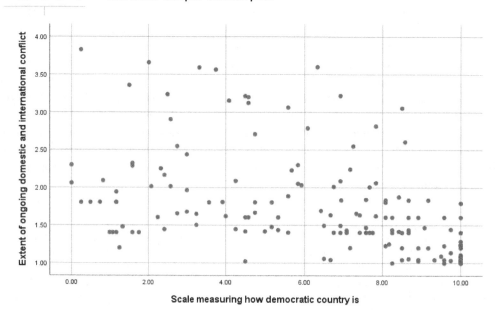

FIGURE 8-6   Adding a Linear Regression Line to a Scatterplot

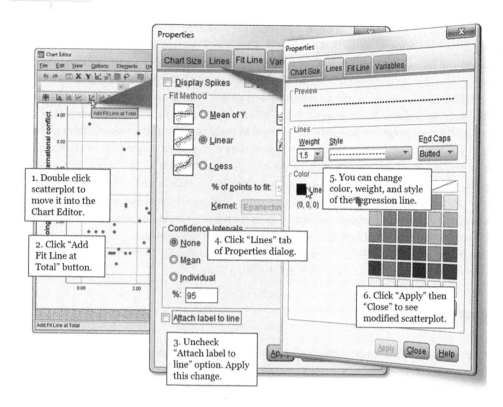

FIGURE 8-7   Removing Non-essential Elements Using Chart Editor

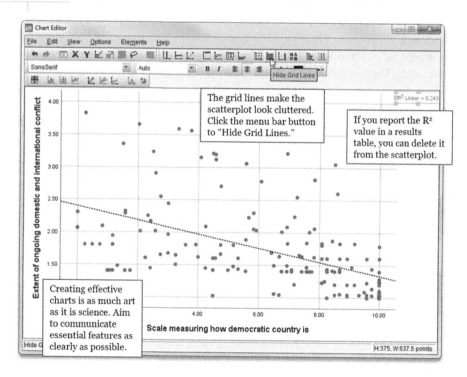

Now that we've added the linear regression line, let's remove the grid of horizontal and vertical grid lines and margin information that clutter the scatterplot. The Chart Editor features a convenient "Hide Grid Lines" button (see Figure 8-7); click that button and the grid lines disappear. To remove the "R2 Linear = 0.243" margin note, click on it once so SPSS highlights that element (see Figure 8-7). Now you can delete that box by pressing your keyboard's delete key or selecting Edit: Delete in the Chart Editor. After removing these non-essential elements, you can close the Chart Editor and see the modified scatterplot in the Viewer (it should look like Figure 8-3 now).

The Chart Editor allows researchers to fine-tune graphics to communicate essential information more clearly. By adding a linear regression line and removing some non-essential elements, we have improved the scatterplot considerably, but one could make further improvements. In practice, creating effective graphics is an iterative process; you start with a basic graphic, revise it, evaluate the revised graphic, and then make further revisions. Applying this idea to our sample scatterplot, we might turn our attention to the axis labels (are the axis labels as clear and descriptive as they could be?) or the numeric labels on each axis (do we really need two decimal places?). The Chart Editor allows us to fine-tune the properties of each graphic element.[11] Our guiding motivation should always be to communicate essential aspects of the data as effectively as possible.

Before exiting the Chart Editor, you may want to save your chart preferences as a template, which can be opened and applied to future scatterplot-editing tasks.[12]

MULTIPLE REGRESSION

Screencast

Multiple
Regression

In the preceding section we explained variation in the level of conflict in countries around the world with a measure of how democratic countries are. The more democratic the country, the less violent it is. This appears to be a strong finding, based on the impressive inferential statistics and model fit, but the reasons for conflict around the world are likely multi-faceted. Indeed, political scientists rarely attempt to explain variation in some outcome of interest with just one independent variable (although most will start with a simple bivariate regression, as we have done).

Consider, for example, an explanation for conflict based on economic self-interest. In some countries, the national economy is dependent on trading goods and services with other countries.[13] In the World dataset, the variable trade_percent_gdp measures the relative value of trade to a country as a percentage of gross domestic product (GDP). Higher values of trade_percent_gdp mean countries are more dependent on international trade. (Trade as a percentage of GDP can exceed 100 percent in countries where the trade economy is larger than the domestic economy.) Countries that depend on trade have strong economic reasons to cultivate good relations with other countries and minimize conflicts that could disrupt trade. Perhaps some of the pacifying effect we attributed to democracy in the preceding bivariate is economic self-interest of democracies dependent on international trade.

---

[11] To edit the axis labels, click on the axis label in the Chart Editor to highlight it and then click again to edit. To delete the unnecessary and distracting digits to the right of the decimal points in the axes tick-mark labels, double-click on a number tick mark and find the Number Format tab of the Properties dialog. Click in the Decimal Places box (which may be empty) and type 0. Click Apply.

[12] With the Chart Editor still open, click File ▶ Save Chart Template. In the Save Chart Template window, click in the All Settings box, which selects all chart features. Now uncheck the box next to Text Content. (You don't want SPSS to apply the same axis titles to all of your scatterplots.) Click Continue. Find a good place to save the template (and concoct a descriptive name for the file), which SPSS saves with the .sgt extension. Do the following to apply the template to future editing projects: In the Chart Editor, click File ▶ Apply Chart Template, find the .sgt file, and click Open. Experience teaches that SPSS will apply most of the template's features to the new graphic, although some minor editing may still be required.

[13] If you're interested in seeing which countries are most and least dependent on international trade, refer to the procedure discussed in the section on "Obtaining Case-level Information with Case Summaries" in Chapter 2.

Multiple regression analysis is designed to disentangle the confounding effects of two (or more) independent variables. Multiple regression will estimate the effect of each independent variable on the dependent variable, controlling for the effects of all other independent variables in the model.

To conduct multiple regression analysis with SPSS, select <u>Analyze</u> ▸ <u>Regression</u> ▸ <u>Linear</u> to return the Regression window. If our earlier bivariate regression selections aren't already in place, move conflict_index into the Dependent field and democ_fh_polity into the Independent(s) field. Now move trade_percent_gdp into the Independent(s) box (see Figure 8-8) and click OK.

This analysis provides the information we need to isolate the partial effect of each independent variable on the dependent variable. As before, SPSS outputs four tables to the Viewer, two of which are particularly interesting to us.

Model Summary

Model	R	R Square	Adjusted R Square	Std. Error of the Estimate
1	0.580ᵃ	0.337	0.328	0.54053

a. Predictors: (Constant), International trade as percentage of GDP, Scale measuring how democratic country is

Coefficientsᵃ

Model		Unstandardized Coefficients B	Unstandardized Coefficients Std. Error	Standardized Coefficients Beta	t	Sig.
1	(Constant)	2.736	0.124		21.996	0.000
	Scale measuring how democratic country is	-0.099	0.014	-0.459	-6.956	0.000
	International trade as percentage of GDP	-0.005	0.001	-0.308	-4.659	0.000

a. Dependent Variable: Extent of ongoing domestic and international conflict

FIGURE 8-8   Conducting Multiple Regression Analysis

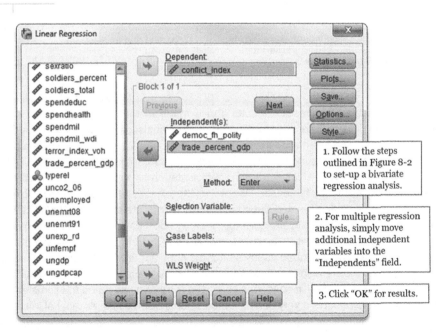

This analysis provides the information we need to isolate the partial effect of each independent variable on the dependent variable. The multiple regression equation is as follows:

$$\text{Conflict Index} = 2.736 - 0.099 \times \text{Democracy Scale} - 0.005 \times \text{Trade Percent GDP}$$

Let's focus on the regression coefficients for each of the independent variables. The coefficient on democ_fh_polity, −0.099, tells us the effect of democ_fh_polity on conflict_index, controlling for trade_percent_gdp. Recall that in the bivariate analysis, a 1-point increase in democ_fh_polity was associated with a 0.106-unit decrease in the expected conflict_index value

A CLOSER LOOK: REPORTING REGRESSION RESULTS IN TABLES

The default SPSS-format tables for regression results do not adhere to the standard design of numerical tables in political science journals. If you're reporting results in a paper or presentation, we encourage you to edit your tables of results so that they follow political science norms. Rather than report all four tables, consolidate the results into one well-formatted table. Using our multiple regression analysis results as an example, we might report our results in the following form:

TABLE   Multiple Regression Analysis of Conflict Index

	Coefficient
Democracy Scale	−0.099***
	(0.104)
Importance of Trade	−0.005***
	(0.001)
Constant	2.736***
	(0.124)
N	156
Adjusted R^2	0.328

Notes: Dependent variable is extent of ongoing domestic and international conflict in country; standard errors reported in parentheses.
*** = $P < .001$ (two-tailed tests)

The formatted table of regression results above modified the standard SPSS output in a number of respects. It is not strictly necessary to report t-statistics because they can be easily calculated by dividing coefficients by their standard errors. Standard errors can be reported in parentheses under the corresponding coefficient (if you do so, make note of this at the bottom of the table). Standardized coefficients (beta coefficients) aren't typically reported so we have deleted them from our results table (see "What Are Standardized Regression Coefficients?" in Chapter 9). P-values are often omitted but it is common to indicate statistically significant results using one, two, or three asterisks (we're only noting the symbols actually used). The constant term is the last coefficient reported (even though software often reports it first). The sample size (N) and model fit statistics can be added as rows after the constant term. The variable labels can be shortened so long as they remain clear and accurate. Decimal places should be vertically aligned and the table borders should be in academic style. The table font should be the same as the font used in the text. The product is a very concise, professional display of the essential information.

in a country. When we control for trade_percent_gdp, we find a slight reduction in this effect—to a 0.099-unit decrease in conflict_index per unit increase in democ_fh_polity. Even so, the regression coefficient on democ_fh_polity, with a t-statistic of −6.956 and a P-value less than .001, remains statistically significant.

The partial effect of trade_percent_gdp on the level of conflict observed in countries tells a similar story. According to the multiple regression results, a 1-percentage-point increase in the value of trade as a percentage of GDP decreases the expected value of conflict_index by 0.005. This may seem like a small effect size, but keep in mind that the observed values of trade_percent_gdp range from 21 percent (Nigeria) to 419 percent (Luxembourg), while the observed values of conflict_index range only from 1 (several countries) to 3.827 (Syria). The t-statistic for this partial regression coefficient is −4.659, which corresponds to a P-value of less than .001. Economic self-interest, like democracy, appears to have a statistically significant negative relationship to violence in countries around the world.

In multiple regression, adjusted R-squared communicates how well all the independent variables explain the dependent variable. By knowing two things about countries—how democratic they are and how much they depend on trade—we can account for .328 (about 33 percent) of the variation in the level of conflict we observe globally. This is an improvement over the explanatory leverage of democracy alone (which explained about 24 percent of the variation in conflict_index).

VISUALIZING MULTIPLE REGRESSION ANALYSIS WITH BUBBLE PLOTS

Once you have created a scatterplot for a dependent variable and one independent variable, you can add "bubbles" that weight the scatterplot markers according to values on a second independent variable. A bubble plot of the running multiple regression analysis example in this chapter would define the y-axis by values of conflict_index, the x-axis by values of the independent variable democ_fh_polity, and vary the size of the markers, which represent countries, in proportion to the value of the control variable trade_percent_gdp (see Figure 8-9). This enables one to visualize the relationship among three variables in a two-dimensional space. Watch the screencast to learn how to create a bubble plot with SPSS.

Screencast
Bubble Plots

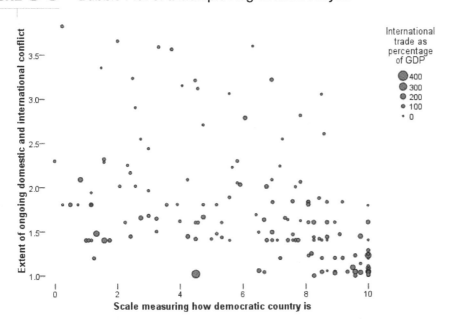

FIGURE 8-9   Bubble Plot of a Multiple Regression Analysis

Name: _Anna Jeffries_   Date: _11/23/22_

E-mail: _anna.jeffries@spartans.ut.edu_   Section: _____

CHAPTER 8 EXERCISES

1. (Dataset: NES. Variables: ft_Trump_pre, ft_Police, ft_Rep, ft_Obama, ft_HClinton_pre, nesw.) We have worked with feeling thermometer ratings several times already. As you know, feeling thermometer questions on the NES ask respondents to rate something on a scale from 0 to 100, with 0 being very cold/negative feelings, 50 representing neutral feelings, and 100 being very warm/positive feelings.

    Let's look at the correlations among several feeling thermometers to get an idea of how people view different subjects. If people think subjects are similar, they should express similar sentiments about them. Perhaps knowing how someone feels about one subject can help us predict how they might feel about a variety of subjects.

    A. Use the Analyze ▶ Correlate ▶ Bivariate procedure to generate a correlation matrix for the following feeling thermometers in the NES dataset: ft_Trump_pre, ft_Police, ft_Rep, ft_Obama, and ft_HClinton_pre. Be sure to weight observations using nesw so your results are nationally representative. Fill in the missing Pearson correlation coefficients in the following table.

	ft_Trump_pre	ft_Police	ft_Rep	ft_Obama	ft_HClinton_pre
ft_Trump_pre	1.00				
ft_Police	.333 ?	1.00			
ft_Rep	0.64	.374	1.00		
ft_Obama	-.724 ?	-.294	-0.53	1.00	
ft_HClinton_pre	-.654	-0.24	-.49	.82	1.00

    B. According to the correlation coefficient, as feeling thermometer scores for the police increase, feeling thermometer scores for Republicans (circle one)

        increase.   (decrease.)

    C. According to the correlation coefficient matrix, which of the following variables has the strongest correlation (either negatively or positively) with feeling thermometer scores for Donald Trump? (circle one)

        Police   Republicans   (Obama)   H. Clinton

    D. According to the correlation coefficient matrix, the following two feeling thermometer scores

have the strongest correlation (either negatively or positively): _ft_obama_ and _ft_HClinton_pre_.

2. (Dataset: States. Variables: vep16_turnout, clinton16.) An article of faith among Democratic Party strategists (and a source of apprehension among Republican strategists) is that high voter turnouts help Democratic candidates. Why should this be the case? According to the conventional wisdom, Democratic electorates are less likely to vote than are Republican voters. Thus, low turnouts naturally favor Republican candidates. As turnouts push higher, the reasoning goes, a larger number of potential Democratic voters will go to the polls, creating a better opportunity for Democratic candidates. Therefore, as turnouts go up, so should the Democratic percentage of the vote.[14]

    A. Use the Analyze ▶ Regression ▶ Linear procedure to test this conventional wisdom. The States dataset contains vep16_turnout, the percentage of the state voting-eligible population that turned out to vote in the 2016 presidential election. This is the independent variable. Another variable, clinton16, the percentage of the vote cast for Democratic candidate Hillary Clinton, is the dependent variable.

    Use linear regression analysis to examine the relationship between voter turnout and Hillary Clinton's vote share. Complete the following table.

	Coefficient	Standard Error	t-ratio	P-value
% Voter turnout	.432 ?	.2236 ?	1.916	.061 ?
Constant term	17.123 ?	13.988	1.22	0.227
N	.266 ?			
R-squared	.071 ?			
Adjusted R-squared	.052 ?			

---

[14] See Michael D. Martinez and Jeff Gill, "The Effects of Turnout on Partisan Outcomes in US Presidential Elections 1960–2000," *Journal of Politics* 67, no. 4 (2005): 1248–1274. Martinez and Gill find that the Democratic advantage from higher turnouts has declined over time.

B. Based on your results, the regression equation for estimating the percentage voting for Hillary Clinton is (fill in the blanks, put the constant, _cons, in the last blank)

Clinton Voter Percentage = _17.12_ + _.432_ × Percentage Turnout + _vep16_turnout_

	Coefficient	Standard Error	t-ratio	P-value
% Pro-choice	-.148 ?	.043 ?	3.49 ?	.001 ?
Constant term	14.899 ?	2.30	6.478	< .001 ?
N	.445 ?			
R-squared	.198 ?			
Adjusted R-squared	.182 ?			

C. Consider your findings in parts A and B. One may conclude that (complete one option)

❏ The conventional wisdom is correct because

_____

_____

✓ The conventional wisdom is incorrect because _the n is not statistically significant because it is smaller than .7_

3. (Dataset: States. Variables: abortlaw2017, prochoice_percent.) As you are no doubt aware, in its momentous decision in *Roe v. Wade* (1973), the U.S. Supreme Court declared that states may not outlaw abortion. Even so, many state legislatures have enacted restrictions and regulations that, while not banning abortion, make an abortion more difficult to obtain. Other states, however, have few or no restrictions. What factors might explain these differences in abortion laws among the states? We know that the public remains divided on this issue. Public opinion in some states is more favorable toward permitting abortion, whereas public opinion is less favorable in other states. Does public opinion guide state policy on this issue?

The States dataset contains abortlaw2017, which measures the number of abortion restrictions a state has enacted into law. Values on abortlaw2017 range from 0 (least restrictive) to 13 (most restrictive). This is the dependent variable. The dataset also has the variable, prochoice_percent, the percentage of the mass public that is pro-choice (thus opposed to putting restrictions on abortion access). This is the independent variable.

A. If you were to use regression analysis to test the idea that public opinion on abortion affects state abortion policy, you would expect to find (check one)

✓ a negative sign on prochoice_percent's regression coefficient.

❏ a positive sign on prochoice_percent's regression coefficient.

B. Using SPSS's Analyze ▶ Regression ▶ Linear procedure, analyze the relationship between abortlaw2017 and prochoice_percent. Complete the following table.

C. According to the results, the regression equation for estimating the number of abortion restrictions is (fill in the blanks, put the constant, _cons, in the last blank)

Number of Restrictions = _14.9_ − _.148_ × Percentage Pro-choice + _prochoice_percent_

D. According to the data, 70 percent of Virginia residents are pro-choice. In Tennessee, by contrast, only 40 percent of the public holds this view. Based on the regression equation (fill in the blanks),

You would estimate that Virginia would have _fewer_ abortion restrictions.

You would estimate that Tennessee would have _more_ abortion restrictions.

E. Adjusted R-squared is equal to _.182_. This means that _the variance in abortion restrictions is affected by the prochoice percent._

F. Run the Graphs ▶ Legacy Dialogs ▶ Scatter/Dot procedure to obtain a scatterplot with a linear prediction overlay. Make sure the x-axis and y-axis are appropriately labeled. Also, change the color and pattern of the linear prediction line. If you prefer, make other enhancements to the graph's appearance. Print the graphic.

4. (Dataset: States. Variables: abortlaw2017, prochoice_percent, womleg_2017.) Suppose that a critic, upon examining the variables in the States dataset and viewing your results in Exercise 3, expresses skepticism about the relationship between mass-level abortion attitudes and the number of state-level restrictions on abortion:

"There is a key aspect of state governance that you have not taken into account: the percentage of state legislators who are women (womleg_2017). If you were to examine the correlation coefficients among abortlaw2017, prochoice_percent, and womleg_2017, you will find two things. First, the correlation between abortlaw2017 and womleg_2017 will be negative and pretty strong. . . say, at least −0.50. Second, the correlation between prochoice_percent and womleg_2017 will be positive and fairly strong—at least +0.50. Third, when you perform a multiple regression analysis of abortlaw2017, using prochoice_percent and womleg_2017 as independent variables, you will find that womleg_2017 is statistically significant, while prochoice_percent will fade to statistical insignificance."

A. Use the Analyze ▶ Correlate ▶ Bivariate procedure to obtain a correlation matrix for abortlaw2017, prochoice_percent, and womleg_2017. Write the correlation coefficients next to the question marks in the following table.

	No. of abortion restrictions	Percent mass public pro-choice	Percent female legislators
No. of abortion restrictions (abortlaw2017)	1.00		
Percent mass public pro-choice (prochoice_percent)	−.449 ?	1.00	
Percent female legislators (womleg_2017)	−.944?	.249 ?	1.00

B. Consider the skeptical critic's first claim regarding the relationship between womleg_2017 and abortlaw2017. According to the correlation coefficient, this claim is (circle one and explain your answer)

(correct)   incorrect

because the correlation is ~~somewhat~~ *negative &* strong at −.449.

C. Consider the skeptical critic's second claim regarding the relationship between womleg_2017 and prochoice_percent. According to the correlation coefficient, this claim is (circle one and explain your answer)

correct   (incorrect)

because The claim is weak at .249

D. Use the Analyze ▶ Regression ▶ Linear procedure to estimate the multiple regression model suggested by the critic. Write the correct values next to the question marks in the following table.

	Coefficient	St. Error	t-ratio	P-value
% Pro-choice	−.110 ?	.039?	−2.88	.007 ?
% Women legislators	−.195 ?	.049?	−3.940	<.001
Constant term	17.716?	2.14	8.30	<.001
N	.631 ?			

	Coefficient	St. Error	t-ratio	P-value
R-squared	.398 ?			
Adjusted R-squared	.372			

E. Based on the evidence in part D, is the critic's third claim regarding the multiple regression analysis correct? (circle one and explain your answer):

(Correct)   Incorrect

because the constant & % women legislators are both <.001

F. Create a bubble plot that depicts the relationship between abortlaw2017 (y-axis) and prochoice_percent (x-axis), weighted by womleg_2017. This is a special graphing procedure demonstrated in a screencast video. Print the graph.

5. (Dataset: GSS. Variables: tolerance, educ, age, polviews, wtss.) What factors affect a person's level of tolerance of unpopular groups? Consider three hypotheses:

Hypothesis 1: In a comparison of individuals, older people will be less tolerant than younger people.

Hypothesis 2: In a comparison of individuals, those with higher levels of education will have higher levels of tolerance than those with lower levels of education.

Hypothesis 3: In a comparison of individuals, conservatives will be less tolerant than liberals.

The GSS dataset includes the following variables, as described in the table below.

GSS Variable	Label	Coding	Status in This Exercise
tolerance	Tolerance	0 (low) to 6 (high)	Dependent variable
age	R's Age (years)	18 to 89	Independent variable
educ	Highest Year of School	0 to 20	Independent variable
polviews	Ideological Self-Placement	1 (ExtrmLib) to 7 (ExtrmCons)	Independent variable

A. Use the Analyze ▶ Regression ▶ Linear procedure to run a multiple regression analysis with the dependent variable and independent variables specified above. (Don't forget to weight observations using wtss.) After you run the model, run the script to obtain adjusted R-squared. Fill in the following table.

	Coefficient	Standard Error	t-ratio	P-value
Age	-.01 ?	.002 ?	-3.897 <.001 ?	
Education	.169 ?	.015	11.67 <.001 ?	
Political ideology	-0.12	.029 ?	4.16 ? <.001 ?	
Constant term	2.885 ?	.279	8.71 ? <.001 ?	
N	.319 ?			
R-squared	.202 ?			

B. Based on the evidence in part A, does it appear that Hypothesis 1 has merit? (circle one and explain your answer)

Yes   No

because

_____

_____

_____

C. Based on the evidence in part A, does it appear that Hypothesis 2 has merit? (circle one and explain your answer)

Yes   No

because

_____

_____

_____

D. Based on the evidence in part A, does it appear that Hypothesis 3 has merit? (circle one and explain your answer)

Yes   No

because

_____

_____

_____

E. The adjusted R-squared statistic for the multiple regression model you estimated in part A equals

.1 _____.

F. Use the regression equation to estimate the tolerance score for the typical respondent, which we will define as a person having the median values of all the independent variables. Run Analyze ▶ Descriptive Statistics ▶ Frequencies with the statistics option (for medians) to obtain the median values for each independent variable. Write the medians in the following table (the median of polviews already appears in the table).

	age	educ	polviews
Median	47.0 ?	13.0 ?	4

G. When you use the median values to estimate the tolerance score for the typical person, you obtain an estimate equal to (fill in the blank) __5.0__.

6. (Dataset: States. Variables: HR_conserv11, Conserv_public.) Two congressional scholars are discussing the extent to which members of the U.S. House of Representatives stay in touch with the voters in their states.

Scholar 1: "When members of Congress vote on important public policies, they are closely attuned to the ideological makeups of their states. Members from states having lots of liberals will tend to cast votes in the liberal direction. Representatives from states with mostly conservative constituencies, by contrast, will take conservative positions on important policies."

Scholar 2: "You certainly have a naïve view of congressional behavior. Once they get elected, members of congress adopt a 'Washington, D.C., state of mind,' perhaps voting in the liberal direction on one policy and in the conservative direction on another. One thing is certain: The way members vote has little to do with the ideological composition of their states."

Think about an independent variable that measures the percentage of self-described "conservatives" among the mass public in a state, with low values denoting low percentages of conservatives and high values denoting high percentages of conservatives. And consider a dependent variable that gauges the degree to which the state's House delegation votes in a conservative direction on public policies. Low scores on this dependent variable tell you that the delegation tends to vote in a liberal direction, and high scores say that the delegation votes in a conservative direction.

A. Below is an empty graphic shell showing the relationship between the independent variable and the dependent variable. Draw a regression line inside the shell that depicts what the relationship should look like if Scholar 1 is correct.

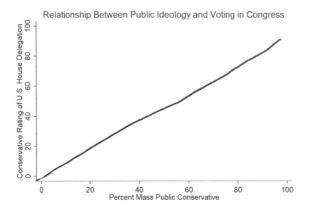

B. Below is another graphic shell showing the relationship between the independent variable and the dependent variable. Draw a regression line inside the shell that depicts what the relationship should look like if Scholar 2 is correct.

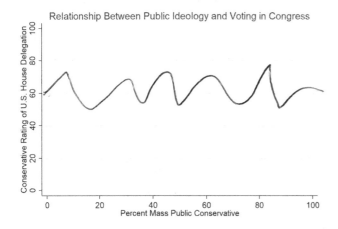

C. The States dataset contains the variable Conserv_public, the percentage of the mass public calling themselves conservative. This is the independent variable. The

dataset also contains HR_conserv11, a measure of conservative votes by states' House members. Scores on this variable can range from 0 (low conservatism) to 100 (high conservatism). This is the dependent variable. Use the Analyze ▶ Regression ▶ Linear procedure to estimate the relationship between the variables.

According to the regression equation, a 1-percentage-point increase in conservatives in the mass public is associated with (check one)

☑ about a 27-point decrease in House conservatism scores.

☑ about a 2-point increase in House conservatism scores.

☐ about an 8-point increase in House conservatism scores.

D. If you were to use this regression to estimate the mean House conservatism score for states having 30 percent conservatives, your estimate would be (circle the closest estimate)

30   35   40   ⟨45⟩   50

E. The adjusted R-squared for this relationship is equal to .582. This tells you that about 60 percent of the variation in HR_conserv11 is explained by Conserv_public.

F. Use the Graphs ▶ Legacy Dialogs ▶ Scatter/Dot procedure to obtain a scatterplot with a linear prediction overlay. Remember that HR_conserv11 is the y-axis variable, and Conserv_public is the x-axis variable. Make sure the y-axis and x-axis are appropriately labeled and change the pattern of the linear prediction line. If you prefer, make other enhancements to the graph's appearance. Print the graph.

G. Based on your inspection of the regression results, the scatterplot and linear prediction line, and adjusted R-squared, which congressional scholar is more correct?

☑ Scholar 1 is more correct because There is a good correlation between the conservatism of the public and the HR conservative rating.

☐ Scholar 2 is more correct because _____

That concludes the exercises for this chapter.

9

Dummy Variables and Interaction Effects

 Watch screencasts of the guided examples in this chapter. **edge.sagepub.com/pollock**

Procedures Covered

<u>T</u>ransform ▶ Create Dummy Variables

<u>A</u>nalyze ▶ <u>R</u>egression ▶ <u>L</u>inear (with dummy variables)

<u>T</u>ransform ▶ <u>C</u>ompute Variable (if optional case selection condition)

<u>A</u>nalyze ▶ <u>R</u>egression ▶ <u>L</u>inear (with interaction variable)

<u>G</u>raphs ▶ <u>L</u>egacy Dialogs ▶ <u>S</u>catter/Dot (fit lines at subgroups)

W ith SPSS, you can easily adapt regression analysis to different research situations. One of the great virtues of regression analysis is the flexibility it offers researchers who want to explain variation in a dependent variable as a function of variables measured at different levels.

In one situation, you might have nominal or ordinal independent variables with multiple values. Independent variables of this type can be incorporated into regression analysis. In this chapter you will learn how to use dummy variables in regression analysis. In a second research situation, you might suspect that the effect of one independent variable on the dependent variable is not the same for all values of another independent variable—that is, interaction is going on in the data. With some slight adjustments to how we specify independent variables, SPSS will run multiple regression to estimate the size and statistical significance of interaction effects. In this chapter you will learn how to perform and interpret multiple regression with interaction effects.

Screencast

Regression with Dummy Variables

REGRESSION WITH MULTIPLE DUMMY VARIABLES

Recall from the discussion of indicator variables in Chapter 3 that a dummy variable can take on only two values, 1 or 0. Each case being analyzed either has the characteristic being measured (a code of 1) or does not have it (a code of 0). For example, a dummy variable for gun ownership might code gun owners as 1 and non-gun owners as 0. Everybody who is coded 1 has the characteristic of being a gun owner, and everybody who is coded 0 does not have that characteristic.

To appreciate why this 0 or 1 coding is the essential feature of dummy variables, consider the following regression model, which is designed to test the hypothesis that gun owners give President Donald Trump higher feeling thermometer ratings than will non-gun owners:

$$\text{Trump feeling thermometer} = a + b \times (\text{gun owner})$$

In this formulation, gun ownership is measured by a dummy variable, "gun owner," which is coded 0 for non-gun owners and coded 1 for gun owners. Since non-gun owners are scored 0 on the dummy, the constant or intercept, a, will tell us the average Trump rating among non-gun owners. Why so? Substituting 0 for the dummy yields: $a + b \times 0 = a$. Any value of b multiplied by 0 equals 0. In the language of dummy variable regression, non-gun owners are the "omitted" category, the category whose mean value on the dependent variable is captured by the intercept, a. The regression coefficient, b, will tell us how much to adjust the intercept for gun owners—that is, when the dummy switches from 0 to 1. Thus, just as in any regression, b will estimate the average change in the dependent variable for a unit change in the independent variable. Since in this case a unit change in the independent variable is the difference between non-gun owners (coded 0 on gun_own) and gun owners (coded 1 on gun_own), then the regression coefficient will reflect the mean difference in Trump ratings between non-gun owners and gun owners.

It is important to be clear on this point: The coefficient, b, *does not* communicate the mean Trump rating among gun owners. Rather, it estimates the mean *difference* between non-gun owners and gun owners.[1] (Of course, an estimated value of the dependent variable among gun owners can be easily arrived at by summing a and b: $a + b \times 1 = a + b$.) As with any regression coefficient, we can rely on the b coefficient's t-ratio and P-value to test the null hypothesis that there is no statistically meaningful difference between gun owners and non-gun owners in thermometer ratings of President Trump. (Spoiler alert: there is a statistically significant difference.)

Let's open the NES dataset to conduct linear regression analysis with gun ownership as the independent variable and Trump thermometer ratings as the dependent variable. Conveniently, gun_own is coded 0 for non-gun owners and 1 for gun owners, but you shouldn't assume a nominal or ordinal variable is properly coded for dummy variable regression; always check variable information first.[2]

To conduct linear regression analysis with a dummy variable, we'll use the same procedure we used in Chapter 8: select Analyze ▶ Regression ▶ Linear (see Figure 8-2). Move ft_Trump_post into the Dependent field, and move gun_own into the Independent(s) field. Click OK.[3]

According to the Coefficients table, the regression equation is as follows:

$$\text{Trump feeling thermometer} = 37.426 + 11.650 \times (\text{gun owner})$$

How would we interpret these estimates? As always, the constant term estimates the value of the dependent variable when the independent variable is 0. Non-gun owners have a value of 0 on the gun owner dummy variable; therefore, we expect non-gun owners to give Trump a 37.426 feeling

---

[1] The b coefficient in this example is comparable to the difference of mean Trump support between non-gun owners and gun owners (controlling for race of respondent) you calculated in Chapter 5.

[2] Remember, you can right-click the variable name in most windows to access variable information. You'll often see nominal variables where the excluded category is coded 1 and observations with the characteristic are coded 2. When a variable with this numeric coding is used in multiple regression, the a intercept term will not equal the expected value of the dependent variable in the reference group (the expected value is $a + b$). How can we address this problem? One solution is to recode the original variable into a new dummy variable with numeric values 0 (for non-gun owners) and 1 (for gun owners).

[3] Don't forget to weight cases using the nesw variable.

Model Summary

Model	R	R Square	Adjusted R Square	Std. Error of the Estimate
1	.157[a]	.025	.025	34.687

a. Predictors: (Constant), Does R own a gun? (v161496)

Coefficients[a]

Model		Unstandardized Coefficients B	Std. Error	Standardized Coefficients Beta	t	Sig.
1	(Constant)	37.426	.728		51.388	.000
	Does R own a gun? (v161496)	11.650	1.244	.157	9.366	.000

a. Dependent Variable: Feeling therm: Donald Trump (post, v162079)

thermometer score. The regression coefficient on the gun owner dummy variable, 11.650, communicates the mean change in the dependent variable when the dummy switches from 0 to 1. We can use this value to estimate the mean Trump rating for gun owners: 37.426 + 11.650 = 49.076. Was the observed difference between gun owners and non-gun owners produced by random sampling error? Not according to the P-value, which is less than .001.

Does gun ownership account for a lot of the variation in Trump's thermometer ratings? Not exactly. According to the R-squared criteria, gun ownership alone accounts for about 2.5 percent of the variation in the dependent variable. (Because we used a large sample and only one predictor, we get the same reported R-squared and adjusted R-squared values.) Clearly, there must be other variables "out there" that contribute to the explanation of Trump's ratings. Let's expand our regression model by taking race and ethnicity into account.

The Race3 variable in the NES dataset assigns whites numeric code 1, blacks numeric code 2, and Hispanics numeric code 3. (If you forget how to check the numeric code of variable values, see the "A CLOSER LOOK: Variables Utility" box in Chapter 1.) We cannot use Race3 in this form in a regression; SPSS will interpret these numeric codes literally and estimate a line from whites to blacks to Hispanics.

We actually need to create not one but *two* dummy variables from the Race3 variable. Why two? Here is a general rule about dummy variables: If the variable you want to "dummify" has k categories, then you will need $k - 1$ dummies to measure the variable. Because Race3 has three unique values, we need at least two dummy variables to estimate a multiple regression. One of these variables, which we will call racedum_1, is equal to 1 for whites and 0 for blacks and Hispanics. The second dummy variable, racedum_2, is equal to 1 for blacks and 0 for whites and Hispanics. Hispanic respondents, then, can be uniquely identified as having values of 0 on racedum_1 and racedum_2. Consider the following recoding protocol:

Race3, Three Categories	Old Value (Race3)	New Value (racedum_1)	New Value (racedum_2)
White	1	1	0
Black	2	0	1
Hispanic	3	0	0
Missing	Missing	Missing	Missing

FIGURE 9-1   Creating a Series of Dummy Variables

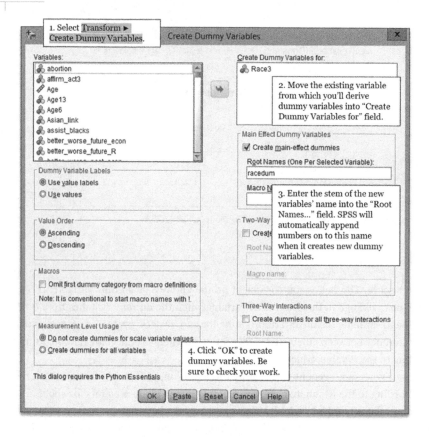

To create multiple dummy variables from a nominal or ordinal variable with more than two unique values, select Transform ► Create Dummy Variables to call up the Create Dummy Variables window.[4] We want to "dummify" the existing Race3 variable, so we'll move it into the "Create Dummy Variables for" field. Our new dummy variables are based on the values of Race3 (rather than the interaction of Race3 and some other variable), so we'll leave the "Create main-effect dummies" option checked and we'll type "racedum" in the "Root Names" field. The root name will be the stem of our new dummy variable names; SPSS will automatically append _1, _2, . . . _k onto the root name so each one of our k new dummy variables will have a unique name. Replicate Figure 9-1 on your computer and click the OK button.

The Viewer output simply confirms that SPSS has generated our new dummy variables:

Variable Creation

	Label
racedum_1	Race3=White
racedum_2	Race3=Black
racedum_3	Race3=Hispanic

---

[4] Alternatively, one can create dummy variables one at a time following the procedure for creating indicator variables discussed in Chapter 3. Creating indicator variables using the Transform ► Recode into Different Variables procedure may be more efficient when the original nominal variable has only two unique values or only one dummy variable is needed.

Before incorporating these new variables into multiple regression analysis of feelings about Donald Trump, it would be prudent to check our work. Run a quick Analyze ▸ Descriptive Statistics ▸ Frequencies on Race3, racedum_1, and racedum_2.

White/Black/Hisp (v161310x)

		Frequency	Percent	Valid Percent	Cumulative Percent
Valid	White	2530	69.3	75.3	75.3
	Black	399	10.9	11.9	87.1
	Hispanic	432	11.8	12.9	100.0
	Total	3361	92.1	100.0	
Missing	System	288	7.9		
Total		3649	100.0		

Race3=White

		Frequency	Percent	Valid Percent	Cumulative Percent
Valid	0	831	22.8	24.7	24.7
	1	2530	69.3	75.3	100.0
	Total	3361	92.1	100.0	
Missing	System	288	7.9		
Total		3649	100.0		

Race3=Black

		Frequency	Percent	Valid Percent	Cumulative Percent
Valid	0	2962	81.2	88.1	88.1
	1	399	10.9	11.9	100.0
	Total	3361	92.1	100.0	
Missing	System	288	7.9		
Total		3649	100.0		

According to the frequency distribution table of Race3, the NES dataset has 2,530 white respondents (75.3% of sample), 399 black respondents (10.9% of sample), and 432 Hispanic respondents (11.9% of sample). According to the frequency distribution table of racedum_1, 2,530 respondents (75.3% of sample) are coded 1 on this dummy variable. According to the frequency distribution table of racedum_2, 399 respondents (10.9% of sample) are coded 1 on this dummy variable. The recodes check out. Why are we ignoring racedum_3? We'll answer this question after we estimate a multiple regression model using our new dummy variables.

Now we are ready to run a multiple regression analysis of ft_Trump_post, using gun_own, racedum_1, and racedum_2 as independent variables. Select Analyze ▸ Regression ▸ Linear. The variable ft_Trump_post should still be in the Dependent field and gun_own in the Independent(s) field, so leave them in place (or move them into place now if your Linear Regression window has been reset). Move two of our new race/ethnicity dummies, racedum_1 and racedum_2, into the Independent(s) panel (see Figure 9-2). Click OK.

FIGURE 9-2   Regression with Multiple Dummy Variables

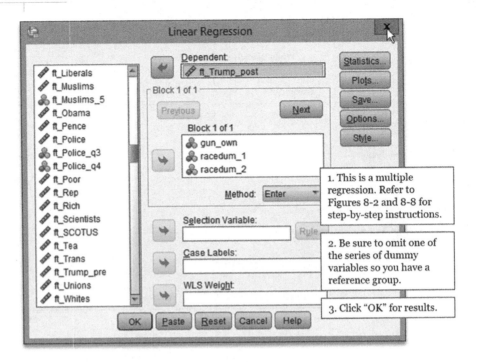

Model Summary

Model	R	R Square	Adjusted R Square	Std. Error of the Estimate
1	.293ª	.086	.085	33.685

a. Predictors: (Constant), Race3=Black, Does R own a gun? (v161496), Race3=White

Coefficientsª

Model		Unstandardized Coefficients B	Std. Error	Standardized Coefficients Beta	t	Sig.
1	(Constant)	26.783	1.671		16.031	.000
	Does R own a gun? (v161496)	9.233	1.264	.125	7.303	.000
	Race3=White	16.712	1.798	.206	9.297	.000
	Race3=Black	-6.447	2.382	-.060	-2.707	.007

a. Dependent Variable: Feeling therm: Donald Trump (post, v162079)

The regression equation is as follows:

$$\text{TrumpFT} = 26.783 + 9.233 \times (\text{gun owner}) + 16.712 \times (\text{white}) - 6.447 \times (\text{black})$$

By estimating the effects of race/ethnicity and gun ownership, these results give us the expected Trump ratings of *six different types* of people. Table 9-1 breaks down how the multiple regression equation yields expected Trump ratings for six different types of people.

TABLE 9-1   Trump Ratings Predicted by Multiple Regression

Case	Constant (baseline)	Gun Difference	White Difference	Black Difference	Expected Rating
Hispanic non-gun owners	26.783	0	0	0	26.783
White non-gun owners	26.783	0	+16.712	0	43.495
Black non-gun owners	26.783	0	0	−6.447	20.336
Hispanic gun owners	26.783	+9.233	0	0	36.016
White gun owners	26.783	+9.233	+16.712	0	52.728
Black gun owners	26.783	+9.233	0	−6.447	29.569

As always, the intercept/constant term is the expected value of the dependent variable when the value of all the independent variables is 0. Think about who falls into the reference category: individuals who do not own a gun, are not white, and are not black. The reference category in this estimation is Hispanic non-gun owners and they're expected to rate Trump at 26.783. On average, gun owners rate Trump 9.233 points higher on a feeling thermometer, once we take race/ethnicity into account. Notice that the estimated effect of gun ownership is lower than estimated in the bivariate regression (11.650), which means some of the difference we initially attributed to gun ownership is better understood as racial/ethnic differences in gun ownership. Taking the difference between gun owners and non-gun owners into account, we find that blacks, on average, rate Trump 6.447 points lower than Hispanics do and whites rate him 16.712 points higher than Hispanics do. Based on these results, we should expect blacks who own guns to rate Trump higher than blacks who don't own guns; similarly, we should expect Hispanics who own guns to rate Trump higher than Hispanics who don't own guns. All told, gun ownership and race/ethnicity explain 8.5 percent of the variation in Trump's feeling thermometer ratings.

It should be clear from our discussion of the multiple regression results that we did not exclude Hispanics from our analysis. We made them the reference/baseline category and compared expected Trump ratings from black and white respondents to Hispanics. When you estimate a multiple regression equation with dummy variables and a constant term, one of the values of the "dummified" variable must serve as the reference category, otherwise there is no unique equation that solves the least-squares problem.[5]

Before going on to the next section, you may want to exercise your new skills by creating new dummies and further expanding the model. In any event, before proceeding be sure to save the dataset.

A CLOSER LOOK: CHANGING THE REFERENCE CATEGORY

When you conduct regression analysis with a nominal- or ordinal-level independent variable, one value of the independent variable(s) will serve as the reference group. The expected value of the dependent variable in the reference group equals the constant term and the partial regression coefficients tell us how much difference can be expected when the independent variable values

(Continued)

---

[5] If you try to estimate a multiple regression equation with a constant term and dummy variables that exhaust all the possible cases, it is mathematically impossible to identify a single solution. If $y = a + b_1 \times (\text{white}) + b_2 \times (\text{black}) + b_3 \times (\text{Hispanic})$ and every respondent is white, black, or Hispanic, then $y = (a + d) + (b_1 - d) \times (\text{white}) + (b_2 - d) \times (\text{black}) + (b_3 - d) \times (\text{Hispanic})$, where d is any number is also true, permitting an infinite number of possible solutions. We must either omit one category of the dummified variable or the constant term.

(Continued)

change. The expected values will be the same regardless of which value is the reference category, but you may find that changing your reference category helps you test your hypotheses and communicate your results more clearly.

When we analyzed the effect of both gun ownership and race/ethnicity on sentiment about Donald Trump, Hispanic non-gun owners were the baseline category. If we hypothesized that minorities give Trump lower feeling thermometer scores than whites do (controlling for gun ownership), we can change the reference category to white non-gun owners to facilitate the comparison. To change the reference category, we would omit the racedum_1 variable, which identifies white respondents, and include the racedum_3 variable, which identifies Hispanic respondents. Try making this change to the multiple regression with dummy variables seen in Figure 9-2 to replicate the results of this analysis.

Model Summary

Model	R	R Square	Adjusted R Square	Std. Error of the Estimate
1	.762[a]	.580	.545	2.191

a. Predictors: (Constant), permit * term_limits, Percent public "Always allow" abortion, Does state have term limits for legislators?

Coefficients[a]

Model		Unstandardized Coefficients		Standardized Coefficients		
		B	Std. Error	Beta	t	Sig.
1	(Constant)	16.184	1.685		9.606	.000
	Percent public "Always allow" abortion	-.247	.044	-.758	-5.646	.000
	Does state have term limits for legislators?	.130	2.780	.019	.047	.963
	permit * term_limits	.029	.074	.155	.389	.699

a. Dependent Variable: Number of restrictions on abortion

As you can see, the model summary statistics don't change, nor does the expected effect of owning a gun. In this analysis, however, the constant term, 43.495, represents the expected Trump feeling thermometer score of white non-gun owners and the partial regression coefficients clearly show that black and Hispanic respondents give Trump significantly lower scores than whites do.

INTERACTION EFFECTS IN MULTIPLE REGRESSION

Screencast

Interaction Effects in Multiple Regression

Multiple regression is a linear and additive technique. It assumes a linear relationship between the independent variables and the dependent variable. It also assumes that the effect of one independent variable on the dependent variable is the same for all values of the other independent variables in the model. In the regression we just estimated, for example, multiple regression assumed that the effect of owning a gun on Trump sentiment is the same for all races/ethnicities. Stated a bit differently, the multiple regression assumed that racial/ethnic differences in Trump evaluation are the same for gun owners and non-gun owners. This assumption works fine for additive relationships. However, if interaction is taking place—for example, if the gap between gun owners and non-gun owners is significantly larger among whites than among blacks or Hispanics—then multiple regression will not capture this effect. Before researchers model interaction effects by using multiple regression, they have usually performed preliminary analyses that suggest such effects are occurring in the data.

In this section, we'll consider the effect of a legislative reform often seen as a cure for political dysfunction: term limits. Some state legislators can only hold office for a limited number of terms or years. Advocates see term limits as a way to get politicians to act differently. If they aren't always working toward re-election, they should be able to act in the public interest rather than serve special interests and single-issue voters. According to this view, term limits change the relationship between public opinion and public policy. We would expect legislatures in states without term limits to be more responsive to voters' policy preferences than legislatures in states with term limits.

The States dataset, states.sav, includes three variables we can use to evaluate the effect of term limits. The permit variable tells us the percentage of people in each state who think women should be permitted to have abortions under all circumstances; the permit variable measures public opinion. The variable abortlaw2017 is the number of legal restrictions on abortion access state legislatures have enacted (out of 14 possible restrictions). An indicator variable, term_limits, identifies states with term limits in place. Public opinion on abortion should affect public policy, but the impact of public opinion on policy outcomes might be weaker in states with term limits than it is in states without term limits.

We would begin building the model in a familiar way, by estimating the effects of each independent variable, permit and term_limits, on the dependent variable, the number of legal restrictions on abortion (abortlaw2017):

$$\text{Abortion restrictions} = a + b_1 \times (\text{Public opinion}) + b_2 \times (\text{Term limits})$$

This is a simple additive model. The constant, a, estimates abortlaw2017 for states with a value of 0 on both independent variables—0 percent public support for unfettered abortion access and no term limits. The parameter b_1 estimates the effect of each percentage-point increase in pro-choice opinion. The parameter b_2 tells us the effect of a one-unit increase in the term_limits variable (which is the difference between not having term limits and having term limits, because the only values of this variable are 0 and 1).

Think about why the simple additive model does not adequately represent the relationship between public opinion, term limits, and public policy described above. Notice that in the simple additive model, the b_1 coefficient is unaffected by the value of term limits. In the simple additive model, public opinion has the same effect on policy in states with term limits and without term limits; similarly, term limits have the same effect on policy regardless of the degree to which public opinion is pro-choice. We need to adjust the regression model to allow the effect of public opinion on policy, estimated by the b_1 coefficient, to vary based on whether legislators face term limits.

In multiple regression, this adjustment is accomplished by including an interaction variable as an independent variable. The interaction variable is the product of the independent variables thought to interact with one another. For the problem at hand, the interaction term is equal to permit × term_limits. Let's include this term in the model we just discussed and see what it looks like:

$$\text{Abortion restrictions} = a + b_1 \times (\text{Public opinion}) + b_2 \times (\text{Term limits}) + b_3$$
$$\times (\text{Public opinion} \times \text{Term limits})$$

All states that are coded 0 on term_limits will have a value of 0 on the interaction variable. The interaction term equals the value of permit in states with term limits, so the value of b_3 will estimate how term limits change the effect of public opinion on public policy.

Let's work through the research problem and get SPSS to estimate the multiple regression model with an interaction term for us. Because the States dataset does not have the interaction variable we need for our model, we will use Compute to calculate it. So, our first step will be using the Transform ▶ Compute Variable procedure to create an interaction variable. Then, we will run Regression to estimate the additive effects and the interaction effect.

To create an interaction variable, select Transform ▶ Compute Variable. You may recall using this procedure in Chapter 3 to compute an additive index. We'll use this procedure to generate a new variable with values equal to the product of the term_limits and permit variables. We will name the interaction variable "interact." Type "interact" in the Target Variable field (see Figure 9-3). In the Numeric Expression field, we'll build the mathematical expression used to compute the new variable: permit * term_limits. You can type that expression into the Numeric Expression field, but we suggest building it by moving the permit variable from the left-hand side list into this field, pressing the * button, and then moving the term_limits variable over to complete the expression (moving the variable names reduces opportunities for typos).

Before clicking OK and computing the variable, there are a couple details to attend to. We want to label the variable we're creating and make sure SPSS doesn't compute values when data are missing. To label the new interaction variable, click the Type & Label button. In the Compute Variable: Type and Label window, type "permit * term_limits" in the Label field. Click Continue, returning to the Compute Variable window.

Whenever you create a new variable by multiplying one variable by another (as we are doing), and at least one of the variables can take on the value of 0 (as is the case here), you need to make sure that the computation is restricted to cases that have non-missing values on both variables.[6] In the Compute Variable window, click the button labeled "If (optional case selection condition)," as shown in Figure 9-3. The grayed-out Compute Variable: If Cases window appears. Select the radio button next to "Include if case satisfies condition." Doing so wakes up the window. Click in the box and type "NOT MISSING(permit) & NOT MISSING(term_limits)." You can also build this expression using the variable list and menu of functions. Click Continue to return to the Compute Variable. Click OK. SPSS creates the interaction variable, interact.

SPSS will simply execute the variable computation we specified. To make sure you've created the interaction term correctly, apply the Analyze ▶ Descriptive Statistics ▶ Frequencies procedure on the interact variable. What you should get is shown on p. 204 in the table called Permit * Term_Limits.

The interact variable records the percentage of people in states with term limits who think abortion should be legal in all circumstances. For states without term limits, the interact variable equals 0.

To conduct a multiple regression analysis with an interaction term, select Analyze ▶ Regression ▶ Linear once again. Click the Reset button to clear the panels for our new analysis. Move abortlaw2017 into the Dependent field. Move the permit, term_limits, and interact variables into the Independent(s) field, as shown in Figure 9-4. Whenever you add an interaction term as an independent variable in multiple regression analysis, you must include the base terms you multiplied to create the interaction term as independent variables. Click OK.

What do these results tell us about the relationship between public opinion, term limits, and public policy? In all states, public opinion has a statistically significant effect on abortion policy. For every 1-percent increase in pro-choice opinion, states enact 0.247 fewer abortion restrictions. So, a 4-percent increase in pro-choice public opinion correlates to one less legal restriction on abortion access. The partial regression coefficient for permit has a t-statistic of −5.646 and a

---

[6] In calculating a multiplicative product, SPSS will assign a valid code of 0 to any case that has a missing value on one of the variables and a value of 0 on the other variable. For example, a state that has a missing value on permit and has a value of 0 on term_limits will be assigned a valid, analyzable value on the interaction variable—a value of 0. This observation should be treated as missing but instead ends up in the analysis. SPSS also returns a valid code of 0 for any expression that divides 0 by a missing value: "Most numeric expressions receive the system-missing value when any one of the values in the expression is missing. Some arithmetic operations involving 0 *can be evaluated* even when the variables have missing values. These operations are: 0 * missing = 0; 0 / missing = 0," from *IBM SPSS Statistics 22 Command Syntax Reference* (Chicago: IBM Corporation, 2013), 95 (emphasis added). Avoid this flaw by restricting the Compute procedure to cases having non-missing values on both variables.

FIGURE 9-3   Computing an Interaction Variable

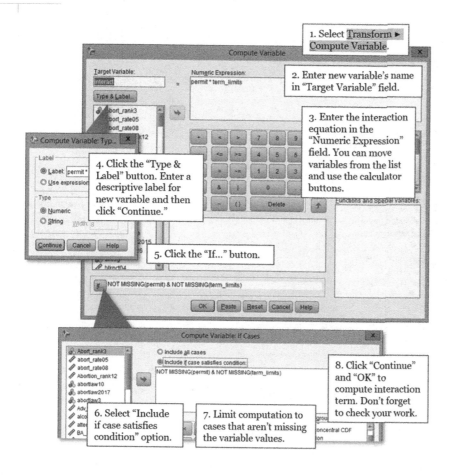

1. Select Transform ▶ Compute Variable.

2. Enter new variable's name in "Target Variable" field.

3. Enter the interaction equation in the "Numeric Expression" field. You can move variables from the list and use the calculator buttons.

4. Click the "Type & Label" button. Enter a descriptive label for new variable and then click "Continue."

5. Click the "If..." button.

6. Select "Include if case satisfies condition" option.

7. Limit computation to cases that aren't missing the variable values.

8. Click "Continue" and "OK" to compute interaction term. Don't forget to check your work.

Permit * Term_limits

		Frequency	Percent	Valid Percent	Cumulative Percent
Valid	.00	28	56.0	70.0	70.0
	15.50	1	2.0	2.5	72.5
	21.10	1	2.0	2.5	75.0
	25.20	1	2.0	2.5	77.5
	30.40	1	2.0	2.5	80.0
	34.10	1	2.0	2.5	82.5
	34.30	1	2.0	2.5	85.0
	37.80	2	4.0	5.0	90.0
	42.90	1	2.0	2.5	92.5
	46.20	1	2.0	2.5	95.0
	46.30	1	2.0	2.5	97.5
	52.80	1	2.0	2.5	100.0
	Total	40	80.0	100.0	
Missing	System	10	20.0		
Total		50	100.0		

FIGURE 9-4   Multiple Regression Analysis with an Interaction Term

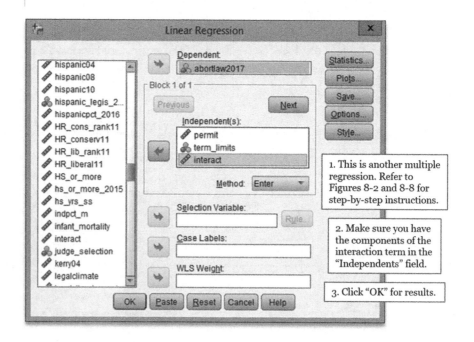

Model Summary

Model	R	R Square	Adjusted R Square	Std. Error of the Estimate
1	.762[a]	.580	.545	2.191

a. Predictors: (Constant), permit * term_limits, Percent public "Always allow" abortion, Does state have term limits for legislators?

Coefficients[a]

Model		Unstandardized Coefficients B	Unstandardized Coefficients Std. Error	Standardized Coefficients Beta	t	Sig.
1	(Constant)	16.184	1.685		9.606	.000
	Percent public "Always allow" abortion	-.247	.044	-.758	-5.646	.000
	Does state have term limits for legislators?	.130	2.780	.019	.047	.963
	permit * term_limits	.029	.074	.155	.389	.699

a. Dependent Variable: Number of restrictions on abortion

P-value of less than .001. The effect of term limits, however, is not statistically significant. Notice that the partial regression coefficient for the interaction term, 0.029, has a *t*-statistic of 0.389 and a *P*-value of .699. The presence of term limits does not appear to significantly alter the effect of public opinion on public policy.[7]

---

[7] The $n = 40$ here because the permit variable is only available for 40 states.

Let's plug the coefficient estimates into our model of abortion policy. This will help you understand how to interpret interaction effects and will set up our discussion of graphing interaction effects in the next section.

$$\text{Abortion restrictions} = 16.184 - 0.247 \times (\text{Public opinion})$$
$$+ 0.130 \times (\text{Term limits}) + 0.029 \times (\text{Public opinion} \times \text{Term limits})$$

Consider how this model applies to states without term limits—that is, when term_limits = 0. Any number multiplied by 0 is 0, so the model simplifies considerably.

Without Term Limits:

$$\text{Abortion restrictions} = 16.184 - 0.247 \times (\text{Public opinion})$$

Now consider states *with* term limits; that is, when term_limits = 1. First, we'll plug in the 1s and then group like terms together.

With Term Limits:

$$\text{Abortion restrictions} = 16.184 - 0.247 \times (\text{Public opinion}) + 0.130 + 0.029 \times (\text{Public opinion})$$
$$= 16.314 - 0.218 \times (\text{Public opinion})$$

Based on this analysis, the effect of public opinion on abortion policy is statistically indistinguishable in states with and states without term limits. The interaction term is not statistically significant. These findings undercut the claims that term limits change the way legislatures make policy, but the usual disclaimers apply. We encourage you to explore other policy areas.

A CLOSER LOOK: WHAT ARE STANDARDIZED REGRESSION COEFFICIENTS?

By this point, you have seen several examples of SPSS regression results. You may have noticed that the Coefficients table reports both unstandardized and standardized regression coefficients. What's the difference?

We have focused our discussion on unstandardized regression coefficients. Unstandardized regression coefficients, which are so widely used the "unstandardized" modifier is unnecessary, tell you the expected effect of a one-unit change in an independent variable on the dependent variable in whatever scale the variables are measured on. In the analysis of state restrictions on abortion, the partial regression coefficient on the permit variable tells you how many more/fewer laws against abortion one would expect when the percentage of the public that supports abortion for any reason increases 1 point.

Standardized regression coefficients, sometimes called "beta" coefficients, are based on standardized versions of the dependent and independent variables. In Chapter 3, you standardized the World dataset's trade_percent_gdp variable. When all the variables in a regression analysis are standardized, the standardized regression coefficients tell you how many standard deviations the dependent variable can be expected to increase/decrease when an independent variable increases by one standard deviation. When variables are standardized, their mean value is 0. In regression analysis, the expected value of the dependent variable when all independent variables have their mean values is the mean value of the dependent variable. Therefore, in standardized

(Continued)

(Continued)

regression analysis, when the value of all independent values equals 0, the expected value of the dependent variable is 0, so there is no constant term (the value of the constant term is 0).

What's the point of standardized regression coefficients? When you have multiple independent variables, standardized regression coefficients can help you identify which variable has the biggest effect on the dependent variable. You can't compare unstandardized partial regression coefficients directly because one independent variable may have considerable variation on a 0–100 scale while another is almost always 0 and a few 1s. When the partial regression coefficients are standardized, you can compare the effect of the typical variation of one variable to the effect of the typical amount of variation of another variable.

GRAPHING LINEAR PREDICTION LINES FOR INTERACTION RELATIONSHIPS

A point emphasized throughout this book is that visual representations can often help to simplify and clarify complex relationships. This is particularly true for interaction effects in multiple regression analysis. Graphing regression lines for an interaction relationship is a great complement to a table of coefficients and inferential statistics.

The SPSS procedure used to create this kind of graphic is very similar to that discussed in Chapter 8 to create a scatterplot with a regression line imposed on top of the data points. In our running example involving public opinion on abortion, term limits, and the number of restrictions on abortion at the state level, the dependent variable is abortlaw2017, the independent variable is permit, and we want to show how the term limits interact with the opinion-policy relationship. However, instead of fitting one regression line to all the observations, we'll add one line for states with term limits and another line for states without them (see Figure 9-5).

To produce a scatterplot of observations with regression lines summarizing an interaction effect, select Graphs ▶ Legacy Dialogs ▶ Scatter/Dot. Make sure Simple Scatter is selected in the Scatter/Dot dialog and then click the Define button to call up the increasingly familiar Simple Scatterplot window (see Figure 9-6). Our dependent variable, abortlaw2017, defines the y-axis. Our multiple

FIGURE 9-5 Scatterplot Showing Multiple Regression Analysis with an Interaction Effect

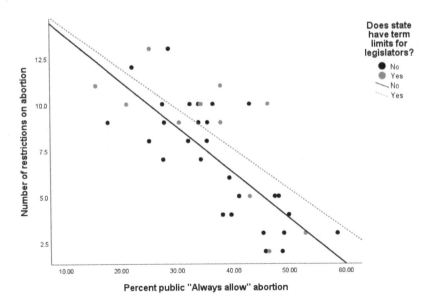

FIGURE 9-6   Creating a Scatterplot with Markers Defined by Variable Values

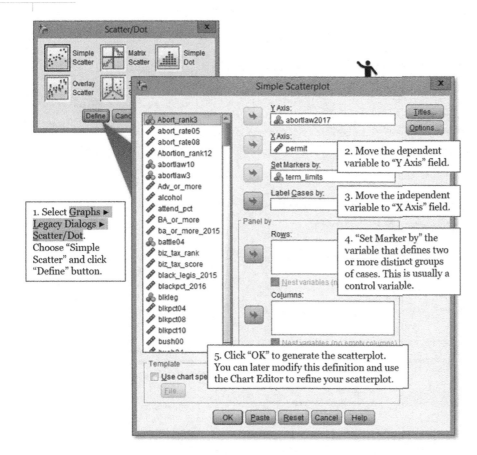

regression model had three independent variables. When you make a scatterplot, your *x*-axis variable should be measured at the interval level so the points are spread out and clearly visible. In the running example, the permit variable is measured at the interval level so move it into the *x*-axis field. We want to be able to visually distinguish states with term limits from those without term limits so move the term_limits variable into the "Set Markers by" field; this defines two separate subgroups of observations. Click the OK button and SPSS will generate a scatterplot we'll need to refine with the Chart Editor to show the (statistically insignificant) interaction effect.

Double-click the scatterplot in the Viewer to move it into the Chart Editor (see Figure 9-7). Here, we'll add fit lines that show the relationship between public opinion and abortion policy in each type of state (and edit these lines so they're more easily distinguished). We'll also edit the scatterplot to better distinguish between states with term limits and states without term limits by changing the color of their respective markers.

To add regression lines that show the expected effect of changes in the permit variable on the number of abortion restrictions in states with term limits and in states without term limits, click the Chart Editor's "Add Fit Line at Subgroups" button. By default, SPSS will display each subgroup's markers and fit line with a unique color. If your graphic will be rendered in grayscale, you'll want to edit the marker and line colors to make it easier to distinguish subgroups. Recall from Chapter 5 that the Chart Editor allows you to select one line or set of markers at a time and edit its properties (see Figure 5-7). To communicate the comparison clearly, match the style and color of a subgroup's markers and fit line. In Figure 9-5, for example, we use black markers and a solid black line for states without term limits and lighter markers and a dashed fit line for states with term limits. To avoid clutter and duplicating information contained in a multiple regression

FIGURE 9-7   Creating a Scatterplot with Regression Lines for the Interaction Effect Added

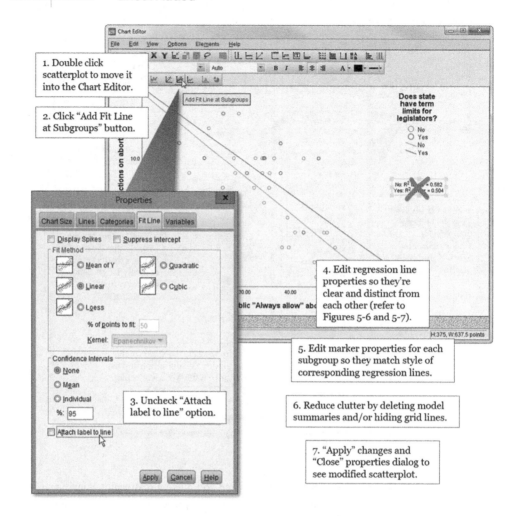

results table, we suggest omitting the fit line labels and model summaries.[8] To do this, you can uncheck the "Attach label to line" option of the fit line properties and then select and delete the model summaries (see Figure 9-7). If grid lines are displayed by default, we recommend clicking the "Hide Grid Lines" button to show the fit lines more clearly.

---

[8] The separate model summaries raise an interesting point: the fit lines produced by estimating separate regression lines for each sample (states with term limits and states without term limits). This will yield the same slope and intercept terms as we derived from estimating a multiple regression model with an interaction term, but dividing the observations into two groups is a less efficient use of the data than estimating a multiple regression with an interaction term based on all available observations.

Name: Anna Jeffries   Date: 12/1/22

E-mail: anna.jeffries@spartans.ut.edu   Section: _____

CHAPTER 9 EXERCISES

1. (Dataset: World. Variables: legal_quality, legal_origin.) In this exercise, you will use multiple regression with dummy variables to analyze the relationship between the quality of a country's current legal system and its legal origins. The World dataset (file name: world.sav) contains legal_quality, an interval-level measure of the quality of a country's legal system that ranges from 0 (lowest quality) to 1 (highest quality). The dataset also contains legal_origin, a five-category nominal variable that indicates the legal origin of the country's commercial code.

Variable	Percent Coded 1	Percent Coded 0	N Coded
legal_origin_dum_1	30.4?	69.6?	139?
legal_origin_dum_2	92.6?	47.4?	139?
legal_origin_dum_3	9.6?	90.4?	139?
legal_origin_dum_4	3.7?	96.3?	139?
legal_origin_dum_5	3.7?	96.3?	139

A. Apply the Analyze ▶ Descriptive Statistics ▶ Frequencies procedure to the variable legal_origin to obtain a better idea of the legal origins commercial codes around the world. Fill in the missing cells of the frequency distribution table below.

Legal Origin	Numeric Code	Frequency	Percentage
English Common Law	1	41?	~~34.3~~ 30.4
French Commercial Code	2	71	~~48~~ ?52.6
Socialist/ Communist Laws	3	13	9.63%
?German Commercial code Scandinavian	4	5?	3.7?
Scandinavian Commercial Code	5	5	3.7?

B. Although the values of legal_origin have numeric codes, it's not an interval-level variable. To incorporate this independent variable into multiple regression analysis, you'll need to create a series of dummy variables based on the values of legal_origin. Apply the Transform ▶ Create Dummy Variables procedure to the legal_original variable to create dummy variables. Use the stem legal_origin_dum to identify the new variables. Check your work by doing frequency analysis on these variables and filling out the table below.

C. Use the Analyze ▶ Regression ▶ Linear procedure to estimate a multiple regression model that explains the legal_quality as a function of legal_origin, and add all but one of these dummy variables as independent variables in the multiple regression model. (Leave out the dummy variable that identifies the legal origin that's the reference category in the results table below.) Use your results to complete the table below.

leave out 1.

	Coefficient	Standard Error	t-ratio	P-value
French Commercial Code	-.070?	.033?	-2.114?	.036?
Socialist/ Communist Laws	-.116?	.054?	-2.150?	.033?
German Commercial Code	0.25	.08?	3.11	.002?
Scandinavian Commercial Code	.37?	.08?	4.595?	<.001?
Constant term	.558?	.027?	21.05	<.001
N	.526?			
R-squared	.277?			
Adjusted R-squared	.255?			

D. The baseline/reference category in the multiple regression model you estimated to complete part C is the following legal origin: *English common law* The expected value of legal quality in countries with this legal origin is ~~SPSS~~ 1.436

E. Change the baseline/reference category to the most common legal origin (French Commercial Code) to compare the difference of other legal origins to the most typical legal origin. Estimate a multiple regression model with French Commercial Code as the baseline/reference category. How do the following legal origins compare to the French Commercial Code? Check one box in each row.

Compared to French Commercial Code Origin	Significantly Lower Quality	Not Significantly Different	Significantly Higher Quality
English Common Law			✓
Socialist/Communist Laws	✓		
German Commercial Code			✓
Scandinavian Commercial Code			✓

2. (Dataset: World. Variables: free_overall, gdp_cap3.) In this exercise, you will use multiple regression with dummy variables to analyze the relationship between economic development and economic freedom. The World dataset (file name: world.dta) contains free_overall, an interval-level measure of freedom that ranges from 0 (least free) to 100 (most free). The dataset also contains gdp_cap3, a three-category ordinal measure of per capita GDP, an indicator of economic development. The gdp_cap3 variable is coded 1 for low-GDP countries, 2 for middle-GDP countries, and 3 for high-GDP countries.

A. Imagine estimating a multiple regression model that explains variation in free_overall as a function of gdp_cap3. Because gdp_cap3 is an ordinal-level variable with three values, one would estimate a multiple regression with dummy variables for two of gdp_cap3's values, leaving out the third value to serve as the reference category. The equation for this model would look something like this:

$$\text{free\_overall} = a + b_1 \times (\text{Low GDP}) + b_2 \times (\text{Middle GDP})$$

Use the terms a, b_1, and b_2 in this equation (alone or in combination) to fill in the blanks in the following table.

The mean difference between the lowest and highest-GDP countries	?
The mean of the dependent variable for the highest-GDP countries	?
The mean of the dependent variable for the lowest-GDP countries	?
The mean difference between the highest and middle-GDP countries	?
The mean of the dependent variable for the middle-GDP countries	?

B. Although the values of gdp_cap3 have numeric codes, it's not an interval-level variable. To incorporate this independent variable into multiple regression analysis, you'll need to create a series of dummy variables based on the values of gdp_cap3. Apply the Transform ▶ Create Dummy Variables procedure to the gdp_cap3 variable to create dummy variables. Use the stem gdp_cap3_dum to identify the new variables. Check your work by doing frequency analysis on these variables and filling out the table below.

Variable	Value on gdp_cap3	Percent Coded 1	Percent Coded 0	N Coded
gdp_cap3_dum_1		?	?	?
gdp_cap3_dum_2		?	?	?
gdp_cap3_dum_3		?	?	?

C. Use the Analyze ▶ Regression ▶ Linear procedure to estimate the regression equation for estimating free_overall (fill in the blanks, putting the constant in the first blank):

$$\text{free\_overall} = \underline{\qquad} + \underline{\qquad} \times (\text{Low GDP}) + \underline{\qquad} \times (\text{Middle GDP})$$

D. Use the regression coefficients to arrive at estimated mean values of free_overall for countries at each level of per capita GDP. Write the estimates in the following table.

GDP per capita	Estimated Mean on free_overall Scale
Low	?
Middle	?
High	?

E. Examine the *t*-ratio and *P*-value on the partial regression coefficient for low-GDP countries. Do the low-GDP per capita countries score significantly lower on free_overall than do the highest-GDP per capita countries? (circle one)

No   Yes

Briefly explain:

_____

_____

F. Examine the *t*-ratio and *P*-value on the partial regression coefficient for middle-GDP countries. Do the middle-GDP per capita countries score significantly lower on free_overall than do the highest-GDP per capita countries? (circle one)

No   Yes

Briefly explain:

_____

_____

G. Change the baseline/reference category to low- or middle-GDP countries and estimate the regression model of economic freedom and development again to determine whether low-GDP per capita countries score significantly lower on free_overall than do the middle-GDP per capita countries. Do low-GDP per capita countries score significantly lower on free_overall than do middle-GDP per capita countries? (circle one)

No   Yes

Briefly explain:

_____

_____

H. According to adjusted *R*-squared, GDP per capita accounts for _____ percent of the variation in free_overall.

3. (Dataset: World. Variables: gini10, hi_gdp, gdp_10_thou, democ_regime.) As a country becomes richer, do more of its citizens benefit economically? Or do economic resources become inequitably distributed across society? The answer may depend on the type of regime in power. Democratic regimes, which need to appeal broadly for votes, may adopt policies that redistribute wealth. Dictatorships, by contrast, are less concerned with popular accountability and thus might hoard economic resources among the ruling elite, creating a less equitable distribution of wealth. This explanation suggests a set of interaction relationships. It suggests that when we compare poorer democracies with

richer democracies, richer democracies will have a *more equitable* distribution of wealth. However, it also suggests that when we compare poorer dictatorships with richer dictatorships, richer dictatorships will have a *less equitable* distribution of wealth. In this exercise you will investigate this set of relationships.

The World dataset contains the variable gini10, which measures the extent to which wealth is inequitably distributed in society. Gini10 can take on any value between 0 (equal distribution of wealth) and 100 (unequal distribution of wealth). So, lower values of gini10 denote less economic inequality, and higher values of gini10 denote greater economic inequality. This is the dependent variable. The dataset also has variables that measure economic prosperity: an interval-level measure, gdp_10_thou, reflects each country's per capita gross domestic product in $10,000s; a dummy variable, hi_gdp, classifies each country as low GDP (coded 0) or high GDP (coded 1). The hi_gdp variable will serve as the measure of the independent variable, level of wealth. A dummy variable, democ_regime, categorizes each country as a dictatorship (coded 0 on democ_regime) or democracy (coded 1 on democ_regime) and is the control variable.

A. Exercise a skill you learned in Chapter 5. To see whether interaction is occurring, obtain a controlled mean comparison table that shows the relationship between gini10 and hi_gdp, controlling for democ_regime. Write the mean values of gini10 next to the question marks in the table that follows.

Economic Status	Is regime a democracy?	
	No	Yes
Low GDP	40.49 ?	44.46 ?
High GDP	44.76 ?	36.8389 ?

B. Examine the table in part A. It appears that interaction (circle one)

is   (is not)

occurring in the data. Explain your reasoning. There is not a large difference between democracies and non-democracies and their GDP

C. The World dataset contains rich_democ, an interaction variable computed by the expression hi_gdp*democ_regime. The rich_democ variable takes on the value of 1 for high-GDP democracies and the value of 0 for all other countries. Use the Transform ▶ Compute

Variable procedure (using the if . . . optional case selection condition setting) to generate a new variable equal to the interaction of the variables gdp_10_thou (the interval-level measure of economic prosperity) and democ_regime. Name this variable interact_democ_gdp (or something similarly descriptive). To check your work, and practice a skill you learned in Chapter 4, use the Analyze ▶ Compare Means ▶ Means procedure to compare the mean value of the interaction term interact_democ_gdp for democracies and non-democracies. Complete the mean comparison table below.

Is regime a democracy?	Mean Value of Interaction Term		N	
No	.000	?	99	?
Yes	.8698	?	90	?

D. Use the Analyze ▶ Regression ▶ Linear procedure to estimate a multiple regression model with gini10 as the dependent variable and gdp_10_thou, democ_regime, and interact_democ_gdp as independent variables. Use your results to fill in the blanks for this equation for gini10 (put the constant in the first blank):

$$\text{gini10} = \underline{41.01} + \underline{.669} \times \text{gdp\_10\_thou} + \underline{2.917} \times \text{democ\_regime} + \underline{-5.339} \times \text{interact\_democ\_gdp}$$

E. Suppose someone claimed that, from the standpoint of statistical significance, low-GDP dictatorships have a significantly more equitable distribution of wealth than do low-GDP democracies.

gini gdp=0

This claim is (circle one) $= 41.01 + 2.917 \times democ + -5.339 \times interac$

(**correct**)   ~~incorrect~~

because

_____
_____
_____

F. Suppose someone claimed that as GDP increases, wealth becomes significantly more equitably distributed in democracies but not in dictatorships.

This claim is (circle one)

(**correct**)   incorrect

because

_____
_____
_____

G. Use the Graphs ▶ Legacy Dialogs ▶ Scatter/Dot procedure (with the fit line at subgroups option) to produce a graphic that shows the interaction between wealth and regime type on economic inequality. The y-axis should correspond to gini10 values, and the x-axis should correspond to gdp_10_thou values. Fit one regression line to the plot for democracies and another regression line to the plot for dictatorships. Request appropriate options for titles, labels, and the legend in the Chart Editor. Print the graph.

4. (Dataset: GSS. Variables: polviews, race2, homosex, wtss.) If one were trying to predict party identification based on opinions on *social issues*, such as homosexuality, one would expect most blacks to be Republicans. Indeed, blacks are considerably more likely to oppose homosexuality than are whites. According to the 2016 GSS data, for example, over 70 percent of blacks say that homosexuality is "always wrong" compared with 50 percent of whites. Yet on the 2016 GSS's party identification scale (which ranges from 1 to 7, with higher scores denoting stronger Republican identifications), blacks average around 2, compared with an average of 4 for whites. Why? A plausible idea is that social issues lack *salience* for blacks. Issues such as homosexuality may matter for whites—whites who think homosexuality is wrong are more likely to be Republicans than are whites who do not think it is wrong—but they have no effect for blacks.[9] According to this argument, blacks who think homosexuality is wrong are no more likely to be Republican than are blacks who do not think homosexuality is wrong. Or so the argument goes. Is this idea supported by the 2016 GSS data? Let's find out.

You can model the varying effect of social issues on party identification with an interaction variable. Consider the 7-point party identification scale (partyid) as a dependent variable, ranging from "Strong Democrat" at 1 to "Strong Republican" at 7. Now bring in two independent variables: race2 (whites have numeric code 0, blacks have numeric code 1) and homosex, a 4-point ordinal measure of acceptance of homosexuality (scored 1 if the respondent said homosexuality is "always wrong," 2 if "almost always wrong," 3 if "sometimes wrong," and 4 if "not wrong at all"). Finally, think about (but don't generate yet) an interaction variable that shows how the effect of social issues on party identification differs among blacks. Examine the regression model that follows:

$$\text{partyid} = a + b_1 \times (\text{if black}) + b_2 \times \text{homosex} + b_3 \times \text{homosex}^*(\text{if black})$$

A. To gauge the varying effect of social issues on party identification for whites and blacks, you need to compare

[9] See Quentin Kidd, Herman Diggs, Mehreen Farooq, and Megan Murray, "Black Voters, Black Candidates, and Social Issues: Does Party Identification Matter?" *Social Science Quarterly* 88, no. 1 (2007): 165–176.

the expected effect of the homosex variable for whites to the expected effect of the homosex variable for blacks.

Which of the following represents the expected effect of a one-unit increase in homosex on party identification for whites? (circle one)

a b_1 $a + b_1$ $a + b_2$ b_2

    b_3 $b_2 + b_3$ $a + b_3$

Which of the following represents the expected effect of a one-unit increase in homosex on party identification for blacks? (circle one)

a b_1 $a + b_1$ $a + b_2$ b_2

    b_3 $b_2 + b_3$ $a + b_3$

B. Remember that higher scores on partyid denote stronger Republican identifications. If the salience argument is correct—the idea that greater acceptance of homosexuality leads to lower Republican identification among whites but not blacks—then the effect of an increased value of homosex on partyid for whites will be (circle one)

     negative.   positive.   zero.

If the salience argument is correct, then the effect of an increased value of homosex on partyid for blacks will be (circle one):

     negative.   positive.   zero.

C. Use the Transform ▶ Compute Variable procedure (with the if . . . optional case selection condition setting) to generate a new variable equal to the interaction of the variables homosex and race2. Name this variable interact_race_homosex (or something similarly descriptive). To check your work, and practice a skill you learned in Chapter 4, use the Analyze ▶ Compare Means ▶ Means procedure to compare the mean value of the interaction term interact_race_homosex for whites and blacks. Complete the mean comparison table below. (Remember to weight observations with wtss.)

Value of race2	Mean Value of Interaction Term	N
White	?	?
Black	?	?

D. Use the Analyze ▶ Regression ▶ Linear procedure to estimate the multiple regression model specified above. For simplicity, treat the independent variable homosex as an interval-level variable. Fill in the missing values in the following table of results. (Remember to weight observations with wtss.)

	Coefficient	Standard Error	t-ratio	P-value
Homosex	?	?	?	?
Black	−3.16	?	?	?
Homosex–Black interaction	?	?	?	?
Constant term	?	0.13	33.13	<.001
N	?			
R-squared	?			

E. Which of the variables in the model have statistically significant effects on partyid? (check all that apply)

❑ Homosex

❑ Black

❑ Homosex–Black Interaction

F. The expected effect of a one-unit increase in homosex on party identification for whites equals _____. The expected effect of a one-unit increase in homosex on party identification for blacks equals _____.

G. Consider all the evidence you have adduced. Based on the evidence, the salience idea appears to be (circle one)

     correct.   incorrect.

Explain your answer.

_____
_____
_____
_____
_____
_____
_____

That concludes the exercises for this chapter. Before exiting SPSS, be sure to save your datasets.

10

Logistic Regression

 Watch screencasts of the guided examples in this chapter. **edge.sagepub.com/pollock**

Procedures Covered

Analyze ▶ Regression ▶ Binary Logistic

Transform ▶ Compute Variable (Predicted probabilities)

Graphs ▶ Legacy Dialogs ▶ Line (Multiple/ Summaries of separate variables)

Y ou now have an array of SPSS skills that enable you to perform the appropriate analysis for just about any situation you will encounter. To analyze the relationship between two categorical variables—variables measured at the nominal or ordinal level—you would enlist Crosstabs. If the dependent variable is an interval-level scale and the independent variable is categorical, then mean comparison analysis would be one way to go. Alternatively, you might create a dummy variable (or variables), specify a linear regression model, and use the Analyze ▶ Regression ▶ Linear procedure to estimate the effects of the categorical variable(s) on the dependent variable. Finally, if both the independent and dependent variables are interval level, then linear regression analysis or Analyze ▶ Correlate ▶ Bivariate would be appropriate techniques. There is, however, a common research situation that you are not yet equipped to tackle.

In its most specialized application, logistic regression is designed to analyze the relationship between an interval-level independent variable and a binary dependent variable. A binary variable, as its name suggests, can assume only two values. Binary variables are just like the dummy variables you created and analyzed earlier in this book. Either a case has the attribute or behavior being measured or it does not. Voted/did not vote, married/not married, favor/oppose same-sex marriage, and South/non-South are examples of binary variables.

THINKING ABOUT ODDS, LOGGED ODDS, AND PROBABILITIES

Consider a binary dependent variable of keen interest to students of political behavior: whether people voted in an election. This variable, of course, has only two values: Either individuals voted (coded 1 on the binary variable) or they did not vote (coded 0).

Now think about an interval-level independent variable often linked to turnout, years of education. We would expect a positive relationship between the independent and dependent variables: as years of education increase, the probability of voting should increase as well. People with fewer years of schooling should have a relatively low probability of voting, and this probability should increase with each additional year of education.

We certainly can conceptualize the voting–education relationship as positive. However, for statistical and substantive reasons, we cannot assume that it is linear—that is, we cannot assume that a 1-year change in education occasions a consistent increase in the probability of voting. Garden-variety regression, often called ordinary least squares or OLS regression, assumes a linear relationship between the independent and dependent variables.[1] Thus, we cannot use Analyze ▶ Regression ▶ Linear to analyze the relationship between education and the probability of voting. But as luck and statistics would have it, we can assume a linear relationship between education and the *logged odds* of voting. Let's put the relationship into logistic regression form and discuss its special properties:

$$\text{Log(odds of voting)} = a + b \times (\text{education})$$

Logged odds provide an essential link between binary outcomes and regression analysis, so it's important to understand what logged odds are. The odds of an event happening are a ratio between the likelihood of an event happening to the likelihood of an event not happening. The odds of an event occurring can be defined by the following equation:

$$\text{Odds of voting} = \frac{P}{1-P}$$

where P is the probability that someone votes. You may have seen odds placed on sporting events. If the odds of a team winning the Superbowl are placed at 2:1, that means oddsmakers think they're twice as likely to win as they are to lose.

The odds of an event occurring range between 0 and positive infinity, with 1 representing even-odds. One is not the midway point between 0 and positive infinity so we work with logged odds. Logged numbers, also called logarithms, are a mathematical transformation based on exponents. The natural log of a number equals the exponent that raises base e (approximately 2.718) to that number. If $y = e^x$, then $\log(y) = x$. Logged odds have some convenient properties that make jumping through these mathematical hoops worthwhile: the logged odds of a 50-50% event (1:1 odds) equals 0; the logged odds of an event with odds less than 1:1, or less probable than 0.5, is a negative number; the logged odds of an event with odds greater than 1:1, or more probable than 0.5, is a positive number.

It is often helpful to translate odds or logged odds into probabilities. A bit of algebraic rearrangement gives us the following equation for probability of an event occurring:

$$P = \frac{\text{Odds}}{1 + \text{Odds}}$$

To connect this formula for calculating probability back to the terms of our logistic regression model, we can exponentiate both sides of the logistic regression equation to obtain the following expression:

$$\text{Odds of voting} = e^{a + b \times (\text{education})}$$

---

[1] In arriving at the estimated effect of the independent variable on the dependent variable, linear regression finds the line that minimizes the square of the distance between the observed values of the dependent variable and the predicted values of the dependent variable—predicted, that is, based on value of the independent variable. The regression line is often referred to as the "least squares" line or "ordinary least squares" line.

FIGURE 10-1   Relationship between Probabilities, Odds, and Logged Odds

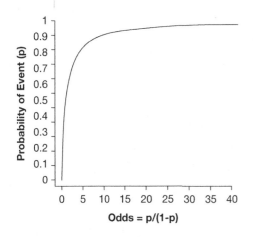
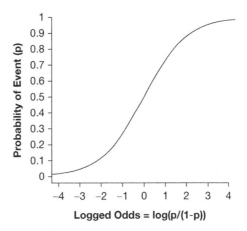

Substituting this expression into the formula for probability, we get the following non-linear equation for the probability of voting:

$$P = \frac{e^{a + b\times(\text{education})}}{1 + e^{a + b\times(\text{education})}}$$

Figure 10-1 shows the relationship between probabilities, odds, and logged odds.

Just as in OLS regression, the constant or intercept (a), estimates the dependent variable (in this case, the logged odds of voting) when the independent variable is equal to 0—that is, for people with no formal education. And the logistic regression coefficient (b) will estimate the change in the logged odds of voting for each 1-year increase in education. What is more, the analysis will produce a standard error for b, permitting us to test the null hypothesis that education has no effect on turnout. Finally, SPSS output for logistic regression will provide R-square–type measures, giving us an idea of the strength of the relationship between education and the likelihood of voting. In all these ways, logistic regression is comfortably akin to linear regression.

However, logistic regression output is more difficult to interpret than are OLS results. In ordinary regression, the coefficients of interest, the constant (a) and the slope (b), are expressed in actual units of the dependent variable.[2] With logistic regression, by contrast, the coefficients of interest are expressed in terms of the *logged odds* of the dependent variable, which is hardly a familiar way of describing outcomes of interest. In the logistic regression framework, the constant (a) will tell us the logged odds of voting when education is 0, and the regression coefficient (b) will estimate the change in the logged odds for each unit change in education. Logged odds, truth be told, have no intuitive appeal. Thus, we often must translate logistic regression results into language that makes better intuitive sense like odds or, better yet, probabilities. In fact, we'll use the non-linear equation for probability above to graph the results of logistic regression analysis with multiple independent variables.

ESTIMATING LOGISTIC REGRESSION MODELS

To work through a guided example of logistic regression analysis, open the NES dataset. For this example, we'll analyze individual opinions on a gay rights issue that came before the U.S. Supreme Court in the case of *Masterpiece Cakeshop v. Colorado Civil Rights Commission*: whether businesses

Screencast

Logistic
Regression
Analysis

---

[2] If we were to use OLS to investigate the relationship between years of education (X) and income in dollars (Y), the regression coefficient on education would communicate the dollar-change in income for each 1-year increase in education. With OLS, what you see is what you get.

FIGURE 10-2   The Logistic Regression Window

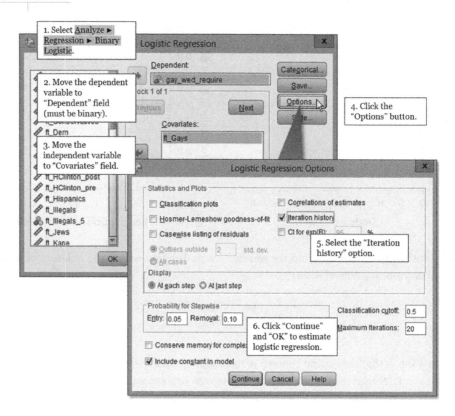

that provide wedding services should be required to provide services to gay couples or should be allowed to refuse to serve them.[3] Respondents' opinions are recorded in the gay_wed_require variable.[4] Those who believe businesses that provide wedding services should be required to serve gay couples are coded as 1s; those who do not think these businesses should be required to serve gay couples are coded as 0s. For this demonstration, we'll use NES respondents' sentiments toward gays measured on a feeling thermometer as the independent variable.

To conduct logistic regression analysis with SPSS, select Analyze ▶ Regression ▶ Binary Logistic, opening the Logistic Regression window (Figure 10-2). Find gay_wed_require in the variable list and move it into the Dependent field. Next, move ft_Gays into the Covariates field. (In logistic regression, independent variables are often called covariates.)

For this logistic regression analysis, we will request some additional diagnostic information. In the Logistic Regression window, click the Options button. The Logistic Regression: Options window opens (see Figure 10-2). Click the box next to "Iteration history." This option will produce output

---

[3] The case started when a Colorado bakery refused to create a wedding cake for a gay couple. According to the state's civil rights agency, under Colorado law, the bakery cannot refuse to provide the couple service because they are gay. The baker argues that he is exercising his constitutionally protected right to freely exercise his religious beliefs. Does the Colorado law go too far? On June 4, 2018, the U.S. Supreme Court held that Colorado's civil rights agency did not give the baker a fair hearing, a narrow ruling that effectively postpones ruling on the constitutional question.

[4] For all guided examples and exercises in this chapter, the binary dependent variables are naturally coded 0 or 1. To get logistic regression to work, SPSS must have 0/1 binaries. However, here is a bit of SPSS trivia. When running Analyze ▶ Regression ▶ Binary Logistic, SPSS will check to make sure that the dependent variable has only two values. The values could be 0 and 1, 3 and 5, 2 and 6, or any two (but only two) unique values. If the two values are not 0 and 1, then SPSS will temporarily recode the variable for the immediate purposes of the analysis, encoding one value of the dependent as 0 and the other as 1. SPSS output informs you which natural code it changed to 0 and which it changed to 1. The encoding does not alter your permanent dataset codes.

that helps to illustrate how logistic regression works. Click Continue, returning to the main Logistic Regression window. Click OK.

In typical fashion, SPSS has given us a wealth of information. Eleven tables now populate the Viewer. For the essential purposes of this book, you need to be conversant with only three or four of these tables. Scroll to the bottom of the output, to the tables labeled "Model Summary" and "Variables in the Equation." Here you will find the main results of this logistic regression analysis. If you get different numbers, remember to weight observations using the nesw variable.

Model Summary

Step	-2 Log likelihood	Cox & Snell R Square	Nagelkerke R Square
1	4309.147[a]	.153	.204

a. Estimation terminated at iteration number 4 because parameter estimates changed by less than .001.

Variables in the Equation

	B	S.E.	Wald	df	Sig.	Exp(B)
Step 1[a] Feeling therm: Gay men and lesbians (v162103)	.033	.002	464.396	1	.000	1.033
Constant	-2.066	.102	411.686	1	.000	.127

a. Variable(s) entered on step 1: Feeling therm: Gay men and lesbians (v162103).

Note: Classification table not shown.

Just as in Analyze ▶ Regression ▶ Linear, the numbers in the column labeled "B" are the estimates for the constant and the regression coefficient. Plug these estimates into our model:

$$\log(\text{odds for service requirement}) = -2.066 + 0.033 \times (\text{ft\_Gays})$$

What do these coefficients tell us? Again, the constant says that for a person who rates gays 0 on a feeling thermometer, the lowest possible score, the estimated logged odds of his or her believing wedding businesses should be required to serve gay couples is equal to −2.066. This is the baseline likelihood, expressed in logged odds.[5]

The coefficient on the ft_Gays variable indicates that the logged odds of supporting the requirement to serve gay couples increases by .033 for each 1-point increase in sentiment toward gays. So, as expected, as the independent variable increases, the likelihood of supporting the requirement to serve increases.

Does sentiment toward gays have a statistically significant effect on the likelihood of supporting the requirement to serve? In OLS regression, SPSS determines statistical significance by calculating a *t*-statistic and an accompanying *P*-value. In logistic regression, SPSS calculates a Wald statistic (which is based on chi-square) and reports a *P*-value for Wald. Interpretation of this *P*-value, displayed in the column labeled "Sig.," is directly analogous to ordinary regression. If the *P*-value is greater than .05, do not reject the null hypothesis; conclude that the independent variable does not have a significant effect on the dependent variable. If the *P*-value is less than or equal to .05, reject the null hypothesis and infer that the independent variable has a significant relationship with the dependent variable. In our output, the *P*-value for ft_Gays is less than .001, so we can conclude that, yes, sentiment toward gays does have a statistically significant effect on the likelihood of supporting the requirement to serve.

---

[5] To translate the logged odds into odds, you can exponentiate the constant: $e^{-2.066} = .127$. Thus, the *odds* that someone who rates gays 0 on a feeling thermometer supporting the requirement to serve gay couples are .127 to 1. The *probability* of their supporting the requirement to serve is therefore $0.127 / (.127 + 1) = 0.112$.

The logistic regression output from SPSS helpfully reports how a one-unit change in an independent variable affects the odds of the outcome of interest occurring. Consider the rightmost column of the Variables in the Equation table, the column labeled "Exp(B)." Here SPSS has reported the value 1.033 for the independent variable, ft_Gays. Where did this number originate? SPSS obtained this number by raising the natural log base e to the power of the logistic regression coefficient, .033. This procedure translates the logged odds regression coefficient into an *odds ratio*. An odds ratio tells us by how much the odds of the dependent variable change for each unit change in the independent variable.

- An odds ratio of less than 1 means that the odds decrease as the independent variable increases (a negative relationship).

- An odds ratio equal to 1 means that the odds do not change as the independent variable increases (no relationship).

- An odds ratio of greater than 1 means that the odds of the dependent variable increase as the independent variable increases (a positive relationship).

An odds ratio of 1.033 means that a one-unit increase in ft_Gays increases the odds that someone supports the requirement to serve by 1.033.

The value of the odds ratio can be used to obtain an even more understandable estimate, the *percentage change in the odds* for each unit change in the independent variable. Mercifully, simple arithmetic accomplishes this task. Subtract 1 from the odds ratio, and multiply by 100. In our current example: $(1.033 - 1) \times 100 = 3.3$. So, we can now say that each 1-point increment in sentiment toward gays increases the odds of supporting the requirement to serve by 3.3 percent. As you can see, when the relationship is positive—that is, when the logistic regression coefficient is greater than 0 and the odds ratio is greater than 1—figuring out the percentage change in the odds requires almost no thought. Just subtract 1 from the odds ratio and move the decimal point two places to the right.

A word of caution about odds ratios: be alert for negative relationships, when the odds ratio is less than 1. (In the exercises at the end of this chapter, you will interpret negative relationships.) Suppose, for example, that the change in odds ratio were equal to 0.25, communicating a negative relationship between the independent variable and the probability of the dependent variable. The percentage change in the odds would be equal to $(0.25 - 1) \times 100 = -75$, indicating that a one-unit change in the independent variable decreases the odds of the dependent variable by 75 percent.

How strong is the relationship between sentiment toward gays generally and the likelihood of supporting the requirement to serve gay couples? Consider the table labeled "Model Summary," above. OLS researchers are quite fond of R-square, the overall measure of strength that gauges the amount of variation in the dependent variable that is explained by the independent variable(s). For statistical reasons, however, the notion of "explained variation" has no direct analog in logistic regression. Even so, methodologists have proposed various "pseudo R-square" measures that gauge the strength of association between the dependent and independent variables, from 0 (no relationship) to 1 (perfect relationship). SPSS reports two of these: the Cox and Snell R-square and the Nagelkerke R-square.

---

[6] Cox–Snell's maximum achievable value depends on the analysis at hand, but it can never exactly equal 1. For a binary dependent variable in which the probabilities of 0 and 1 are equal (probability of 0 =.5 and probability of 1 =.5), Cox–Snell reaches a maximum of only .75 for a model in which all cases are predicted perfectly. Nagelkerke's adjustment divides the calculated value of Cox–Snell by the maximum achievable value of Cox–Snell, returning a coefficient that varies between 0 and 1. See D. R. Cox and E. J. Snell, *The Analysis of Binary Data* (London: Chapman and Hall, 1989); N. J. D. Nagelkerke, "A Note on a General Definition of the Coefficient of Determination," *Biometrika* 78, no. 3 (September 1991): 691–692.

Cox–Snell is the more conservative measure—that is, its maximum achievable value is less than 1. The Nagelkerke measure adjusts for this, and so it generally reports a higher pseudo R-square than does Cox–Snell.[6] These two measures are never wildly different, and they do give the researcher a ballpark feel for the strength of the relationship. With values in the range of .153 to .204, you could conclude that sentiment toward gays generally is a major factor in whether people think wedding businesses should be required to serve gay couples.

One other measure is reported in the Model Summary table, "–2 Log likelihood," which is equal to 4,309.147. In some ways, this is the most important measure of strength produced by logistic regression. By itself, however, the magnitude of –2 log likelihood doesn't mean very much. But scroll up a bit, so that you can view the tables labeled "Iteration History" and "Omnibus Tests of Model Coefficients" in the Viewer.[7]

Iteration History[a,b,c,d]

| | | | | Coefficients |
| | | | | Feeling therm: Gay men and lesbians |
Iteration		-2 Log likelihood	Constant	(v162103)
Step 1	1	4320.447	-1.738	.028
	2	4309.183	-2.047	.033
	3	4309.147	-2.066	.033
	4	4309.147	-2.066	.033

a. Method: Enter

b. Constant is included in the model.

c. Initial-2 Log Likelihood: 4894.854

d. Estimation terminated at iteration number 4 because parameter estimates changed by less than .001.

Omnibus Tests of Model Coefficients

		Chi-square	df	Sig.
Step 1	Step	585.706	1	.000
	Block	585.706	1	.000
	Model	585.706	1	.000

In figuring out the most accurate estimates for the model's coefficients, logistic regression uses a technique called maximum likelihood estimation (MLE).[8] When it begins the

---

[7] When you request iteration history, SPSS will by default produce two histories—one appearing near the beginning of the output beneath the label "Block 0: Beginning Block" and one appearing later beneath the label "Block 1: Method = Enter." In most situations, all the information you will need can be found under the Block 1 entry. The text shows the Block 1 entry.

[8] The mathematics of maximum-likelihood estimation is complicated. The general intuition can be compared to the least squares criteria in linear regression. With linear regression, we estimate coefficients that best fit observations based on the criteria of minimizing squared errors. Squared errors measure how much the observations deviate from the expected values of a regression model. Similarly, with MLE, we estimate coefficients that best fit observations using the criteria of maximizing likelihood. The more an observation deviates from the expected values of the logistic regression model, the lower its logged likelihood. In linear regression, the coefficients that satisfy the least squares criteria also satisfy the maximum likelihood criteria, but MLE can be used for a broader range of non-linear models like logistic regression.

analysis, MLE finds out how well it can predict the observed values of the dependent variable without using the independent variable as a predictive tool. You can get an idea of how well a model explains the outcome by comparing the initial log likelihood (the know-nothing model) with the final log likelihood (the know-something model). If sentiment toward gays did not help explain support for the requirement to serve gay couples, then the final log likelihood would be about the same as the initial log likelihood. If, by contrast, sentiment toward gays greatly improved the model's explanatory power, then the initial and final log likelihoods would be very different—the final log likelihood would be much closer to 0 than the initial log likelihood.[9]

The number labeled "Initial −2 Log Likelihood" (equal to 4,894.854 and found in note c beneath the Iteration History table) summarizes this "know-nothing" prediction. MLE then brings the independent variable into its calculations, running the analysis again—and again and again—to find the best possible predictive fit between ft_Gays and the likelihood of supporting the requirement to serve gay couples. According to the Iteration History table, SPSS ran through four iterations, finally deciding that it had maximized its ability to predict the outcome of interest with this independent variable. This final-step fit statistic, 4,309.147, is recorded in the Iteration History table and it also appears in the Model Summary table. This final number represents the "know-something" model—that is, it summarizes how well we can predict someone's opinion on requiring wedding businesses to serve gay couples by knowing how they rate gays on a feeling thermometer.

The amount of explanatory leverage gained by including ft_Gays as a predictor is determined by subtracting the final-step −2 log likelihood (4,309.147) from the initial −2 log likelihood (4,894.854). If you performed this calculation by hand, you would end up with 585.707, which appears in the Omnibus Tests of Model Coefficients table next to "Model" (off by .001 due to rounding error).[10] This number, which could be succinctly labeled "Model Chi-Square," is a chi-square test statistic. In the "Sig." column of the Omnibus Tests of Model Coefficients table, SPSS has reported a P-value of <.001 for this chi-square statistic. Here is our conclusion: Compared with how well we can predict opinions about requiring wedding businesses to serve gay couples without knowing sentiment toward gays generally, including ft_Gays as a predictor significantly enhances the performance of the model.

By now you are aware of the interpretive challenges presented by logistic regression analysis. In running the good-old Analyze ▶ Regression ▶ Linear procedure, you had a mere handful of statistics to report and discuss: the constant, the regression coefficient(s) and accompanying P-value(s), and adjusted R-square. That's about it. With Analyze ▶ Regression ▶ Binary Logistic, however, there are more statistics to record and interpret. Above is a tabular summary of the results of the running analysis of support for requiring wedding businesses to serve gay couples. You could use the tabular format shown in Table 10-1 to report the results of any logistic regressions you perform.

---

[9] Because the likelihood of an observation can vary between 0 and 1, the logs of likelihoods can vary between large negative numbers (any likelihood of less than 1 has a negatively signed log) and 0 (the log of 1 is equal to 0). As a model's predictive power improves, therefore, log likelihoods approach 0. Multiplying log likelihood by −2 makes it analogous to using variance to measure OLS model fit and yields a chi-square statistic for the logistic regression model.

[10] This change in log likelihood from the know-nothing model to the last iteration of the know-something model can also be used to calculate yet another measure of logistic regression model fit: the pseudo R-square measure equal to the proportion reduction in −2 log likelihood. In this example, pseudo R-square = 585.707 / 4,894.854 = .120.

TABLE 10-1   Logistic Regression Model Estimates and Summary

Model estimates	Coefficient	St. Error	P-value	Odds ratio	Percent change in odds
Feeling therm: Gays & lesbians	0.033	0.002	<0.001	1.033	3.3%
Constant	−2.066	0.141	<0.001		
N	3,535				
Chi-Square[1]	585.706		<0.001		
Cox-Snell R-Square	.153				
Nagelkerke R-Square	.204				

Source: 2016 NES

LOGISTIC REGRESSION WITH MULTIPLE INDEPENDENT VARIABLES

In this section, we'll add an explanatory variable to our logistic regression analysis of support for requiring wedding business to serve gay couples. Sentiment toward gays generally, although clearly an important predictor of supporting the requirement, left a lot of the variation in opinions on this issue unexplained, indicating that other factors might also contribute to the explanation.

Logistic regression, like OLS regression, can accommodate multiple predictors of a binary dependent variable. In addition to sentiment toward gays, we might also evaluate the effect of party identification on support for requiring wedding businesses to serve gay couples. Consider this logistic regression model:

$$\log(\text{odds of service requirement})=a + b_1 \times(\text{ft\_Gays}) + b_2 \times(\text{Dem}) + b_3 \times(\text{Repub})$$

Again, we are in an OLS-like environment. As before, the feeling thermometer rating for gays measures individuals' sentiments about gays generally. From a substantive standpoint, we would again expect the coefficient b_1 to be positive: As feeling thermometer scores for gays increase, so too should the logged odds of supporting the requirement to serve gay couples. Just as in OLS, b_1 will estimate the effect of sentiment toward gays on support for the requirement to serve gay couples, controlling for the effect of other independent variables.

We may also expect some partisan differences with respect to gay rights. The partyid3 variable in the NES dataset differentiates between Democrats, Republicans, and Independents. Democrats tend to favor the rights of gay couples over the rights of wedding business owners, while Republicans tend to favor the rights of wedding business owners over those of gay couples. Independents make a logical reference category. Thus, we should find a positive sign on the coefficient for the Democrat indicator variable, b_2, and a negative sign on the coefficient for the Republican indicator variable. The partial regression coefficients b_2 and b_3 will estimate the effect of identifying as a Democrat or Republican, respectively, on the logged odds of an individual supporting the requirement to serve, controlling for the effect of sentiment toward gays generally.

Finally, the various measures of the model's explanatory power—Cox–Snell, Nagelkerke, and model chi-square—will give us an idea of how well both independent variables explain public opinion on this issue.

---

[1] Alternatively, this row could be labeled "Change in −2 log likelihood."

FIGURE 10-3   Logistic Regression Analysis with Multiple Independent Variables

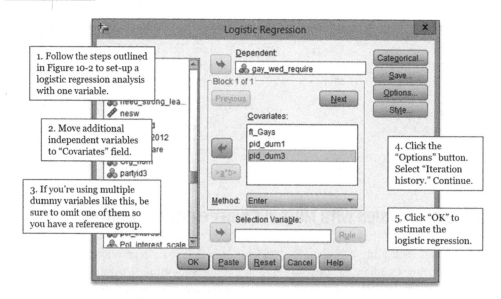

Let's see what happens when we add party identification to our model. Select <u>Analyze</u> ▶ <u>Regression</u> ▶ Binary Logistic. Everything should still be in place from our previous run: gay_wed_require is in the Dependent field and ft_Gays is in the Covariates box. We'll simply add party identification as an additional covariate. It's tempting to add partyid3 to the list, but it's an ordinal-level independent variable with just three unique values; we're better off using dummy variables to identify Democrats (the pid_dum1 variable) and Republicans (pid_dum3) and using Independents as the omitted/reference category (see Figure 10-3). The Options should still be set to show iteration history (see Figure 10-2). Click OK to run the analysis.

Scroll to the bottom of the output and view the results displayed in the Model Summary and Variables in the Equation tables.

Model Summary

Step	-2 Log likelihood	Cox & Snell R Square	Nagelkerke R Square
1	4058.661ª	.207	.277

a. Estimation terminated at iteration number 4 because parameter estimates changed by less than .001.

Variables in the Equation

		B	S.E.	Wald	df	Sig.	Exp(B)
Step 1ª	Feeling therm: Gay men and lesbians (v162103)	.029	.002	337.541	1	.000	1.029
	partyid3==Dem	.597	.088	46.309	1	.000	1.816
	partyid3==Rep	-.901	.098	84.999	1	.000	.406
	Constant	-1.775	.113	244.874	1	.000	.170

a. Variable(s) entered on step 1: Feeling therm: Gay men and lesbians (v162103), partyid3==Dem, partyid3==Rep.

Let's plug these estimates into our model:

$$log(\,odds\,of\,service\,requirement\,)=-1.775 + 0.029\times(\,ft\_Gays\,) + 0.597\times(\,Dem\,)-0.901\times(\,Repub\,)$$

Interpreting the signs and statistical significance of these coefficients follows a straightforward multiple regression protocol. The coefficient on ft_Gays, 0.029, tells us that, controlling for party identification, each additional point on the feeling thermometer toward gays increases the logged odds of supporting the requirement to serve gay couples by 0.029. If someone identifies as a Democrat, the logged odds of that person supporting the requirement to serve is 0.597 greater than someone who identifies as an Independent. The logged odds of someone who identifies as a Republican supporting the requirement to serve is 0.901 less than someone who identifies as an Independent. According to the Wald chi-square and accompanying P-values, each independent variable is significantly related to the dependent variable.

Now consider SPSS's helpful translations of the coefficients, from logged odds to odds ratios, which are displayed in the "Exp(B)" column. After controlling for party identification, the effect of sentiment toward gays generally is slightly moderated. Each additional point on the feeling thermometer toward gays increases the odds ratio by 1.029 and boosts the odds of supporting the requirement to serve gay couples by about 2.9 percent: $(1.029 - 1) \times 100 = 2.9$. If one were to compare individuals having the same sentiment toward gays but who differed in party identification, the odds of the Democrat identifier supporting the service requirement would be 1.816 times those of an Independent, while the odds of the Republican identifier supporting the service requirement would be 0.406 times those of an Independent. Translate 1.816 into a percentage change in the odds: $(1.816 - 1) \times 100 = 81.6$ percent greater odds. Translate 0.406 into a percentage change in the odds: $(0.406 - 1) \times 100 = 59.4$ percent lower odds.[12]

Iteration History[a,b,c,d]

Iteration		-2 Log likelihood	Constant	Feeling therm: Gay men and lesbians (v162103)	partyid3==Dem	partyid3==Rep
Step 1	1	4080.949	-1.417	.023	.520	-.737
	2	4058.803	-1.745	.028	.592	-.888
	3	4058.661	-1.774	.029	.597	-.901
	4	4058.661	-1.775	.029	.597	-.901

a. Method: Enter

b. Constant is included in the model.

c. Initial -2 Log Likelihood: 4876.897

d. Estimation terminated at iteration number 4 because parameter estimates changed by less than .001.

Omnibus Tests of Model Coefficients

		Chi-square	df	Sig.
Step 1	Step	818.236	3	.000
	Block	818.236	3	.000
	Model	818.236	3	.000

[12] When using interval-level independent variables with many values, you will often obtain logistic regression coefficients and odds ratios that appear to be quite close to null hypothesis territory (coefficients close to 0 and odds ratios close to 1) but that nonetheless trump the null hypothesis. Remember that logistic regression, like OLS, estimates the marginal effect of a one-unit increment on the logged odds of the dependent variable. In the current example, it's important to keep in mind that the ft_Gays variable ranges between 0 and 100, while the dummy variables identifying Democrats and Republicans only vary between 0 and 1.

According to the Cox–Snell (.207) and Nagelkerke (.277) *R*-square statistics, adding party identification to the model increased its explanatory power, at least when compared with the simple analysis using ft_Gays as the sole predictor. The value of −2 log likelihood, 4,058.661, is best viewed through the lens of the chi-square test, which you will find by scrolling up to the tables labeled "Omnibus Tests of Model Coefficients" and "Iteration History."

The initial know-nothing model—estimating the likelihood of supporting the requirement to serve gay couples without using ft_Gays or party ID as predictors—returned a −2 log likelihood of 4,876.897 (see notes to the Iteration History table). After bringing the independent variables into play and running through four iterations, SPSS's MLE settled on a −2 log likelihood of 4,058.661, an improvement of 818.236. This value, which is a chi-square test statistic, is statistically significant ("Sig." <.001). This tells us that, compared with the know-nothing model, both independent variables significantly improve our ability to predict the outcome.

GRAPHING PREDICTED PROBABILITIES WITH ONE INDEPENDENT VARIABLE

You now know how to perform basic logistic regression analysis, and you know how to interpret the logistic regression coefficient in terms of an odds ratio and in terms of a percentage change in the odds. No doubt, odds ratios are easier to comprehend than are logged odds. And percentage change in the odds seems more understandable still. Having said this, most investigators prefer to think in terms of probabilities.

In the first analysis we ran, logistic regression assumed that there is a linear relationship between sentiment toward gays and the logged odds of supporting the requirement to serve gay couples. This linearity assumption permitted us to arrive at an estimated effect that best fits the data. The change in logged odds may be linear, but the logistic regression model assumes a non-linear relationship between sentiment toward gays and the probability of supporting the requirement to serve gay couples. That is, it assumed that for people who lie near the extremes of the independent variable—respondents with extremely cold or extremely warm feelings about gays—a 1-point increase in sentiment toward gays will have a weaker effect on the probability of supporting the requirement to serve gay couples than will a 1-point increase for respondents in the middle range of the independent variable. People with extremely cold sentiments are unlikely to support requiring businesses to serve gay couples, so a 1-unit increase in sentiment toward gays probably won't have a huge effect. The same holds for people with extremely positive sentiments. They are already quite likely to support requiring businesses to serve gay couples, and a 1-unit increase should not greatly enhance this probability. It is in the middle range of the independent variable where changes in sentiment should have the most potent marginal impact, pushing individuals over the decision threshold from "do not support" to "support." So, the effect of a 1-unit change in sentiment is not linear; the marginal effect of sentiment toward gays depends on where respondents "are" on the sentiment variable.

Even though we cannot identify a single coefficient that summarizes the effect of sentiment toward gays on the probability of supporting the service requirement, we can use SPSS to calculate a predicted probability of supporting the service requirement for respondents at each level of the feeling thermometer toward gays. How does this work? Recall from the first section of this chapter that there are math equations linking odds, logged odds, and probabilities. For graphing purposes, we transform the linear equation of logged odds into a predicted probability curve.

Recall that we estimated the following relationship when ft_Gay was the sole independent variable in our logistic regression analysis:

$$\log(\text{odds of service requirement}) = -2.066 + 0.033 \times (\text{ft\_Gays})$$

Let's estimate this logistic regression model with one explanatory variable again and request that SPSS calculate and save the predicted probability of supporting the requirement to serve gay couples for each respondent. Select <u>A</u>nalyze ▶ <u>R</u>egression ▶ <u>B</u>inary Logistic once again. If the selections from our logistic regression analysis with multiple explanatory variables are still in place, move pid_dum1 and pid_dum3 back to the variable list, leaving only ft_Gays in the Covariates box and gay_wed_require in the Dependent box (see Figure 10-2). Now click the Save button in the Logistic Regression window. This opens the Logistic Regression: Save window (Figure 10-4).

In the Predicted Values panel, click the Probabilities box. Click Continue, which returns you to the Logistic Regression window. One more thing. We won't be discussing iteration history on this run, so click Options and uncheck the "Iteration history" box (see Figure 10-2). Click Continue. You are ready to go. Click OK.

SPSS generates output that is identical (except for the iteration history) to our earlier run. So where are the predicted probabilities that we requested? Because we just ran the analysis, SPSS has taken us to the Viewer. Return to the Variable View of the Data Editor. Scroll to the bottom of the Variable View. As you know, this is where SPSS puts the new variables that you create using Recode or Compute. There you will find a new variable bearing the name "PRE_1" and the label "Predicted probability" (Figure 10-5).

SPSS has performed just as requested. It ran the analysis, generated the logistic regression output, and silently saved a new variable, the predicted probability of supporting the requirement to serve gay couples for each case in the dataset. We will want to have a look at PRE_1. But first we need to give it a more descriptive label. Click in the Label cell and type a more informative variable label, such as "Predicted probability support service requirement."

How does this new variable, PRE_1, help us to describe changes in the estimated probability of supporting the requirement that wedding businesses serve gay couples as ft_Gays increases? SPSS now has a predicted probability of supporting the service requirement at each observed value of the ft_Gays variable, from 0 degrees to 100. There are two complementary ways to describe the relationship between ft_Gays and PRE_1. First, we can select <u>A</u>nalyze ▶ Co<u>m</u>pare Means ▶ <u>M</u>eans and ask SPSS to calculate the mean values of PRE_1 (dependent variable) for each value of ft_Gays (independent variable). A mean comparison table will show us by how much the estimated probability of supporting the service requirement increases between groups of respondents with different sentiments about gay people (see Figure 4-8 for reference). Second, we can obtain a line chart of the same information. To obtain a line chart, select <u>G</u>raphs ▶ <u>L</u>egacy Dialogs ▶ <u>L</u>ine (Simple) and click ft_Gays into the "Category Axis" box. Then, in the Line Represents section, select the "Other statistic" option and move PRE_1 into the Variable panel (refer to Figure 4-9 as necessary). This allows us

FIGURE 10-4   Requesting Predicted Probabilities

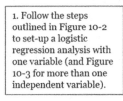

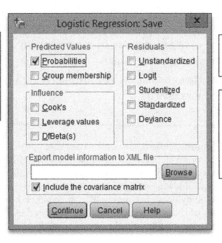

FIGURE 10-5   Predicted Probability Saved as a New Variable in the Data Editor

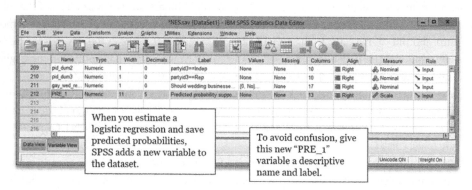

to visualize the non-linear relationship between sentiment toward gays and the predicted probability of believing wedding businesses should be required to serve gay couples.

Both the mean comparison and line chart methods of analyzing predicted probabilities should be familiar to you, as we covered them in earlier chapters, so go ahead and perform the analyses. In the mean comparison results below, the values of ft_Gays appear in ascending order down the left-hand column, and mean predicted probabilities (somewhat distractingly, to 7-decimal-point precision) are reported in the column labeled "Mean." Notice that between ft_Gays scores 64 and 65, the predicted probability of supporting the requirement to serve switches from less than .5 to greater than .5.

The mean comparison table is useful, but the number of unique values of ft_Gays in the sample make it unwieldy. The line chart (Figure 10-6) adds clarity and elegance to the relationship. The slight kinks in the curve occur at ft_Gays values that aren't observed in the sample (like 9, 21, 27, 28, and 44).

To get a feel for predicted probabilities, scroll back and forth between the tabular analysis and the graphic output. What happens to the predicted probability of voting as ft_Gays increases? As you can see in Figure 10-6, the relationship between scores on the feeling thermometer and the predicted probability of supporting the requirement to serve gay couples is not a straight line. There is a slight S-shaped curve. Suppose that you had to pick a 1-point increment in feeling thermometer scores that has the largest impact on the probability of supporting the requirement to serve gay couples. What would that increment be? Study the results and think about the phenomenon you are analyzing. Remember that the dependent variable is measured as a binary decision. A person either supports requiring service or thinks businesses should be allowed to refuse service. You may have noticed that, between 63 and 64 degrees on the feeling thermometer, the predicted probabilities increase from .493 to .502, a difference of .009 and the largest marginal increase in the data. And it is between these two values of the ft_Gays that, according to the analysis, the binary decision shifts in favor of supporting the requirement to serve gay couples—from a probability of less than .50 to a probability of greater than .50. The interval between 63 and 64 degrees is the "sweet spot"—the interval with the largest impact on the predicted probability, and the interval in which the predicted probability switches from less than .50 to more than .50.[13]

---

[13] The largest marginal effect of the independent variable on the probability of the dependent variable is sometimes called the *instantaneous effect*. In our example, the instantaneous effect is equal to .009, and this effect occurs between 63 and 64 degrees on ft_Gays. The effect of a one-unit change in the independent variable on the probability of the dependent variable is always greatest for the interval containing a probability equal to .5. The instantaneous effect, calculated by hand, is equal to b*0.25, in which b is the value of the logistic regression coefficient. For a discussion of the instantaneous effect, see Fred C. Pampel, *Logistic Regression: A Primer*, SAGE University Papers Series on Quantitative Applications in the Social Sciences, series no. 07-132 (Thousand Oaks, CA: SAGE, 2000), 24–26.

Report

Predicted probability support service requirement

Feeling therm: Gay men and lesbians (v162103)	Mean	N	Std. Deviation
0	.1124575	227	.00000000
1	.1157834	29	.00000000
2	.1191944	15	.00000000
3	.1226919	4	.00000000
4	.1262774	7	.00000000
5	.1299521	6	.00000000
...			
50	.3963025	982	.00000000
51	.4041999	108	.00000000
52	.4121472	25	.00000000
53	.4201406	15	.00000000
54	.4281761	7	.00000000
55	.4362496	6	.00000000
56	.4443571	2	.00000000
57	.4524943	8	.00000000
58	.4606570	2	.00000000
59	.4688409	5	.00000000
60	.4770415	210	.00000000
61	.4852546	23	.00000000
62	.4934756	12	.00000000
63	.5017001	5	.00000000
64	.5099238	5	.00000000
65	.5181420	12	.00000000
...			
95	.7426124	17	.00000000
96	.7488505	7	.00000000
97	.7549872	17	.00000000
98	.7610219	18	.00000000
99	.7669538	30	.00000000
100	.7727824	489	.00000000
Total	.4855417	3597	.19717626

Note: Table output edited for brevity.

Although most political researchers like to get a handle on predicted probabilities, as we have just done, there is no agreed-upon format for succinctly summarizing logistic regression results in terms of probabilities. One commonly used approach is to report the so-called full effect of the independent variable on the probability of the dependent variable. The full effect is calculated by subtracting the probability associated with the lowest observed value of the independent variable from the probability associated with the highest value of the independent variable. According to

FIGURE 10-6   Line Chart for Predicted Probabilities

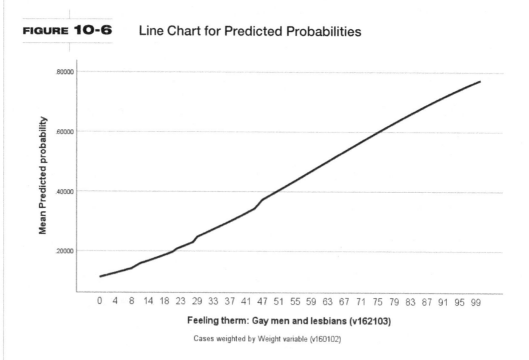

our mean comparisons, the predicted probability that someone with a 0 ft_Gays score supports the requirement that wedding businesses serve gay couples is .112, and the predicted probability for those with a 100 ft_Gays score is .773. The full effect would be .773 − .112 = .661. So, measured across its full range of observed values, feelings about gays generally boost the probability of supporting the requirement to serve by .661.

Saving and graphing predicted probabilities using the Logistic Regression: Save option works fine for simple models with one independent variable. By examining these predicted probabilities, you can summarize the full effect of the independent variable on the dependent variable. Furthermore, you can describe the interval of the independent variable having the largest impact on the probability of the dependent variable. Of course, SPSS will also gladly save predicted probabilities for logistic regression models having more than one independent variable. With some specialized exceptions, however, these predicted probabilities are not very useful for summarizing the effect of each independent variable on the probability of the dependent variable, controlling for the other independent variables in the model. As noted earlier, although logistic regression assumes that the independent variables have an additive effect on the logged odds of the dependent variable, the technique also assumes that the independent variables have an interactive effect on the probability of the dependent variable. How can we summarize these interaction effects? We answer this question in the next section.

GRAPHING PREDICTED PROBABILITIES WITH MULTIPLE INDEPENDENT VARIABLES

One might reasonably ask, "Controlling for party identification, what is the effect of a 1-point increase in sentiment toward gays on the probability of having the opinion that wedding businesses should be required to serve gay couples?" Inconveniently, with logistic regression the answer is always, "It depends."

In logistic regression models having more than one independent variable, graphing predicted probabilities presents special challenges. The technique assumes that the independent variables have additive effects on the logged odds of the dependent variable. Thus, for any combination of values of the independent variables, one obtains an estimated value of the logged odds of the dependent variable by adding up the partial effects of the predictor variables. However, logistic regression also assumes that the independent variables have interactive effects on the probability of the dependent variable. For example, in the case of Republican identifiers (who have a lower probability of supporting the requirement to serve gay couples), the technique might estimate a large effect of increasing sentiment toward gays on the probability of supporting the requirement to serve gay couples. For those who identify as Democrats (who have a higher probability of supporting the requirement to serve gay couples), logistic regression may find a weaker effect of increasing sentiment on the probability of supporting the requirement to serve gay couples. So, the effect of each independent variable on the probability of the dependent variable will depend on the values of the other predictors in the model.

These challenges notwithstanding, researchers have proposed several intuitively accessible ways to represent probabilities.[14] One approach is to report changes in the probability of the dependent variable across the values of a particularly interesting independent variable, while holding all other independent variables constant at their sample-wide means. Thus, one retrieves marginal effects at the means (MEMs). In the current example, we might estimate the probability of supporting the requirement to serve gay couples at each value of ft_Gays, from 0 to 100, while holding partisan identification constant at its typical values. This would allow us to answer the question, "For the 'typical' respondent (in terms of partisan identification), how does the probability of supporting the requirement to serve gay couples change as sentiment toward gays increases?"

A second, more nuanced approach is to report changes in the probability of the dependent variable across the range of an interesting independent variable—and to do so separately, for discrete categories of another independent variable. Thus, one presents marginal effects at representative values (MERs). In the current example, we might estimate the probability of supporting the requirement to serve gay couples at each value of ft_Gays, from 0 to 100, for each value of partyid3: Democrat, Independent, and Republican. This requires plotting three separate lines on a figure. This would enable us to answer these questions: "In what ways does sentiment toward gays affect the probability of supporting the requirement to serve gay couples for Democrats? How do these effects differ from the effect of sentiment toward gays on Independents or Republicans?"

Marginal Effects at the Means

In the MEMs approach, the analyst examines the effect of each independent variable while holding the other independent variables constant at their sample means. In this way, we can get an idea of the effect of each variable on individuals who are "average" on all of the other variables being studied. Unfortunately, the Analyze ▶ Regression ▶ Binary Logistic procedure will not calculate the predicted probabilities associated with each value of an independent variable while holding the other variables constant at their sample means.[15] That's the bad news. The good news is that the desired probabilities can be obtained using Transform ▶ Compute Variable, and they are readily analyzed using Compare Means.

---

[14] The discussion and terminology here draw on the insights of Richard Williams, "Using the Margins Command to Estimate and Interpret Adjusted Predictions and Marginal Effects," *The Stata Journal* 12, no. 2 (2012): 308–331.

[15] In calculating predicted probabilities for multivariate logistic regression models, SPSS returns estimated probabilities for subjects having each combination of values on the independent variables. It does not calculate the probabilities associated with each value of a given independent variable while holding the other predictors constant.

Here is the logistic regression model that SPSS estimated for the running logistic regression analysis example with multiple independent variables:

$$\log(\text{odds of service requirement}) = -1.775 + 0.029 \times (\text{ft\_Gays}) + 0.597 \times (\text{Dem}) - 0.901 \times (\text{Repub})$$

We can enlist this equation for two tasks. First, we can plug in the sample mean of ft_Gays and calculate the effect of partisan identification on the probability of supporting the requirement to serve gay couples. Second, we can plug in the sample means of the party identifier variables and calculate the effect of ft_Gays on the probability of supporting the requirement to serve gay couples. Here we will work through the second task only—figuring out the effect of sentiment toward gays on the probability of supporting the requirement to serve gay couples for people with typical partisan identification.

Before proceeding, of course, we need to obtain the sample means of the party identifier variables. Applying the Analyze ▶ Descriptive Statistics ▶ Frequencies procedure to partyid3, we see that .355 of respondents identify as Democrats, .365 identify as Independents, and .280 identify as Republicans.[16]

We have already seen that probabilities may be retrieved from logged odds via this conversion, extended for multiple independent variables:

$$\text{Probability} = \frac{e^{a + b_1 \times x_1 + b_2 \times x_2 + b_3 \times x_3}}{1 + e^{a + b_1 \times x_1 + b_2 \times x_2 + b_3 \times x_3}}$$

This equation can be applied to the running example to logistic regression results into predicted probabilities for any plugged-in value of ft_Gays, holding other predictors constant at their mean values:

$$\text{Probability} = \frac{e^{-1.775 + .029 \times \text{ft\_Gays} + .597 \times .355 - .901 \times .280}}{1 + e^{-1.775 + .029 \times \text{ft\_Gays} + .597 \times .355 - .901 \times .280}}$$

which simplifies to:

$$\text{Probability} = \frac{e^{-1.815 + .029 \times \text{ft\_Gays}}}{1 + e^{-1.815 + .029 \times \text{ft\_Gays}}}$$

Using this formula, we could calculate predicted probabilities for varying ft_Gays values by hand—first finding the predicted probability of voting for individuals with ft_Gays values of 0, then calculating the predicted probability of people with ft_Gays values of 1, and so forth until reaching 100. But let's ask SPSS to do the work for us.

What do we want SPSS to do? We want SPSS to calculate the predicted probability of supporting the requirement to serve gay couples for respondents at each level of ft_Gays, holding party identifiers constant at their sample means. Select Transform ▶ Compute Variable. Because we are holding party ID constant but allowing ft_Gays to vary, we will name this variable pre_ftgays. Type "pre_ftgays" in the Target Variable box. In the Numeric Expression box, type this expression: "Exp(−1.815 + .029*ft_Gays) / (1 + Exp(−1.815 + .029*ft_Gays)),", as shown in Figure 10-7.[17] Next, click the Type & Label button. In the Compute Variable: Type & Label Dialog's Label field,

---

[16] While individual observations never have these values, only 0 or 1, they can serve as typical values for the purposes of visualizing the expected effect of sentiment toward gays at an aggregate level.

[17] SPSS has a large repertoire of built-in statistical functions. The function Exp(numerical expression) returns the natural log base *e* raised to the power of the numerical expression. This is precisely what we want here.

FIGURE 10-7   Computing a Predicted Probability for Different Values
of an Independent Variable at the Mean Value of Another
Independent Variable

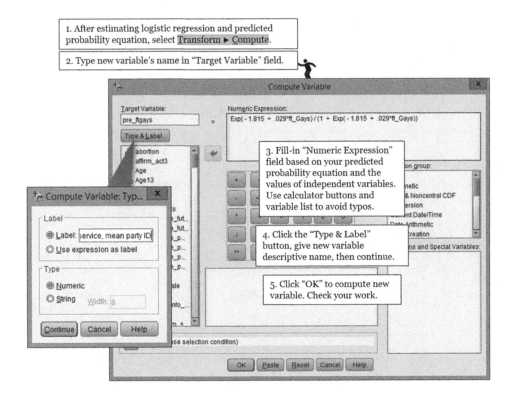

give pre_ftgays a descriptive label like "Pred prob: require service, mean party ID." Click the Continue button and then OK. SPSS computes a new variable, pre_ftgays, and enters this variable into the dataset.

Finally, we have the estimates that permit us to examine the effect of sentiment toward gays on the probability of having the opinion that wedding businesses should be required to serve gay couples for respondents with typical party identifications. These predicted probabilities have been added to the dataset as pre_ftgays. SPSS computes pre_ftgays for each observation, but does so for a respondent with typical party ID values, effectively ignoring individual-level variation in party ID to provide a better picture of the marginal effect of ft_Gays for typical respondents.

As was the case with graphing predicted probabilities with one independent variable, there are two complementary ways to describe the relationship between education and pre_ftgays and the predicted probability of supporting the requirement to serve gay couples: a mean comparison table and a line chart. To create a mean comparison table, select Analyze ▶ Compare Means ▶ Means. Click our newly computed variable, pre_ftgays, into the Dependent List, and click ft_Gays into the Independent List. Click OK.

What is the effect of sentiment toward gays generally on having the opinion that wedding businesses should be required to serve gay couples? Notice that people who rate gays at 0 on the feeling thermometer have a .140 probability of supporting the requirement compared with a probability of about .747 for individuals who rate gays at 100. Thus, holding party ID constant at its typical values, we find that the full effect of education is equal to .747 − .140 = .607. Controlling for party ID has moderated the full effect of ft_Gays somewhat (the comparable effect was .661 without controlling for party ID). Note that the transition between less than and more than .5 probability now occurs between 62 and 63 on the ft_Gays scale.

Report

Pred prob: require service, mean party ID

Feeling therm: Gay men and lesbians (v162103)	Mean	N	Std. Deviation
0	.1400	227	.00000
1	.1436	29	.00000
2	.1472	15	.00000
3	.1508	4	.00000
4	.1546	7	.00000
5	.1584	6	.00000
...			
50	.4097	982	.00000
51	.4168	108	.00000
52	.4238	25	.00000
53	.4309	15	.00000
54	.4381	7	.00000
55	.4452	6	.00000
56	.4524	2	.00000
57	.4596	8	.00000
58	.4668	2	.00000
59	.4740	5	.00000
60	.4813	210	.00000
61	.4885	23	.00000
62	.4958	12	.00000
63	.5030	5	.00000
64	.5102	5	.00000
65	.5175	12	.00000
...			
95	.7191	17	.00000
96	.7249	7	.00000
97	.7307	17	.00000
98	.7363	18	.00000
99	.7419	30	.00000
100	.7474	489	.00000
Total	.4875	3597	.17917

Note: Table output edited for brevity.

A line chart of the predicted probability of having the opinion that wedding businesses should be required to serve gay couples at varying levels of ft_Gay for someone with typical partisan identification looks similar to the one produced above, except on close inspection, we see that the probability starts a bit higher at the low end of the scale and ends a bit lower on the high end of the ft_Gays scale (Figure 10-8).

FIGURE 10-8   Predicted Probabilities for Different Values of an Independent
                   Variable at the Mean Value of Other Independent Variables

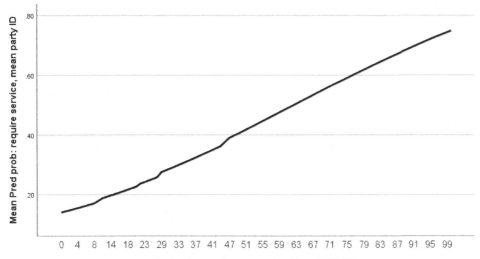

Feeling therm: Gay men and lesbians (v162103)

Cases weighted by Weight variable (v160102)

Marginal Effects at Representative Values

Analyzing marginal effects at mean values is perhaps the most prevalent methodology for describing predicted probabilities. However, for some research questions, MEMs may prove inadequate. Suppose that, based on a controlled cross-tabulation, we have reason to think that sentiment toward gays has a different effect on Democrats, Independents, and Republicans. If we were to estimate and compare the effects of ft_Gays among three groups of respondents—Democrats, Independents, and Republicans—what would the comparison reveal? In this section, we'll demonstrate how to show the marginal effect of sentiment toward gays on the outcome of interest for each value of party identification.

Our plot of marginal effects at representative values (MERs) should depict the logistic regression estimates with multiple independent variables:

$$log(odds\ of\ service\ requirement) = -1.775 + 0.029 \times (ft\_Gays) + 0.597 \times (Dem) - 0.901 \times (Repub)$$

In the MEMs method, we used these estimates to compute the probability of believing wedding businesses should be required to serve gay couples at varying ft_Gays values for a typical partisan identification. In the MERs method, we have SPSS compute three estimated probabilities for the effect of ft_Gays on the outcome of interest—one for Independents, another for Democrats, and a third for Republicans. Consider the expressions that follow, which transform the logged odds equations into non-linear equations for predicted probabilities. In Table 10-2, we show the mathematical equations on the left and the corresponding statements we execute in SPSS on the right.

To obtain these estimates, we'll need to make three circuits through the Transform ▶ Compute Variable procedure, each requiring a fair amount of typing in the Numeric Expression box—although you may have already figured out how to copy and paste commands to reduce the keyboard drudgery. The first statement will estimate the probability of supporting the requirement to serve gay couples at each value of ft_Gays for Independents. And it asks SPSS to save these predicted probabilities in a new variable, pre_indep. The second statement estimates the

Screencast

Working with
Probabilities,
Marginal Effects
at Representative
Values (MERs)

TABLE 10-2   Equations for Computing MERs

Mathematical Equation	SPPS Statement
$\text{probability}_{\text{Indep}} = \dfrac{e^{-1.775 + .029 \times ft_{Gays}}}{1 + e^{-1.775 + .029 \times ft_{Gays}}}$	pre_indep = Exp(–1.775 + .029*ft_Gays) / (1 + Exp(–1.775 + .029*ft_Gays))
$\text{probability}_{\text{Dem}} = \dfrac{e^{-1.178 + .029 \times ft_{Gays}}}{1 + e^{-1.178 + .029 \times ft_{Gays}}}$	pre_dem = Exp(–1.178 + .029*ft_Gays) / (1 + Exp(–1.178 + .029*ft_Gays))
$\text{probability}_{\text{Repub}} = \dfrac{e^{-2.676 + .029 \times ft_{Gays}}}{1 + e^{-2.676 + .029 \times ft_{Gays}}}$	pre_repub = Exp(–2.676 + .029*ft_Gays) / (1 + Exp(–2.676 + .029*ft_Gays))

Report

Mean

Feeling therm: Gay men and lesbians (v162103)	Pred prob: require service, Independents	Pred prob: require service, Democrats	Pred prob: require service, Republicans
0	.1449	.2354	.0644
1	.1486	.2407	.0662
2	.1523	.2460	.0680
3	.1560	.2514	.0698
4	.1599	.2569	.0718
5	.1638	.2625	.0737
...			
40	.3509	.4955	.1801
41	.3576	.5027	.1844
...			
61	.4985	.6436	.2876
62	.5057	.6502	.2936
...			
92	.7095	.8161	.4980
93	.7154	.8204	.5052
...			
99	.7495	.8446	.5486
100	.7549	.8484	.5558
Total	.4963	.6234	.3083

Note: Output edited for brevity.

probability of the dependent variable at each value of ft_Gays for Democrats, and it too will save a new variable, pre_dem. The third statement does the same for Republicans, saving its work as pre_repub. Go ahead and Compute these three variables (refer to Figure 10-7 as necessary for an example of computing predicted probabilities). Label each variable appropriately so you'll be able to distinguish them later.

Let's examine our new predicted probabilities with a mean comparison table. Select Analyze ▶ Compare Means ▶ Means, putting ft_Gays in the Independent List and all three new variables, pre_indep, pre_dem, and pre_repub, in the Dependent List. To simplify the mean comparison table and make it more readable, click the Options button and move Standard Deviation and Number of Cases back into the Statistics list. SPSS will return a bare-bones mean comparison table.

Consider the dramatically different effects of ft_Gays for these party identifications. The full effect of ft_Gays is about the same for Independents (.7549 − .1449 = .6100) and Democrats (.8484 − .2354 = .6130), but it is less for Republicans (.5558 − .0644 = .4914). Also, notice that the ft_Gays increment with the largest marginal effect—the increment in which the probability of supporting the requirement to serve switches from less than .50 to more than .50—occurs between 61 and 62 for Independents, 40 and 41 for Democrats, and 92 and 93 for Republicans.

When you use the MERs method to explore complex relationships, you will want to complement your analyses with appropriate graphic support. Consider Figure 10-9, a multiple line chart that has spent some "editing" time in the Chart Editor.

This chart instantly communicates the remarkably different ways in which sentiment toward gays affects the probability of having the opinion that wedding businesses should be required to serve gay couples for different values of party identification. With one minor exception, the skills you developed earlier in this book will allow you to obtain an unedited version of this graphic. Using the editing skills you already have—and acquiring additional skills through practice and experimentation—you can create the edited version.

FIGURE 10-9   Edited Line Chart with Multiple Predicted Probability Curves

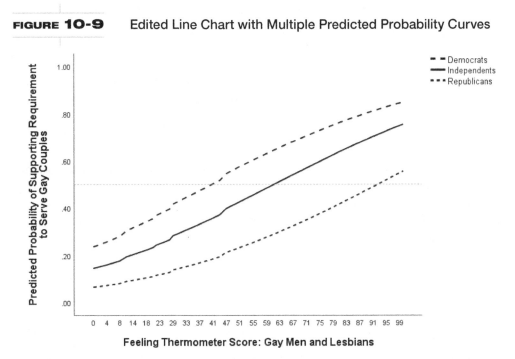

Cases weighted by Weight variable (wtss)

FIGURE 10-10   Creating Line Chart with Multiple Predicted Probability Curves

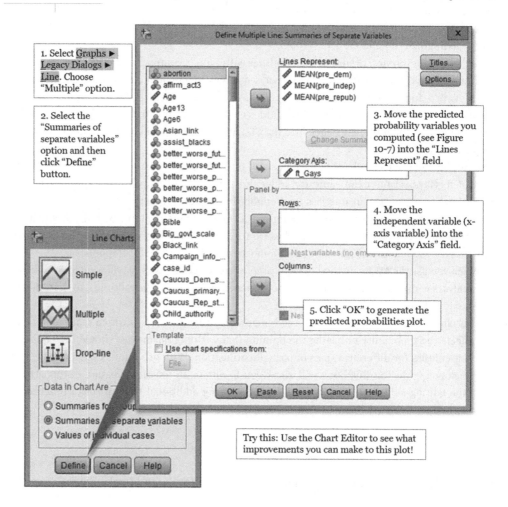

1. Select Graphs ▶ Legacy Dialogs ▶ Line. Choose "Multiple" option.

2. Select the "Summaries of separate variables" option and then click "Define" button.

3. Move the predicted probability variables you computed (see Figure 10-7) into the "Lines Represent" field.

4. Move the independent variable (x-axis variable) into the "Category Axis" field.

5. Click "OK" to generate the predicted probabilities plot.

Try this: Use the Chart Editor to see what improvements you can make to this plot!

To create a line chart with multiple predicted probability curves, select Graphs ▶ Legacy Dialogs ▶ Line (Figure 10-10). In the Line Chart dialog, select Multiple. Here is something new: Instead of the default setting, "Summaries for groups of cases," select the radio button next to "Summaries of separate variables," as shown in Figure 10-10. Click Define. The Summaries of Separate Variables window should look familiar.

The variable whose effects we want to display, ft_Gays, goes in the Category Axis field. The three predicted-probability variables, pre_indep, pre_dem, and pre_repub, go in the Lines Represent field. SPSS offers to graph mean values of pre_indep, pre_dem, and pre_repub, which fits our purpose. There's nothing more to it. Clicking OK produces the requested graphic result (Figure 10-11). This is a line chart with a lot of potential. Before moving on to the exercises, see what improvements you can make.[18]

---

[18] You may want to experiment with a few choices in the Chart Editor's Options menu: Y Axis Reference Line, Text Box, and Hide Legend. SPSS sometimes produces charts that are too "square." A chart with a width of between 1.3 and 1.5 times its height may be more pleasing to the eye. In any event, you can alter the aspect ratio (the ratio of width to height) in the Chart Size tab of the Properties window. After unchecking the box next to "Maintain aspect ratio," click in the Width box and type a number that is between 1.3 and 1.5 times the value appearing in the SPSS Height box.

FIGURE **10-11**   Multiple Line Chart of Two Logistic Regression Curves

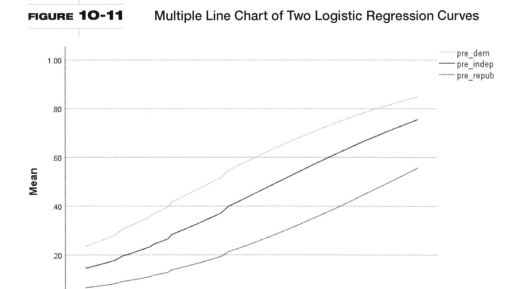

Feeling therm: Gay men and lesbians (v162103)

Cases weighted by Weight variable (v160102)

Name: _____   Date: _____

Email: _____   Section: _____

CHAPTER 10 EXERCISES

1. (Dataset: World. Variables: death_penalty_status, democ_fh_polity, gdp_10_thou, women13, muslim.) Why do some countries continue to impose the death penalty, while others have abolished it? We are likely to hear different hypotheses, depending on who we ask.

   Political Hypothesis: In a comparison of countries, those that are more democratic are less likely to impose the death penalty than countries that are less democratic. (Independent variable: democ_fh_polity.)

   Economic Hypothesis: In a comparison of countries, those with a higher per capita GDP are less likely to impose the death penalty than countries with a lower GDP. (Independent variable: gdp_10_thou.)

   Feminist Hypothesis: In a comparison of countries, those with more women in elected offices are less likely to impose the death penalty than those with fewer women in elected offices. (Independent variable: women13.)

   Religious Hypothesis: In a comparison of countries, those that are predominately Muslim are more likely to impose the death penalty than those that are not predominately Muslim. (Independent variable: muslim.)

   For this exercise, you will use logistic regression analysis with multiple independent variables to test these hypotheses about the use of the death penalty around the world.

   A. The dependent variable in this exercise, death_pen_country, is a variable coded 0 for countries that have abolished or don't use the death penalty and 1 for countries that use the death penalty. The variable death_penalty_status has four values, so you'll want to use the Transform ▶ Recode into Different Variables procedure to create a new variable named death_pen_country with the desired coding (numeric values 1–3 → 0 and 4 → 0).

   To make sure you've generated the dependent variable death_pen_country correctly, apply the Analyze ▶ Descriptive Statistics ▶ Frequencies procedure to it in order to fill in the blanks in the frequency distribution table that follows.

Does country use death penalty?	Frequency	Percentage
No	117	?
Yes	?	?
Total	?	100%

   B. Which of the values below best approximates the *odds* that a randomly selected country uses the death penalty? (circle one)

   7:10   1:2   3:10   3:7   7:3   2:1

   C. Use the Analyze ▶ Regression ▶ Binary Logistic procedure to estimate a logistic regression model with death_pen_country as the dependent variable and democ_fh_polity, gdp_10_thou, women13, and muslim as the four independent variables. Fill in the following results table.

	Coefficient	Standard Error	z	P-value
Democracy	?	?	?	?
Per capita GDP (in $10,000s)	0.63	?	?	?
Percentage of women in legislature	?	?	?	?
Predominately Muslim	?	?	?	?
Constant term	1.30	?	?	?
N	?			
Cox and Snell R-squared	?			
Model chi-squared	?	Prob > chi-squared	?	

   D. The Exp(B) values reported by SPSS can help you interpret logistic regression results. Use the results of your logistic regression analysis to fill in the blanks in the following table. In the far-right column, indicate the percentage change in logged odds associated with a one-unit increase in each independent variable.

Independent Variable	Exp(B)	Percentage Change in Logged Odds
Democracy	?	?
Per capita GDP (in $10,000s)	1.88	?
Percentage of women in legislature	?	?
Predominately Muslim	?	?

E. Based on your results, which of the hypotheses about why some countries use the death penalty and others do not are supported by the evidence? Use the .05 significance level as your cut-off for deciding whether the data support the research hypotheses. (check one box in each row)

Expected Effect on Using the Death Penalty	Significantly Less Likely	No Significant Difference	Significantly More Likely
More democratic countries	?	?	?
Higher per capita GDP	?	?	?
More women in legislature	?	?	?
Predominately Muslim countries	?	?	?

2. (Dataset: States. Variables: medicaid_expansion, demstate09, unemploy, preg_teen_rate.) Medicaid is a government-run program that provides health insurance to poor people. Medicaid is administered by state governments and jointly funded by the states and the federal government. The Affordable Care Act (ACA) made federal funds available to allow states to expand Medicaid eligibility to cover state residents making up to 133 percent of poverty-line income but could not require states to expand Medicaid eligibility.[19] The federal government offered to pay the full cost of

---

[19] Originally, the Affordable Care Act was written in a way that would cut all federal Medicaid funding to states that refused to expand their Medicaid eligibility but the U.S. Supreme Court held in *National Federation of Independent Business v. Sebelius* that the federal government may not use its spending power in such a heavy-handed manner.

---

expanded Medicaid coverage for 3 years and 90 percent of the cost thereafter.[20] Some states chose to take federal money and expand their Medicaid coverage, while other states decided not to take the money and keep eligibility limited to people making less than the poverty line.

Why did some state governments accept federal funding and expand Medicaid eligibility, while other state governments declined the federal offer? In this exercise, you'll use the States dataset and logistic regression analysis with multiple independent variables to analyze state policy decisions.

A. The dependent variable in this analysis is named medicaid_expansion. States that did not adopt expanded Medicaid eligibility are coded 0 and states that adopted expanded guidelines following the ACA are coded 1. Run the Analyze ▶ Descriptive Statistics ▶ Frequencies procedure on medicaid_expansion to fill in the blanks in the following frequency distribution table.

Did state expand Medicaid?	Frequency	Percentage
No	?	?
Yes	?	?
Total	50	100%

B. What *proportion* of states adopted new Medicaid eligibility guidelines after the ACA to expand Medicaid enrollment? (circle one)

0.19   0.31   0.38   0.50   0.62

C. Consider some plausible explanations for why a state may opt to accept ACA funds to expand Medicaid coverage rather than decline the federal funds offered.

Partisan Politics. The ACA is so closely identified with President Barack Obama that it is often called Obamacare. Participating in the ACA initiative to expand Medicaid enrollment is a partisan issue identified with the Democrats; Republican legislatures can be expected to reject the offer. We can measure the partisan composition of state legislatures (before the ACA was enacted) with the demstate09 variable.

Economic Needs. Medicaid is primarily intended for poor people; the purpose of the ACA was to make near-poor people eligible for Medicaid. Thus, expanding Medicaid would tend to help states with higher unemployment

---

[20] For more information, see https://www.medicaid.gov/affordable-care-act/index.html.

more than states with low unemployment. The variable unemploy provides state unemployment rates.

Medical Needs. Medicaid is a health insurance program. Expanding Medicaid may provide greater benefits to states with greater health care needs than states with lesser health care needs. There are a number of ways to measure the relative health of state populations. Teen pregnancies present a challenge for state-operated health insurance for low-income populations (preg_teen_rate is the independent variable).

Use the Analyze ▶ Regression ▶ Binary Logistic procedure to estimate a logistic regression model with medicaid_expansion as the dependent variable and demstate09, unemploy, and preg_teen_rate as independent variables. Use your results to fill in the blank cells of the following table.

	Coefficient	Standard Error	P-value
Percentage of legislature Democrats	?	?	?
Unemployment rate	?	?	?
Teen pregnancy rate	−0.03	?	?
Constant term	−6.05	3.04	?
N		?	
Cox and Snell R-squared		?	
Model chi-squared		?	Prob > chi-squared	?

D. The Exp(B) values reported by SPSS can help you interpret logistic regression results. Use the results of your logistic regression analysis to fill in the blanks in the following table. In the far-right column, circle whether a one-unit increase in each independent variable increases, decreases, or does not significantly affect the odds that a state expanded Medicaid.

	Exp(B)	Effect on odds of Medicaid expansion (circle one)
Percentage of legislature Democrats	?	Increase Decrease Not Sig.

	Exp(B)	Effect on odds of Medicaid expansion (circle one)
Unemployment rate	?	Increase Decrease Not Sig.
Teen pregnancy rate	?	Increase Decrease Not Sig.

E. Use the Transform ▶ Compute Variable procedure to compute the predicted probability of expanding Medicaid at varying values of demstate09 and mean values of unemploy and preg_teen_rate. Give the new variable a descriptive name like pred_medexp_means. You should compute this variable's values from the results you reported in part C and the mean values of unemploy and preg_teen_rate. To verify your work on this part, fill in the blanks in the following equation (see the "Marginal Effects at the Means" section in the text for examples):

$$\text{pred\_medexp\_means} = \frac{e^{(\underline{\quad} + \underline{\quad} \times \text{demstate09})}}{1 + e^{(\underline{\quad} + \underline{\quad} \times \text{demstate09})}}$$

F. Use the Graphs ▶ Legacy Dialogs ▶ Line procedure to create a graphic showing the predicted probability of expanding Medicaid at varying values of demstate09 and mean values of unemploy and preg_teen_rate. The y-axis of your graph should correspond to the pred_medexp_means variable you created in part E; the x-axis should correspond to demstate09 values ranging from 0 to 100. Using this chapter's examples as guides, request all appropriate options. Print the graph.

G. Based on your results, which, if any, of the following explanations for states' Medicaid expansion decisions is supported by the data to a reasonable degree of certainty. (circle all that apply)

Partisan Politics   Economic Needs   Medical Needs

3. (Dataset: GSS. Variables: cappun, polviews, sex, income16, attend, wtss.) In Exercise 1, we asked "Why do some countries continue to impose the death penalty, while others have abolished it?" It's tempting to apply the insights we discovered from analyzing countries to individuals. For example, if we found that countries with more women in government are less likely to use the death penalty, it's tempting to think that on an individual level, women must be more inclined to oppose the death penalty than men are; but aggregate-level relationships may not hold at the individual level. Fortunately, we can analyze individual-level survey data from at least one country to gain some

insight on why some people support the death penalty, while others oppose capital punishment.

The GSS asks respondents whether they favor or oppose the death penalty for murder. Responses are encoded in the cappun variable. (We looked at this variable in a Chapter 6 exercise, as you may recall.) In this exercise, we'll use logistic regression analysis to see if politics, income, gender, or religion help explain individual opinions about the death penalty.

A. The variable cappun assigns numeric code 1 to respondents who favor the death penalty and 2 to respondents who oppose the death penalty. To use logistic regression, the dependent variable must be coded 0/1. To interpret results consistently with Exercise 1, people who favor the death penalty should be coded 1 and those who oppose it should be coded 0. Use the Transform ▶ Recode into Different Variables procedure to create a new variable named cappun_supporter with the desired coding (numeric values 1 → 1 and 2 → 0).

To make sure the dependent variable cappun_supporter is coded correctly, apply the Analyze ▶ Descriptive Statistics ▶ Frequencies procedure to it and fill in the blanks in the following frequency distribution table. Be sure to weight observations with wtss so the statistics are nationally representative.

Support capital punishment?	Numeric Value	Frequency	Percentage
No	?	?	?
Yes	?	?	60.92%
Total		2,695	100%

B. Why do some people support capital punishment for murderers? In Exercise 1, we consider four possible reasons that countries might use capital punishment: politics, economics, gender, and religion. Let's apply similar considerations to individual-level decisions about capital punishment. As an individual-level political variable, use polviews; for an economic variable, use income16; to assess gender differences, use the nominal-level variable sex; for a religion variable, use attend. (For more concise results, treat polviews, income16, and attend as interval-level variables.)

Use the Analyze ▶ Regression ▶ Binary Logistic procedure to estimate a logistic regression model with cappun_supporter as the dependent variable and polviews, income16, sex, and attend as the independent variables. Be sure to weight observations with wtss so the results are nationally representative and fill in the blanks in table below.

	Coefficient	Standard Error	P-value
Political ideology	?	?	?
Household income	?	?	?
Female gender	?	?	?
Church attendance	?	?	?
Constant term	−1.01	0.23	<0.001
N	?		
Cox and Snell R-squared	?		?
Model chi-squared	?	Prob > chi-squared	?

C. The Exp(B) values reported by SPSS can help you interpret logistic regression results. Use the results of your logistic regression analysis to fill in the blanks in the following table. In the far-right column, indicate the percentage change in logged odds associated with a one-unit increase in each independent variable.

	Exp(B)	Percentage Change in Logged Odds
Political ideology	?	?
Household income	?	?
Female gender	?	?
Church attendance	?	?

D. Use the Transform ▶ Compute Variable procedure to compute the predicted probabilities of men and women supporting capital punishment at varying values of polviews and mean values of income16 and attend. You should compute two new variables; give them descriptive names like pred_cappun_men and pred_cappun_women. To verify your work on this part, fill in the blanks in the following equations (see the "Marginal Effects at Representative Values" section in the text for examples):

$$\text{pred\_cappun\_men} = \frac{e^{(\underline{\quad} + \underline{\quad} \times \text{polviews})}}{1 + e^{(\underline{\quad} + \underline{\quad} \times \text{polviews})}}$$

$$\text{pred\_cappun\_women} = \frac{e^{(\underline{\quad} + \underline{\quad} \times \text{polviews})}}{1 + e^{(\underline{\quad} + \underline{\quad} \times \text{polviews})}}$$

E. Use the Graphs ▶ Legacy Dialogs ▶ Line procedure to create a multiple line chart showing the predicted probabilities of men and women supporting capital punishment at varying values of polviews and mean values of income16 and attend. The y-axis of your graph should correspond to the probability that an individual supports capital punishment based on the logistic regression analysis; the x-axis should correspond to polviews values ranging from 1 (extremely liberal) to 7 (extremely conservative). Your graph should have two separate predicted probability curves: one for men and another for women (which means you need to compute two different predicted probabilities from your results). Print the graph.

F. Based on your results, which, if any, of the following factors explain why some people support capital punishment? Base your conclusions on the logistic regression analysis and the convention .05 statistical significance threshold. (circle all that apply)

Politics   Income   Gender   Religion

4. (Dataset: World. Variables: democ_regime, frac_eth, gdp_10_thou.) In Chapter 5, you tested the following hypothesis: In comparing countries, those having lower levels of ethnic heterogeneity are more likely to be democracies than are those having higher levels of ethnic heterogeneity. This hypothesis says that as heterogeneity goes up, the probability of democracy goes down. You then reran the analysis, controlling for a measure of countries' economic development, gross domestic product per capita. For this independent variable, the relationship is thought to be positive: As economic development increases, so does the likelihood that a country will be democratic. In the current exercise, you will re-examine this set of relationships, using a more powerful method of analysis, logistic regression.

The World dataset contains democ_regime, frac_eth, and gdp_10_thou. The variable, democ_regime, is coded 1 if the country is a democracy and coded 0 if it is not a democracy. This is the dependent variable. One of the independent variables, frac_eth, can vary between 0 (denoting low heterogeneity) and 1 (high heterogeneity). The other independent variable, gdp_10_thou, measures gross domestic product per capita in units of $10,000.

A. Use the Analyze ▶ Regression ▶ Binary Logistic procedure to estimate a logistic regression model with democ_regime as the dependent variable and two independent variables: frac_eth and gdp_10_thou. Write the correct value next to each question mark in the following table.

	Coefficient	Standard Error	P-value
Ethnic fractionalization	?	?	?
GDP per capita (in $10,000s)	?	?	?
Constant term	0.54	?	?
N	?		
Nagelkerke R-squared	?		
Model chi-squared	?	Prob > chi-squared	?

B. Study the Exp(B) value that SPSS reports for the frac_eth variable. Controlling for gdp_10_thou, a one-unit change in frac_eth, from low heterogeneity to high heterogeneity (check one)

❑ increases the odds of democracy by about 20 percent.

❑ decreases the odds of democracy by about 20 percent.

❑ decreases the odds of democracy by about 70 percent.

Controlling for frac_eth, each $10,000 increase in per capita gross domestic product (check one)

❑ increases the odds of democracy by about 110 percent.

❑ increases the odds of democracy by about 220 percent.

❑ increases the odds of democracy by about 40 percent.

C. For this part, you will calculate the full effect of ethnic fractionalization on the probability a country is a democracy. For this analysis, you can hold gdp_10_thou constant at its mean value (0.6258). As an empirical matter, the most homogeneous country in the World dataset has a value of 0 on frac_eth, and the most heterogeneous country has a value of approximately 0.9 on frac_eth. The predicted probability of democracy for a highly homogeneous country (frac_eth = 0) with an average level of gdp_10_thou equals _____. The predicted probability of democracy for a highly heterogeneous country (frac_eth = 0.9) with an average level of gdp_10_thou equals _____. The difference between the values you've written in the two preceding blanks is the full effect of ethnic fractionalization within the sample values: _____.

D. Use the Graphs ▶ Legacy Dialogs ▶ Line procedure to graphically display the effect of ethnic fractionalization on the probability a country is a democracy (for countries with mean per capita GDPs). Using this chapter's examples as guides, request all appropriate options. Be sure to change the labels as necessary. Print the graph.

That concludes the exercises for this chapter. Before exiting SPSS, be sure to save your datasets.

11

Doing Your Own Political Analysis

Procedures Covered

File ▶ New ▶ Data

Edit ▶ Paste

In working through the guided examples in this book, and in performing the exercises, you have developed some solid analytic skills. The datasets you have analyzed here could, of course, become the raw material for your own research. You would not be disappointed, however, if you were to look elsewhere for excellent data. High-quality social science data on a wide variety of phenomena and units of analysis—individuals, census tracts, states, countries—are easily accessible via the Internet and might serve as the centerpiece for your own research. Your school, for example, may be a member of the Inter-university Consortium for Political and Social Research (ICPSR), the premier organizational clearinghouse for datasets of all kinds.[1] In this chapter we will take a look at various sources of available data and provide practical guidance for inputting them into SPSS.

To get you thinking about doing your own research, we begin by laying out the stages of the research process and by offering some manageable ideas for original analysis. We then consider different data sources and procedures for inputting the data into the Data Editor. Finally, we describe a serviceable format for an organized and presentable research paper.

SEVEN DOABLE IDEAS

Let's begin by describing an ideal research procedure and then discuss some practical considerations and constraints. In an ideal world, you would

1. Observe an interesting behavior or relationship and frame a research question about it;

2. Develop a causal explanation for what you have observed and construct a hypothesis;

3. Read and learn from the work of other researchers who have tackled similar questions;

---

[1] You can browse ICPSR's holdings at www.icpsr.umich.edu.

4. Collect and analyze the data that will address the hypothesis; and

5. Write a research paper or article in which you present and interpret your findings.

In this idealized scenario, the phenomenon that you observe in stage 1 drives the whole process. First, think up a question, then research it and obtain the data that will address it. As a practical matter, the process is almost never this clear cut. Often someone else's idea or assertion may pique your interest. For example, you might read articles or attend lectures on a variety of topics—democratization in developing countries, global environmental issues, ideological change in the Democratic or Republican Party, the effect of election laws on turnout and party competition, and so on—that suggest hypotheses you would like to examine. So you may begin the process at stage 3, then return to stage 1 and refine your own ideas. Furthermore, the availability of relevant data, considered in stage 4, almost always plays a role in the sorts of questions we address.

Suppose, for example, that you want to assess the organizational efforts to mobilize African Americans in your state in the last presidential election. You want precinct-level registration data, and you need to compare these numbers with the figures from previous elections. You would soon become an expert in the bureaucratic hassles and expense involved in dealing with county governments, and you might have to revise your research agenda. Indeed, for professional researchers and academics, data collection in itself can be a full-time job. For students who wish to produce a competent and manageable project, the so-called law of available data can be a source of frustration and discouragement.

A doable project often requires a compromise between stage 1 and stage 4. What interesting questions can you ask, given the datasets available with this book? To help you get started doing your own political analysis, we'll discuss the following seven possible lines of research.

Political Knowledge and Interest

As you may have learned in other political science courses, scholars continue to debate the levels of knowledge and political awareness among ordinary citizens. Do citizens know the length of a U.S. senator's term of office? Do they know what constitutional protections are guaranteed by the First Amendment? Do people tend to know more about some things—Internet privacy or abortion policy, for example—and less about other things, such as foreign policy or international politics? Political knowledge is a promising variable because the researcher is likely to find some people who know a lot about politics, some who know a fair amount, and others who know very little.[2] One could ask, "What causes this variation?"

The NES dataset contains a number of variables that measure respondents' political knowledge. Some variables measure respondents' knowledge of particular topics, like the terms of senators and presidents, whereas other variables are constructed to differentiate respondents' political knowledge at the ordinal or interval level. See Appendix Table A-2 for an alphabetical list of all variables in the NES dataset.

Self-Interest and Policy Preferences

It is widely thought that people support policies to advance their personal interests. This view is consistent with the economist's view that people generally act in a way that maximizes their personal happiness. There's often no conflict between self-interest and public interest. For example, if you think the federal government should do more to curb global warming, you probably think that limiting greenhouses gasses is in everybody's interest, not just yours. Sometimes, however, our general views on public policy conflict with our self-interest. For example, one might generally favor

---

[2] For excellent guidance on the meaning and measurement of political knowledge, see Michael X. Delli Carpini and Scott Keeter, "Measuring Political Knowledge: Putting First Things First," *American Journal of Political Science* 37, no. 4 (November 1993): 1179–1206.

protecting the environment, but if a proposal to do so decreases the value of one's personal property, self-interest may prevail over public interest.

There is a good body of political science research on the role of self-interest in the formulation of policy preferences. The empirical research is mixed.[3] The NES and GSS datasets offer students a number of opportunities to explore how self-interest affects the formulation of individual policy preferences. To pursue this line of research, consider the variables that record personal information about the GSS and NES survey respondents, such as their age, occupation, parental status, and so forth. There are many such variables. Then consider how different personal characteristics would alter policy preferences if the respondent was motivated by self-interest and look for a variable that measures individual preferences on these policies. For example, do gun owners have significantly different preferences with respect to gun control than do non-gun owners? Do parents express fundamentally different preferences on public school education policies than non-parents? The datasets provided with this book offer numerous opportunities to test the theory that people act in a politically self-interested manner.

When you conduct this research, we suggest you consider and try to control for the possibility that respondents' policy preferences reflect their own conception of public interest, which may coincide with their own self-interest at times. You might, for example, incorporate some measure of political ideology or party identification to help isolate the extent to which selfishness compels people to disregard their general political views.

Economic Performance and Election Outcomes

Here is one of the most widely discussed ideas in political science: how the state of the economy before an election affects election results. If the economy is strong, the candidate of the incumbent party does well, probably winning the election. If the economy is performing poorly, the incumbent party's nominee pays the price, probably losing. There are a couple of intriguing aspects to this idea. For one thing, it works well—but not perfectly. Moreover, the economy–election relationship has several researchable layers.

Focusing on state-by-state results in presidential elections, you can imagine a simple two-category measure of the dependent variable (the incumbent party wins or the incumbent party loses) or an interval-level measure of the dependent variable (the percentage of state residents who vote for the incumbent president's party). Now consider some potential independent variables that measure the strength of the economy in the states, such as the state unemployment rate. Or you could modify and refine the basic idea, as many scholars have done, by adding additional noneconomic variables you believe to be important. To what extent do demographic factors or varying opinions on social issues challenge the view that elections are a referendum on the president's handling of the economy? You'll find the variables you need to get started with this research in the States dataset.

Electoral Turnout in Comparative Perspective

The record of voter turnout in American presidential elections is relatively low. The situation in other democratic countries is strikingly different. Turnouts in some Western European countries average well above 70 percent. Why? More generally, what causes turnout to vary between countries? Some scholars have focused on institutional differences in electoral systems. Many countries, for example, have systems of proportional representation in which narrowly focused parties with relatively few supporters nonetheless can gain representation in the legislature. The variable pr_sys in the World dataset identifies countries with proportional representation systems. Are citizens more likely to be mobilized to vote under such institutional arrangements? You could see if other variables are associated with differences in turnout around the world.

---

[3] See e.g. Robin Wolpert and James Gimpel, "Self-Interest, Symbolic Politics, and Public Attitudes Toward Gun Control," *Political Behavior* 20, no. 3 (1998): 241–262.

This area of research might also open the door for some informed speculation on your part. What sort of electoral reforms, if instituted in the United States, might enhance electoral turnout? What other (perhaps unintended) consequences might such reforms have?

Interviewer Effects on Public Opinion Surveys

The GSS and NES surveys ask participants some sensitive and controversial questions. These surveys, for example, ask people questions about racism, sexism, and homosexuality. These are important topics, but one of the challenges that researchers face when they attempt to discern public opinions on sensitive topics is the human tendency to give socially acceptable answers on certain topics. What's acceptable or expected behavior depends on social context. Behavior that is normal at a football game is not acceptable during a church service.

Public opinion researchers do their best to avoid influencing how people respond to surveys, but surveys are inevitably administered in some context that may affect how people respond to questions, particularly sensitive and controversial topics. For example, a survey can be administered in person, over the phone, or over the Internet. Do people give significantly different responses to a live person than they do to an Internet survey? Identify an NES variable you think would be affected by context and compare responses obtained face to face with those obtained over the Internet (using the mode variable).

The GSS dataset includes a number of variables about the person conducting the interview, such as the interviewer's age, race, ethnicity, and gender. How might the interviewer's race, ethnicity, and/or gender define the parameters of social acceptability in the interview? Identify a question in the GSS dataset you think could be affected by who conducted the interview and see if who asked the question affected the answers given.

Religion and Politics

All four datasets include variables related to religion and religious practices, facilitating research into the relationship between religion and politics. Most political science research on religion and politics will treat religion as the independent variable and analyze how religious beliefs influence political outcomes. The GSS and NES datasets include variables related to respondents' religious beliefs, or lack thereof, and one can analyze how individuals' beliefs affect their political attitudes and opinions. Similarly, the States and World datasets include aggregate-level measures of religious beliefs and practices, allowing researchers to examine how varying religious practices affect state or national politics.

A couple words of caution are in order for those interested in researching how religion affects politics. First, it's important for the researcher to control for other variables, such as political ideology, that offer alternative explanations for the observed political outcomes. In some cases, conservative political ideology may offer a better explanation of variation in a dependent variable than do religious beliefs. Second, if one analyzes aggregate-level data from the States or World dataset, it is important to make inferences about individuals from aggregate-level results. For example, if one finds that states with more frequent church attendance have significantly more gun violence than states with fewer attenders, one should not infer that people who go to church frequently are more violent than others are. This mistake is known as the ecological fallacy.

There are also some opportunities to examine attitudes and opinions related to religion as the dependent variable. For example, the GSS dataset asks respondents whether someone with an anti-religion message should be permitted to teach in college (colath), speak in the respondent's community (spkath), or have a book in the library (libath). These are interesting questions because they raise First Amendment issues about the proper role of religion in public affairs. We would discourage political science students from analyzing religious affiliations and beliefs as a dependent variable to determine what causes someone to believe in God or go to church. The nature and origins of religious beliefs are certainly important topics, but these topics are largely outside the scope of political science.

Race and Politics

Race is one of the most enduring and difficult issues in politics. There are many ways to analyze the relationship between race and politics using the datasets that accompany this book. To help students identify potential research topics, we'll first discuss research designs that use race (or ethnicity) as an independent variable and then discuss designs where race-related variables are the outcome of interest.

How does race affect political beliefs and outcomes? Do individuals who identify as racial or ethnic minorities express significantly different political views than others do? Both the GSS and NES datasets include variables identifying respondents' race and ethnicity. Do states or countries with greater proportions of racial or ethnic minorities have different political outcomes than those with lesser proportions of minorities? You can find data to conduct this inquiry in both the States and World datasets. Because race is such an enduring and important issue, the results of this kind of analysis are usually interesting whether one finds that race makes or does not make a significant difference. At the same time, we encourage students interested in the effect of race on politics to read the words of caution above (about studying the effect of religion on politics), which are equally applicable here.

One can also examine race-related political beliefs, attitudes, or outcomes as the dependent variable in political science research. In the GSS dataset, one can find variables measuring respondents' support for affirmative action and government relief, belief in racial stereotypes, and sense of shared fate. The NES dataset also contains a number of variables measuring respondents' opinions and attitudes about racial discrimination and minority communities in the United States. Some predictors, like respondents' race and party identification, should seem obvious and you should include these explanations in your analysis. Can you identify other significant predictors of race-related political beliefs and attitudes? Consider examining the influence of factors like age, employment status, and education.

IMPORTING DATA INTO SPSS

Each of the research topics outlined above represents a practical compromise between posing an interesting question, obtaining available data, and using SPSS to perform the analysis. However, as you will no doubt discover, data sources vary in their "input friendliness"—some data are easy to input into SPSS, and other data require more typing. This section reviews different data sources and input procedures.

SPSS Formatted Datasets

The least labor-intensive sources provide SPSS-format datasets (*.sav files) that are ready to download and analyze. One such source, the ICPSR's data clearinghouse at the University of Michigan, was mentioned at the beginning of this chapter.[4] But many other sites exist, often maintained by scholars, academic departments, and private foundations. For example, try the Political Science Data website, www.poliscidata.com, maintained by one of the authors of this books (Edwards). You can find datasets related to different topics as well as links to datasets made available by individual political scientists and political science journals. If you're interested in comparative politics or international relations, visit Pippa Norris's website.[5] Are you interested in the political beliefs and civic behavior of young people? The Center for Information and Research on Civic

---

[4] http://www.icpsr.umich.edu

[5] http://www.pippanorris.com

Learning and Engagement (CIRCLE) provides excellent data (and links to data) in SPSS format.[6] More generally, the University of California–Berkeley's Survey Documentation and Analysis (SDA) website—a clearinghouse for the General Social Surveys, the American National Election Studies, and census microdata—allows you to download customized datasets and codebooks in a variety of formats, including SPSS.[7]

Opening an SPSS-format dataset is simple. We covered this skill in Chapter 1. Download the dataset to your computer, just as you downloaded the four datasets that accompany this book, and either double-click the *.sav file to open it or, with SPSS running, select File ▶ Open ▶ Data and find the downloaded dataset.

Other Supported Data Types

In addition to datasets saved as SPSS-format *.sav files, SPSS supports a variety of other common file types. Data stored in other supported file types can be imported into SPSS with relatively little fuss. These other supported file types generally fall into two categories:

- *Text file types.* Researchers frequently save datasets as text files as a kind of lowest common denominator among statistics software programs. Text file types supported by SPSS include *.txt, *.csv, *.dat, and *.tab. These types of files store data in long lines of text, one observation per line, with variables separated by commas or tab spacing. To import datasets stored in text format, select File ▶ Open ▶ Data and "Files of type: Text." SPSS will then guide you through a text import wizard to make sure the variables and observations are organized properly.

- *Other statistics software formats.* SPSS can import datasets saved in the file types of other popular programs, including Stata and SAS files. To import datasets stored in another program's file type, select File ▶ Open ▶ Data and the file type for that software. If the file type is not supported, you should look for the target dataset saved in a text file type or open the target dataset in its native software and save it in an SPSS-friendly file type.

When you import data in other supported file types, be sure to view the imported data in SPSS's Data Editor (refer to Chapter 1 for a discussion of SPSS's Data Editor). Make sure the Data View shows numbers where you expect to see numbers and text where you expect to see text. In the Variable View, you may notice that a dataset imported from another supported file format is not carefully labeled. This is particularly true of bare-bones text-format datasets that contain no variable or value labels. You may want to edit labels of variables you analyze so your results display more clearly (see the "Working with Variable Labels" section in Chapter 3).

Microsoft Excel Datasets

Much of the data available on the Internet are not SPSS ready but are instead saved in spreadsheets, predominately in Microsoft Excel format. In these situations, you can import the spreadsheet as a supported file type or copy/paste the data from Excel into the SPSS Data Editor. There are a few caveats to keep in mind, however.

Many of the Excel files you will find on the Internet contain a lot of non-importable text and graphics junk. SPSS recognizes two basic forms of data, numeric and string. Numeric data contain only numbers, including numbers with decimals. String data contain letters, words, symbols, or commas. Although some string data are essential—case identifiers, such as state or country names, are obvious examples—SPSS much prefers to analyze numeric data, not strings. Some editing and cleaning may be necessary.

---

[6] http://www.civicyouth.org/ResearchTopics/research-products-cat/data-sets/

[7] http://sda.berkeley.edu/archive.htm

FIGURE 11-1 Opening an Excel Dataset and Evaluating Its SPSS Friendliness

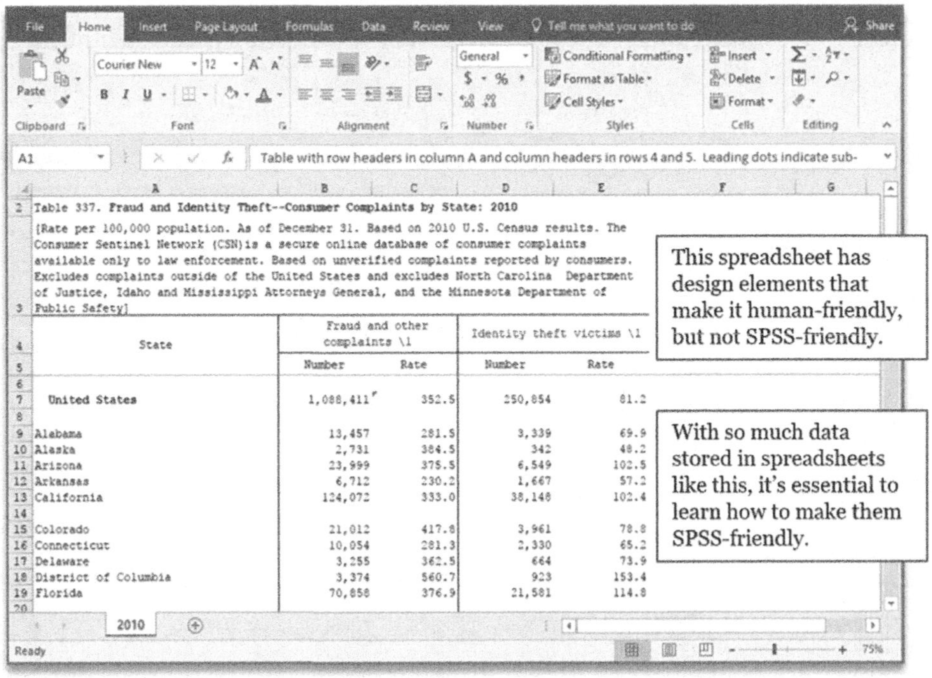

Source: United States Census Bureau

Consider Figure 11-1, which shows an Excel file downloaded from a U.S. Census site.[8] This spreadsheet records consumer complaints of fraud and identity theft, by state. This set could be saved as a .csv file, but SPSS would not import it correctly without first editing the spreadsheet. The large text header, the long column labels, the eye-pleasing blank rows, and even the commas in the values in the "Number" columns are all features designed to make the file easy for humans to peruse and interpret. Unfortunately, these features are not SPSS friendly.

Now consider Figure 11-2, an SPSS-friendly version of the same data. This dataset is symmetrical. Each column has a brief label, the blank rows are gone, and the large number values no longer contain commas. (In imported data, numbers with decimal points are fine, but numbers with commas are not.) Once the data are saved in this format, you can import them into SPSS or copy and paste them into SPSS's Data Editor.

In the current example, the numbers reported with comma separators would be read as string data, not numeric data. To remove the commas, and thereby convert the data from string to numeric, follow the steps illustrated in Figure 11-3.

To prepare an SPSS-friendly spreadsheet, follow these steps:

1. Select the desired data columns and rows. Make sure that the data selection is rectangular—that each row contains the same number of columns.

2. Open a blank Excel worksheet. Paste the selected data into the new file. To delete blank rows, select the row, right-click, and click on Delete. Depending on how you plan to use the data, you may want to remove any non-state entries, such as the District of Columbia and Puerto Rico.

3. To remove commas from data values, select the columns. To select multiple nonadjacent columns, press and hold <Ctrl>.

---

[8] http://www2.census.gov/library/publications/2011/compendia/statab/131ed/tables/12s0337.xls

FIGURE 11-2 SPSS-Friendly Excel Spreadsheet

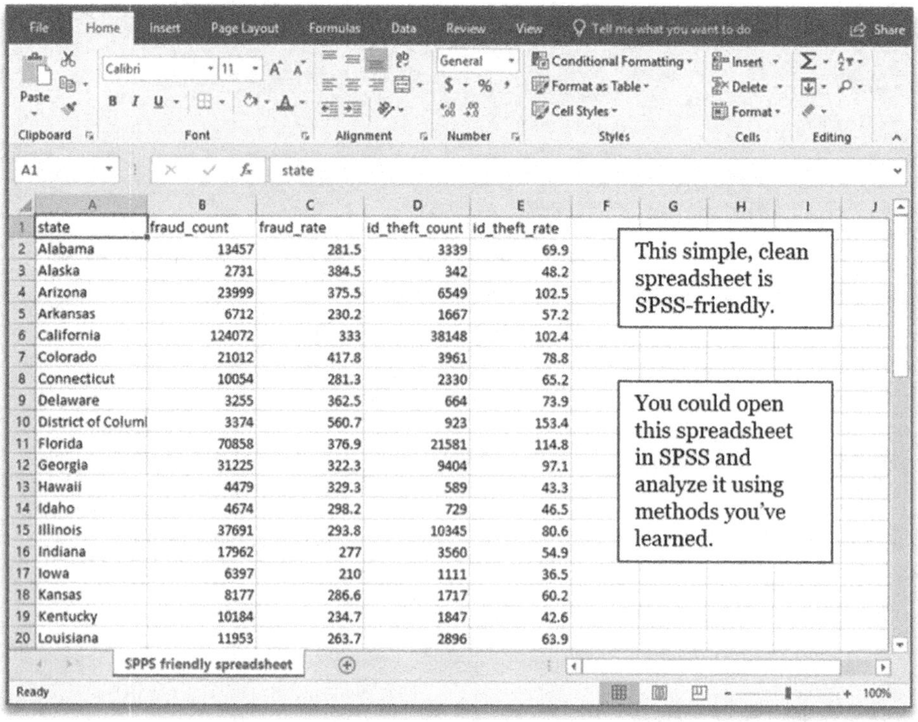

state	fraud_count	fraud_rate	id_theft_count	id_theft_rate
Alabama	13457	281.5	3339	69.9
Alaska	2731	384.5	342	48.2
Arizona	23999	375.5	6549	102.5
Arkansas	6712	230.2	1667	57.2
California	124072	333	38148	102.4
Colorado	21012	417.8	3961	78.8
Connecticut	10054	281.3	2330	65.2
Delaware	3255	362.5	664	73.9
District of Columl	3374	560.7	923	153.4
Florida	70858	376.9	21581	114.8
Georgia	31225	322.3	9404	97.1
Hawaii	4479	329.3	589	43.3
Idaho	4674	298.2	729	46.5
Illinois	37691	293.8	10345	80.6
Indiana	17962	277	3560	54.9
Iowa	6397	210	1111	36.5
Kansas	8177	286.6	1717	60.2
Kentucky	10184	234.7	1847	42.6
Louisiana	11953	263.7	2896	63.9

Source: United States Census Bureau

4. From Excel's Home panel, select Number → Category: Number. Make sure that the Use 1000 Separator box is unchecked. (Excel may already have unchecked the box.) In Decimal places, type an appropriate value. In the example, the numbers we are re-formatting do not have decimal places, so a value of 0 is appropriate.[9]

5. Insert a new row at the top of the data file. To accomplish this, select the current top row (the data line for Alabama), right-click, and click on Insert. Type descriptive variable names at the top of each column.

Once you've fixed all the SPSS-unfriendly elements on the spreadsheet data you want to analyze, save the SPSS-friendly spreadsheet. You have two options for importing an SPSS-friendly spreadsheet into SPSS. First, you can select File ▶ Open ▶ Data and select the Excel-format spreadsheet. This will call up the Read Excel File window (see Figure 11-4). If you've named variables in the spreadsheet on the first row, be sure to check the option "Read variable names from first row of data."

To copy/paste the edited Excel data into the SPSS Data Editor, follow these steps, which are illustrated in Figure 11-5.

1. Select the Excel data rows that you want to paste into SPSS. Make sure that the selection is rectangular—that is, ensure that each row contains the same number of columns. Avoid selecting column headers and labels. Also, do not use Excel's row-number markers to make

[9] Depending on the exact character of the data, you may also want to modify the value in the Decimal places box. If the data contain decimals, then specify the number of decimal places. In the current example, the numbers in the edited columns do not contain decimals, so we would type "0" in the Decimal places box.

FIGURE 11-3   Creating an SPSS-Friendly Excel Spreadsheet

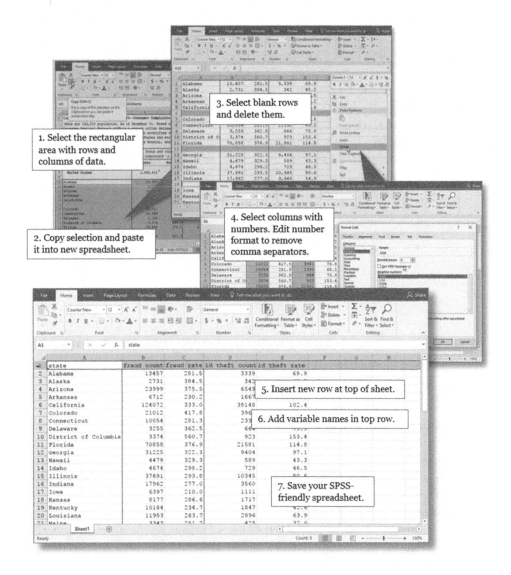

the selection. (This copies the desired columns, plus a number of empty columns.) Rather, select the data by clicking inside the matrix. In the current example, we would begin the selection by clicking on "Alabama," selecting the five columns to the right, and selecting down through the last state, "Wyoming." After completing the selection, click the Copy icon on the Excel menu bar.

2. On the SPSS menu bar, select File ▶ New ▶ Data.

3. If SPSS's Data Editor opens in the Variable View, select the Data View tab. Click in the upper-left cell of the Data View.

4. Select Edit ▶ Paste or right-click the upper-left cell and select the Paste option. SPSS copies the Excel data into the Data Editor and supplies generic variable names. Switch to the Variable View and provide descriptive names and labels for the variables.

FIGURE 11-4   Import an SPSS-Friendly Excel Spreadsheet into SPSS

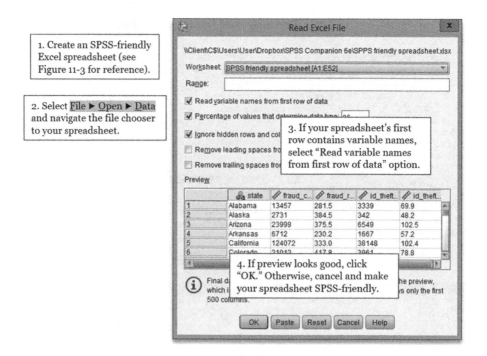

HTML Table Data

As we have just seen, if the data are available in Excel format, it is a relatively simple matter to copy/paste into SPSS. The next remove is this: If the data are in HTML format, it is a relatively simple matter to copy/paste into Excel—or directly into SPSS, if all the data are already SPSS-friendly. Often a side trip through Excel is necessary. Note, however, that the HTML-to-Excel procedure works best with Internet Explorer, but it may not work consistently with Mozilla Firefox or Google Chrome.

By way of illustration, consider the Freedom House's Freedom on the Net 2016 Scores for 65 countries around the world. This table offers an interval-level measurement of Internet freedom based on obstacles to access, limits on content, and violation of user rights.

As shown in Figure 11-6, to convert this table to an SPSS-friendly format, we would select the data, copy them to the clipboard, and paste them into Excel. Once in Excel, check the first row, which should contain the variable names. Verify that the variable names are properly aligned and acceptable. You may want to shorten variable names and eliminate white spaces. In addition, make sure numbers in your spreadsheet are rendered as numeric values, rather than text; if large numbers have separating commas, you'll want to remove the separating commas at this stage. Once you are satisfied that things look okay, save the dataset as an .xls or .csv file and use either the GUI or copy/paste it into SPSS.

WRITING IT UP

Several of the datasets described thus far would provide great raw material for analysis. After you input your data, you can let the creative juices flow—describe the variables, perform cross-tabulation and mean comparison analyses, run linear regression and logit models. Rewarding findings are guaranteed.

FIGURE 11-5   Copying and Pasting from Excel into SPSS

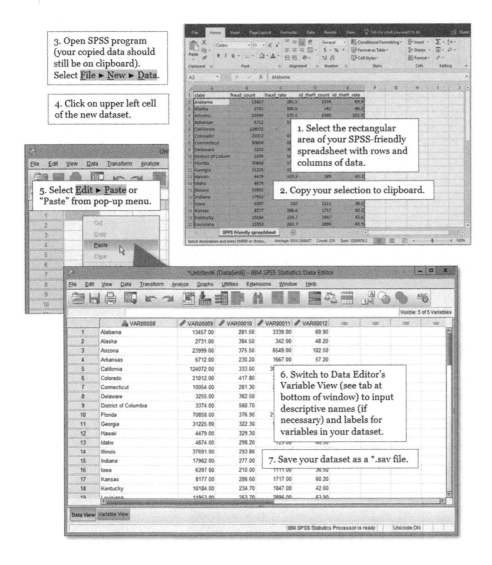

At some point the analysis ends, and the writing must begin. It is at this point, as well, that two contradictory considerations often collide. On one hand, you have an embarrassment of riches. You have worked on your research for several weeks, and you know the topic well—better, perhaps, than does anyone who will read the paper. There may be a large amount of material that you want to include in your paper. On the other hand, you want to get it written, and you do not want to write a book. It's impossible to produce a polished research paper in one try so don't think you have to write your paper in the order suggested here. In our experience, most scholars write papers "from the inside-out," meaning you start by describing the variables of interest, perhaps using some of the methods suggested in Chapter 2, even though your variable descriptions will end up in the middle of your finished product. Get started early to give yourself an opportunity to be creative and try different things. You can edit and revise your writing to produce a polished final draft.

The two questions most frequently asked by students are, "How should my paper be organized?" and "How long should it be?" (These questions are not necessarily asked in this order.) Of course,

FIGURE 11-6   Converting an HTML-Format Table to an SPSS-Friendly File

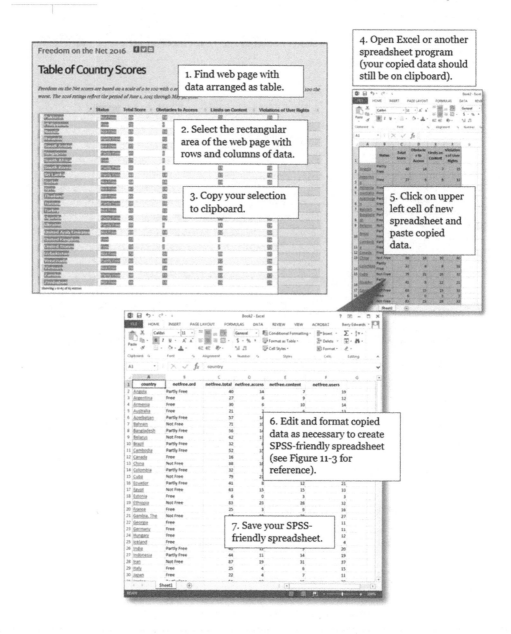

different projects and instructors might call for different requirements. Here is a rough outline for a well-organized paper of sixteen to twenty-four double-spaced pages (in twelve-point font).

I. The research question (3–4 pages)

    A. Introduction to the problem (1 page)

    B. Theory and process (1–2 pages)

    C. Propositions (1 page)

II. Previous research (2–4 pages)

    A. Descriptive review (1–2 pages)

    B. Critical review (1–2 pages)

III. Data and hypotheses (3–4 pages)

    A. Data and variables (1–2 pages)

    B. Measurement (1 page)

    C. Hypotheses (1 page)

IV. Analysis (4–7 pages, including tables)

    A. Descriptive statistics (1–2 pages)

    B. Bi-variate comparisons (1–2 pages)

    C. Controlled comparisons (2–3 pages)

V. Conclusions and implications (3–5 pages)

    A. Summary of findings (1 page)

    B. Implications for theory (1–2 pages)

    C. Limitations and suggestions for future research (1–2 pages)

The Research Question

Because of its rhetorical challenges, the opening section of a paper is often the most difficult to write. In this section the writer must both engage the reader's interest and describe the purpose of the research. Here is a heuristic device that may be useful: In the first page of the write-up, place the specific research problem in the context of larger, clearly important issues or questions. For example, suppose your research is centered on the landmark healthcare legislation passed by Congress in 2010. A narrowly focused topic? Yes. A dry topic? Not at all. The opening page of this paper could frame larger questions about the sometimes conflicting roles of congressional party leadership and constituency interests in shaping the behavior of representatives and senators. Thus, your analysis will advance our knowledge by illuminating one facet of a larger, more complex question.

Following the introduction, the writer begins to zero in on the problem at hand. The "theory and process" section describes the logic of the relationships you are studying. Many political phenomena, as you have learned, have competing or alternative explanations. You should describe these alternatives, and the tension between them, in this section. Although a complete description of previous research does not appear in this section, you should give appropriate attribution to the most prominent work. These references tie your work to the scholarly community, and they raise the points you will cover in a more detailed review.

You should round out the introductory section of your paper with a brief statement of purpose or intent. Think about it from the reader's perspective. Thus far you have made the reader aware of the larger context of the analysis, and you have described the process that may explain the relationships of interest. If this process has merit, then it should submit to an empirical test of some kind. What test do you propose? The "Propositions" section serves this role. Here you set the parameters of the research—informing the reader about the units of analysis, the concepts to be measured, and the type of analysis to be performed.

Previous Research

Here you provide an intellectual history of the research problem, a description, and a critique of the published research on which the analysis is based. You first would describe these previous analyses in some detail. What data and variables were used? What were the main findings? Did different researchers arrive at different conclusions? Political scientists who share a research interest often agree on many things. Yet knowledge is nourished through criticism, and in reviewing previous work you will notice key points of disagreement—about how concepts should be measured, what are the best data to use, or which variables need to be controlled. In the latter part of this section of the paper, you would review these points and perhaps contribute to the debate. Here we need to make a practical point: The frequently asked question "How many articles and books should be reviewed?" has no set answer. It depends on the project. However, here is an estimate: A well-grounded yet manageable review should discuss at least four references.

Data, Hypotheses, and Analysis

Together, the sections "Data and Hypotheses" and "Analysis" form the heart of the project, and they have been the primary concerns of this book. By now you are well versed in how to describe your data and variables and how to frame hypotheses. You also know how to set up a cross-tabulation or mean comparison table, and you can make controlled comparisons and interpret your findings.

In writing these sections, however, you should bear in mind a few reader-centered considerations. First, assume that the reader might want to replicate your study—collect the data you gathered, define and measure the concepts as you have defined and measured them, manipulate the variables just as you have computed and recoded them, and produce the tables you have reported. By explaining precisely what you did, your write-up should provide a clear guide for such a replication.

Second, devote some space to a statistical description of the variables. Often you can add depth and interest to your analysis by briefly presenting the frequency distributions of the variables, particularly the dependent variable.

Finally, exercise care in constructing readable tables. You can select, copy, and paste the tables generated by SPSS directly into a word processor, but they always require further editing for readability. As we have attempted to emphasize throughout this text, sometimes all you need are basic tables and figures; however, when you're sharing your work in a presentation or paper, format your tables and figures properly and take advantage of SPSS's myriad options to refine your graphics so they communicate the essence of your analysis as clearly as possible.

Conclusions and Implications

No section of a research paper can write itself. But the final section comes closest to realizing this optimistic hope. Here you discuss the analysis on three levels. First, you provide a condensed recapitulation. What are the main findings? Are the hypotheses borne out? Were there any unexpected findings? Second, you describe where the results fit in the larger fabric of scholarly research on the topic. In what ways are the findings consistent with the work of previous researchers? Does your analysis lend support to one scholarly perspective as opposed to another? Third, research papers often include suggestions for further research. There are always limitations to any analysis that should be discussed candidly. Indeed, you may have encountered some methodological problems that still must be worked out, or you might have unearthed a noteworthy substantive relationship that could bear future scrutiny. You should describe these new issues or questions. Here, too, you are allowed some room to speculate—to venture beyond the edge of the data and engage in a little "What if?" thinking. After all, the truth is still out there.

Name: _____ Date: _____

E-mail: _____ Section: _____

CHAPTER 11 EXERCISES

1. Identify three websites where you can download SPSS-format (.sav) datasets for political science research. For each site, please provide the name of the site, its web address (URL), and a brief description of the SPSS-format datasets you can download from the site.

   A. Name of website: _____

   Website address: _____

   What SPSS-format datasets can you download from this website?

   _____

   _____

   _____

   B. Name of website: _____

   Website address: _____

   What SPSS-format datasets can you download from this website?

   _____

   _____

   _____

   C. Name of website: _____

   Website address: _____

   What SPSS-format datasets can you download from this website?

   _____

   _____

   _____

2. You can import datasets saved in many different formats into SPSS by selecting File ▶ Open ▶ Data, including datasets saved in Stata, Excel, SAS, and text file formats. Each of these different dataset file formats can be identified by their file name extensions. Please identify the file name extensions for these other importable file formats by completing the table below.

Dataset File Format	File Name Extension(s)
Stata	?
Excel	?
SAS	?
Text	?

3. A political science major is interested in analyzing factors that increase voter turnout in elections. There is at least one variable in each of the four companion datasets that measures voter turnout. In the World and States datasets, there are aggregate-level measures of voter turnout. Variables in the GSS and NES datasets indicate whether a respondent voted in a given election. Use the appendices of this book to help this student identify variables that could be used in this analysis.

Companion Dataset	Variables That Measure Voter Turnout
World	?
States	?
GSS	?
NES	?

4. Another political science major is interested in analyzing the relationship between religion and politics. There is at least one variable in each of the four companion datasets that measures how religious the unit of analysis is. In the World and States datasets, there are aggregate-level measures of how religious countries and states are. In the GSS and NES datasets, we can find measures of how religious individuals are. Use the appendices of this book to help this student identify variables that could be used in this analysis.

Companion Dataset	Variables That Measure Religiosity
World	?
States	?
GSS	?
NES	?

5. The North Carolina Center for Public Policy Research (NCCPPR) is a nonpartisan organization that publishes some unique and interesting information about North Carolina state politics. Among other things, the NCCPPR creates and compiles a ranking of the most influential lobbyists in the state.[10] Below, you can see a screenshot of one page of their lobbyist rankings.

This ranking could be used to do your own political analysis of lobbyist influence in state politics, but the rankings in the format you see here aren't quite SPSS ready. Describe how you would get this table SPSS ready.

_____

_____

_____

_____

_____

6. Do political scientists write journal articles in the order you read them (i.e. abstract, introduction, literature

review, theory and hypothesis, data and methods, results, discussion, conclusion)? Explain why political scientists do or do not write articles in the order they're read.

_____

_____

_____

_____

_____

7. When you do your own political analysis, you should write a literature review. Does a good literature review summarize all the books and articles that are related to your research topic? Please explain your answer.

_____

_____

_____

_____

_____

Rankings of The Most Influential Lobbyists in the North Carolina General Assembly, in Rank Order

Lobbyist	2013 Ranking	Lobbyist	2013 Ranking	Lobbyist	2013 Ranking
Brubaker, Harold	1	Tilson, Hugh H., Jr.	21	Martin, Lisa D.	41
Simpson, Dana E.	2	Ballantine, Patrick	22	Crouch, Kimberly (Kim) Y.	42
Fetzer, Tom	3	Lanier, Joseph (Joe) H.	23	Heron, Douglas (Doug) G.	43
Ellen, Andy	4	McClure, Christopher (Chris)	24	Adams, Julia	44
Kaplan, Harrison (Harry) J.	5	Wilson, Constance (Connie) K.	25	Zechini, Richard (Rick) A.	45
Kostrzewa, Theresa	6	Horne, B. Davis (Dave), Jr.	26	Page, Paula G.	46
Hawkins, Kathy G.	7	Kent, Timothy (Tim) D.	27	Hollis, Christopher (Chris) S.	47
Harrell, James (Jim) A., III	8	Melton, Ken	28	Scoggin, William (Bill)	48
Tillett, Johnny L.	9	Carpenter, J. Michael (Mike)	29	Thomas, Catherine (Cady) Louise	49
Salamido, Gary J.	10	Fleming, R. Mark	30	Fitzgerald, Tami	50
Harris, Lori Ann	11	Clary, Debbie A.	31	Broughton, James (Jimmy) W.C.	51
Cooper, John J.	12	Metcalf, John	32	Davis, Estherine K.	52
Barnhart, Jeff	13	Sevier, Thomas (Tommy) Wayne, Jr.	33	Cashion, Jake	53
Metcalf, Steve	14	Simpson, David (Dave) N.	34	Valauri, Susan R.	54
Neely, Charles (Chuck) B., Jr.	15	DeVivo, Laura H.	35	Moore, Thomas	55
Baggett, Hurshell (Chip) Eugene	16	Adams, Tony L.	36	Carr, Jon P.	56
McMillan, John B.	17	Steen, Fred F. II	37	Babcock, Nathan	57
Bode, John T.	18	Sands, Alexander (Sandy) P., III	38	Parker, Phillip Jacob (Jake), Jr.	58
Bone, Frederick (Fred) T.	19	Cozort, Jack	39	Isley, Philip	59
Stevens, Richard	20	Hicks, Joy A.	40	Doster, Betty	60

[10] See https://nccppr.org/rankings-of-the-most-influential-lobbyists-in-the-2013-north-carolina-general-assembly/.

Appendix, Table A-1

Variables in the GSS Dataset in Alphabetical Order[1]

Variable Name	Description
abany	Abortion if Woman Wants for Any Reason
abany_r	Binary coding of abany (1=yes, 0=no)
abdefect	Abortion if Strong Chance of Serious Defect
abdefect_r	Binary coding of abdefect (1=yes, 0=no)
abhlth	Abortion if Woman's Health Seriously Endangered
abhlth_r	Binary coding of abhlth (1=yes, 0=no)
abnomore	Abortion if Married--Wants No More Children
abnomore_r	Binary coding of abnomore (1=yes, 0=no)
abortion	Abortion Scale, Legal under how many conditions?
abpoor	Abortion if Low Income—Can't Afford More Children
abpoor_r	Binary coding of abpoor (1=yes, 0=no)
abrape	Abortion if Pregnant as Result of Rape
abrape_r	Binary coding of abrape (1=yes, 0=no)
absingle	Abortion if Not Married
absingle_r	Binary coding of absingle (1=yes, 0=no)
affrmact	Favor Preference in Hiring Blacks?
age	Age of Respondent
age5	Five age groups
artexbt	Did Respondent Go to an Art Exhibit in Last 12 Months?
assisted	Support for Assisted Suicide
attend	How Often Respondent Attends Religious Services
authoritarianism	Authoritarianism scale
ballot	Ballot Used for Interview

Variable Name	Description
bible	Feelings About the Bible
bigbang	Science Knowledge: The Universe Began with a Huge Explosion
bigbang_r	Binary coding of bigbang (1=true, 0=false, don't know)
bigbang2	Universe Expanding Since It Began: True or False
birthmo	Month in Which Respondent Was Born
bored	How Often Does Respondent Have Extra Time?
born	Was Respondent Born in This Country
boyorgrl	Science Knowledge: Father Gene Decides Sex of Baby
boyorgrl_r	Binary coding of boyorgrl (1=true, 0=false, don't know)
brlawfl	Do Private Companies Comply With Regulations
brnotax	Do Private Companies Avoid Taxes
cappun	Favor or Oppose Death Penalty for Murder
caseid	ID Number
cctv	Civil Liberties - Video Surveillance
childs	Number of Children
chldidel	Ideal Number of Children
class	Subjective Class Identification
closeblk	How Close Feel to Blacks
closewht	How Close Feel to Whites
clssmtes	Use Classmates
cohort	Year of Birth
colath	Allow Anti-Religionist to Teach
colcom	Should Communist Teacher Be Fired

(Continued)

[1] To find detailed information on coding and question wording, visit the following link at the University of California–Berkeley's Social Data Archive and search the alphabetical variable list: http://sda.berkeley.edu/D3/GSS16/Doc/hcbk.htm.

(Continued)

Variable Name	Description
colhomo	Allow Homosexual to Teach
colmil	Allow Militarist to Teach
colmslm	Allow Anti-American Muslim Clergymen Teaching in College
colrac	Allow Racist to Teach
comprend	Respondent's Understanding of Questions
compuse	Respondent Use Computer
conarmy	Confidence in Military
conbus	Confidence in Major Companies
conclerg	Confidence in Organized Religion
condrift	Science Knowledge: The Continents Have Been Moving
condrift_r	Binary coding of condrift (1=true, 0=false, don't know)
coneduc	Confidence in Education
confed	Confidence in Exec Branch of Fed Govt
confinan	Confidence in Banks & Financial Institutions
conjudge	Confidence in United States Supreme Court
conlabor	Confidence in Organized Labor
conlegis	Confidence in Congress
conmedic	Confidence in Medicine
conpress	Confidence in Press
consci	Confidence in Scientific Community
contv	Confidence in Television
coop	Respondent's Attitude Toward Interview
courts	Courts Dealing with Criminals
degree	Respondent's Highest Degree
denom	Specific Denomination
discwk5	Discrimination at Work in Past 5 Years
divlaw	Divorce Laws: Should It Be Harder to Get a Divorce?
earthsun	Science Knowledge: The Earth Goes Around the Sun
earthsun_r	Binary coding of earthsun (1=false, 0=true, don't know)

Variable Name	Description
easyget	How Difficult Was Case to Get
educ	Highest Year of School Completed
electron	Science Knowledge: Electrons Are Smaller Than Atoms
electron_r	Binary coding of electron (1=true, 0=false, don't know)
emailhr	E-mail Hours per Week
emailmin	E-mail Minutes per Week
emonitor	Civil Liberties - Monitor E-mails
envir_spend	Spending for environment
eqwlth	Should Govt Reduce Income Differences
evolved	Science Knowledge: Human Beings Developed from Animals
evolved_r	Binary coding of evolved (1=true, 0=false, don't know)
evolved2	Elephants Evolved from Earlier Species: True or False
facebook	Use Facebook
fair	People Fair or Try to Take Advantage
fair_r	Numeric coding of fair (3=fair, 2=depends, 1=take advantage)
famorjob	Would You Sacrifice Job Opportunities for Family
fechld	Mother Working Doesn't Hurt Children
fechld_rev	Mother Working Doesn't Hurt Children (reversed)
feelevel	Amount of Fees Paid
fefam	Better for Man to Work, Woman Tend Home
female	Is Respondent female?
femrole	Female role work/family
fepol	Women Not Suited for Politics
fepresch	Preschool Kids Suffer if Mother Works
finalter	Change in Financial Situation
finrela	Opinion of Family Income
flexhrs1	Importance of Flexible Hours at Work
flickr	Use Flickr

Variable Name	Description
form	Form of Split Questionnaire Asked
formwt	Weight Deal with Experimental Randomization
found	Case Was Retrievable in 2012
fund	How Fundamentalist Is Respondent Currently
future_scale	Adult Hope Scale (AHS)
gendereq	Gov Resp to Promote Equality
genegen	How Dangerous Modifying Genes in Crops
getahead	Opinion of How People Get Ahead
givinffor	Should Govt Collect Foreigner Info Without Knowledge
givinfusa	Should Govt Collect Citizen Info Without Knowledge
googlesn	Use Google
govtinfo	Should Govt Info Be Public
grass	Should Marijuana Be Made Legal
gunlaw	Favor or Oppose Gun Permits
gvinflu1	What People or Org Have Most Influence
gvinflu2	What People or Org Have 2nd Most Influence
hapmar	Happiness of Marriage
happy	General Happiness
harass5	Harassment at Work in Past 5 Years
health	Condition of Health
helpblk	Should Govt Aid Blacks?
helpful	People Helpful or Looking Out for Selves
helpnot	Should Govt Do More or Less?
helpoth	To Help Others
helppoor	Should Govt Improve Standard of Living?
helpsick	Should Govt Help Pay for Medical Care?
hispanic	Hispanic Specified
hlthstrt	Would You Say the Respondent's Health in General Is Excellent, Good, Fair, or Poor

Variable Name	Description
homosex	Homosexual Sex Relations
hope1	I Could Get Out of a Jam
hope2	I Am Energetically Pursuing My Goals
hope3	There Are Many Ways Around Problems I Face
hope4	I See Myself as Successful
hope5	I Can Think of Many Ways to Reach My Current Goals
hope6	I Am Meeting My Current Goals
hotcore	Science Knowledge: The Center of Earth Is Very Hot
hotcore_r	Binary coding of hotcore (1=true, 0=false, don't know)
huadd	Housing Unit (Hu) at Address?
huaddwhy	Why There Is No Hu at This Address
hunt	Does Respondent or Spouse Hunt
hunt1	Does Respondent or Spouse or Partner Hunt
id	Respondent ID Number
if12who	Who Would Respondent Have Voted for in 2012 Election
income16	Total Family Income
incuspop	What Interviewer Believes the Income Status of This Housing Unit Is, Relative to
intage	Age of Interviewer
intethn	Race of Interviewer
inthisp	Is Interviewer Spanish, Hispanic or Latino
intmbile	Use Internet/Apps from Phone or Tablet
intrace1	Interviewer's Race1
intrace2	Interviewer's Race2
intrace3	Interviewer's Race3
intrecnt	Used Internet/Apps Yesterday
intsex	Sex of Interviewer
intstart	Year Starting to Use Internet/Apps
intuse	Use Internet/Apps More Than Occasionally
intwkdyh	Hours of Internet Use on Weekdays
intwkdym	Minutes of Internet Use on Weekdays

(Continued)

(Continued)

Variable Name	Description	Variable Name	Description
intwkenh	Hours of Internet Use on Weekends	lotr5	I Rarely Count on Good Things Happening to Me
intwkenm	Minutes of Internet Use on Weekends	lotr5_rev	Numeric coding of lotr5 (5=strongly disagree . . . 1=strongly agree)
intyrs	Interviewer Years of Service as an Interviewer at N.O.R.C.	lotr6	I Expect More Good Things to Happen to Me Than Bad
issp	Filter for ISSP Cases	lowpay	I Would Accept Job for Lower Pay
kidsinhh	Does Interviewer Believe That There Are Children Under the Age of 15 Present at Respondent's Household	marital	Marital Status
		mobile16	Geographic Mobility Since Age 16
kidssol	Respondent's Kids Living Standard Compared to Respondent	mode	Interview Done In-Person or Over the Phone
lasers	Science Knowledge: Lasers Work by Focusing Sound Waves	nataid	National Spending Amount: Foreign Aid
lasers_r	Binary coding of lasers (1=false, 0=true, don't know)	natarms	National Spending Amount: Military, Armaments, and Defense
leasthrs	Fewest Hours/Week Worked in Past Month	natchld	National Spending Amount: Assistance for Childcare
letdie1	Allow Incurable Patients to Die	natcity	National Spending Amount: Solving Problems of Big Cities
letin1	Number of Immigrants to America Nowadays Should Be	natcrime	National Spending Amount: Halting Rising Crime Rate
libath	Allow Anti-Religious Book in Library	natdrug	National Spending Amount: Dealing with Drug Addiction
libcom	Allow Communists Book in Library		
libhomo	Allow Homosexuals Book in Library	nateduc	National Spending Amount: Improving Nation's Education System
libmil	Allow Militarists Book in Library	natenrgy	National Spending Amount: Developing Alternative Energy Sources
libmslm	Allow Anti-American Muslim Clergymen's Books in Library	natenvir	National Spending Amount: Improving & Protecting Environment
librac	Allow Racists Book in Library	natfare	National Spending Amount: Welfare
life	Is Life Exciting or Dull	natheal	National Spending Amount: Improving & Protecting Nations Health
linkedin	Use Linkedin		
lngthinv	How Long Was Interview	natmass	National Spending Amount: Mass Transportation
lot_scale	Life Orientation Test	natpark	National Spending Amount: Parks and Recreation
lotr1	In Uncertain Times I Usually Expect the Best		
lotr2	If Something Can Go Wrong for Me It Will	natrace	National Spending Amount: Improving the Conditions of Blacks
lotr2_rev	Numeric coding of lotr2 (5=strongly disagree . . . 1=strongly agree)	natroad	National Spending Amount: Highways and Bridges
lotr3	I'm Always Optimistic About My Future		
lotr4	I Hardly Ever Expect Things to Go My Way	natsci	National Spending Amount: Supporting Scientific Research
lotr4_rev	Numeric coding of lotr4 (5=strongly disagree . . . 1=strongly agree)		

Variable Name	Description
natsoc	National Spending Amount: Social Security
natspac	National Spending Amount: Space Exploration Program
news	How Often Does Respondent Read Newspaper
obamavote	Voted for Obama in 2012
obey	To Obey
other	Other Protestant Denominations
oversamp	Weights for Black Oversamples
owngun	Have Gun in Home
parsol	Respondent's Living Standard Compared to Parents
partyid	Party Identification
phase	Subsampling: Two-Phase Design
phone	Does Respondent Have Telephone
pillok	Birth Control to Teenagers 14–16
pinterst	Use Pinterest
pistol	Pistol or Revolver in Home
polgbeco	What Is Your View on Politics in U.S. & World
polviews	Ideological Self-Identification
popular	To Be Well Liked or Popular
pornlaw	Feelings About Pornography Laws
pray	How Often Does Respondent Pray
prayer	Bible Prayer in Public Schools
premarsx	Sex Before Marriage
pres12	Vote Obama or Romney
prvdhlth	Who Provides for Sick People
prvdold	Who Provides for Old People
prvdschl	Who Provides School Education
racdif1	Differences Due to Discrimination
racdif2	Differences Due to Inborn Disability
racdif3	Differences Due to Lack of Education
racdif4	Differences Due to Lack of Will
race	Race of Respondent

Variable Name	Description
race2	Is Respondent White or Black?
racehisp	Race with Hispanic (2000 and Later)
racethas	Points Assigned to Asian American
racethbl	Points Assigned to Black/African American
racethhi	Points Assigned to Hispanic/Latino
racethna	Points Assigned to Native American/ American Indian
racethot	Points Assigned to Other
racethwh	Points Assigned to White
radioact	Science Knowledge: All Radioactivity Is Man-Made
radioact_r	Binary coding of radioact (1=false, 0=true, don't know)
rank	Respondent's Self Ranking of Social Position
rcontact	Do You Have Personal Contact at Work
reg16	Region of Residence, Age 16
region	Region of Interview
relig	Respondent's Religious Preference
reliten	Strength of Affiliation
res16	Type of Place Lived in When 16 Years Old
respond	Estimate of the Probability That This Household Will Respond to the Survey
rgroomed	Respondent Grooming Rating
rhlthend	Respondent Health Rating
rifle	Rifle in Home
rincom16	Respondent's Income
rlooks	Respondent Physical Attractiveness Rating
rowngun	Does Gun Belong to R
rsampcode	Revised Sampcode
rushed	How Often Respondent Feels Rushed
rweight	Respondent Weight Rating
sampcode	Sampling Error Code
sample	Sampling Frame and Method
samplerc	Sample - Recoded
satfin	Satisfaction with Financial Situation

(Continued)

(Continued)

Variable Name	Description
science_quiz	Total number of scientific knowledge questions answered correctly
sei10	R's Socioeconomic Index (2010)
sei10educ	Percentage of Some College Educ in Occ10 Based on ACS 2010
sei10inc	Percentage of $45k+ Earners in Occ10 Based on ACS 2010
sethrs	How Are Your Working Hours Decided
sex	Respondent's Sex
sexeduc	Sex Education in Public Schools
sexornt	Sexual Orientation
shotgun	Shotgun in Home
sibs	Number of Brothers and Sisters
size	Size of Place in 1000s
snapchat	Use Snapchat
snsmyear	Year First Joined SNS
socbar	Spend Evening at Bar
socfrend	Spend Evening with Friends
social_disconnect	Social disconnectedness scale
social_media	Respondent belongs to how many social media networks?
social_trust	Social trust
socommun	Spend Evening with Neighbor
socrel	Spend Evening with Relatives
spanint	If No Spanish, Respondent Could Have Been Interviewed in English
spanking	Favor Spanking to Discipline Child
spanself	If This Interview Had Only Been Available in English, Would You?
spend18	Additive index of 18 national budget items
spkath	Allow Anti-Religionist to Speak
spkath_r	Binary version of spkath (1=allow, 0=no allow)
spkcom	Allow Communist to Speak
spkcom_r	Binary version of spkcom (1=allow, 0=no allow)
spkhomo	Allow Homosexual to Speak

Variable Name	Description
spkhomo_r	Binary version of spkhomo (1=allow, 0=no allow)
spkmil	Allow Militarist to Speak
spkmil_r	Binary version of spkmil (1=allow, 0=no allow)
spkmslm	Allow Muslim Clergymen Preaching Hatred of the US
spkmslm_r	Binary version of spkmslm (1=allow, 0=no allow)
spkrac	Allow Racist to Speak
spkrac_r	Binary version of spkrac (1=allow, 0=no allow)
srcbelt	Src Beltcode
suicide1	Suicide if Incurable Disease
suicide2	Suicide if Bankrupt
suicide3	Suicide if Dishonored Family
suicide4	Suicide if Tired of Living
tax	Respondent's Federal Income Tax
teensex	Sex Before Marriage -- Teens 14–16
thnkself	To Think for One's Self
tolerance	Free speech for unpopular groups
trust	Can People Be Trusted
trust_r	Numeric version of trust (3=can trust, 2=depends, 1=cannot trust)
tumblr	Use Tumblr
tvhours	Hours per Day Watching TV
twitter	Use Twitter
unemp	Ever Unemployed in Last Ten Years
union	Does Respondent or Spouse Belong to Union
union1	Does Respondent or Spouse or Partner Belong to Union
unionhh	Someone in household belong to union?
unionsbd	Strong Trade Unions Are Bad for U.S. Economy
uscitzn	Is Respondent a U.S. Citizen?
usewww	Respondent Use WWW Other Than E-mail
usualhrs	How Many Hours/Week Do You Usually Work

Variable Name	Description
uswar	Expect U.S. in War Within 10 Years
uswary	Expect U.S. in World War in 10 Years
version	Version of Questionnaire
vetyears	Years in Armed Forces
vine	Use Vine
viruses	Science Knowledge: Antibiotics Kill Viruses as Well as Bacteria
viruses_r	Binary coding of viruses (1=false, 0=true, don't know)
vote12	Did Respondent Vote in 2012 Election
vpsu	Variance Primary Sampling Unit
vstrat	Variance Stratum
webmob	Respondent Uses Home Internet Through Mobile Device
whatsapp	Use Whatsapp
wordsum	Number Words Correct in Vocabulary Test

Variable Name	Description
workhard	To Work Hard
wrkgovt	Govt or Private Employee
wrkslf	Respondent Self-Employed or Works for Somebody
wrkstat	Labor Force Status
wrkwayup	Blacks Overcome Prejudice Without Favors
wtss	Weight Variable
wtssall	Weight Variable
wtssnr	Weight Variable
wwwhr	WWW Hours per Week
wwwmin	WWW Minutes per Week
xmarsex	Sex with Person Other Than Spouse
xnorcsiz	Expanded N.O.R.C. Size Code
year	GSS Year for This Respondent
zodiac	Respondent's Astrological Sign

Appendix, Table A-2

Variables in the NES Dataset in Alphabetical Order[1]

Variable Name	Variable Description[2]	Variable Name	Variable Description[2]
abortion	Abortion opinion (v161232)	case_id	2016 Case ID (v160001)
affirm_act3	Affirmative action in universities (v161204x)	Caucus_Dem_state	Does Respondent reside in Democratic caucus state?
Age	Age group (v161267)	Caucus_Rep_state	Does Respondent reside in Republican caucus state?
Age6	Age group (v161267x)	Caucus_primary_state_type	Caucus / primary / state type
Age13	Age group (v161267x)		
Asian_link	Asian Respondents: Is life affected by what happens to Asians? (v162226)	Child_authority	Should child follow self or authority? (v162239–42/41 rev coded)
assist_blacks	Government assistance to blacks (v161198)	climate_1	Climate change: Natural causes or Human activity? (v161222)
better_worse_future_econ	Econ better/worse next year (v161141x)	climate_2	Government action on rising temperatures (v161224)
better_worse_future_R	Respondent better/worse off next year (v161111)	Climate_scale	Climate liberalism (v161222, v161224)
better_worse_past_econ	Econ better/worse past year (v161140x)	Clinton_Sanders	Primary vote for Clinton or Sanders?
better_worse_past_econ_2	Economy better or worse?	Clinton_vote	Clinton or Trump?
		Clinton_vote_100	Vote for Clinton in 2016? (0/100)
better_worse_past_R	Respondent better/worse off than 1 year ago (v161110)	Community_issue	Did Respondent attend meeting on school/community issue in past 12 months? (v162196)
better_worse_past_R_2	R's financial situation better or worse?	Community_volunteer	Has Respondent done any volunteer work in past 12 months? (v162197)
Bible	Is Bible word of God or men? (v161243)	Community_work	Has Respondent done community work in past 12 months? (v162195)
Big_govt_scale	Pro Big Government Scale (v162183,v162184_rev,v162185)		
Black_link	Black Respondents: Is life affected by what happens to Blacks? (v162225)	cong_approve	Approve Congress? (v161080x)
		cong_incumb_approve	Approve House incumbent? (v162114x)
Campaign_info_sources	From how many sources did Respondent hear about campaign? (v161363a–e)	Contact_party	Was Respondent contacted by party about campaign?

[1] We've retained a number of technical variables that may be of interest to some researchers but are largely beyond the scope of the text: V160101 (Pre-election weight—full sample), V160101f (Pre-election weight—FTF sample), V160101w (Pre-election weight—Web sample), V160102 (Post-election weight—full sample, this is the same as nesw), V160102f (Post-election weight—FTF sample), V160102w (Post-election weight—Web sample), V160201 (Stratum—full sample), V160201f (Stratum—FTF sample), V160201w (Stratum—Web sample), V160202 (Variance of primary sampling unit [PSU]—Full sample), V160202f (Variance PSU—FTF sample), V160202w (Variance PSU—Web sample), V160502 (Completed Pre only or completed Pre and Post interviews), V161001 (Pre-election: FTF only: Consent to audio recording), and V161002 (Pre-election: FTF only: Interviewer Observation: Is Respondent male or female).

[2] The codes in parentheses in variable descriptions correspond to variable names in the ANES 2016 Time Series Survey. We've renamed and/or recoded many variables to make the dataset more user-friendly. For specific coding and question wording, go to the following link and search codebooks: http://www.electionstudies.org/studypages/anes_timeseries_2016/anes_timeseries_2016.htm.

Variable Name	Variable Description[2]
defense_spend	Defense spending (v161181)
Discrim_scale	Perceived discrimination (v162357,58,61,62,64,66)
Econ_pessimism	Economic pessimism (v161110–v161111)
educ4	Education (v1270 collapsed)
Education	Highest level of education (v161270)
egalit_3	Egalitarianism, 3 categories
egalitarianism	Egalitarianism scale (v162243–162246)
envir_jobs	Environment or jobs (v161201)
F_scale	Fascism Scale (v162169–v162170: Get rid of rotten apples / Country needs strong leader to take us back to true path)
Female	Is Respondent female? (v161342)
Female_bond	Working mother's bond with child (v162229), numeric codes reversed
Female_role	Moms: Better/worse stay home? Working mom bond with child? High = Non-traditional values (v162229, v162230)
fracking	Approve/Disapprove fracking (v161223)
Free_trade	Does Respondent favor or oppose free trade agreements? (v162176)
ft_Asians	Feeling thermometer: Asian-Americans (v162310)
ft_BClinton	Feeling thermometer: Bill Clinton (v161093)
ft_Blacks	Feeling thermometer: Blacks (v162312)
ft_BLM	Feeling thermometer: Black Lives Matter (v162113)
ft_Business	Feeling thermometer: Big business (v162100)
ft_Christians	Feeling thermometer: Christians (v162107)
ft_Congress	Feeling thermometer: Congress (v162104)
ft_Conservatives	Feeling thermometer: Conservatives (v162101)
ft_Dem	Feeling thermometer: Democratic Party (v161095)
ft_Feminists	Feeling thermometer: Feminists (v162096)
ft_Fund	Feeling thermometer: Christian fundamentalists (v162095)

Variable Name	Variable Description[2]
ft_Gays	Feeling thermometer: Gay men and lesbians (v162103)
ft_HClinton_post	Feeling thermometer: Hillary Clinton (post-election, v162078)
ft_HClinton_pre	Feeling thermometer: Hillary Clinton (pre-election, v161086)
ft_Hispanics	Feeling thermometer: Hispanics (v162311)
ft_Illegals	Feeling thermometer: Illegal immigrants (v162313)
ft_Illegals_5	Feeling thermometer: Illegal immigrants simplified to 5 categories
ft_Jews	Feeling thermometer: Jews (v162108)
ft_Kane	Feeling thermometer: Tim Kane (v161090)
ft_Liberals	Feeling thermometer: Liberals (v162097)
ft_Muslims	Feeling thermometer: Muslims (v162106)
ft_Muslims_5	Feeling thermometer: Muslims simplified to 5 categories
ft_Obama	Feeling thermometer: Barack Obama (v161092)
ft_Pence	Feeling thermometer: Mike Pence (v161091)
ft_Police	Feeling thermometer: Police (v162110)
ft_Poor	Feeling thermometer: Poor people (v162099)
ft_Rep	Feeling thermometer: Republican Party (v161096)
ft_Rich	Feeling thermometer: Rich people (v162105)
ft_Scientists	Feeling thermometer: Scientists (v162112)
ft_SCOTUS	Feeling thermometer: U.S. Supreme Court (v162102)
ft_Tea	Feeling thermometer: Tea Party (v162109)
ft_Trans	Feeling thermometer: Transgender people (v162111)
ft_Trump_post	Feeling thermometer: Donald Trump (post, v162079)
ft_Trump_pre	Feeling thermometer: Donald Trump (pre, v161087)
ft_Unions	Feeling thermometer: Unions (v162098)
ft_Whites	Feeling thermometer: Whites (v162314)

(Continued)

(Continued)

Variable Name	Variable Description[2]
gay_adopt	Should gay and lesbian couples be allowed to adopt?
gay_job_discrim	Should laws protect gays lesbians against job discrimination?
Gay_laws_scale	Gay laws (higher codes more conservative / v161227, 1229x–1231)
gay_marriage	Respondent's position on gay marriage (v161231)
gay_wed_serve	Business wedding services to same sex couples (v161227x recoded)
GOTV	Anyone talk to Respondent about registering or getting out to vote
grass	Should marijuana be legal? (v162179)
gun_control2	Should fed government make it more difficult to buy a gun?
gun_imp	How important is gun issue to Respondent? (v161188)
gun_own	Does Respondent own a gun? (v161496)
Hispanic_link	Hispanic Respondents: life be affected by what happens to Hispanics (v162224)
HR_vote_party	Party of 2016 U.S. House of Representatives vote (v162067x)
immig_birthright	Favor birthright citizenship? (v161194x)
immig_chldrn	Send back children brought illegally? (v161195x)
immig_chldrn_rec	Send back children brought illegally? (recoded)
immig_scale	Pro-immigration Scale (v161194x,95x,96x)
immig_scale_4	Pro-immigration Scale (v161194x,95x,96x) (Binned)
immig_wall	Build wall with Mexico? (v161196x)
Income	Income (v161361x)
income_gap	Income gap larger/smaller income gap today (v161138)
income_gap_action	Does Respondent favor or oppose government reducing income inequality? (v162148)
income3	Income (v161361x)
income4	Income
income5	Income
income7	Income
interview_mode	Mode of interview (v160501)

Variable Name	Variable Description[2]
intl_force	Willing to use force to solve international problems (v161154)
isolationism	Country would be better off if we just stayed home (v161153)
jobs_stndLiving	Jobs/standard of living (v161189)
Kids	Does Respondent have children? (v162296x)
libcon3	Ideological self-placement, 3 categories
libcon7	Ideological self-placement (v161126)
libcon7_Dem	Ideological placement: Democratic Party (v161130)
libcon7_Rep	Ideological placement: Republican Party (v161131)
libcon10	Left-Right self-placement (CSES v162289)
marital	Respondent Marital status (v161268)
Married	Is Respondent married? (v161268)
ME_Isis	Send troops to fight ISIS? (v161213x)
ME_refugees	Allow Syrian refugees? (v161214x)
Misogyny	Misogyny scale (v161507–v161510)
Misogyny4	Misogyny scale (v161507–v161510) (Binned)
nativism	Nativism scale (v162271–162274)
nativism2	Nativism, 2 categories
nativism4	Nativism, 4 categories
need_strong_leader	Country needs strong leader to take us back to true path (v162170), numeric codes reversed
nesw	Weight variable (v160102)
nesw_rnd	Weight variable, rounded to nearest integer
Obama_2012	Obama in 2012? (v161006)
ObamaCare	Respondent Favor/Oppose 2012 health care law (v161114x)
Org_num	Number of organizations Respondent belongs to (v162194)
partyid3	Party Identification, 3 categories (v161158x)
partyid7	Party Identification, 7 categories (v161158x)
pol_interest	Interest in politics/campaigns (v161003, v161004)
Pol_interest_scale	Political Interest Scale (v161003,v161004,v161009)

Variable Name	Variable Description[2]
political_trust	How often trust government in Wash to do what is right? (v161215)
polknow	Pol knowledge (v162072,73a,74a,75a,76b)
polknow2	RECODE of polknow variable
pres_econ	Approve president's handling econ? (v161083x)
pres_foreign	Approve president's handling foreign relations? (v161084x)
pres_hlth	Approve president's handling health care? (v161085x)
pres_job	Approve president's job? (v161082x)
Primary_party	Did Respondent vote Democratic or Republican in primary/caucus?
primary_voter	Did Respondent vote in primary of caucus? (v161021)
primary_who	Which candidate did Respondent support? (v161021a)
Race_all	Summary: Racial self-identification (v161310x)
Race2	White/Black (v161310x)
Race3	White/Black/Hispanic (v161310x)
racial_resentment_scale	Racial resentment (v162211–v162214)
racial_resentment_scale_4	Racial resentment, 4 categories
region	Region of residence
Relig_attend	How often does Respondent attend religious services? (v161244, 45, 45a)
Relig_imp	Religion important to Respondent? (v161241–42)
rid_rotten_apples	Country would be great by getting rid of rotten apples (v162169), numeric codes reversed
sex_orient	Sexual orientation of Respondent (v161511)
sex_orient_fmfrnd	Gay, lesbian, or bisexual among family and friends? (v161512)
Sexism_trad	Traditional Sexism (v161507–v161510)
social_trust	How often can people be trusted? (v161219)
Spend_Child	Spending: Child care (v161210)
Spend_Crime	Spending: Dealing with crime (v161208)
Spend_Enviro	Spending: Protecting the environment (v161212)

Variable Name	Variable Description[2]
Spend_Poor	Spending: Aid to the poor (v161211)
Spend_Scale	Spending on 8 government programs (v161205–v161212)
Spend_Schools	Spending: Public schools (v161206)
Spend_SciTech	Spending: Science and technology (v161207)
spend_serv	Government spending/services (v161178)
Spend_SocSec	Spending: Social Security (v161205)
Spend_Welfare	Spending: Welfare programs (v161209)
spend8	Increase spending on 8 programs (v161205–v161212)
Ticket_splitter	Did Respondent split Pres and HR vote? (v16062x, 067x)
torture	Favor/oppose torture for suspected terrorists (v162295)
trans_bathroom	Transgender bathroom policy (v161228)
Trump	Vote for Trump in 2016? (0/100)
Trump_OtherRep	Primary vote for Trump or other Republican?
version	Is ANES 2016 Time Series release
Voted_2012	Did Respondent vote in 2012? (v161005)
Voted_2016	Did Respondent vote in 2016? (v162032x)
Voter_type	Voter type (note: primary voters also include caucus goers)
Voter_type_primary_caucus	Nomination participation: Democratic primary, Democratic caucus, Republican primary, or Republican caucus?
voting_duty	Voting as duty or choice (v161151x)
voting_duty2	Recode of voting_duty
white_black_4	White therm-Black therm, binned into 4 categories
whites_minus_blacks	White therm-Black therm
Who_2012	Obama or Romney? (v161006)
Who_2016	Major party vote (v162062x)
Who_2016_full	Vote 2016 summary (all candidates) (v162062x)
wordsum	Vocabulary test: Number words correct (v161497–v161506)

Appendix, Table A-3

Variables in the States Dataset by Topic

INDEX

Variable Name	Description
state	State name
stateid	Two-letter postal abbreviation for state name

ABORTION RELATED

abort_rank3	Abortion restrictions (3 category ranking)
abort_rate05	Abortions per 1,000 women (2005)
abort_rate08	Number of abortions per 1,000 women aged 15–44 (2008)
abortion_rank12	2012 Abortion rank (Americans United for Life)
abortlaw3	Abortion restrictions (three tiers of number of restrictions)
abortlaw10	Number of restrictions on abortion (2010)
abortlaw2017	Number of restrictions on abortion (out of 14 possible restrictions, based on Guttmacher Institute's Overview of State Abortion Law 2017)[1]
permit	Percent public that would always permit abortion (2004 NES)
ProChoice	Percent public pro-choice
prochoice_percent	Percentage of adults who say abortion should be legal in all/most cases (2014)[2]
ProLife	Percent public pro-life

CIVIC CULTURE

volunteer_hrs_pc	Volunteer hours per resident[3]
volunteer_percent	Volunteer rate. From Corporation for National & Community Service[4]

COURTS

corrections_incarc_rate	Population incarcerated per 100,000 state residents (in 2015). U.S. Bureau of Justice Statistics
corrections_total_rate	Population under correctional supervision per 100,000 state residents (incarcerated or community supervision) (in 2015). U.S. Bureau of Justice Statistics[5]
crime_rate_burglary	Burglary rate, per 100,000 population (2014) (burglary is entry into a home/building illegally with intent to commit a crime). From Uniform Crime Statistics
crime_rate_murder	Murder and non-negligent manslaughter rate, per 100,000 population (2014). From Uniform Crime Statistics
crime_rate_property	Property crime rates, per 100,000 population (includes burglary, larceny, motor vehicle theft, 2014). From Uniform Crime Statistics
crime_rate_violent	Violent crime rate, per 100,000 population (2014). From Uniform Crime Statistics[6]
deathpen_executions	Executions since 1976 (as of Aug 2017). From Death Penalty Information Center[7]

---

[1] https://data.guttmacher.org/states

[2] http://www.pewforum.org/religious-landscape-study/compare/views-about-abortion/by/state/

[3] https://www.nationalservice.gov/vcla/volunteer-hours-resident-states

[4] https://www.nationalservice.gov/vcla/state-rankings-volunteer-rate

[5] https://www.bjs.gov/content/pub/pdf/cpus15.pdf

[6] https://www.ucrdatatool.gov/Search/Crime/State/RunCrimeOneYearofData.cfm

[7] https://deathpenaltyinfo.org/number-executions-state-and-region-1976

deathpen_exonerations	Death penalty exonerations since 1973. From Death Penalty Information Center[8]
judge_selection	Method used to select appellate court judges. From BallotPedia[9]
legalclimate	State legal climate rating 2015. From Institute for Legal Reform[10]
legalclimate_rank	State legal climate ranking 2015. From Institute for Legal Reform

DEMOGRAPHICS[11]

blackpct_2015	Percentage white (2015)
blkpct04	Percent black (2004)
blkpct08	Percent black (2008)
blkpct10	Percent black (2010)
density	Population density (2010)
hispanic04	Percent Hispanic (2004)
hispanic08	Percent Hispanic (2008)
hispanic10	Percent Hispanic (2010)
hispanicpct_2015	Percentage Hispanic (2015)
over64	Percent population over age 64
over64_2016	Percent population over age 64 in 2016
pop_18_24	Percent population aged 18–24 (2004)
pop_18_24_10	Percent population aged 18–24 (2010)
pop_18_24_2016	Percentage population ages 18–24 (2015)
pop2000	State population, 2000
pop2010	State population, 2010
pop2010_hun_thou	State population, 2010 (in 100k)
pop2016 (in 100k)	State population, 2016 (in 100k)

popchng0010	State population, 2000–2012
popchngpct	State population percentage, 2000–2010
urban	Percent urban population (2000)
whitepct_2015	Percentage white (2015)

EDUCATION

adv_or_more	Percent of population with advanced degree or higher
ba_or_more	Percent of population with college degree or higher
ba_or_more_2015	Percent population college degree or higher (2015). U.S. Census Bureau American Community Survey
college	Percent of population with college or higher
hs_or_more	Percent population high school education or higher
hs_or_more_2015	Percent population high school education or higher (2015). U.S. Census Bureau American Community Survey
hs_yrs_ss	Years of social studies required to graduate high school (2014). From the Center for Information and Research on Civic Learning and Engagement[12]
schools_avg_salary	Average salary of public school teachers (2016). From the National Education Association
schools_spend	Expenditure per student in average daily attendance (2017). From the National Education Association
schools_st_ratio	Students enrolled per teacher (2016). From the National Education Association[13]

(Continued)

---

[8] https://deathpenaltyinfo.org/documents/FactSheet.pdf

[9] https://ballotpedia.org/Judicial_selection_in_the_states

[10] http://www.instituteforlegalreform.com/states

[11] All state-level demographic data from the U.S. Census Bureau.

[12] http://civicyouth.org/high-school-civics-requirements-and-assessments-vary-across-the-u-s/

[13] http://www.nea.org/assets/docs/2017_Rankings_and_Estimates_Report-FINAL-SECURED.pdf

(Continued)

ECONOMY

biz_tax_rank	State business tax climate ranking (2017). From The Tax Foundation
biz_tax_score	State business tax climate rating (2017). From The Tax Foundation[14]
defexpen	Federal defense expenditures per capita
earmarks_pcap	Earmarks per capita (in dollars)
gini_2016	Gini index score 2016. Compiled by United Health Foundation from U.S. Census Bureau data
gini_rank_2016	Income equality ranking (based on Gini index 2016). Compiled by United Health Foundation from U.S. Census Bureau data[15]
govt_worker	Percentage workforce government workers (2012)
min_wage	State minimum wage; states without minimum wage coded as 0. From the National Conference of State Legislatures[16]
prcapinc	Per capita income
rtw	Right to work state?
unemploy	Unemployment rate (2004)
unemploy2016	State unemployment rate in Nov. 2016 from U.S. Bureau of Labor Statistics[17]
union_2016	Percent of workers who are union members (2016) from U.S. Bureau of Labor Statistics[18]
union04	Percent workers who are union members (2004)
union07	Percent workers who are union members (2007)
union10	Percent workforce unionized (2010)

ELECTIONS AND REPRESENTATION

battle04	Battleground state in 2004?
black_legis_2015	Percent of state legislators who are African American (in 2015 session). From National Conference of State Legislatures[19]
blkleg	Percent of state legislators who are black
bush00	Percent voting for Bush in 2000
bush04	Percent voting for Bush in 2004
citizen_ideology	Citizen ideology index (2013). Based on Berry, Ringquist, Fording, and Hanson (1998)[20]
clinton16	Vote share for Clinton in 2016 election
clinton16_ev	Electoral College votes for Clinton in 2016 election
conpct_m	Percent mass public Conservative
cons_hr06	Conservatism score, U.S. House delegation (2006)
cons_hr09	Conservatism score, U.S. House delegation (2009)
conserv_advantage	Conservative advantage, mass public (2012)
conserv_public	Percent mass public conservative (2013)
cook_index	Cook Index: Higher scores mean more Democratic
cook_index3	3 quantiles of cook_index
dem_advantage	Democratic advantage, mass public (2012)
dem_hr09	Percent U.S. House delegation Democratic (2009)
demhr11	Percent HR delegation Democratic (2011)

---

[14] https://taxfoundation.org/2017-state-business-tax-climate-index/

[15] https://www.americashealthrankings.org/explore/2016-annual-report/measure/gini/state/ALL

[16] http://www.ncsl.org/research/labor-and-employment/state-minimum-wage-chart.aspx

[17] https://www.bls.gov/news.release/archives/laus_12162016.htm

[18] https://www.bls.gov/news.release/union2.t05.htm

[19] http://www.ncsl.org/research/about-state-legislatures/who-we-elect-an-interactive-graphic.aspx

[20] https://rcfording.wordpress.com/state-ideology-data/

demnat06	Percent U.S. House and Senate Democratic (2006)
dempct_m	Percent mass public Democratic
demstate_2017	Percent of state legislators who are Democrats (in 2017 session). From National Conference of State Legislatures[21]
demstate06	Percent of state legislators who are Democrats (2006)
demstate09	Percent of state legislators who are Democrats (2009)
demstate13	Percent state legislature Democrats (2013)
evm	State electoral vote: McCain (2008)
evo	State electoral vote: Obama (2008)
evo2012	Obama's Electoral College vote
evr2012	Romney's Electoral College vote
gb_win00	Did Bush win electoral vote, 2000?
gb_win04	Did Bush win electoral vote, 2004?
gore00	Percent voting for Gore 2000
hispanic_legis_2015	Percent of state legislators who are Hispanic/Latino (in 2015 session). From National Conference of State Legislatures[22]
hr_cons_rank11	Conservativism ranking of House of Representatives delegation (2011, American Conservative Union)
hr_conserv11	Conservativism rating of House of Representatives delegation (2011, American Conservative Union)
hr_lib_rank11	Liberalism ranking of House of Representatives delegation (2011, Americans for Democratic Action)
hr_liberal11	Liberalism rating of House of Representatives delegation (2011, Americans for Democratic Action)
indpct_m	Percent mass public Independent

kerry04	Percent voting for Kerry 2004
legis_prof_rank	Legislative professionalism rank for 2015. From Squire (2017)
legis_prof_score	Legislative professionalism score for 2015. From Squire (2017)[23]
libpct_m	Percent mass public Liberal
mccain08	Percent voting for McCain 2008
modpct_m	Percent mass public Moderate
nader00	Percent voting for Nader 2000
obama_win08	Did Obama win electoral vote, 2008?
obama_win12	Did Obama win the state in 2012?
obama08	Percent voting for Obama 2008
obama2012	Obama vote share in 2012
polarization_house	Polarization in state legislature, measured as distance between party medians in state's House chamber in 2014. From Shor and McCarthy (2015)
polarization_senate	Polarization in state legislature, measured as distance between party medians in state's Senate chamber in 2014. From Shor and McCarthy (2015)
policy_innovation_rate	Policy adoption rate score (1958–2009) calculated by Boehmke and Skinner (2012) to measure state policy innovativeness.[24] The proportion of all policies that started diffusing in the time period (1959–2009) adopted by each state
reppct_m	Percent mass public Republican
romney2012	Romney vote share in 2012
seniority_sen2	Does state have influential U.S. Senator?
state_govt_rank	Overall quality of state government administrative functions (composite of fiscal stability, budget transparency, government digitalization, and state integrity rankings). From U.S. News and World Report[25]

(Continued)

[21] http://www.ncsl.org/research/about-state-legislatures/partisan-composition.aspx

[22] http://www.ncsl.org/research/about-state-legislatures/latino-legislators.aspx

[23] http://journals.sagepub.com/doi/abs/10.1177/1532440017713314

[24] https://dataverse.harvard.edu/dataset.xhtml?persistentId=hdl:1902.1/18507

[25] https://media.beam.usnews.com/b5/c5/ecf250de4930b201f74063d5150e/171206-best-states-overall-rankings-2017.pdf

(Continued)

term_limits	Does state have term limits for legislators? 0=no, 1=yes. From National Conference of State Legislatures[26]
to_0004	Percentage point change in turnout from 2000 to 2004
to_0408	Percentage point change in turnout from 2004 to 2008
to_0812	Percentage point change in turnout from 2008 to 2012
trnout00	Turnout in 2000 presidential election
trnout04	Turnout in 2004 presidential election
trump16	Vote share for Trump in 2016 election
trump16_ev	Electoral College votes for Trump in 2016 election
vep00_turnout	Percent turnout of voting eligible population in 2000
vep04_turnout	Percent turnout of voting eligible population in 2004
vep08_turnout	Percent turnout of voting eligible population in 2008
vep12_turnout	Percent turnout of voting eligible population in 2012
vep14_turnout	Percent turnout of voting eligible population in 2014. From United States Election Project[27]
vep16_turnout	Percent turnout of voting eligible population in 2016. From United States Election Project
voter_id_law	Voter identification law in effect in 2017. From National Conference of State Legislatures[28]
womleg_2007	Percent of state legislators who are women (2007)
womleg_2010	Percent of state legislators who are women (2010)
womleg_2011	Percent of state legislators who are women (2011)
womleg_2017	Percent of state legislators who are women (2017). From the National Conference on State Legislatures

GAY RIGHTS

gay_policy	Billman's policy scale (4 ordinal categories)
gay_policy_con	Does state have "most conservative" gay policies?
gay_policy2	RECODE of gay_policy (Billman's policy scale)
gay_support	Lax-Phillips opinion index
gay_support3	Gay rights: public support (3 categories)
lgbtq_equality_laws	Number of laws passed that advance LGBTQ equality, according to 2016 Human Rights Campaign State Equality Index[29]

GEOGRAPHY

division	Census division (9 different regions of country)
region	Census region (4 categories)
south	Southern state?

GUN RELATED

gun_check	Background checks for gun purchases per 100,000 population (2012)
gun_dealer	Gun dealers per 100,000 population
gun_murder10	Gun murder rate (2010)
gun_rank_rev	Recode of gun_rank11 so higher number ranks = more gun restrictions
gun_rank3	Recode of gun_rank11 (3 ordinal categories)
gun_rank11	Brady gun rank (2011)
gun_rank2015	Brady Campaign ranking (2015)
gun_scale11	Brady gun law scale (2011)
gunlaw_rank	Brady Campaign rank (2008)
gunlaw_rank3_rev	Number of restrictions (2008)

---

[26] http://www.ncsl.org/research/about-state-legislatures/chart-of-term-limits-states.aspx

[27] http://www.electproject.org/home/voter-turnout/voter-turnout-data

[28] http://www.ncsl.org/research/elections-and-campaigns/voter-id.aspx

[29] http://www.hrc.org/resources/2016-state-equality-index-view-your-states-scorecard

gunlaw_scale	Brady Campaign score (2008)
gunlaw_scale2015	Brady Campaign score (2015)[30]

HEALTH

alcohol	Alcohol consumption in gallons per capita (2007)
carfatal	Motor vehicle fatalities (per 100,000 population)
carfatal07	Motor vehicle fatalities per 100,000 population (2007)
cig_tax	Cigarette tax per pack (2007)
cig_tax_3	Cigarette tax per pack: 3 categories (2007)
cig_tax12	Cigarette tax per pack (2012)
cig_tax12_3	Cigarette tax per pack: 3 categories (2012)
cigarettes	Packs smoked bimonthly per adult (2003)
drug_death_rate	Drug overdose death rate per 100,000 adults (2015). From the Centers for Disease Control[31]
infant_mortality	Number of infant deaths per 1,000 live births (deaths before age one year) (2016). Compiled by United Health Foundation[32]
medicaid_expansion	Status of state action on Medicaid expansion pursuant to Affordable Care Act (as of Jan. 1 2017). From the Kaiser Family Foundation[33]
obesity_percent	Percentage of adults with a body mass index of 30.0 or higher based on reported height and weight. Compiled by United Health Foundation[34]
opioid_rx_rate	Retail opioid prescriptions dispensed per 100 persons (2016). From the Centers for Disease Control[35]

pot_policy	Marijuana laws
pot_policy_2017	Marijuana laws (2017). From the National Conference of State Legislatures[36]
preg_teen_rate	Number of pregnancies per 1,000 women aged 15–19, 2011. From Guttmacher Institute[37]
preg_uninten_rate	Unintended pregnancy rate per 1,000 women 15–44: 2010. From Guttmacher Institute
smokers12	Percentage of population who smoke
suicide_rate	Number of deaths due to intentional self-harm per 100,000 population. Compiled by United Health Foundation[38]
uninsured_pct	Percentage without health insurance (2012)
uninsured_pct_2015	Percentage without health insurance (2015). From U.S. Census Bureau, American Community Survey

RELIGION

attend_pct	Percent frequently attend religious services (Pew)
relig_cath	Percentage Catholic (2012)
relig_high	Percentage high religiosity (2012)
relig_import	Percent religion "A great deal of guidance"
relig_import_2016	Overall index of religiosity (2016). From Pew Research[39]
relig_low	Percentage low religiosity (2012)
relig_prot	Percentage Protestant (2012)
religiosity	Religious observance-belief scale (Pew)
religiosity3	Religiosity (3 categories)
secularism	Secularism scale (Pew)
secularism3	3 quantiles of secularism

---

[30] http://www.crimadvisor.com/?page=scorecard

[31] https://www.cdc.gov/drugoverdose/data/statedeaths.html

[32] https://www.americashealthrankings.org/explore/2016-annual-report/measure/IMR/state/ALL

[33] http://www.kff.org/health-reform/state-indicator/state-activity-around-expanding-medicaid-under-the-affordable-care-act/

[34] https://www.americashealthrankings.org/explore/2016-annual-report/measure/Obesity/state/ALL

[35] https://www.cdc.gov/drugoverdose/maps/rxstate2016.html

[36] http://www.ncsl.org/research/health/state-medical-marijuana-laws.aspx

[37] https://data.guttmacher.org/states

[38] https://www.americashealthrankings.org/explore/2016-annual-report/measure/Suicide/state/ALL

[39] http://www.pewresearch.org/fact-tank/2016/02/29/how-religious-is-your-state

Appendix, Table A-4

Variables in the World Dataset by Topic

IDENTIFIERS

Variable Name	Description
arda	Country numerical code
cabrv	Three-letter abbreviation of country name
ccode	Numeric country code based on the ISO-3166-1 standard
country	Country/territory name (title case)
natcode	Name of country (lower case)
region	Region name
regionun	United Nations region
unname	United Nations country/territory name

DEMOGRAPHICS

ciapop	Total population (CIA)
ciapopgr	Percent population growth rate (CIA)
frac_eth	Ethnic factionalization (Alesina et al., 2003)
frac_eth2	Ethnic factionalization, divided into High and Low categories
frac_eth3	Level of ethnic fractionalization: 3 categories (Low, Medium, High)
frac_lang	Language factionalization (Alesina et al., 2003)
frac_relig	Religious factionalization (Alesina et al., 2003)
immigrants_percent	Percentage of population born in another county. From World Bank's World Development Indicators
lifeex_f	Life expectancy at birth among females (CIA) CIALIF_F
lifeex_m	Life expectancy at birth among males (CIA) CIALIF_M
lifeex_total	Life expectancy at birth, total population (CIA) cialifex
migration_net	Number of immigrants minus number of emigrants annually. Positive numbers mean more people coming into country than leaving it. From World Bank's World Development Indicators

old06	Percentage of population ages 65 and above, 2006 (WB 2007)
old2003	Percentage of population ages 65 and above, 2003 (WB 2004)
pop_0_14	Percentage of population age 0–14 (CIA) CIAPSTR1
pop_15_64	Percentage of population age 15–64 (CIA) CIAPSTR2
pop_65_older	Percent of population age 65 and older (CIA) CIAPSTR3
pop_age	Median age in years, 2010 UNMAGE10
pop_age_1990	Median age in years, 1990 UNMAGE90
pop_total	Total population in millions, 2010 (UN) UNPOP10
pop_urban	Percentage of the population living in urban areas, 2010 (UN) UNURB10
pop03	Population (in millions), 2003 (World Bank 2004)
pop08	Population (in millions), 2008 WB
pop08_3	Population (in millions), WB (Banded)
popcat3	Size of country by population (3-categories)
refugees_from	Refugees from the country who live in other countries. From World Bank's World Development Indicators
refugees_in	Refugees from other countries in the country. From World Bank's World Development Indicators
sexratio	Sex ratio at birth (male births per 100 female births), 2010 UNSEXR10
ungr9095	Percent average annual population growth, 1990 to 1995
unmort_f	Number of adult female deaths per 1,000 females, 2008
unmort_m	Number of adult male deaths per 1,000 males, 2008
unpop30	Projected 2030 population in millions
unpop90	Total population in millions, 1990
unsexr90	Sex ratio at birth (male births per 100 female births), 1990 (UN)
urban03	Percentage urban population, 2003

urban06	Percentage urban population, 2006
untfr95	Total fertility rate (births per woman), 1990–1995 (UN)
yng2003	Percentage of population ages 0–14, 2003
young06	Percentage of population ages 0–14, 2006 (WB 2007)

ECONOMY

business_starts	Number of new corporations registered annually. From World Bank's World Development Indicators
ciagdpag	Composition of GDP: Agricultural sector (CIA)
ciagdpin	Composition of GDP: Industrial sector (CIA)
ciagdpsv	Composition of GDP: Service sector (CIA)
ciainfla	Inflation rate (percentage increase in consumer prices) (CIA)
ciaingro	Industrial production growth rate (annual percentage increase in industrial production) (CIA)
ciaunemp	Unemployment rate (CIA)
debt	Public debt as a percentage of GDP (CIA) ciapdebt
debt_wdi	National debt as a percentage of GDP. From World Bank's World Development Indicators
econ_compete	Measure of global economic competitiveness. From World Economic Forum
free_business	Heritage Foundation rating: business freedom (2010)
free_corrupt	Heritage Foundation rating: corruption (2010)
free_finance	Heritage Foundation rating: financial freedom (2010)
free_fiscal	Heritage Foundation rating: fiscal freedom (2010)
free_govspend	Heritage Foundation rating: government spending (2010)
free_invest	Heritage Foundation rating: invest freedom (2010)
free_labor	Heritage Foundation rating: labor freedom (2010)

free_monetary	Heritage Foundation rating: monetary freedom (2010)
free_overall	Heritage Foundation rating: overall economic freedom (2010)
free_overall_4	4 quantiles of free_overall
free_property	Heritage Foundation rating: property rights (2010)
free_trade	Heritage Foundation rating: free trade (2010)
gas_production	In millions of barrels of oil equivalent. From Michael Ross's Oil and Gas Data, 1932–2014[1]
gdp08	GDP in billions in 2008 (World Bank)
gdp_10_thou	GDP per capita in 10K US$ (2002)
gdp_cap2	GDP per capita (US$): 2 categories (2002)
gdp_cap3	GDP per capita (US$): 3 categories (2002)
gdpcap08_2	GDP per capita (US$) in 2008, 2 categories
gdpcap2_08	GDP per capita (US$) in 2008, 2 categories (may be redundant)
gdpcap3_08	GDP per capita (US$) in 2008 (Binned)
gdppcap08	GDP per capita in 2008 (World Bank)
gdppcap08_3	3 quantiles of gdppcap08 (as numeric)
gini04	Gini coefficient, 2004 (UN 2004)
gini04_4	Gini coefficient, 2004 (UN 2004), 4 categories
gini08	Gini coefficient, 2008 (UN 2008)
gini10	Gini coefficient, 2000–2010 (UN)
govt_help_cap	Capacity of state to provide for needy citizens. From Fund for Peace, Fragile States Index
hi_gdp	High GDP dummy
oil	Oil production, in barrels per day (CIA) CIAOIL_P
oil_production	In metric tons. From Michael Ross's Oil and Gas Data, 1932–2014
organized_crime	Average rating of the impact of organized crime on the economy, ranges 1–7 (lower values = more impact). From World Economic Forum
poverty	Percentage of the population below the poverty line
self_employed	Percentage of labor force that is self-employed. From World Bank's World Development Indicators

(Continued)

[1] https://dataverse.harvard.edu/dataset.xhtml?persistentId=doi:10.7910/DVN/ZTPW0Y

(Continued)

soldiers_percent	Percentage of labor force in the military. From World Bank's World Development Indicators
soldiers_total	Total number of people in the military. From World Bank's World Development Indicators
spendmil	Public expenditure on the military as a percentage of GDP, 2008 (UN)
spendmil_wdi	Public expenditure on the military as a percentage of GDP. From World Bank's World Development Indicators
trade_percent_gdp	International trade as percentage of GDP in 2016 (for countries without 2016 data, most recent non-missing data used, typically 2015). From World Bank
unemployed	Percentage of labor force that is unemployed (available/seeking employment but not employed). From World Bank's World Development Indicators
unemrt08	Employment to population ratio, percentage of the total population ages 15–64, 2008
unemrt91	Employment to population ratio, percentage of the total population ages 15–64, 1991
unexp_rd	Public expenditure on research and development as a percentage of GDP (UN)
unfempf	Ratio of female to male formal employment rates
ungdp	Gross domestic product (GDP) in billions of U.S. dollars, 2008 (UN)
ungdpcap	Gross domestic product (GDP) per capita in U.S. dollars, 2008 (UN)
ungdpppp	Gross domestic product (GDP) in billions of U.S. dollars (adjusted for purchasing power) (UN)
unin_inc	Inequality-adjusted income index, 2010 (UN)
unions	Union density (www.ilo.org)
unpovnpl	Percentage of population below national poverty line, 2000–2008 (UN)

unremitp	Per capita remittance inflows in U.S. dollars, 2008
unremitt	Remittance inflows as a percentage of GDP, 2008

EDUCATION

ciaedex	Percent of GDP spent on education (CIA)
educ_f_avgyrs	Average Schooling Years, Female (25+). From Educational Attainment Dataset by Barro and Lee[2]
educ_f_none	Percentage of Females with No Schooling (25+). From Educational Attainment Dataset by Barro and Lee
educ_m_avgyrs	Average Schooling Years, Male (25+). From Educational Attainment Dataset by Barro and Lee
educ_m_none	Percentage of Males with No Schooling (25+). From Educational Attainment Dataset by Barro and Lee
educ_quality	Average rating of quality of educational system, ranges 1–7 (higher values = better quality). From World Economic Forum
literacy	Literacy rate (CIA)
schools_internet	Average rating of internet availability in schools, ranges 1–7 (higher values = more extensive). From World Economic Forum
spendeduc	Public expenditure on education as a percentage of GDP (UN)
unineduc	Inequality-adjusted education index, 2010
unlit	Adult literacy rate (percentage of population age 15 or older) (UN)
unseced	Percentage of the population ages 25 and older with at least secondary education (UN)

ENVIRONMENT

carbon_footprint	Carbon footprint. Area of forest land required to sequester the country's carbon emissions. From Global Footprint Network
eco_footprint	Total ecological footprint. From Global Footprint Network

[2] http://www.barrolee.com/

energy_ renew_ percent	Percentage of country's energy that is non-fossil fuel (i.e. solar, wind, nuclear). From World Bank's World Development Indicators	dem_score14	Democracy score, higher scores more democratic (Economist 2014)
envir_treaties	Number of environmental treaties agreed to. From Environmental Treaties and Resource Indicators[3]	democ	Is government a democracy? (Based on regime_type3)
		democ08	Democracy score, 2008 (UNPOLFRE)
ocean_health	Measure of health of oceans adjacent to country. From Ocean Health Index[4]	democ11	Democracy score, 2011 (UN)
unco2_06	Carbon dioxide emissions per capita in 2006, in tons (UN)	democ_bin_ bmr	Is country democratic? A dichotomous coding of democracy. Boix, Miller, and Rosato (2013)
		democ_fh_ polity	Scale measuring how democratic country is. Averages Freedom House and Polity scores, transformed to 0–10 scale

GOVERNMENT AND POLITICS

		democ_regime	Is regime a democracy? (1990)
autoc	Autocracy score	democ_ regime08	Is government a democracy? (may be redundant)
colony	Colony of what country? (CIA)	district_size3	Average number of members per district (World Values Survey)
confidence	Confidence in institutions scale (World Values Survey)	dnpp_3	Effective number of parliamentary parties
const_age	Age of the country's constitution (as of 2012). From Institutions and Election Project[5]	dpi_cemo	Is chief executive a military officer? 0=no, 1=yes. From World Bank's Database of Political Institutions
corrupt_ perception	Corruption perception index. From Transparency International[6]	dpi_pr	Does country use a proportional representation system? 0=no, 1=yes. From World Bank's Database of Political Institutions
coup_attempts	Number of attempted coups d'etats since 1950. From Jonathan Powell[7]		
coups	Number of successful coups d'etats since 1950. From Jonathan Powell	dpi_system	National political system (0=Presidential, 1=Assembly-elected President, 2=Parliamentary). From World Bank's Database of Political Institutions
decent08	Democratic decentralization, 2008 (UN)		
decentralization	Decentralization scale	durable	Number of years since the last regime transition (Polity)
dem_economist	Full or partial democracy? (Economist, 2014)	effectiveness	Government effectiveness scale (Kaufmann, 2002)
dem_level4	Regime type (Economist, 2014)	election_ integrity	Average of expert evaluation of integrity of country's electoral system. From Electoral Integrity Project[8]
dem_other	Percentage of other democracies in region		
dem_other5	Percentage of other democracies in region: 5 categories	election_ violence_post	Were there riots and protest after election? From National Elections Across Democracy and Autocracy[9]
dem_rank14	Democracy rank, lower number ranks more democratic (Economist 2014)		

(Continued)

---

[3] http://sedac.ciesin.org/entri/

[4] http://www.oceanhealthindex.org/

[5] https://havardhegre.net/iaep/

[6] https://www.transparency.org/research/cpi/overview

[7] http://www.jonathanmpowell.com/

[8] https://www.electoralintegrityproject.com/

[9] http://www.nelda.co/

(Continued)

election_violence_pre	Were there riots and protest before election? From National Elections Across Democracy and Autocracy	peace_index_rank	Ranking of peacefulness of country (1=most peaceful). From Visions of Humanity Global Peace Index 2017
enpp_3	Effective number of parliamentary parties	peace_index_score	Measure of overall peacefulness of country (higher scores=less peaceful). From Visions of Humanity Global Peace Index 2017
enpp3_democ	Effective number of parliamentary parties: 3 categories	pol_terror_scale_ai	Political terror scale. Ordinal scale from 1–5 of how much government terrorizes country's citizens, with 1 corresponding to very little oppression by government. From Amnesty International
enpp3_democ08	Effective number of parliamentary parties (World Values Survey)		
eu	EU member state (yes/no)		
fhrate04_rev	Freedom House rating of democracy (reversed)	pol_terror_scale_hrw	Political terror scale. Ordinal scale from 1 to 5 of how much government terrorizes country's citizens, with 1 corresponding to very little oppression by government. From Human Rights Watch
fhrate08_rev	Freedom House 1–7 scale reversed, rescaled 0–12		
govt_quality	Measure of the quality of government. From International Country Risk Guide of Political Risk Group[10]		
		polity	Higher scores more democratic (Polity)
icc_treaty_ratified	Has country ratified the international treaty that established the International Criminal Court (ICC)? (1=yes). From International Committee of the Red Cross[11]	pr_sys	Proportional representation system? (Institute for Democracy and Electoral Assistance)
		press_freedom_fh	Measure of freedom of the country's press. Based on Freedom House Freedom of the Press Report 2015, fit to 0–10 range
indy	Year of independence (CIA)		
ipu_wom13_all	Percent Women in lower house of legislature, all countries, 2013 (Inter-parliamentary Union)	press_freedom_rsf	Measure of freedom of the country's press. From Reporters Sans Frontiers
		regime_type3	Regime type (Cheibub's Democracy Dictatorship dataset)
laws_protect_prop	Measure of legal protections for private property rights, ranges from 0–10 with higher values corresponding to greater legal protection of property rights. From Fraser Institute	rights_assn	Freedom of assembly and association, Ordinal Scale 0–2. From CIRI Human Rights Data Project[13]
		rights_dommov	Freedom of domestic movement, Ordinal Scale 0–2. From CIRI Human Rights Data Project
liberty_index_eiu	From the Economist Intelligence Unit's Index of Democracy		
media_access_cand	Does country provide free or subsidized media access for political candidates? (1=yes) From Institute for Democracy and Electoral Assistance[12]	rights_formov	Freedom of foreign movement, Ordinal Scale 0–2. From CIRI Human Rights Data Project
		rights_law_index	Measure of violations of human right and rule of law. From Fund for Peace, Fragile States Index
media_access_parties	Does country provide free or subsidized media access for political parties? (1=yes) From Institute for Democracy and Electoral Assistance		
		rights_speech	Freedom of speech, Ordinal Scale 0–2. From CIRI Human Rights Data Project
oecd	OECD member state? (yes/no)		

---

[10] http://www.prsgroup.com/

[11] https://ihl-databases.icrc.org/ihl/INTRO/585?OpenDocument

[12] https://www.idea.int/data-tools

[13] http://www.humanrightsdata.com/

rights_treaties	Number of international human rights treaties ratified (out of 16 possible). From UNHRC[14]
unjourn	Number of verified cases of journalists imprisoned in 2009 (UN)
vdem_delib_comp	Deliberative component of V-Dem Country Scores for 2016[15]
vdem_edi	Electoral democracy index, V-Dem Country Scores for 2016
vdem_equality_comp	Egalitarian component of V-Dem Country Scores for 2016
vdem_ldi	Liberal democracy index, V-Dem Country Scores for 2016
vdem_ldi_rank	Liberal democracy ranking, based on liberal democracy index, V-Dem Country Scores for 2016
vdem_liberal_comp	Liberal component of V-Dem Country Scores for 2016
vdem_partic_comp	Participatory component of V-Dem Country Scores for 2016
votevap00s	Turnout: elections in 2000s (Institute for Democracy and Electoral Assistance)
votevap90s	Turnout: elections in 1990s (Institute for Democracy and Electoral Assistance)
women05	Percent women in lower house of legislature, democracies only, 2005 (Inter-parliamentary Union)
women09	Percent women in lower house of legislature, democracies only, 2009 (Inter-parliamentary Union)
women13	Percent Women in lower house of legislature, democracies only, 2013 (Inter-parliamentary Union)

HEALTH

fertility	Total fertility rate: Number children born per woman (CIA)
hiv_percent	Percentage of population aged 15–49 with HIV. From World Economic Forum

infant_mortality	Number infants dying before age one per 1,000 live births. From World Bank's World Development Indicators
spendhealth	Public expenditure on health as a percentage of GDP (UN)
unnoncom	Age-standardized death rates from non-communicable diseases per 100,000 people (UN)

INTERNET

internet_freedom	Measure of Internet freedom in country; combines measures of obstacles to access, limits on content, and violations of user rights. Ranges 0 to 100 (with 100=most freedom, which is inverse of Freedom House coding)
internet_status	Status of Internet freedom in country (1=Not Free, 2=Partly Free, 3=Free). Freedom House's Freedom on the Net 2016 Report
schools_internet	Average rating of Internet availability in schools, ranges 1–7 (higher values = more extensive). From World Economic Forum
unnetgro	Percent growth in the number of Internet users, population based, 2000–2008 (UN)
unnetuse	Internet users per 100 people, 2008 (UN)

JUSTICE SYSTEM

bribe_judge	Proportion of survey respondents from country reporting that they or member of family paid bribe to legal/judicial system in last year. From Global Corruption Barometer
bribe_police	Proportion of survey respondents from country reporting that they or member of family paid bribe to police in last year. From Global Corruption Barometer

(Continued)

---

[14] http://indicators.ohchr.org/

[15] https://www.v-dem.net/media/filer_public/b0/79/b079aa5a-eb3b-4e27-abdb-604b11ecd3db/v-dem_annualreport2017_v2.pdf

(Continued)

death_penalty_status	Legal status of death penalty (1=Abolished, 2=Abolished Except for Extraordinary Crimes, 3=Abolished in Practice, 4=Uses Death Penalty). From Death Penalty Information Center
homicide_rate	Number of intentional homicides per 100,000 persons From UNODC Global Study on Homicide 2013 (where 2012 data missing from report, last reported year used, typically 2011)
imprisonment_rate	Number incarcerated per 100,000 persons. From World Prison Brief[16]
indep_judiciary	Does country have an independent judiciary? (1=yes). From Political Constraints Index Dataset[17]
judicial_indep_wef	Average rating of judicial independence, ranges 1–7. From World Economic Forum
legal_origin	Legal origin of commercial code of country (1=English Common Law, 2=French Commercial Code, 3=Socialist/Communist Laws, 4=German Commercial Code, 5=Scandinavian Commercial Code). From LaPorta, Lopez de-Silanes, Shleifer, and Vishny (1998)[18]
legal_quality	Measure of quality of country's legal institutions. Institutional Quality Dataset[19]
rights_injud	Independence of the judiciary, Ordinal Scale 0–2. From CIRI Human Rights Data Project

RELIGION

gfi2008	Government favoritism of religion index
gfi_08r	Government favoritism of religion index, rounded to nearest integer
govregrel	Government regulation of religion index, 2008 (ARDA's coding of the 2008 U.S. State Department's International Religious Freedom Reports)

gri_08r	Government regulation of religion index, 2008, rounded to nearest integer
i_gvtfav	Government favoritism of religion index, ordinal ranking
i_gvtreg	Government regulation of religion index, ordinal ranking
i_socreg	Modified Social Regulation of Religion Index, 2008, ordinal ranking
msri2008	Modified social regulation of religion index, 2008 (higher score means higher less regulation)
msri_08r	Modified Social Regulation of Religion Index, 2008, rounded to nearest integer
muslim	Are Muslims predominate religious group?
religion	Largest religion by proportion (UN)
rights_relfree	Freedom of Religion. From CIRI Human Rights Data Project
typerel	Predominant religion
vi_rel3	Percent saying religion very important, 3 categories

SOCIAL/DEVELOPMENT

civil_war	Civil war intensity, 2008
conflict_index	Measure of extent of ongoing domestic and international conflict. From Visions of Humanity
conflict_internal	Number of internal conflict between govt and groups in country without invention from other countries. From UCDP/PRIO Database[20]
conflict_internat	Number of internal conflict between govt and groups in country with intervention from other countries (on one of both sides). From UCDP/PRIO Database

---

[16] http://www.prisonstudies.org/highest-to-lowest/prison_population_rate?field_region_taxonomy_tid=All

[17] https://mgmt.wharton.upenn.edu/faculty/heniszpolcon/polcondataset/

[18] https://scholar.harvard.edu/shleifer/publications/law-and-finance

[19] https://sites.google.com/site/aljazkuncic/research

[20] https://www.prio.org/Data/Armed-Conflict/UCDP-PRIO/

global_social	Social globalization measured by personal contacts of citizens, information flows, and cultural proximity. From KOF Index of Globalization
happiness	Measure of how happy citizens are. From World Happiness Report
hdi	Human development index (HDI) value, 2010 (UN)
hdi05	Human Development Index (HDI) value, 2005 (UN)
hdi_rank_change	Change in Human Development Index (HDI) rank from 2005 to 2010
human_develop	Measure of level of human development in country. Human development dimensions include having long and healthy lives, being knowledgeable, and enjoying a decent standard of living. From UNDP Human Development Report[21]
human_flight	Measure of human flight and brain drain from country. From Fund for Peace, Fragile States Index
militarization	Measure of extent of militarization (e.g., military spending, weapons owned). From Visions of Humanity
pmat12_3	Post-materialism, 3 categories (World Values Survey)
protact3	Protest activity (World Values Survey)
refugees_impact	Measure of impact of population displacement on country. From Fund for Peace, Fragile States Index
rich_democ	Rich democracy, interaction of Hi_gdp*democ_regime
terror_index_voh	Measure of the impact of terrorism on the county. From Visions of Humanity[22]
violence_cost	Economic cost of violence on national economy. Measured as a percentage of GDP. From Visions of Humanity

unmobcov	Percentage of the population covered by a mobile phone network, 2008 (UN)
unnewsp	Daily newspapers per thousand people, 2004 (UN)
unsathlt	Percentage of population who are satisfied with their personal health (UN)
unsati	Overall life satisfaction, most recent measure during 2006–2009 (0–10, higher means more satisfied) (UN)
unsatif	Overall life satisfaction among females, most recent measure during 2006–2009 (UN)
unsatjob	Percentage of employed who are satisfied with their job (UN)
unsatliv	Percentage who are satisfied with their standard of living (UN)

WOMEN'S RIGHTS

gender_equal3	Gender empowerment measure, 3 categories (World Values Survey)
gender_unequal	Gender Inequality Index value, 2008 (UN) UN_GII
gender_unequal_rank	Gender Inequality Index rank, 2008 (UN) UN_GII_R
rights_wecon	Women's economic rights, Ordinal Scale 0–2. From CIRI Human Rights Data Project
rights_wopol	Women's political rights, Ordinal Scale 0–2. From CIRI Human Rights Data Project
rights_worker	Women's social rights, Ordinal Scale 0–2. From CIRI Human Rights Data Project
womyear	Year women first enfranchised (Inter-parliamentary Union)
womyear2	Women's suffrage (Inter-parliamentary Union)

[21] http://hdr.undp.org/

[22] http://visionofhumanity.org/indexes/terrorism-index/

Made in United States
Orlando, FL
02 September 2022

21926087R00167